PLANT BASED
Cookbook

Simple & Satisfying Plant-Based Recipes
To Give Your Taste Buds A Treat

Ashley Colman

CONTENTS

SALADS & ENTRÉES **34**

SOUPS & STEWS 49

SNACKS & SIDES..67

LUNCH **92**

DINNER 116

DESSERTS **128**

MEASUREMENTS & CONVERSIONS **134**

INTRODUCTION

Imagine having the energy and vigor you had as a teenager. Staying alert and productive all day long. A life with fewer aches and illnesses.

Can you eat your way to a better life? Yes!

If you give your body the fuel and materials it needs, you will greatly reduce the wear and tear our modern stress-filled world puts on it. As a result, you'll have higher resilience to avoidable illnesses and diseases.

There is a lot of chatter about what diet is best for you. However, all the top long-term diets have one thing in common: They all have a heavy focus on plant-based foods.

Today, we will go over everything you need to benefit from a plant-based diet. Let's get started!

WHAT IS A PLANT-BASED DIET?

A plant-based diet is when you get most or all of your calories and nutrition from plants. For some people, this means cutting out meats, or even all animal-based products altogether. In general, it is a lifestyle choice, with conscious food choices. A few examples are:

- **Flexitarian**: Focuses on plant-based foods, but it also leaves room for some animal-based products like meat, eggs, and dairy.

- **Pescatarian**: Focuses on plant-based foods, but allows for fish in the diet.

- **Vegetarian**: Avoids all animal flesh, though they may leave their meal plans open to eggs or dairy products. Some eat both, while others only allow one or the other.

- **Vegan**: Avoids all animal-based products. Some make it an entire lifestyle, avoiding even fur, weather, and some cosmetics made from animals.

- **Mediterranean Diet:** People on the Mediterranean diet make fresh produce, lean meats, and plant products like olive oil the base for their meals.

- **Whole foods Diet:** People on a whole food diet completely shun processed foods, and they strive to eat mostly raw plant-based products.

- **Plant-Forward**: Cooking and eating that emphasizes plant-based foods, but is not limited to them. Meats are not the main feature of meals.

These are just a few of the various lifestyle diets out there that focus on eating fresh plants. For the purpose of this book, we'll focus on a purely plant-based diet. Feel free to incorporate everything you learn here in a diet that works best for your situation.

How does a plant-based diet work?

First off, unlike many diets out there, a plant-based diet is not a "magic bullet." Instead, it is simple nutrition and biology!

We have way too many processed foods in our diet. Too much salt. Too many alien chemicals our bodies were not designed to digest. Too many calories for way too little gain. Then our body strains itself trying to sort through too much junk, chemicals it can not identify, and way too few resources to function. No wonder we're sick and tired!

Our bodies are made to process plant-based foods. And we can attain everything our body needs from the right combinations of plants. Vitamins, minerals, antioxidants, amino acids, fiber, anti-inflammatories- everything is right there in your gardens and produce aisle!

Your body breaks down the plants into the nutritional blocks you need, and then it uses those blocks to build, fuel, and protect itself. The fresher these ingredients are, the better your body can process them.

What are the benefits?

There are dozens of benefits to a plant-based diet. Here are a few of our favorites.

- **Every Food has Individual Benefits!** Blueberries are heart-healthy and decrease inflammation. Kale is full of the essential vitamins your immune system needs. Quinoa contains amino acids you used to get from meats… we could fill a library with all the knowledge and studies!!

- **Heart Health.** Studies show plant-based diets can reduce the plaque buildup and inflammation that contributes to heart disease. In fact, A Harvard study revealed it can reduce the risk by up to 40%!

- **Diabetes.** A plant-based diet is full of complex carbs and the nutrients needed to regulate blood sugar. Studies have revealed these better life choices help regulate or prevent Type 2 diabetes.

- **Brain Health.** A plant-based diet is rich in antioxidants, omega-three fatty acids, and other brain-boosting nutrients. Studies show that it can improve brain function and slow the progress of degenerative diseases.

- **Mood Booster.** While it is not a replacement for therapy, studies show that a plant-based diet can help reduce the biological aspects of low mood and depression! It can even reduce your depression symptoms by up to 35%!

These are just a few highlights. Every aspect of your life is affected by the quality of nutrition you fuel your body with. There are hundreds of studies on the positive effects of a nutrient-rich plant-based diet on everything from sleep quality to reduced cancer risk.

How to transition to a plant-based diet?

1. **Research the Best Plant-Based Journey for You.** Talk to your doctor and a registered dietician or nutritionist to find the best options for you and your medical background.

2. **Take out the Trash.** You can't eat it if it is not there. Throw out ALL processed foods from your fridge or pantry. Also, throw out all animal-based food products that do not match your plant-based diet choices. Do not buy when you eat out or go grocery shopping.

3. **Plan Ahead.** What will you do at a pizza celebration, wedding, birthday, etc? How will you handle unhealthy food gifts and gift cards? What will your responses be to people that you know will have something to say about your choices? Who will you turn to celebrate milestones and when you need a morale boost on sticking to your diet? Knowing how you will keep processed foods away from your plate will help you stick to your new lifestyle!

4. **Start with Breakfast.** Scientific studies show that eating a good breakfast improves both physical and mental health! Start off with simple things like oatmeal topped with blueberries, and swapping milk for soy or almond milk.

5. **Swap snacks and sugary drinks for better alternatives.** Change out chips for crunchy nuts and fruits. Exchange sodas for green tea and herbal infusions.

6. **Substitute the meat-based products.** Try out recipes that substitute dairy, eggs, and meats in your diet. Try a few alternatives to each thing until you find something that works great for you.

7. **Make Plants the Star. Modern meals tend to put the focus on meat.** Make meat a topping or condiment if you have it at all. Instead, focus the meal on things like leafy greens, vegetables, beans, and whole grains.

8. **Try one new plant-based ingredient a week.** This helps with a variety of things:
   - Adjust to the new lifestyle
   - Increase variety to close nutritional gaps
   - Identify any food sensitivities quickly by narrowing down what changed in your diet that week.
   - Keep the diet fresh and interesting to avoid slipping into old habits

9. **Light to Moderate Daily Exercise.** Just eating isn't enough. You also have to move your body to stimulate your metabolism. Even a 15-minute walk up and down your street can do wonders for your health.

What to avoid?

Here are some things to avoid to get the most out of your plant-based diet:

1. **Avoid most or all animal products.** You can get more nutrition without the unhealthy fats and cholesterol through plants. If you do look to animal products, use them as a condiment rather than the centerpiece of the meal.

2. **Avoid refined sugars.** They are processed until there is no nutrition whatsoever. It is empty calories your body burns way too fast, causing the crash and brain fog we feel soon after eating it.

3. **White flour.** Like sugar, white flour is processed until it is nothing but calories that burn too fast. On top of that, most white flours are full of chemicals and heavy metals.

4. **Highly processed vegetable oils.** The more a thing is processed, the more alien it is to the body. Plus the processing removes all the nutritional benefits of the ingredients! Instead of vegetable oil, try using an omega-3 rich virgin olive oil.

5. **Excess.** Too much of anything is bad for you, even plants. Make sure to eat a large variety of plant products and avoid hyper-focusing on one or two foods.

6. **Ignoring your doctor.** If you have prescriptions or a medical condition, make sure to consult your doctor before making a huge change in your diet. Your treatment, care regiment, or prescriptions may require specific dietary guidelines.

   For example, people on blood thinners need to be careful about their vitamin K intake with certain medications. Keep your doctor in the loop so they can monitor your progress and adjust your medications as needed.

7. **Getting in a rut.** If you narrow your diet to the same meal rotations week after week, you risk nutritional deficiency. Try a new ingredient every week and vary your meals to close the gaps.

8. **Too many changes too fast.** It can be tempting to change everything all in one go, but that can lead to overwhelm and discouragement. Plus you might run into food sensitivities you did not know you had. Making small changes over time lets you integrate the new lifestyle naturally AND helps you pinpoint the foods that do not agree with you.

WHAT SHOULD I EAT?

Not sure where to start? Pick an option from the list below!

Breakfast

- A Green smoothie
- Fruit cup with whole-grain toast
- Homemade granola with fruit
- French toast, substituting egg batter with vegan solutions. Top with antioxidant-rich strawberries and almonds.
- Overnight oatmeal with almond butter and fruit
- Nondairy yogurt with granola
- Vegan scrambles, substituting eggs for tofu
- Red Lentil Pancakes and ½ cup blueberries
- Blueberry millet porridge
- Avocado toast with fresh fruit

Lunch

- Mediterranean Grain Bowl
- Quinoa vegetable soup
- 2-3 cups worth of salad: 2-3 leafy greens, 3-4 other vegetables, topped with nuts, berries, and olive oil.
- Veggie pinwheels on whole-grain tortillas
- Bean and millet chili with 3-5 veggies mixed in
- Whole-grain lunch wrap with fresh veggies, chickpeas, and beans or lentils.
- Vegetable hummus wrap
- ALT (Avacado, lettuce, tomato) sandwich with a fruit salad

Dinner

- Black bean enchiladas with wild rice
- Vegan pizza with a chickpea crust
- Lightly grilled mushrooms in homemade bbq sauce on a whole grain bun, with sweet potatoes and one cup of salad (2-3 leafy greens, 3-5 veggies, and topped with nuts, berries, and olive oil.)
- Veggie Pasta with homemade tomato and garlic sauce
- Veggies lightly stir-fried in olive oil and topped on veggie pasta or brown rice.
- Sweet potato curry rice
- Stuffed peppers with one cup salad and fruit

Snacks and Desserts

- Blended Frozen Banana "ice cream" topped with fruit or berries
- Banana shake with almond or homemade peanut butter.
- Apple slices with non-dairy yogurt
- A handful of mixed nuts
- Dried fruit (watch out for sweetened processed ones!)
- Sliced pears with cinnamon
- Hummus with carrots, olives, or celery
- Fruit cup with plant-based yogurt
- Baby veggies with avocado dip
- Fruit smoothie with blueberries or cranberries

FINAL THOUGHTS

A plant-based diet is not dooming yourself to a life of iceberg lettuce. In fact, it can be easy, fun, and full of tasty experiences. Not to mention all the health benefits along the way!

Look into the right plant-based diet for you, and give it a try today! You won't regret it.

To your health.

Note: Before you start with the plant-based diet or any other diet, always consult your doctor or medical professional to be sure that it's safe for you.

BREAKFAST & SMOOTHIES

Oat & Peach Smoothie

Ingredients for 4 servings

1 cup chopped peaches	1 cup water
1 banana	2 tbsp parsley, chopped
¼ cup rolled oats	1 cup chopped spinach
1 tbsp chia seeds	1 carrot, peeled
1 cup raspberries	1 tbsp grated fresh ginger
½ cup almond milk	

Directions and Total Time: 15 minutes

Place all ingredients in your blender and purée until smooth. Serve in glasses and enjoy!

Broccoli Sprout Smoothie

Ingredients for 2 servings

1 banana	2 soft Medjool dates, pitted
2 cups kale, chopped	1 tbsp hemp hearts
½ cup frozen strawberries	¼ tsp ground cinnamon
½ cup coconut milk	¼ tsp ground cardamom
1 cup broccoli sprouts	1 tbsp grated fresh ginger

Directions and Total Time: 15 minutes

Place all ingredients in your blender, adding 1 cup of water or more for a lighter version. Serve immediately and enjoy!

Tropical Matcha Smoothie

Ingredients for 2 servings

1 cup chopped pineapple	3 picked mint leaves
1 cup chopped mango	½ cup coconut milk
1 cup chopped kale	½ cup orange juice
½ avocado	1 tsp matcha tea powder

Directions and Total Time: 15 minutes

Place all ingredients in your blender and purée until totally smooth. Serve in glasses and enjoy!

Refresh Smoothie

Ingredients for 2 servings

1 peeled apple, chopped	1 cup water
1 cup apple juice	½ cup ice
1 cup strawberries	1 cup chopped spinach
1 cup chopped cucumber	¼ cup fresh mint, chopped
½ cup coconut water	

Directions and Total Time: 15 minutes

Put all ingredients in your blender and blitz until you obtain the desired consistency. Pour the smoothie into glasses and serve immediately.

Sunrise Smoothie

Ingredients for 2 servings

1 peeled grapefruit, segmented	1 cup strawberries
1 banana	1 peeled carrot, chopped
1 cup chopped mango	1 cup grapefruit juice
1 cup chopped peach	

Directions and Total Time: 15 minutes + chilling time

Put all the ingredients into your blender and blitz until smooth, adding water if needed. Chill for 30 minutes before serving.

Wake-Up Smoothie

Ingredients for 4 servings

1 banana	1 cup spinach, chopped
¼ cup plant protein powder	½ cup coconut milk
1 tbsp flaxseed	1 cup water
1 tbsp cocoa powder	1 tsp maca powder
1 tbsp peanut butter	1 tsp cocoa nibs
1 tbsp agave nectar	

Directions and Total Time: 15 minutes

Add all the ingredients to your blender and pureé until smooth. Divide the smoothie between glasses and serve.

Watermelon & Raspberry Smoothie

Ingredients for 2 servings

1 cup strawberries	1 tbsp chia seeds
1 cup chopped watermelon	½ cup almond milk
1 cup raspberries	2 tbsp fresh mint, chopped

Directions and Total Time: 15 minutes

Place all the ingredients in your blender, add 1 cup of water and blitz until smooth. Serve and enjoy!

Work-Out Smoothie

Ingredients for 2 servings

1 banana	2 tbsp raisins
1 tbsp almond butter	1 tsp maple syrup
¼ tsp ground cinnamon	1 tbsp ground flaxseed
¼ tsp ground nutmeg	1 ½ cups orange juice

Directions and Total Time: 15 minutes

Blitz all the ingredients in your blender until smooth. Serve chilled.

Morning Oats

Ingredients for 1 serving

½ cup rolled oats	¼ tsp ground cinnamon
1 tbsp chia seeds	1 tbsp hazelnuts, chopped
1 tbsp date syrup	1 banana, sliced

Directions and Total Time: 10 minutes + soaking time

In a mixing bowl, place the oats, chia seeds, date syrup, and cinnamon. Pour enough cool water over the oats to submerge them, and stir to combine. Leave to soak for 1 hour. Top with banana and hazelnuts before serving.

Vanilla-Coconut Latte

Ingredients for 1 serving

½ cup full-fat coconut milk	¼ tsp vanilla extract
2 tsp coconut oil	1 scoop collagen powder
1 ½ cups hot coffee	
1 tbsp plant-based butter	
½ tsp ground cinnamon	

Directions and Total Time: 10 minutes

Pour the coconut milk and coconut oil into a pan over medium heat. Put the hot coffee, hot coconut milk mix, plant-based butter, cinnamon, and vanilla in a blender and hit blend and high for 15-30 seconds. Put the collagen and blend on the lowest setting. Serve and enjoy!

Chocolate-Oat Cookies

Ingredients for 5 servings

1 tbsp ground flaxseed	¼ tsp ground nutmeg
2 tbsp peanut butter	A pinch of salt
2 tbsp date syrup	½ cup rolled oats
1 peeled apple, shredded	¼ cup dark chocolate chips
1 tsp ground cinnamon	

Directions and Total Time: 30 minutes

Preheat oven to 350°F. Place the ground flaxseed in a small bowl and cover it with enough water; let sit to dissolve. Beat the peanut butter with date syrup in a bowl until creamy, then add the apple.

Pour in the flaxseed mixture. Sift the cinnamon, nutmeg, and salt into a separate bowl, then stir into the wet mixture. Fold in the oats and chocolate chips. Scoop out about 10 balls of dough and press lightly to flatten. Arrange the cookies on a parchment-lined baking sheet at least 2-3 inches apart. Bake for 12 minutes or until golden brown. Transfer the cookies to a wire rack to cool completely. Keep in an airtight container for up to 3 days.

Pumpkin Crumble Muffins

Ingredients for 6 servings

2 tbsp nut butter	2 cups whole-grain flour
1 ½ cups pumpkin purée	1 tsp baking powder
1/3 cup coconut sugar	1 tsp ground cinnamon
½ cup almond milk	A pinch of salt
2 tbsp ground flaxseed	½ cup walnuts, chopped
1 tsp apple cider vinegar	¼ cup dark chocolate chips
1 tsp pure vanilla extract	1 tbsp date sugar

Directions and Total Time: 35 minutes

Preheat the oven to 350°F. Lightly spray 12-cup muffin tin with cooking oil. Add nut butter, pumpkin puree, coconut sugar, almond milk, flaxseed, vinegar, and vanilla in a blender jar. Puree until well mixed. Sift flour, baking powder, cinnamon, salt, and chopped walnuts into a large bowl. Stir in the wet ingredients until it just comes together. Divide the batter between the muffin cups. Top with chocolate chips and date sugar. Bake for 15-20 minutes until a toothpick in the middle of the muffin comes out clean. Let cool for a few minutes. Serve.

"Cheesy" Granola

Ingredients for 6 servings

2 cups uncooked rolled oats	2 tsp dried thyme
1 cup chopped walnuts	1 tsp garlic powder
1 cup chopped raw almonds	¼ tsp chili powder
6 tbsp olive oil	Salt and black pepper to taste
¼ cup vegan Parmesan	

Directions and Total Time: 25 minutes

Preheat the oven to 375°F. Combine all of the ingredients in a large bowl. When well mixed, spread out onto a parchment-lined baking sheet and bake for 10 minutes. Toss the mixture with a spatula and bake for another 5 minutes until golden. Let cool. Serve and enjoy!

Berry Muesli Bowl

Ingredients for 5 servings

1 cup rolled oats	¼ cup chopped dried figs
1 cup quinoa flakes	¼ cup shredded coconut
2 cups puffed cereal	¼ cup non-dairy chocolate
¼ cup sunflower seeds	chips
¼ cup walnuts	1 tsp ground cinnamon
¼ cup raisins	½ cup applesauce
¼ cup dried pitted cherries	½ cup berries

Directions and Total Time: 20 minutes

Place the rolled oats, quinoa flakes, puffed cereal, sunflower seeds, walnuts, raisins, cherries, figs, coconut, chocolate chips, and cinnamon in a container and shake. Transfer the muesli to a bowl and add in with applesauce and berries. Stir to combine, then serve.

Date-Apple French Toast

Ingredients for 2 servings

2 tsp coconut oil	1 tbsp maple date syrup
½ tsp ground cinnamon	1 apple, cored and thinly sliced
½ tsp orange zest	2 slices whole-grain bread

Directions and Total Time: 40 minutes

Preheat the oven to 350°F. Combine coconut oil, cinnamon, orange zest, and date syrup in a large bowl. Toss in apple slices and coat. Transfer the apples to a medium skillet over medium heat. Cook until it has softened, or about 5 minutes. Place the apples on a plate and cook the bread in the same skillet. Cook for 2 or 3 minutes, then flip the bread. Cook for another 2 to 3 minutes. Arrange the cooked bread on a baking sheet and top with the apples. Bake for 15-20 minutes. Serve.

Crunchy Granola

Ingredients for 6 servings

3 cups uncooked rolled oats	4 tbsp cane sugar
½ cup vegan butter, melted	3 tsp ground cinnamon
¼ cup chopped raw cashews	½ tsp vanilla extract
¼ cup agave syrup	½ tsp sea salt

Directions and Total Time: 20 minutes + cooling time

Preheat the oven to 375°F. Combine oats, butter, cashews, agave syrup, 2 tbsp sugar, 2 tsp cinnamon, vanilla, and salt in a bowl. When well mixed, spread it out on a parchment-lined baking sheet. Bake for 10 minutes. Toss the mixture with a spatula and bake for another 5 minutes until golden. While the granola is cooking, mix the remaining sugar and cinnamon in a small bowl. Remove the baking sheet from the oven and sprinkle the cinnamon sugar over the granola. Let cool completely.

Morning Sunshine Muffins

Ingredients for 6 servings

2 tbsp almond butter	1 tsp pure vanilla extract
¼ cup almond milk	½ tsp ground cinnamon
1 tangerine, peeled	½ tsp ground ginger
1 carrot, coarsely chopped	¼ tsp ground nutmeg
2 tbsp chopped dried apricots	¾ cup rolled oats
3 tbsp molasses	1 tsp baking powder
2 tbsp ground flaxseed	2 tbsp raisins
1 tsp apple cider vinegar	2 tbsp sunflower seeds

Directions and Total Time: 45 minutes

Preheat the oven to 350°F. Lightly spray a 12-cup muffin tin with cooking oil. Add almond butter, milk, tangerine, carrot, apricots, molasses, flaxseed, vinegar, vanilla, cinnamon, ginger, and nutmeg to a food processor blender. Puree until mostly smooth. Process the oats in a clean blender jar or food processor until it resembles flour. Pour into a large bowl along with baking powder. Stir in wet ingredients until just comes together. Fold in raisins and sunflower seeds. Divide the batter among the muffin cups. Bake for 30 minutes or until a toothpick in the middle of the muffin comes out clean. Extra time may be needed depending on the weight of your tin.

Kiddo French Toasts with Blueberry Syrup

Ingredients for 6 servings

1 banana, mashed	A pinch of salt
1 cup almond milk	6 slices whole-grain bread
1 tsp pure vanilla extract	1 cup blueberries
¼ tsp lemon zest	2 tbsp orange juice
½ tsp ground cinnamon	1 tbsp maple syrup
1 ½ tsp arrowroot powder	

Directions and Total Time: 60 minutes

Preheat the oven to 350°F.

Beat together banana, almond milk, vanilla, lemon zest, cinnamon, arrowroot, and salt in a shallow bowl or pie pan. Dip the bread in the mixture and arrange in a single layer on a baking dish. Edges can touch if necessary. Pour excess banana mixture over the bread. Bake for 30 minutes until the bread is just brown. While the toast is baking, add blueberries, orange juice, and maple syrup to a small saucepan over medium heat. Use a spoon to break up the berries and let simmer for 15-20 minutes. Stir occasionally until the syrup has reduced. Plate the toast and drizzle with blueberry syrup. Serve warm.

Raspberry-Coconut Smoothie

Ingredients for 1 serving

¼ cup raspberries	1 tsp coconut cream
1 cup coconut milk	1 tbsp date sugar
½ tsp vanilla extract	

Directions and Total Time: 5 minutes

Put the blueberries, coconut milk, vanilla, coconut cream, and date sugar in a blender. Mix completely by blending for 30-60 seconds.

Chocolate-Rice Pudding

Ingredients for 2 servings

1 cup brown rice	1 tbsp almond butter
1 tsp ground cinnamon	1 tbsp hemp seeds
1 cup almond milk	2 tbsp walnuts
1 banana, mashed	¼ cup strawberries
2 tbsp cocoa powder	

Directions and Total Time: 45 minutes

Add brown rice, cinnamon, milk, and 1 cup water to a medium pot over high heat. Once it comes to a boil, reduce the heat to low and simmer. Cover the pot and cook for 25-30 minutes. As the rice is cooking, combine banana, cocoa powder, almond butter, and hemp seeds in a medium bowl. When the rice is done, add 1 cup of the rice to a bowl. Next, add half of the pudding. Finally, top with half of the walnuts and berries. Serve warm.

Mediterranean Sandwiches

Ingredients for 2 servings

1 tbsp wholegrain mustard	2 tbsp minced red onions
1 tbsp umeboshi vinegar	1 tbsp capers, minced
1 (15-oz) can garbanzo beans	1 tsp caper juice
¼ cup vegan mayonnaise	Salt and black pepper to taste
1 celery stalk, thinly sliced	4 bread slices, toasted

Directions and Total Time: 20 minutes

Mash garbanzo beans, mustard, vinegar, mayonnaise, celery, red onion, capers, caper juice, salt, and pepper in a large bowl. Spread ½ of the mixture over one piece of toast, then top with another piece of toast. Repeat for the other sandwich. Serve and enjoy.

Fruity Couscous Bowl

Ingredients for 1 serving

1 tangerine, zested and juiced	1 tbsp agave nectar
¼ cup whole-wheat couscous	1 tbsp fresh mint, minced
1 cup mixed berries	1 tbsp coconut flakes
½ cup cubed cantaloupe	

Directions and Total Time: 15 minutes

Preheat the oven to 350°F. Bring tangerine juice and half of the zest to a boil in a small pot. Add dry couscous to a small bowl and pour the tangerine juice over it. Place a plate or plastic wrap over the bowl to trap the steam for 5 minutes. Combine berries, cantaloupe, agave nectar, and the rest of the zest in another bowl. Remove the cover from the couscous and fluff the soft couscous with a fork. Add the fruit, mint, and coconut to the couscous.

Homemade Fruit & Nut Granola

Ingredients for 4 servings

2 cups rolled oats	½ cup pumpkin seeds
¾ cup rice flour	½ cup shredded coconut
1 tbsp ground cinnamon	1 ¼ cups apple juice
1 tsp ground ginger	½ cup raisins
½ cup walnuts, chopped	½ cup goji berries
½ cup almonds, chopped	

Preheat the oven to 350°F. Combine oats, flour, cinnamon, ginger, walnuts, almonds, pumpkin seeds, and coconut. Pour juice over the oat mixture and stir until just combined. Arrange the granola on a large baking sheet. Bake for 15 minutes, then stir with a spatula to ensure even dryness. Bake for another 30 minutes or until crunchy. Remove the granola and toss in raisins and goji berries. Serve and enjoy. Once cooled, granola can be stored in an airtight container for 2 weeks.

Mushroom & Chickpea Scramble

Ingredients for 1 serving

1 tsp olive oil	1 tsp paprika
½ cup mushrooms, sliced	1 tsp turmeric
Salt and black pepper to taste	1 tbsp nutritional yeast
½ cup green peas	½ cup grape tomatoes, diced
½ cup cooked chickpeas	¼ cup fresh cilantro, chopped

Directions and Total Time: 20 minutes

Preheat the oven to 350°F. Add oil to a large skillet over medium heat. Saute mushrooms and salt for 7-8 minutes, stirring occasionally. Stir in green peas. In a separate bowl, mash chickpeas with a fork, then transfer it to the skillet. Cook for a few minutes until they are heated through. Next, stir in paprika, turmeric, nutritional yeast, and black pepper. Add tomatoes and most of the cilantro and cook until just warm. Garnish with the rest of the cilantro. Serve warm and enjoy.

Cinnamon-Coconut Doughnuts

Ingredients for 6 servings

¼ cup applesauce	¾ cup coconut sugar
¼ cup almond milk	2 ½ tsp cinnamon
2 tbsp safflower oil	½ tsp ground nutmeg
1 ½ tsp vanilla	¼ tsp salt
½ tsp lemon zest	¾ tsp baking powder
1 ½ cups all-purpose flour	

Directions and Total Time: 35 minutes

Preheat air fryer to 350°F. Add applesauce, almond milk, oil, vanilla, and lemon zest. Stir well. In a different bowl, combine flour, ½ cup coconut sugar, ½ tsp cinnamon, nutmeg, salt, and baking powder. Stir well. Add the mixture to the wet mix and blend. Pull off bits of the dough and roll into balls. Place in the greased frying basket, leaving room between as they get bigger. Spray the tops with oil. Air Fry for 8-10 minutes, flipping once.

During the last 2 minutes of frying, place 4 tbsp of coconut sugar and 2 tsp of cinnamon in a bowl and stir to combine. After frying, coat each donut by spraying with oil and toss in the cinnamon-sugar mix. Serve.

Energy Matcha

Ingredients for 1 serving

1 tsp matcha powder	1 tsp coconut oil
½ cup boiling water	1 tsp date sugar
¼ cup coconut milk	½ tsp ground cinnamon

Directions and Total Time: 5 minutes

Pour the boiling water and the matcha in a bowl and stir until well-mixed. Use a frother if you have one. Pour the mix into a blender and add coconut milk, coconut oil, and date sugar in with it. Mix for 15-30 seconds. Add some cinnamon on top and serve.

Root Veggies with Avocado Dip

Ingredients for 2 servings

1 peeled and pitted avocado	1 beet, peeled and cubed
1 tbsp apple cider vinegar	1 daikon, peeled and cubed
1 tsp dried dill	2 baby carrots, cubed
Salt and black pepper to taste	1 tsp dried thyme
1 peeled sweet potato, cubed	¼ tsp cayenne pepper

Directions and Total Time: 40 minutes

Preheat the oven to 350°F. Puree avocado, vinegar, dill, salt, and 2-3 tablespoons of water in a blender until smooth. Set to the side. Add sweet potato, beet, daikon, carrots, and enough water to cover them in a large pot. Bring the water to a boil and continue boiling for 15 minutes. When the vegetables are just soft, drain the water. Season with salt, thyme, cayenne, and black pepper. Arrange the vegetables in a single layer on a large baking sheet. Roast for 10-15 minutes or until browned on the edges. Serve with avocado dip and enjoy.

Easy Oatmeal Bars with Blueberries

Ingredients for 6 servings

2 cups uncooked rolled oats	½ tsp ground cinnamon
2 cups all-purpose flour	1 cup coconut oil, melted
1 ½ cups dark-brown sugar	4 cups blueberries
1 ½ tsp baking soda	¼ cup sucanat
Salt to taste	2 tbsp potato starch

Directions and Total Time: 50 minutes

Preheat the oven to 425°F. Mix oats, flour, sugar, baking soda, salt, and cinnamon in a large bowl. Pour in oil and stir until combined and crumbly. Add blueberries in another large bowl along with sucanat and potato starch. Stir gently until evenly coated. Place 3 cups of the oat mixture into a greased baking pan and press to form the bottom layer. Top with the blueberry mixture. Sprinkle the rest of the crumble mixture over the blueberries. Bake for 40 minutes. Cool completely. Cut into 6 bars.

Peppermint Hot Chocolate

Ingredients for 1 serving

1 cup coconut milk	1 tbsp date sugar
1 ½ tbsp cacao powder	¼ tsp peppermint extract
¼ tsp ground cinnamon	1 tbsp coconut cream

Directions and Total Time: 10 minutes

Pour the coconut milk into a pan and warm it over low heat, allowing it to bubble. As it heats, put the cacao, cinnamon, date sugar, and peppermint extract in a blender. Pour in the coconut milk and blend for 30-60 seconds. Add some coconut whipped cream to the top.

Chocolate Pancakes with Coconut Cream

Ingredients for 4 servings

1 (15-oz) can coconut milk, refrigerated overnight
½ cup confectioners' sugar
1 cup all-purpose flour
1 tbsp baking powder
1 tbsp sucanat
¼ tsp ground cinnamon
1 tsp orange zest
1 cup rice milk
4 tbsp chocolate sprinkles
2 tbsp canola oil

Directions and Total Time: 25 minutes

In a small bowl, scoop out the coconut milk from the can. Use a fork to mash the milk while stirring in confectioners' sugar. Whisk flour, baking powder, sucanat, orange zest, and cinnamon in a large bowl. Fold in rice milk mixture until just combined without overmixing. Fold in 3 tablespoons of chocolate sprinkles. In a large skillet, heat oil over medium heat. Make one pancake at a time with ¼ cup of batter. Cook for 2 minutes until bubbles form in the middle, then flip the pancake. Cook for another 2 minutes until golden and cooked in the middle. Repeat the process with the rest of the batter. Top each serving with chilled coconut whipped cream and chocolate sprinkles. Serve warm.

Maple-Cinnamon Cereal Bowls

Ingredients for 2 servings

1 cup coconut flakes
2 tbsp plant-based butter
1 tbsp ground cinnamon
1 tsp pure maple sugar
2 tbsp cacao nibs
½ cup coconut milk

Directions and Total Time: 15 minutes

Preheat the oven to 325°F. Pour the coconut flakes into a bowl and set to the side. Put the plant-based butter, cinnamon, and pure maple sugar into a skillet and heat over medium heat. All the mix to melt and stir well. Add the mix to the coconut, stir well, then pour the flakes onto a cookie sheet in a single layer. Cook for 5-7 minutes, making sure to stir 2-3 times to avoid burning. When time is up, allow the flakes to chill on the counter. Spoon equal amounts into two bowls, add the cacao nibs, and pour coconut milk. Serve and enjoy!

Avocado-Ginger Smoothie

Ingredients for 1 serving

½ avocado, pitted and peeled
¼ cup almond milk
¼ cup coconut milk
½ tsp ground ginger
1 tsp lime juice
1 tbsp date sugar
½ cup ice

Directions and Total Time: 5 minutes

Put the avocado, almond milk, coconut milk, ginger, lime juice, and date sugar in a blender, then choose high and blend for 30-60 seconds. Put ice in last, blend, and serve.

Tofu French Toast

Ingredients for 4 servings

½ cup oat milk
¼ cup soft tofu
1 ½ tsp vanilla extract
A pinch of sea salt
½ cup organic cane sugar
1 tbsp ground cinnamon
¼ tsp lemon zest
4 tbsp vegan butter
8 pieces sturdy vegan bread
Maple syrup, for serving
1 cup blueberries

Directions and Total Time: 25 minutes

In a shallow bowl or pie plate, whisk milk, tofu, vanilla, and salt until the tofu has broken down and the mixture is smooth. In another shallow bowl or pie plate, whisk sugar, lemon zest, and cinnamon until combined. In a large skillet, melt 1 tablespoon of butter over medium heat. Dip 2 pieces of bread in the milk mixture on both sides. Do not soak. Place the bread in the skillet and cook for about 2 minutes per side. Dip the cooked bread in the cinnamon and sugar mixture on both sides. Shake off any excess. Repeat the process for the rest of the bread. Top with blueberries and syrup. Serve.

Coconut Breakfast

Ingredients for 2 servings

½ cup slivered almonds
1 tbsp coconut flakes
2 tbsp chia seeds
2 tbsp cacao nibs
2 tbsp sunflower seeds
½ cup almond milk

Directions and Total Time: 5 minutes

Mix the almonds, coconut, chia seeds, cacao nibs, and sunflower seeds, then put equal amounts of the mix into two bowls. Add the almond milk and serve.

Almond Bars

Ingredients for 4 servings

2 tbsp plant-based butter, melted
¼ cup almonds nuts
¼ cup nut peanut butter
1 tsp pure maple sugar
2 tbsp shredded coconut

Directions and Total Time: 10 minutes + chilling time

Put the almonds into your food processor and process until they are tiny grains. Mix the crushed nuts, peanut butter, pure maple sugar, and plant-based butter in a bowl and stir, then toss in the shredded coconut. Stir to combine. Lay parchment paper in a loaf pan, making sure to press it inside, then add the mix. Put in the fridge for an hour, then cut the mix into bars. Serve and enjoy!

Vegan Cheddar Grits

Ingredients for 4 servings

2 cups almond milk
Salt and black pepper to taste
1 cup stone-ground cornmeal
¼ tsp garlic powder
¼ cup vegan butter
1 cup vegan cheddar shreds

Directions and Total Time: 30 minutes

Heat milk, 2 cups water, and salt in a large pot over medium heat. Stir in cornmeal and whisk continuously. Reduce the heat to low and cover the pot. Simmer for 20 to 25 minutes while whisking every 3 to 4 minutes to prevent lumps. When the grits are creamy, remove from the heat and whisk in butter, garlic, and pepper. Next, slowly whisk in the vegan cheese. Serve hot and enjoy!

Mashed Potato Taquitos with Hot Sauce

Ingredients for 4 servings

1 potato, peeled and cubed	2 tbsp minced scallions
2 tbsp oat milk	4 corn tortillas
2 garlic cloves, minced	1 cup red chili sauce
Salt and black pepper to taste	1 avocado, sliced
½ tsp ground cumin	2 tbsp cilantro, chopped

Directions and Total Time: 30 minutes

In a pot fitted with a steamer basket, cook the potato cubes for 15 minutes on the stovetop. Pour the potato cubes into a bowl and mash with a potato masher. Add the milk, garlic, salt, pepper, and cumin and stir. Add the scallions and cilantro and stir them into the mixture. Set aside. Preheat air fryer to 390°F. Run the tortillas under water for a second, then place them in the greased frying basket. Air Fry for 1 minute. Lay the tortillas on a flat surface. Place an equal amount of the potato filling in the center of each. Roll the tortilla sides over the filling and place seam-side down in the frying basket. Fry for 7 minutes or until the tortillas are golden and slightly crisp. Serve with chili sauce and avocado slices. Enjoy!

Morning Berry Quinoa Bowl

Ingredients for 4 servings

3 cups cooked quinoa	1 cup blueberries
1 1/3 cups almond milk	½ cup chopped raw walnuts
2 bananas, sliced	¼ cup rice syrup
1 cup raspberries	

Directions and Total Time: 10 minutes

To prepare the bowls, layer the ingredients per bowl as follows. Start with ¾ cup quinoa and drizzle over 1/3 cup milk. Top with ½ banana, ¼ cup raspberries, ¼ cup blueberries, and 2 tablespoons walnuts. Add 1 tablespoon rice syrup over the top of each quinoa bowl. Serve.

Energy Smoothie Bowl

Ingredients for 1 serving

¼ avocado	1 cup apple juice
1 apple	¼ cup fresh blackberries
1 cup roughly chopped kale	1 tbsp chia seeds
2 peeled kiwis, sliced	

Directions and Total Time: 10 minutes

Place the avocado, apple, kale, 1 kiwi, and apple juice in your food processor and pulse until smooth. Pour the mixture into a bowl and top with the remaining kiwi and blackberries. Scatter with chia seeds and serve.

Sweet Corn Bread

Ingredients for 6 servings

1 mashed banana	¼ tsp salt
½ cup cornmeal	¼ tsp baking soda
½ cup pastry flour	½ tbsp lemon juice
1/3 cup sugar	½ cup almond milk
1 tsp lemon zest	¼ cup sunflower oil
½ tbsp baking powder	

Directions and Total Time: 35 minutes

Preheat air fryer to 350°F. Add the cornmeal, flour, sugar, lemon zest, baking powder, salt, and baking soda in a bowl. Stir with a whisk until combined. Add the mashed banana, lemon juice, almond milk, and oil to another bowl and stir well. Add the wet mixture to the dry mixture and stir gently until combined. Spray a baking pan with oil. Pour the batter in and Bake in the fryer for 25 minutes or until golden and a knife inserted in the center comes out clean. Cut into wedges and serve.

Zucchini Vegetarian Tacos

Ingredients for 3 servings

1 small zucchini, sliced	1 (15-oz) can refried beans
1 yellow onion, sliced	6 corn tortillas, warm
¼ tsp garlic powder	1 cup guacamole
Salt and black pepper to taste	1 tbsp cilantro, chopped

Directions and Total Time: 20 minutes

Preheat air fryer to 390°F. Place the zucchini and onion in the greased frying basket. Spray with more oil and sprinkle with garlic, salt, and pepper to taste. Roast for 6 minutes. Remove, shake, or stir, then cook for another 6 minutes, until the veggies are golden and tender. In a small pan, heat the refried beans over low heat. Stir often. When warm enough, remove and set aside. Place a corn tortilla on a plate and fill it with beans, roasted vegetables, and guacamole. Top with cilantro and enjoy!

Morning Apple Biscuits

Ingredients for 6 servings

1 apple	¼ cup peanut butter
1 cup oat flour	1/3 cup raisins
2 tbsp maple syrup	½ tsp ground cinnamon

Directions and Total Time: 15 minutes

Preheat air fryer to 350°F. Grate the apple with a grater. Combine apple, flour, maple syrup, peanut butter, raisins, and cinnamon in a bowl until combined. Make balls out of the mixture. Place them onto parchment paper and flatten them. Bake for 9 minutes until slightly brown.

Vegetarian Quinoa Cups

Ingredients for 6 servings

1 carrot, chopped	2 tbsp lemon juice
1 zucchini, chopped	¼ cup nutritional yeast
4 asparagus, chopped	¼ tsp garlic powder
¾ cup quinoa flour	Salt and black pepper to taste

Directions and Total Time: 25 minutes

Preheat air fryer to 340°F. Combine the vegetables, quinoa flour, water, lemon juice, nutritional yeast, garlic powder, salt, and pepper in a medium bowl, and mix well. Divide the mixture between 6 cupcake molds. Place the filled molds into the air fryer and Bake for 20 minutes, or until the tops are lightly browned, and a toothpick inserted into the center comes out clean. Leave to cool slightly before serving.

Chia Seed Banana Bread

Ingredients for 6 servings

2 bananas, mashed	¼ cup sugar
2 tbsp sunflower oil	½ tsp cinnamon
2 tbsp maple syrup	1 orange, zested
½ tsp vanilla	¼ tsp salt
½ tbsp chia seeds	¼ tsp ground nutmeg
½ tbsp ground flaxseeds	½ tsp baking powder
1 cup pastry flour	

Directions and Total Time: 35 minutes

Preheat air fryer to 350°F. Place the bananas, oil, maple syrup, vanilla, chia, and flaxseeds in a bowl and stir to combine. Add the flour, sugar, cinnamon, salt, nutmeg, baking powder, and orange zest. Stir to combine. Pour the batter into a greased baking pan. Smooth the top with a rubber spatula and Bake for 25 minutes or until a knife inserted in the center comes out clean. Remove and let cool for a minute. Then cut into wedges and serve.

Morning Potato Cakes

Ingredients for 6 servings

4 Yukon Gold potatoes	2 tbsp lemon juice
2 cups kale, chopped	2 tsp dried rosemary
1 cup rice flour	2 tsp shallot powder
¼ cup cornstarch	Salt and black pepper to taste
¾ cup almond milk	½ tsp turmeric powder

Directions and Total Time: 50 minutes

Preheat air fryer to 390°F. Scrub the potatoes and put them in the air fryer. Bake for 30 minutes or until soft. When cool, chop them into small pieces and place them in a bowl. Mash with a potato masher or fork. Add kale, rice flour, cornstarch, almond milk, lemon juice, rosemary, shallot powder, salt, pepper, and turmeric. Stir well. Make 12 balls out of the mixture and smash them lightly with your hands to make patties. Place them in the greased frying basket, and Air Fry for 10-12 minutes, flipping once, until golden and cooked through. Serve.

Vietnamese Gingered Tofu

Ingredients for 4 servings

1 (8-oz) package extra-firm tofu, cubed	
4 tsp shoyu	2 tbsp nutritional yeast
1 tsp onion powder	1 tsp dried rosemary
½ tsp garlic powder	1 tsp dried dill
½ tsp ginger powder	2 tsp cornstarch
½ tsp turmeric powder	2 tsp sunflower oil
Black pepper to taste	

Directions and Total Time: 25 minutes

Sprinkle the tofu with shoyu and toss to coat. Add the onion, garlic, ginger, turmeric, and pepper. Gently toss to coat. Add the yeast, rosemary, dill, and cornstarch. Toss to coat. Dribble with the oil and toss again. Preheat air fryer to 390°F. Spray the fryer basket with oil, put the tofu in the basket and Bake for 7 minutes. Remove, shake gently, and cook for another 7 minutes or until the tofu is crispy and golden. Serve warm.

less Mung Bean Tart

Ingredients for 2 servings

2 tsp soy sauce	½ cup mung beans, soaked
1 tsp lime juice	Salt and black pepper to taste
1 garlic clove, minced	½ minced shallot
½ tsp red chili flakes	1 green onion, chopped

Directions and Total Time: 20 minutes

Add the soy sauce, lime juice, garlic, and chili flakes to a bowl and stir. Set aside. Preheat the air fryer to 390°F. Place the drained beans in a blender along with ½ cup of water, salt, and pepper. Blend until smooth. Stir in shallot and green onion, but do not blend. Pour the batter into a greased baking pan. Bake for 15 minutes in the air fryer or until golden. A knife inserted in the center should come out clean. Once cooked through, cut the "quiche" into quarters. Drizzle with sauce and serve. Enjoy!

Vegan French Toast

Ingredients for 4 servings

1 ripe banana, mashed	2 tbsp ground flaxseed
¼ cup protein powder	4 bread slices
½ cup almond milk	2 tbsp agave syrup

Directions and Total Time: 15 minutes

Preheat air fryer to 370°F. Combine the banana, protein powder, almond milk, and flaxseed in a shallow bowl and mix well. Dip bread slices into the mixture. Place the slices on a lightly greased pan in a single layer and pour any of the remaining mixture evenly over the bread. Air Fry for 10 minutes, or until golden brown and crispy, flipping once. Serve warm topped with agave syrup.

Banana-Blackberry Muffins

Ingredients for 6 servings

1 ripe banana, mashed	2 tbsp coconut sugar
½ cup almond milk	¾ cup flour
1 tsp apple cider vinegar	1 tsp baking powder
1 tsp vanilla extract	½ tsp baking soda
2 tbsp ground flaxseed	¾ cup blackberries

Directions and Total Time: 20 minutes

Preheat air fryer to 350°F. Place the banana in a medium bowl. Stir in almond milk, apple vinegar, vanilla extract, flaxseed, and coconut sugar until combined. In another bowl, combine flour, baking powder, and baking soda. Pour it into the banana mixture and toss to combine. Divide the batter between 6 muffin molds. Top each with blackberries, pressing slightly. Bake for 16 minutes until golden brown and a toothpick comes out clean. Serve cooled.

After-Workout Smoothie

Ingredients for 2 servings

2 bananas, frozen	2 cups unsweetened rice milk
½ cup rolled oats	1 avocado
4 tbsp hemp hearts	1 tsp cinnamon
2 cups baby spinach	

Directions and Total Time: 10 minutes

Place the banana, oats, hemp hearts, spinach, avocado, cinnamon, and rice milk in a blender. Blend until smooth. Drink and enjoy as soon as possible.

Chia-Pineapple Pudding

Ingredients for 2 servings

4 tbsp chia seeds	2 cups pineapple chunks
1 ½ cups unsweetened oat milk	1 cup shredded coconut
½ tsp ground cinnamon	3 tbsp walnuts

Directions and Total Time: 20 minutes

In a large bowl, mix the chia seeds and oat milk and let set for 10 minutes. Add in the cinnamon, pineapples, coconut, and walnuts, stir together, and enjoy.

Bam-Bam Smoothie

Ingredients for 2 servings

2 cups cauliflower florets	2 tbsp chia seeds
2 cups strawberries	1 tsp vanilla extract
Juice of 1 lemon	3 cups almond milk
½ cup hemp hearts	

Directions and Total Time: 15 minutes

In a blender, combine the cauliflower, strawberries, lemon juice, hemp hearts, chia seeds, vanilla, and almond milk. Blend until smooth. Drink as soon as possible.

Nutty Oatmeal with Banana

Ingredients for 2 servings

¼ cup rolled or quick oats	¼ tsp vanilla extract
1/3 cup coconut milk	1 tbsp maple syrup
½ tsp ground cinnamon	¼ cup chopped pecans
⅛ tsp ground nutmeg	1 banana, sliced

Directions and Total Time: 10 minutes + chilling time

In a recipient, mix the oats, coconut milk, cinnamon, nutmeg, vanilla, and maple syrup. Add the pecans and banana to the oatmeal and fold them in. Seal the container and place in the refrigerator and let chill overnight.

Morning Cereal Bowl with Berries

Ingredients for 4 servings

1 cup sliced raspberries	2 tbsp pumpkin seeds
1 cup blackberries	2 tbsp hemp hearts
4 tbsp chopped cashews	½ cup almond milk
4 tbsp chopped almonds	

Directions and Total Time: 10 minutes

In a bowl, combine the raspberries, blackberries, cashews, almonds, pumpkin seeds, and hemp hearts. Pour the milk over the cereal and serve.

Mediterranean Tostada

Ingredients for 2 servings

2 tsp extra-virgin olive oil	10 cherry tomatoes, halved
2 large whole-grain tortillas	2 cups torn spinach
1 diced shalot	½ cup pesto

Directions and Total Time: 20 minutes

Preheat a large nonstick skillet over medium heat. Using ½ tsp of olive oil, brush both sides of the tortilla.

In the skillet, toast the tortilla until crispy on one side, then flip the tortilla and toast the other side. Remove from the pan. Add the remaining ½ tsp of olive oil to the skillet and sauté the shalot and cherry tomatoes for 3-4 minutes, until the shalot is translucent and fragrant.

Add the spinach and sauté for about 1 minute, until wilted. Spread the pesto on the toasted tortilla and then top with the sautéed vegetables.

Spicy Tofu & Pumpkin Hash

Ingredients for 4 servings

3 tbsp extra-virgin olive oil	1 tsp oregano
14 oz extra-firm tofu, crumbled	¼ tsp cumin
2 tbsp tamari sauce	¼ tsp thyme
1 tbsp white wine vinegar	2 cups pumpkin cubes
1 tbsp chili powder	½ cup chopped cilantro
2 tsp paprika	2 avocados, sliced
1 tsp garlic powder	

Directions and Total Time: 30 minutes

Preheat oven to 350°F. Combine 2 tbsp of oil, tamari sauce, vinegar, chili powder, paprika, garlic powder, oregano, cumin, and cloves in a small bowl and mix well. Add the tofu crumbles and toss to coat. Spread the mixture evenly on a greased baking sheet.

Toss the pumpkin with the remaining olive oil in another bowl and add it to the baking sheet. Bake in the oven until the tofu is chewy and the squash is cooked through, stirring halfway through the cooking time, about 25 minutes. Garnish with cilantro and avocado. Enjoy!

Green Hash Browns

Ingredients for 4 servings

1 head broccoli, cut into florets	
5 tbsp plant butter	½ white onion, grated
3 tbsp flax seed powder	Salt and black pepper to taste

Directions and Total Time: 35 minutes

In a small bowl, mix the flax seed powder with 9 tbsp water, and allow soaking for 5 minutes. Pour the broccoli into a food processor and pulse a few times until smoothly grated. Transfer the broccoli into a bowl, add the vegan "flax egg," white onion, salt, and black pepper. Use a spoon to mix the ingredients evenly and set aside 5 to 10 minutes to firm up a bit. Place a large non-stick skillet over medium heat and drop 1/3 of the plant butter to melt until no longer shimmering.

Ladle scoops of the broccoli mixture into the skillet (about 3 to 4 hash browns per batch). Flatten the pancakes to measure 3 to 4 inches in diameter, and fry until golden brown on one side, 4 minutes. Turn the pancakes with a spatula and cook the other side to brown too, another 5 minutes. Transfer the hash browns to a serving plate and repeat the frying process for the remaining broccoli mixture. Serve the hash browns warm with green salad.

Avocado & Tofu Shakshuka

Ingredients for 4 servings

14 oz extra-firm tofu, pressed and sliced
1 (14-oz) can diced fire-roasted tomatoes

2 tbsp olive oil	1 tsp ground cumin
2 tbsp crumbled tofu	1 tsp ground coriander
1 red bell pepper, chopped	2 tbsp chopped parsley
1 shallot, chopped	1 avocado, sliced
1 tsp red pepper flakes	

Directions and Total Time: 30 minutes

Preheat oven to 360°F. Warm the olive oil in a skillet over medium heat. Add and sauté the bell pepper and shallot for 3-5 minutes until slightly tender. Sprinkle with cumin and coriander and stir for 30 seconds. Add the tomatoes and mix well.

Arrange the tofu slices on top, cover the pan with lid, and reduce the heat. Simmer for 10 minutes. Then, remove the lid and transfer the pan to the oven. Bake for 8-10 minutes until the tofu is crisp. Top with crumbled tofu, red pepper flakes, parsley, and sliced avocado. Enjoy!

Eggless Tomato-Kale Frittata

Ingredients for 4 servings

1 cup chickpea flour	2 cups kale leaves, chopped
Salt and black pepper to taste	1 orange bell pepper, chopped
1 tbsp extra-virgin olive oil	1 cup grape tomatoes, halved

Directions and Total Time: 65 minutes

In a mixing bowl, whisk together the chickpea flour with 2 cups of water. Season with salt and pepper; set aside.

Preheat the oven to 400°F. Warm the olive oil in a deep sauté pan over medium heat. Add kale, bell pepper, and tomatoes and stir-fry until the kale is wilted and bright green, about 5 minutes. Pour the whisked chickpea mixture into the pan.

Gently stir with a spatula to evenly distribute the vegetables in the mixture. Place the pan to the oven and bake for 30-40 minutes until firm and golden or when an inserted toothpick in the center comes out clean. Remove the pan from the oven and let sit for 5-10 minutes before slicing. Serve and enjoy!

Homemade Tofu Yogurt Parfaits with Figs

Ingredients for 4 servings

12 oz of soft tofu	½ cup maple syrup, divided
1 banana	4 tbsp chia seeds
¼ cup almond milk	12 figs, thinly sliced
¼ cup lemon juice	

Directions and Total Time: 20 minutes

In a blender, mix the tofu, banana, almond milk, lemon juice, and ¼ cup of maple syrup until smooth. Divide the resulting yogurt between 4 bowls. Add 1 tbsp of chia seeds to each bowl and mix. Top evenly each bowl with the fig slices. To serve, drizzle each bowl with the remaining maple syrup.

Veggie & Tofu Scramble

Ingredients for 4 servings

14 oz extra-firm tofu, pressed and broken into small chunks

1 tbsp extra-virgin olive oil	2 cups baby spinach
1 yellow onion, diced	¼ cup nutritional yeast
2 garlic cloves, minced	1 tsp turmeric
1 red bell pepper, chopped	Salt and black pepper to taste
2 asparagus, chopped	

Directions and Total Time: 20 minutes

Warm the olive oil in a skillet over medium heat. Add the onion, garlic, asparagus, bell pepper, salt, and pepper and sauté for 4-5 minutes, until the onion is translucent. Add the tofu, spinach, nutritional yeast, and turmeric. Stir-fry until the spinach is wilted and the tofu is heated through, about 4-5 minutes. Serve and enjoy!

Sesame Bread

Ingredients for 6 servings

4 tbsp sesame oil	2 tbsp psyllium husk powder
4 tbsp flax seed powder	1 tsp salt
2/3 cup coconut cream cheese	1 tsp baking powder
1 cup coconut flour	1 tbsp sesame seeds

Directions and Total Time: 40 minutes

In a bowl, mix the flax seed powder with 1 ½ cups water until smoothly combined and set aside to soak for 5 minutes. Preheat oven to 400°F. When the vegan "flax egg" is ready, beat in the cream cheese and sesame oil until well mixed. Whisk in the coconut flour, psyllium husk powder, salt, and baking powder until adequately blended. Spread the dough onto a greased baking tray. Allow the mixture to stand for 5 minutes and then brush with some sesame oil. Sprinkle with the sesame seeds and bake the dough for 30 minutes or until golden brown on top and set within. Take out the bread and allow cooling for a few minutes. Slice and serve.

Cherry-Apple Oatmeal Cups

Ingredients for 2 servings

2/3 cup rolled oats	½ tsp ground cinnamon
1 cored apple, diced	¾ cup almond milk
4 pitted cherries, diced	

Directions and Total Time: 20 minutes

Preheat air fryer to 350°F. Mix the oats, apple, cherries, and cinnamon in a heatproof bowl. Add in almond milk and Bake for 6 minutes, stir well and Bake for 6 more minutes until the fruit are soft. Serve cooled.

Exotic Pancakes

Ingredients for 4 servings

2 tsp plant butter	A pinch salt
2 tbsp flax seed powder	1 tbsp coconut sugar
½ cup coconut milk	2 tbsp pure date syrup
¼ cup raspberries, mashed	½ tsp cinnamon powder
½ cup oat flour	2 tbsp coconut flakes
1 tsp baking soda	Fresh raspberries for garnishing

Directions and Total Time: 25 minutes

In a medium bowl, mix the flax seed powder with the 6 tbsp water and thicken for 5 minutes. Mix in coconut milk and raspberries. Add the oat flour, baking soda, salt, coconut sugar, date syrup, and cinnamon powder. Fold in the coconut flakes until well combined.

Working in batches, melt a quarter of the butter in a non-stick skillet and add ¼ cup of the batter. Cook until set beneath and golden brown, 2 minutes. Flip the pancake and cook on the other side until set and golden brown, 2 minutes. Transfer to a plate and make the remaining pancakes using the rest of the ingredients in the same proportions. Top the pancakes with some raspberries.

Yummy Almond Waffles

Ingredients for 4 servings

2 tbsp plant butter	A pinch of salt
1 cup fresh almond butter	1 ½ cups almond milk
2 tbsp flax seed powder	2 tbsp pure maple syrup
2/3 cup almond flour	1 tsp fresh lemon juice
2 ½ tsp baking powder	

Directions and Total Time: 20 minutes

In a medium bowl, mix the flaxseed powder with 6 tbsp water and allow soaking for 5 minutes. Add the almond flour, baking powder, salt, and almond milk. Mix until well combined. Preheat a waffle iron and brush with some plant butter. Pour in a quarter cup of the batter, close the iron and cook until the waffles are golden and crisp, 2-3 minutes. Transfer the waffles to a plate and make more waffles using the same process and ingredient proportions. In a bowl, mix the almond butter with maple syrup and lemon juice. Spread the top with the almond-lemon mixture and serve.

Pistachio-Pumpkin Cake

Ingredients for 4 servings

3 tbsp vegetable oil	½ tsp cinnamon powder
2 tbsp flaxseed powder	½ tsp baking powder
¾ cup canned pumpkin puree	¼ tsp cloves powder
½ cup pure corn syrup	½ tsp allspice powder
3 tbsp pure date sugar	½ tsp nutmeg powder
1 ½ cups whole-wheat flour	2 tbsp chopped pistachios

Directions and Total Time: 70 minutes

Preheat oven to 350°F. In a bowl, mix the flax seed powder with 6 tbsp water and allow thickening for 5 minutes to make the vegan "flax egg." In a bowl, whisk the vegetable oil, pumpkin puree, corn syrup, date sugar, and vegan "flax egg." In another bowl, mix the flour, cinnamon powder, baking powder, cloves powder, allspice powder, and nutmeg powder. Add this mixture to the wet batter and mix until well combined. Pour the batter into a greased loaf pan, sprinkle the pistachios on top, and gently press the nuts onto the batter to stick.

Bake in the oven for 50-55 minutes or until a toothpick inserted into the cake comes out clean. Remove the cake onto a wire rack, allow cooling, slice, and serve.

Creole Kale & Tofu Scramble

Ingredients for 4 servings

¼ cup grated plant-based Parmesan cheese	
2 tbsp plant butter	2 tbsp chopped green onions
1 (14-oz) pack tofu, crumbled	Salt and black pepper to taste
1 red bell pepper, chopped	1 tsp turmeric powder
1 green bell pepper, chopped	1 tsp Creole seasoning
1 tomato, finely chopped	½ cup chopped baby kale

Directions and Total Time: 20 minutes

Melt the plant butter in a skillet over medium heat. Add the tofu. Cook with occasional stirring until the tofu is light golden brown while making sure not to break the tofu into tiny bits but to have scrambled resemblance, 5 minutes. Stir in the bell peppers, tomato, green onions, salt, black pepper, turmeric powder, and Creole seasoning. Sauté until the vegetables soften, 5 minutes. Mix in the kale to wilt, 3 minutes and then half of the plant-based Parmesan cheese. Allow melting for 1 to 2 minutes and then turn the heat off. Top with the remaining cheese and serve warm.

Avocado & Mushroom Panini

Ingredients for 4 servings

1 cup sliced button mushrooms	
4 oz sliced plant-based Parmesan cheese	
1 tbsp olive oil	2 tbsp lemon juice
Salt and black pepper to taste	½ tsp pure maple syrup
1 ripe avocado, sliced	8 slices whole-wheat ciabatta

Directions and Total Time: 30 minutes

Heat the olive oil in a medium skillet over medium heat and sauté the mushrooms until softened, 5 minutes. Season with salt and black pepper. Turn the heat off.

Preheat a panini press to medium heat, 3 to 5 minutes. Mash the avocado in a medium bowl and mix in the lemon juice and maple syrup. Spread the mixture on 4 bread slices, divide the mushrooms and plant-based Parmesan cheese on top. Cover with the other bread slices and brush the top with olive oil. Grill the sandwiches one after another in the heated press until golden brown, and the Parmesan cheese is melted. Serve.

Soy Chorizo & Corn Grits with Cheddar

Ingredients for 6 servings

½ cup grated plant-based cheddar cheese	
2 tbsp peanut butter	1 cup corn kernels
1 cup quick-cooking grits	2 cups vegetable broth
1 cup soy chorizo, chopped	Salt to taste

Directions and Total Time: 25 minutes

Preheat oven to 380°F. Pour the broth in a pot and bring to a boil over medium heat. Stir in salt and grits. Lower the heat and cook until the grits are thickened, stirring often. Turn the heat off, put in the plant-based cheddar cheese, peanut butter, soy chorizo, and corn; mix well. Spread the mixture into a greased baking dish and bake for 45 minutes until slightly puffed and golden brown.

Spicy Tofu Scramble

Ingredients for 4 servings

3 oz grated plant-based Parmesan
2 tbsp plant butter for frying   2 tbsp chopped scallions
8 oz extra firm tofu   Salt and black pepper to taste
1 green bell pepper, chopped   1 tsp Mexican chili powder
1 tomato, finely chopped

Directions and Total Time: 46 minutes

Place the tofu in between two parchment papers to drain liquid for about 30 minutes. Melt the plant butter in a large non-stick skillet until no longer foaming. Crumble the tofu into the plant butter and fry until golden brown, stirring occasionally, making sure not to break the tofu into tiny pieces. The goal is to have the tofu like scrambled eggs, about 4 to 6 minutes.

Stir in the bell pepper, tomato, scallions, and cook until the vegetables are soft, about 4 minutes. Then, season with salt, black pepper, chili powder, and stir in the plant-based Parmesan to incorporate and melt for about 2 minutes. Spoon the scramble into a serving platter.

Chia & Coconut Pudding with Nectarines

Ingredients for 4 servings

1 cup coconut milk   ½ cup granola
½ tsp vanilla extract   2/3 cup chopped nectarine
3 tbsp chia seeds

Directions and Total Time: 5 minutes+ cooling time

In a bowl, mix the coconut milk, vanilla, and chia seeds until well combined. Divide the mixture between 4 breakfast cups and refrigerate for at least 4 hours to allow the mixture to gel. Top with granola and nectarine.

Almond Crêpes with Berry Cream

Ingredients for 4 servings

For the berry cream:
2 tbsp plant butter   ½ cup fresh blueberries
2 tbsp pure date sugar   ½ cup fresh raspberries
1 tsp vanilla extract   ½ cup coconut cream
For the crepes:
3 tbsp plant butter   ¼ tsp salt
2 tbsp flax seed powder   2 cups almond flour
1 tsp vanilla extract   1 ½ cups almond milk
1 tsp pure date sugar   1 ½ cups water

Directions and Total Time: 35 minutes

Melt butter in a pot over low heat. Mix in date sugar and vanilla. Cook until the sugar melts and then toss in berries. Allow softening for 2-3 minutes. Set aside to cool.

In a bowl, mix the flax seed powder with 6 tbsp water and allow to thicken for 5 minutes to make the vegan "flax egg." Whisk in vanilla, date sugar, and salt. Pour in ¼ cup of almond flour and whisk, then a quarter cup of almond milk, and mix until no lumps remain. Repeat the mixing process with the remaining almond flour and almond milk in the same quantities until exhausted.

Mix in 1 cup of water until the mixture is runny like that of pancakes, and add the remaining water until it is lighter. Brush a large non-stick skillet with some butter and place over medium heat to melt. Pour 1 tablespoon of the batter into the pan and swirl the skillet quickly and all around to coat the pan with the batter.

Cook until the batter is dry and golden brown beneath, about 30 seconds. Use a spatula to carefully flip the crepe and cook the other side until golden brown too. Fold the crepe onto a plate and set aside. Repeat making more crepes with the remaining batter until exhausted. Plate the crepes, top with the whipped coconut cream and the berry compote. Serve immediately.

Coconut French Toasts

Ingredients for 2 servings

3 tbsp plant butter   1 ½ tsp baking powder
2 tbsp coconut cream   A pinch of salt
4 tbsp flaxseed   2 tbsp coconut cream
2 tbsp coconut flour   ½ tsp cinnamon powder
2 tbsp almond flour

Directions and Total Time: 16 minutes

For the vegan "flax egg," whisk flax seed powder and 12 tbsp water in two separate bowls and leave to soak for 5 minutes. Grease a glass dish (for the microwave) with 1 tsp plant butter. In another bowl, mix coconut flour, almond flour, baking powder, and salt.

When the flaxseed egg is ready, whisk one portion with the coconut cream and add the mixture to the dry ingredients. Continue whisking until the mixture is smooth with no lumps. Pour the dough into the glass dish and microwave for 2 minutes or until the bread's middle part is done. Take out and allow the bread to cool. Remove the bread and slice in half. Return to the glass dish. Whisk the remaining vegan "flax egg" with the coconut milk whipping cream until well combined. Pour the mixture over the bread slices and leave to soak. Turn the bread a few times to soak in as much of the batter. Melt 2 tbsp of the plant butter in a frying pan and fry the bread slices on both sides. Transfer to a serving plate, sprinkle with cinnamon powder and serve.

Strawberry-Coconut Porridge

Ingredients for 2 servings

1 oz olive oil   1 tbsp coconut flour
5 tbsp coconut cream   1 pinch ground chia seeds
1 tbsp flax seed powder   Thawed frozen strawberries

Directions and Total Time: 12 minutes

In a small bowl, mix the flax seed powder with the 3 tbsp water, and allow soaking for 5 minutes.

Place a non-stick saucepan over low heat and pour olive oil, vegan "flax egg," coconut flour, chia seeds, and coconut cream. Cook the mixture while stirring continuously until your desired consistency is achieved. Turn the heat off and spoon the porridge into serving bowls. Top with 4 to 6 strawberries and serve immediately.

Apple Pancakes

Ingredients for 4 servings

1 tbsp coconut oil	1 tsp sea salt
2 cups almond milk	½ tsp ground cinnamon
1 tsp apple cider vinegar	¼ tsp grated nutmeg
2 ½ cups whole-wheat flour	¼ tsp ground allspice
2 tbsp baking powder	½ cup applesauce
½ tsp baking soda	1 cup water

Directions and Total Time: 30 minutes

Whisk the almond milk and apple cider vinegar in a bowl and set aside. In another bowl, combine the flour, baking powder, baking soda, salt, cinnamon, nutmeg, and allspice. Transfer the almond mixture to another bowl and beat with the applesauce and water. Pour in the dry ingredients and stir. Melt some coconut oil in a skillet over medium heat. Pour a ladle of the batter and cook for 5 minutes, flipping once until golden. Repeat the process until the batter is exhausted. Serve warm.

Pear & Pecan Farro Breakfast

Ingredients for 4 servings

1 tbsp plant butter	1 cup farro
2 cups water	2 peeled pears, chopped
½ tsp salt	¼ cup chopped pecans

Directions and Total Time: 20 minutes

Bring water to a boil in a pot over high heat. Stir in salt and farro. Lower the heat, cover, and simmer for 15 minutes until the farro is tender and the liquid has absorbed. Turn the heat off and add in the butter, pears, and pecans. Cover and rest for 12-15 minutes. Serve.

Lemon-Blackberry Waffles

Ingredients for 4 servings

¼ cup plant butter, melted	1 tsp ground cinnamon
1 ½ cups whole-heat flour	2 cups soy milk
½ cup old-fashioned oats	1 tbsp fresh lemon juice
¼ cup date sugar	1 tsp lemon zest
3 tsp baking powder	½ cup fresh blackberries
½ tsp salt	

Directions and Total Time: 15 minutes

Preheat the waffle iron. In a bowl, mix flour, oats, sugar, baking powder, salt, and cinnamon. Set aside. In another bowl, combine milk, lemon juice, lemon zest, and butter. Pour into the wet ingredients and whisk to combine. Add the batter to the hot greased waffle iron, using approximately a ladleful for each waffle. Cook for 3-5 minutes, until golden brown. Repeat the process until no batter is left. Serve topped with blackberries.

Breakfast Couscous with Dates & Nuts

Ingredients for 4 servings

½ cup chopped macadamia nuts

3 cups apple juice	¼ tsp ground cloves
1 ½ cups couscous	½ cup dried dates
1 tsp ground cinnamon	

Directions and Total Time: 20 minutes

Pour the apple juice into a pot over medium heat and bring to a boil. Stir in couscous, cinnamon, and cloves. Turn the heat off and cover. Let sit for 5 minutes until the liquid is absorbed. Using a fork, fluff the couscous and add the dates and macadamia nuts, stir to combine.

Maple-Walnut Waffles

Ingredients for 4 servings

3 tbsp plant butter, melted	1 tbsp baking powder
1 ¾ cups whole-wheat flour	1 ½p cups soy milk
1/3 cup ground walnuts	3 tbsp pure maple syrup

Directions and Total Time: 15 minutes

Preheat the waffle iron and grease with oil. Combine the flour, walnuts, and baking powder in a bowl. Set aside. In another bowl, mix the milk and butter. Pour into the walnut mixture and whisk until well combined. Spoon a ladleful of the batter onto the waffle iron. Cook for 3-5 minutes, until golden brown. Repeat the process until no batter is left. Top with maple syrup to serve.

Date-Orange Cups

Ingredients for 6 servings

1 tsp vegetable oil	½ tsp ground cinnamon
3 cups bran flakes cereal	½ tsp salt
1 ½ cups whole-wheat flour	1/3 cup brown sugar
½ cup dates, chopped	¾ cup fresh orange juice
3 tsp baking powder	

Directions and Total Time: 30 minutes

Preheat oven to 400°F. Grease a 12-cup muffin tin with oil. Mix the bran flakes, flour, dates, baking powder, cinnamon, and salt in a bowl. In another bowl, combine the sugar and orange juice until blended. Pour into the dry mixture and whisk. Divide the mixture between the cups of the muffin tin. Bake for 20 minutes or until golden brown and set. Cool for a few minutes before removing from the tin and serve.

Almond Muffins with Blueberries

Ingredients for 12 servings

1 tbsp coconut oil melted	1 tsp apple cider vinegar
1 cup quick-cooking oats	1 ½ cups whole-wheat flour
1 cup boiling water	½ cup pure date sugar
½ cup almond milk	2 tsp baking soda
¼ cup ground flaxseed	A pinch of salt
1 tsp almond extract	1 cup blueberries

Directions and Total Time: 30 minutes

Preheat oven to 400°F. In a bowl, stir in the oats with boiling water until they are softened. Pour in the coconut oil, milk, flaxseed, almond extract, and vinegar. Add in the flour, sugar, baking soda, and salt. Gently stir in blueberries. Divide the batter between greased muffin tins. Bake for 20 minutes until lightly brown. Allow cooling for 10 minutes. Using a spatula, run the sides of the muffins to take out. Serve chilled.

Maple Nut & Raisin Granola

Ingredients for 6 servings

5 ½ cups old-fashioned oats	1 cup pure maple syrup
1 ½ cups chopped walnuts	½ tsp ground cinnamon
½ cup shelled sunflower seeds	¼ tsp ground allspice
1 cup golden raisins	A pinch of salt
1 cup shaved almonds	

Directions and Total Time: 20 minutes

Preheat oven to 325°F. In a baking dish, place the oats, walnuts, and sunflower seeds. Bake for 10 minutes. Lower the heat from the oven to 300°F. Stir in the raisins, almonds, maple syrup, cinnamon, allspice, and salt. Bake for an additional 15 minutes. Serve cooled.

Morning Muesli with Chocolate & Blueberries

Ingredients for 5 servings

¼ cup non-dairy chocolate chips	
2 cups spelt flakes	¼ cup chopped dried figs
2 cups puffed cereal	¼ cup shredded coconut
¼ cup sunflower seeds	3 tsp ground cinnamon
¼ cup almonds	½ cup coconut milk
¼ cup raisins	½ cup blueberries
¼ cup dried cranberries	

Directions and Total Time: 10 minutes

In a bowl, combine the spelt flakes, puffed cereal, sunflower seeds, almonds, raisins, cranberries, figs, coconut, chocolate chips, and cinnamon. Toss to mix well. Pour in the coconut milk. Let sit for 1 hour and serve topped with blueberries.

Mango-Almond Quinoa with Raspberries

Ingredients for 2 servings

2 tbsp almond butter	3 tbsp cocoa powder
1 cup quinoa	1 tbsp hemp seeds
1 tsp ground cinnamon	1 tbsp walnuts
1 cup non-dairy milk	¼ cup raspberries
1 large mango, chopped	

Directions and Total Time: 35 minutes

In a pot, combine the quinoa, cinnamon, milk, and 1 cup of water over medium heat. Bring to a boil, low heat, and simmer covered for 25-30 minutes. In a bowl, mash the mango and mix cocoa powder, almond butter, and hemp seeds. In a serving bowl, place cooked quinoa and mango mixture. Top with walnuts and raspberries. Serve.

Walnut & Berry Topped Yogurt

Ingredients for 4 servings

4 cups dairy-free yogurt, cold	2 cups mixed berries, chopped
2 tbsp pure malt syrup	¼ cup chopped walnuts

Directions and Total Time: 10 minutes

In a medium bowl, mix the yogurt and malt syrup until well-combined. Divide the mixture into 4 breakfast bowls. Top with the berries and walnuts. Enjoy immediately.

Spiced Oat Jars with Pecans & Pumpkin Seeds

Ingredients for 5 servings

2 ½ cups old-fashioned rolled oats	
5 tbsp pumpkin seeds	Salt to taste
5 tbsp chopped pecans	1 tsp ground cardamom
5 cups soy milk	1 tsp ground ginger
2 ½ tsp agave syrup	

Directions and Total Time: 10 minutes + chilling time

In a bowl, put oats, pumpkin seeds, pecans, soy milk, agave syrup, salt, cardamom, and ginger and toss to combine. Divide the mixture between mason jars. Seal the lids and transfer to the fridge to soak for 10-12 hours.

Sweet Lemon & Quinoa Muffins

Ingredients for 5 servings

2 tbsp coconut oil, melted	2 ½ cups whole-wheat flour
¼ cup ground flaxseed	1 ½ cups cooked quinoa
2 cups lemon curd	2 tsp baking soda
½ cup pure date sugar	A pinch of salt
1 tsp apple cider vinegar	½ cup raisins

Directions and Total Time: 25 minutes

Preheat oven to 400°F. In a bowl, combine the flaxseed and ½ cup water. Stir in the lemon curd, sugar, coconut oil, and vinegar. Add in flour, quinoa, baking soda, and salt. Put in the raisins, be careful not to be too fluffy. Divide the batter between a greased muffin tin and bake for 20 minutes until golden and set. Allow cooling slightly before removing it from the tin. Serve.

Barley & Oat Porridge with Almonds

Ingredients for 4 servings

2 ½ cups vegetable broth	½ cup slivered almonds
2 ½ cups almond milk	¼ cup nutritional yeast
½ cup steel-cut oats	2 cups old-fashioned rolled oats
1 tbsp pearl barley	

Directions and Total Time: 25 minutes

Pour the broth and almond milk in a pot over medium heat and bring to a boil. Stir in oats, pearl barley, almond slivers, and nutritional yeast. Reduce the heat and simmer for 20 minutes. Add in the rolled oats, cook for an additional 5 minutes, until creamy. Serve chilled.

Kale & Pumpkin Stir-Fry

Ingredients for 2 servings

1 tbsp olive oil	2 garlic cloves, minced
1 cup pumpkin, shredded	½ tsp dried thyme
½ onion, chopped	1 cup chopped kale
1 carrot, peeled and chopped	Salt and black pepper to taste

Directions and Total Time: 25 minutes

Heat the oil in a skillet over medium heat. Sauté onion and carrot for 5 minutes. Add in garlic and thyme and cook for 30 seconds. Place in the pumpkin and cook for 10 minutes until tender. Stir in kale, cook for 4 minutes until the kale wilts. Season with salt and pepper. Serve.

Paradise Smoothie

Ingredients for 4 servings

1 banana	1 cup strawberries
1 cup chopped mango	1 carrot, peeled and chopped
1 cup chopped apricots	1 cup water

Directions and Total Time: 5 minutes

Put the banana, mango, apricots, strawberries, carrot, and water in a food processor. Pulse until smooth; add more water if needed. Divide between glasses and serve.

Powerful Smoothie

Ingredients for 3 servings

1 banana	1 tbsp hemp hearts
½ cup coconut milk	¼ tsp ground cinnamon
1 cup broccoli sprouts	¼ tsp ground cardamom
2 cherries, pitted	1 tbsp grated fresh ginger

Directions and Total Time: 5 minutes

In a food processor, place banana, coconut milk, 1 cup of water, broccoli, cherries, hemp hearts, cinnamon, cardamom, and ginger. Blitz until smooth. Serve in glasses.

Energetic Smoothie

Ingredients for 2 servings

1 cup peeled and diced carrots	2 tbsp maple syrup
1 cup strawberries	2 cups almond milk
1 apple, chopped	

Directions and Total Time: 5 minutes

Place in a food processor all the ingredients. Blitz until smooth. Pour in glasses and serve.

Kiwi & Banana Smoothie

Ingredients for 2 servings

1 banana, sliced	1 orange, cut into segments
2 cups kale	1 cup coconut milk
1 cup sliced kiwi	

Directions and Total Time: 10 minutes

In a food processor, put the banana, kale, kiwi, orange, and coconut milk. Pulse until smooth. Serve in glasses.

Arugula & Blueberry Smoothie

Ingredients for 4 servings

4 cups chopped arugula	Juice of 2 limes
2 cups frozen blueberries	4 tbsp maple syrup
4 cups almond milk	

Directions and Total Time: 5 minutes

In a food processor, blitz the arugula, blueberries, almond milk, lime juice, and maple syrup until smooth.

Mayan Smoothie Bowl

Ingredients for 4 servings

4 bananas, sliced	2 cups fresh raspberries
1 cup papaya	½ cup slivered almonds
1 cup baked granola, crushed	4 cups plant-based milk

Directions and Total Time: 10 minutes

Put bananas, papaya, raspberries, and milk in a food processor and pulse until smooth. Transfer to a bowl and stir in granola. Top with almonds and serve.

Wake-Up Smoothie

Ingredients for 2 servings

1 scoop plant-based protein powder	
1 banana, sliced	1 tbsp chia seeds
1 peach, chopped	1 cucumber, chopped
1 cup almond milk	

Directions and Total Time: 5 minutes

Purée the banana, peach, almond milk, protein powder, chia seeds, and cucumber for 50 seconds until smooth in a food processor. Serve immediately in glasses.

Strawberry-Banana Smoothie

Ingredients for 4 servings

4 bananas, sliced	4 cups kale
4 cups strawberries	4 cups plant-based milk

Directions and Total Time: 5 minutes

In a food processor, add bananas, strawberries, kale, and milk and blitz until smooth. Divide between glasses. Serve.

Hazelnut-Berry Quinoa Bowl

Ingredients for 4 servings

3 cups cooked quinoa	2 cups berries
1 1/3 cups almond milk	½ cup chopped raw hazelnuts
2 bananas, sliced	¼ cup agave syrup

Directions and Total Time: 5 minutes

In a large bowl, combine the quinoa, milk, banana, berries, and hazelnuts. Divide between serving bowls and top with agave syrup to serve.

Popeye´s Smoothie

Ingredients for 2 servings

1 avocado	2 cups almond milk
2 cups baby spinach	Juice of 1 lime
1 cup peach chunks	2 tbsp maple syrup

Directions and Total Time: 5 minutes

In a food processor, combine avocado, spinach, peach, milk, lime juice, and maple syrup. Purée until smooth.

Minty Fruit Smoothie

Ingredients for 3 servings

1 cup strawberries	½ cup coconut milk
1 cup chopped watermelon	1 cup water
1 cup cranberries	1 tsp goji berries
1 tbsp chia seeds	2 tbsp fresh mint, chopped

Directions and Total Time: 5 minutes

In a food processor, put the strawberries, watermelon, cranberries, chia seeds, coconut milk, water, goji berries, and mint. Pulse until smooth. Divide between 3 glasses.

Cinnamon Almond Buckwheat

Ingredients for 4 servings

1 cup almond milk	1 tsp cinnamon
1 cup water	¼ cup chopped almonds
1 cup buckwheat groats	2 tbsp pure date syrup

Directions and Total Time: 20 minutes

Place almond milk, water, and buckwheat in a pot over medium heat and bring to a boil. Lower the heat and simmer covered for 15 minutes. Allow sitting covered for 5 minutes. Mix in cinnamon, almonds, and date syrup.

Chili Swiss Chard & Tofu Scramble

Ingredients for 5 servings

2 tsp olive oil	1 tsp chili powder
1 (14-oz) pack tofu, crumbled	½ tsp ground cumin
1 onion, chopped	½ tsp ground turmeric
3 cloves minced garlic	Salt and black pepper to taste
1 celery stalk, chopped	5 cups Swiss chard
2 large carrots, chopped	

Directions and Total Time: 35 minutes

Heat the oil in a skillet over medium heat. Add in the onion, garlic, celery, and carrots. Sauté for 5 minutes. Stir in tofu, chili powder, cumin, turmeric, salt, and pepper, cook for 7-8 minutes. Mix in the Swiss chard and cook until wilted, 3 minutes. Allow cooling and seal, and serve.

Conga French Toasts

Ingredients for 4 servings

1 tbsp olive oil	1 tsp ground cinnamon
3 bananas	¼ tsp grated nutmeg
1 cup almond milk	4 slices bread
Zest and juice of 1 tangerine	

Directions and Total Time: 25 minutes

Blend the bananas, almond milk, tangerine juice, tangerine zest, cinnamon, and nutmeg until smooth in a food processor. Spread into a baking dish. Submerge the bread slices in the mixture for 3-4 minutes. Heat the oil in a skillet over medium heat. Fry the bread for 5 minutes until golden brown. Serve hot.

Cherry-Pumpkin Granola

Ingredients for 6 servings

½ cup coconut oil, melted	¼ cup ground flaxseed
½ cup maple syrup	½ cup sunflower seeds
1 tsp vanilla extract	½ cup slivered almonds
3 tsp pumpkin pie spice	½ cup shredded coconut
4 cups rolled oats	½ cup dried cherries
1/3 cup whole-wheat flour	½ cup dried apricots, chopped

Directions and Total Time: 45 minutes

Preheat oven to 350°F. In a bowl, combine the coconut oil, maple syrup, and vanilla. Add in the pumpkin pie spice. Put oats, flour, flaxseed, sunflower seeds, almonds, and coconut on a baking sheet and toss to combine. Coat with the oil mixture. Spread the granola out evenly. Bake for 25 minutes. Once ready, break the granola into chunks and stir in the cherries and apricots. Bake another 5 minutes. Allow cooling and serve.

Banana Oats with Pumpkin Seeds

Ingredients for 4 servings

3 cups water	¼ cup pumpkin seeds
1 cup steel-cut oats	2 tbsp maple syrup
2 bananas, mashed	A pinch of salt

Directions and Total Time: 35 minutes

Bring water to a boil in a pot, add in oats, and lower the heat. Cook for 20-30 minutes. Put in the mashed bananas, cook for 3-5 minutes more. Stir in maple syrup, pumpkin seeds, and salt. Serve.

Almond-Raspberry Shake

Ingredients for 4 servings

1 ½ cups almond milk	Juice from half lemon
½ cup raspberries	½ tsp almond extract

Directions and Total Time: 5 minutes

In a blender or smoothie maker, pour the almond milk, raspberries, lemon juice, and almond extract. Puree the ingredients at high speed until the raspberries have blended almost entirely into the liquid. Pour the smoothie into serving glasses. Stick in some straws and serve.

Kiwi Oatmeal Squares

Ingredients for 6 servings

1 cup plant butter, melted	½ tsp ground cinnamon
2 cups uncooked rolled oats	4 cups kiwi, chopped
2 cups all-purpose flour	¼ cup organic cane sugar
1 ½ cups pure date sugar	2 tbsp cornstarch
1 ½ tsp baking soda	¼ tsp salt

Directions and Total Time: 50 minutes

Preheat oven to 380 F. Grease a baking dish. In a bowl, mix the oats, flour, date sugar, baking soda, salt, and cinnamon. Put in butter and whisk to combine. In another bowl, combine the kiwis, cane sugar, and cornstarch until the kiwis are coated. Spread 3 cups of oatmeal mixture on a greased baking dish and top with kiwi mixture and finally put the remaining oatmeal mixture on top. Bake for 40 minutes. Let cool. Serve sliced into squares.

Mango-Pumpkin Rice Pudding with Walnuts

Ingredients for 4 servings

1 cup brown rice	2 tsp pumpkin pie spice
1 ½ cups non-dairy milk	1 mango, chopped
3 tbsp pure date sugar	2 tbsp chopped walnuts

Directions and Total Time: 30 minutes

In a pot over medium heat, add the rice, 2 cups water, milk, sugar, and pumpkin pie spice. Bring to a boil, lower the heat and simmer for 18-20 minutes until the rice is soft and the liquid is absorbed. Put in the mango and stir to combine. Top with walnuts to serve.

Mozzarella & Pesto Twists

Ingredients for 6 servings

1 ½ cups grated plant-based mozzarella cheese
5 tbsp plant butter   ½ tsp salt
1 tbsp flax seed powder   1 tsp baking powder
4 tbsp coconut flour   2 oz vegan pesto
½ cup almond flour   Olive oil for brushing

Directions and Total Time: 35 minutes

First, mix the flax seed powder with 3 tbsp water in a bowl, and set aside to soak for 5 minutes. Preheat oven to 350°F and line a baking sheet with parchment paper. In a bowl, evenly combine the coconut flour, almond flour, salt, and baking powder. Melt the plant butter and cheese in a deep skillet over medium heat and stir in the vegan "flax egg." Mix in the flour mixture until a firm dough forms. Turn the heat off, transfer the mixture in between two parchment papers, and then use a rolling pin to flatten out the dough of about an inch's thickness. Remove the parchment paper on top and spread the pesto all over the dough. Now, use a knife to cut the dough into strips, twist each piece, and place it on the baking sheet. Brush with olive oil and bake for 15 to 20 minutes until golden brown. Remove the bread twist; allow cooling for a few minutes, and serve with almond milk.

Seedy Bread

Ingredients for 6 servings

½ cup melted coconut oil   1 tsp ground caraway seeds
3 tbsp ground flax seeds   1 tsp hemp seeds
¾ cup coconut flour   ¼ cup psyllium husk powder
1 cup almond flour   1 tsp salt
3 tsp baking powder   2/3 cup coconut cream cheese
5 tbsp sesame seeds   ¾ cup coconut cream
½ cup chia seeds   1 tbsp poppy seeds

Directions and Total Time: 55 minutes

Preheat oven to 350°F. Line a loaf pan with parchment paper. For the vegan "flax egg," whisk flax seed powder with ½ cup of water and let the mixture sit to soak for 5 minutes. In a bowl, evenly combine the coconut flour, almond flour, baking powder, sesame seeds, chia seeds, ground caraway seeds, hemp seeds, psyllium husk powder, and salt. In another bowl, use an electric hand mixer to whisk the cream cheese, coconut oil, coconut whipping cream, and vegan "flax egg." Pour the liquid ingredients into the dry ingredients, and continue whisking with the hand mixer until a dough forms. Transfer the dough to the loaf pan, sprinkle with poppy seeds, and bake in the oven for 45 minutes or until a knife inserted into the bread comes out clean. Remove the parchment paper with the bread, and allow cooling on a rack.

Tofu Avocado "Sandwich"

Ingredients for 2 servings

½ oz plant butter   2 oz gem lettuce leaves
1 avocado, sliced   1 oz tofu, sliced
1 large red tomato, sliced   1 tbsp chopped parsley

Directions and Total Time: 10 minutes

Put the avocado on a plate and place the tomato slices by the avocado. Arrange the lettuce (with the inner side facing you) on a flat plate to serve as the base of the sandwich.

To assemble the sandwich, smear each leaf of the lettuce with plant butter, and arrange some tofu slices in the leaves. Then, share the avocado and tomato slices on each tofu. Garnish with parsley and serve.

Creamy Pimiento Biscuits

Ingredients for 4 servings

¼ cup plant butter, cold and cubed
1 cup shredded vegan cheddar cheese
1 tbsp melted plant butter   ½ tsp garlic powder
2 cups whole-wheat flour   ¼ tsp black pepper
2 tsp baking powder   ¾ cup coconut milk
1 tsp salt   1 (4 oz) jar chopped pimientos,
½ tsp baking soda

Directions and Total Time: 30 minutes

Preheat the oven to 450°F and line a baking sheet with parchment paper. Set aside. In a medium bowl, mix the flour, baking powder, salt, baking soda, garlic powder, and black pepper. Add the cold butter using a hand mixer until the mixture is the size of small peas. Pour in ¾ of the coconut milk and continue whisking. Continue adding the remaining coconut milk, a tablespoonful at a time, until dough forms.

Mix in the cheddar cheese and pimientos. (If the dough is too wet to handle, mix in a little bit more flour until it is manageable). Place the dough on a lightly floured surface and flatten the dough into ½-inch thickness.

Use a 2 ½-inch round cutter to cut out biscuits' pieces from the dough. Gather, re-roll the dough once and continue cutting out biscuits. Arrange the biscuits on the prepared pan and brush the tops with the melted butter. Bake for 12-14 minutes, or until the biscuits are golden brown. Cool and serve.

Banana French Toasts with Berry Syrup

Ingredients for 8 servings

1 banana, mashed   A pinch of salt
1 cup coconut milk   8 slices whole-grain bread
1 tsp pure vanilla extract   1 cup strawberries
¼ tsp ground nutmeg   2 tbsp water
½ tsp ground cinnamon   2 tbsp maple syrup
1 ½ tsp arrowroot powder

Directions and Total Time: 40 minutes

Preheat oven to 350°F. In a bowl, stir banana, coconut milk, vanilla, nutmeg, cinnamon, arrowroot, and salt. Dip each bread slice in the banana mixture and arrange on a baking tray. Spread the remaining banana mixture over the top. Bake for 30 minutes until the tops are lightly browned. In a pot over medium heat, put the strawberries, water, and maple syrup. Simmer for 15-10 minutes until the berries break up and the liquid isreduced. Serve topped with strawberry syrup.

Strong Green Smoothie

Ingredients for 2 servings

1 avocado	2 cups soy milk
1 cup chopped cucumber	½-inch piece peeled ginger
2 cups curly endive	2 tbsp chia seeds
2 apples, peeled and cored	1 cup coconut yogurt
2 tbsp lime juice	

Directions and Total Time: 5 minutes

Put in a food processor the avocado, cucumber, curly endive, apple, lime juice, soy milk, ginger, chia seeds, and coconut yogurt. Blend until smooth. Serve.

High Protein Fruit Smoothie

Ingredients for 4 servings

1 tbsp peanut butter	1 cup spinach, chopped
1 cup applesauce	½ cup non-dairy milk
2 tbsp plant protein powder	1 cup water
1 tbsp flaxseed	1 tsp matcha powder
1 tbsp cacao powder	1 tsp cocoa nibs
1 tbsp maple syrup	

Directions and Total Time: 5 minutes

Put in a food processor the applesauce, protein powder, flaxseed, cacao powder, peanut butter, maple syrup, spinach, milk, water, matcha powder, and cocoa nibs. Pulse until smooth. Divide between glasses and serve.

Applesauce & Cranberry Cookies

Ingredients for 2 servings

½ cup rolled oats	2 tbsp pure date sugar
1 tbsp whole-wheat flour	¼ cup applesauce
½ tsp baking powder	2 tbsp dried cranberries

Directions and Total Time: 20 minutes

Combine the oats, flour, baking powder, and sugar in a bowl. Add in applesauce and cranberries. Stir until well combined. Form 2 cookies out of the mixture and microwave for 1 ½ minutes. Serve cooled.

Mango Matcha Smoothie

Ingredients for 4 servings

1 cup chopped pineapple	1 avocado
1 cup chopped mango	2 cups almond milk
1 cup chopped spinach	1 tsp matcha green tea powder

Directions and Total Time: 5 minutes

In a food processor, place the pineapple, mango, spinach, avocado, almond milk, and matcha powder. Blitz until smooth. Divide between 4 glasses and serve. Enjoy!

Chocolate Pudding with Banana & Berries

Ingredients for 4 servings

3 tbsp flaxseed + 9 tbsp water	1 tbsp vanilla caviar
3 tbsp cornstarch	6 oz white chocolate chips
1 cup coconut cream	Whipped coconut cream
2 ½ cups almond milk	Sliced bananas and raspberries
½ pure date sugar	

Directions and Total Time: 20 minutes+ cooling time

In a bowl, mix the flaxseed powder with water and allow thickening for 5 minutes to make the vegan "flax egg."

In a large bowl, whisk the cornstarch and coconut cream until smooth. Beat in the vegan "flax egg" until well combined. Pour the almond milk into a pot and whisk in the date sugar. Cook over medium heat while frequently stirring until the sugar dissolves. Reduce the heat to low and simmer until steamy and bubbly around the edges.

Pour half of the almond milk mixture into the vegan "flax egg" mix, whisk well and pour this mixture into the remaining milk content in the pot. Whisk continuously until well combined. Bring the new mixture to a boil over medium heat while still frequently stirring and scraping all the pot's corners, 2 minutes.

Turn the heat off, stir in the vanilla caviar, then the white chocolate chips until melted. Spoon the mixture into a bowl, allow cooling for 2 minutes, cover with plastic wraps, make sure to press the plastic onto the surface of the pudding, and refrigerate for 4 hours.

Remove the pudding from the fridge, take off the plastic wrap, and whip for about a minute. Spoon the dessert into serving cups, swirl some coconut whipping cream on top, and top with the bananas and raspberries. Enjoy.

Cinnamon Pear Oatmeal

Ingredients for 2 servings

1 ¼ cups apple cider	1 tsp ground cinnamon
1 peeled pear, chopped	1 tbsp pure date syrup
2/3 cup rolled oats	

Directions and Total Time: 20 minutes

Pour the apple cider in a pot over medium heat and bring to a boil. Add in pear, oats, and cinnamon. Lower the heat and simmer for 3-4 minutes until the oatmeal thickens. Divide between bowls and drizzle with date syrup.

Blackberry & Chocolate Smoothie

Ingredients for 2 servings

1 tbsp poppy seeds	2 tbsp pure agave syrup
2 cups soy milk	2 tbsp cocoa powder
2 cups blackberries	

Directions and Total Time: 10 minutes

Submerge poppy seeds in soy milk and let sit for 5 minutes. Transfer it to a food processor and add in the blackberries, agave syrup, and cocoa powder. Blitz until smooth. Serve right away in glasses.

Collard Green & Tofu Crêpes with Mushrooms

Ingredients for 4 servings

2 tbsp extra-virgin olive oil	1/3 cup plant-based milk
1 cup whole-wheat flour	¼ cup lemon juice
1 tsp onion powder	½ cup chopped mushrooms
½ tsp baking soda	½ cup finely chopped onion
¼ tsp salt	2 cups collard greens
1 cup pressed, crumbled tofu	

Directions and Total Time: 25 minutes

Combine the flour, onion powder, baking soda, and salt in a bowl. Blitz the tofu, milk, lemon juice, and oil in a food processor over high speed for 30 seconds. Pour over the flour mixture and mix to combine well. Add in the mushrooms, onion, and collard greens.

Heat a skillet and grease with cooking spray. Lower the heat and spread a ladleful of the batter across the surface of the skillet. Cook for 4 minutes on both sides or until set. Remove to a plate. Repeat the process until no batter is left, greasing with a little more oil, if needed. Serve.

Spinach & Mushroom Omelet

Ingredients for 4 servings

1 cup sautéed button mushrooms

1 cup chickpea flour	1 green bell pepper, chopped
½ tsp onion powder	3 scallions, chopped
½ tsp garlic powder	½ cup chopped fresh spinach
¼ tsp white pepper	1 cup halved cherry tomatoes
1/3 cup nutritional yeast	1 tbsp fresh parsley leaves

Directions and Total Time: 25 minutes

In a bowl, mix the chickpea flour, onion powder, garlic powder, white pepper, and nutritional yeast until well combined. Heat a medium skillet over medium heat and add a quarter of the batter. Swirl the pan to spread the batter across the pan. Scatter a quarter each of the bell pepper, scallions, mushrooms, and spinach on top and cook until the bottom part of the omelet sets, 1-2 minutes. Carefully flip the omelet and cook the other side until set and golden brown. Transfer the omelet to a plate and make the remaining omelets. Serve the omelet with the tomatoes topped with parsley.

Carrot Bread with Chocolate Chips

Ingredients for 4 servings

¼ cup olive oil	2 tbsp flax seed powder
1 ½ cup whole-wheat flour	½ cup pure date sugar
¼ cup almond flour	¼ cup pure maple syrup
¼ tsp salt	¾ tsp almond extract
¼ tsp cloves powder	1 tbsp grated lemon zest
¼ tsp cayenne pepper	½ cup applesauce
1 tbsp cinnamon powder	4 carrots, shredded
½ tsp nutmeg powder	3 tbsp chocolate chips
1 ½ tsp baking powder	2/3 cup black raisins

Directions and Total Time: 75 minutes

Preheat oven to 375°F and line a loaf tin with baking paper. In a bowl, mix all the flour, salt, cloves powder, cayenne pepper, cinnamon powder, nutmeg powder, and baking powder. In another bowl, mix the flax seed powder, 6 tbsp water, and allow thickening for 5 minutes. Mix in the date sugar, maple syrup, almond extract, lemon zest, applesauce, and olive oil.

Combine both mixtures until smooth and fold in the carrots, chocolate chips, and raisins. Pour the mixture into a loaf pan and bake in the oven until golden brown on top or a toothpick inserted into the bread comes out clean, 45-50 minutes. Remove from the oven, transfer the bread onto a wire rack to cool, slice, and serve.

Cauliflower & Potato Hash Browns

Ingredients for 4 servings

4 tbsp plant butter	1 big head cauliflower, riced
3 tbsp flax seed powder	½ white onion, grated
2 large potatoes, shredded	Salt and black pepper to taste

Directions and Total Time: 35 minutes

In a bowl, mix the flaxseed powder and 9 tbsp water. Allow thickening for 5 minutes for the vegan "flax egg." Add the potatoes, cauliflower, onion, salt, and black pepper to the vegan "flax egg" and mix until well combined. Allow sitting for 5 minutes to thicken. Working in batches, melt 1 tbsp of plant butter in a non-stick skillet and add 4 scoops of the hashbrown mixture to the skillet. Make sure to have 1-inch intervals between each scoop.

Use a spoon to flatten the batter and cook until compacted and golden brown on the bottom part, 2 minutes. Flip the hashbrowns and cook further for 2 minutes or until the vegetable cook and is golden brown. Transfer to a paper-towel-lined plate to drain grease. Make the remaining hashbrowns using the remaining ingredients.

Zucchini Hash Browns

Ingredients for 4 servings

2 shredded zucchinis	1 tsp allspice
2 tbsp nutritional yeast	2 tbsp aquafaba

Directions and Total Time: 20 minutes

Preheat air fryer to 400°F. Combine zucchinis, nutritional yeast, allspice, and aquafaba in a bowl. Make 4 patties out of the mixture. Cut 4 pieces of parchment paper, put a patty on each foil, and fold in all sides to create a rectangle. Using a spatula, flatten them and spread them. Then unwrap each foil and remove the hash browns onto the fryer and Air Fry for 12 minutes until golden brown and crispy, turning once. Serve right away.

Caribbean Granola

Ingredients for 5 servings

2 cups rolled oats	½ cup pumpkin seeds
¾ cup whole-wheat flour	½ cup shredded coconut
1 tbsp ground cinnamon	1 ¼ cups orange juice
1 tsp ground ginger	½ cup dried cherries
½ cup sunflower seeds	½ cup goji berries
½ cup hazelnuts, chopped	

Directions and Total Time: 50 minutes

Preheat oven to 350°F. In a bowl, combine the oats, flour, cinnamon, ginger, sunflower seeds, hazelnuts, pumpkin seeds, and coconut. Pour in the orange juice, toss to mix well. Transfer to a baking sheet and bake for 15 minutes. Turn the granola and continue baking until it is crunchy, about 30 minutes. Stir in the cherries and goji berries and store in the fridge for up to 14 days.

Home-Style Cinnamon Rolls

Ingredients for 4 servings

½ (16-oz) pizza dough
1/3 cup dark brown sugar
¼ cup vegan butter, softened
½ tsp ground cinnamon

Directions and Total Time: 40 minutes

Preheat air fryer to 360°F. Line a sheet with parchment paper. Roll out the dough into a rectangle. Using a knife, spread the brown sugar and butter, covering all the edges, and sprinkle with cinnamon. Fold the long side of the dough into a log, then cut it into 8 equal pieces, avoiding compression. Place the rolls, spiral-side up onto the sheet. Let rise for 20 minutes. Grease the rolls with cooking spray and Bake for 8 minutes until golden brown. Serve right away.

Homemade English Muffins

Ingredients for 4 servings

3 tbsp plant butter
2 tbsp flax seed powder
2 tbsp almond flour
½ tsp baking powder
1 pinch of salt

Directions and Total Time: 20 minutes

In a small bowl, mix the flax seed with 6 tbsp water until evenly combined and leave to soak for 5 minutes. In another bowl, evenly combine the almond flour, baking powder, and salt. Then, pour in the vegan "flax egg" and whisk again. Let the batter sit for 5 minutes to set.

Melt plant butter in a frying pan and add the mixture in four dollops. Fry until golden brown on one side, then flip the bread and fry further until golden brown. Serve.

Basic Naan Bread

Ingredients for 6 servings

1/3 cup olive oil
4 tbsp plant butter
4 oz plant butter
¾ cup almond flour
2 tbsp psyllium husk powder
½ tsp salt
½ tsp baking powder
2 garlic cloves, minced

Directions and Total Time: 25 minutes

In a bowl, mix almond flour, psyllium husk, salt, and baking powder. Mix in some olive oil and 2 cups of boiling water to combine the ingredients, like a thick porridge. Stir thoroughly and allow the dough to rise for 5 minutes. Divide it into 6 to 8 pieces and mold into balls. Place the balls on parchment paper and flatten with your hands.

Melt the plant butter in a frying pan and fry the naan on both sides to have a beautiful, golden color. Transfer the naan to a plate and keep warm in the oven. For the garlic butter, add the remaining plant butter to the frying pan and sauté the garlic until fragrant, 3 minutes. Pour the garlic butter into a bowl and serve with the naan.

Mango Naan Bread

Ingredients for 4 servings

1/3 cup olive oil
2 tbsp plant butter for frying
¾ cup almond flour
1 tsp salt + extra for sprinkling
1 tsp baking powder
2 cups boiling water
4 cups chopped mangoes
1 cup pure maple syrup
1 lemon, juiced
A pinch of saffron powder
1 tsp cardamom powder

Directions and Total Time: 40 minutes

In a large bowl, mix the almond flour, salt, and baking powder. Mix in the olive oil and boiling water until smooth, thick batter forms. Allow the dough to rise for 5 minutes. Form balls out of the dough, place each on a baking paper, and use your hands to flatten the dough. Melt the plant butter in a large skillet and fry the dough on both sides until set and golden brown on each side, 4 minutes per bread. Transfer to a plate and set aside for serving. Add mangoes, maple syrup, lemon juice, and 3 tbsp water in a pot and cook until boiling, 5 minutes. Mix in saffron and cardamom powders and cook further over low heat until the mangoes soften. Mash the mangoes with the back of the spoon until relatively smooth with little chunks of mangoes in a jam. Cool completely. Spoon the jam into sterilized jars and serve with the naan bread.

Blueberry Pudding with Chia & Walnuts

Ingredients for 2 servings

¾ cup coconut milk
½ tsp vanilla extract
½ cup blueberries
2 tbsp chia seeds
Chopped walnuts to garnish

Directions and Total Time: 5 minutes + chilling time

In a blender, pour the coconut milk, vanilla extract, and half of the blueberries. Process the ingredients at high speed until the blueberries are incorporated into the liquid. Open the blender and mix in the chia seeds. Share the mixture into two breakfast jars, cover, and refrigerate for 4 hours to allow the mixture to gel. Garnish the pudding with the remaining blueberries and walnuts.

Pineapple French Toasts

Ingredients for 4 servings

2 tbsp maple syrup + extra for drizzling
2 tbsp flax seed powder
1 ½ cups almond milk
½ cup almond flour
2 pinches of salt
½ tbsp cinnamon powder
½ tsp fresh lemon zest
1 tbsp fresh pineapple juice
8 whole-grain bread slices

Directions and Total Time: 55 minutes

Preheat the oven to 400°F and lightly grease a roasting rack with olive oil. Set aside. In a bowl, mix the flax seed powder with 6 tbsp water and allow thickening for 5-8 minutes. Whisk in the almond milk, almond flour, maple syrup, salt, cinnamon powder, lemon zest, and pineapple juice. Soak the bread on both sides in the almond milk mixture and allow sitting on a plate for 3 minutes.

Heat a large skillet over medium heat and place the bread in the pan. Cook until golden brown on the bottom side. Flip the bread and cook further until golden brown on the other side, 4 minutes in total. Transfer to a plate, drizzle some maple syrup on top and serve immediately.

Morning Corn Cakes

Ingredients for 4 servings

4 tbsp olive oil	1 tsp salt
1 tbsp flaxseed powder	2 tsp baking powder
2 cups yellow cornmeal	1 cup vegan mayonnaise

Directions and Total Time: 35 minutes

In a bowl, mix the flax seed powder with 3 tbsp water and allow thickening for 5 minutes to form the vegan "flax egg." Mix in 1 cup of water and then whisk in the cornmeal, salt, and baking powder until soup texture forms but not watery. Heat a quarter of the olive oil in a griddle pan and pour in a quarter of the batter. Cook until set and golden brown beneath, 3 minutes. Flip the cake and cook the other side until set and golden brown too. Plate the cake and make three more with the remaining oil and batter. Top the cakes with mayonnaise.

Orange Crêpes

Ingredients for 4 servings

½ cup melted plant butter	¼ tsp salt
3 tbsp plant butter for frying	2 cups almond flour
2 tbsp flax seed powder	1 ½ cups oat milk
1 tsp vanilla extract	3 tbsp fresh orange juice
1 tsp pure date sugar	2 tbsp maple syrup

Directions and Total Time: 30 minutes

In a medium bowl, mix the flax seed powder with 6 tbsp water and allow thickening for 5 minutes to make the vegan "flax egg." Whisk in the vanilla, date sugar, and salt. Pour in a quarter cup of almond flour and whisk, then a quarter cup of oat milk, and mix until no lumps remain. Repeat the mixing process with the remaining almond flour and almond milk in the same quantities until exhausted. Mix in the plant butter, orange juice, and half of the water until the mixture is runny like pancakes. Add the remaining water until the mixture is lighter. Brush a non-stick skillet with some butter and place over medium heat to melt.

Pour 1 tbsp of the batter into the pan and swirl the skillet quickly and all around to coat the pan with the batter. Cook until the batter is dry and golden brown beneath, about 30 seconds. Flip the crepe and cook the other side until golden brown too. Fold the crepe onto a plate and set aside. Repeat with the remaining batter until exhausted. Drizzle maple syrup on the crepes and serve.

Coconut Breakfast with Berry & Pecans

Ingredients for 2 servings

1 (14-oz) can coconut milk, refrigerated overnight	
1 cup granola	1 cup sliced strawberries
½ cup pecans, chopped	

Directions and Total Time: 15 minutes

Drain the coconut milk liquid. Layer the coconut milk solids, granola, and strawberries in small glasses. Top with chopped pecans and serve right away.

Raspberry Muffins with Orange Glaze

Ingredients for 4 servings

½ cup plant butter, softened	½ cup oat milk
2 tbsp flax seed powder	2 tsp vanilla extract
2 cups whole-wheat flour	1 lemon, zested
1 ½ tsp baking powder	1 cup dried raspberries
A pinch salt	2 tbsp orange juice
2 cups pure date sugar	

Directions and Total Time: 40 minutes

Preheat oven to 400°F and grease 6 muffin cups with cooking spray. In a small bowl, mix the flax seed powder with 6 tbsp water and allow thickening for 5 minutes to make the vegan "flax egg."

In a medium bowl, mix the flour, baking powder, and salt. In another bowl, cream the plant butter, half of the date sugar, and vegan "flax egg." Mix in the oat milk, vanilla, and lemon zest.

Combine both mixtures, fold in raspberries, and fill muffin cups two-thirds way up with the batter. Bake for 20-25 minutes. In a medium bowl, whisk orange juice and remaining date sugar until smooth. Remove the muffins when ready and transfer to them a wire rack to cool. Drizzle the glaze on top to serve.

Maple Oat Bread

Ingredients for 4 servings

4 cups whole-wheat flour	1 tsp baking soda
¼ tsp salt	1 ¾ cups coconut milk, thick
½ cup rolled oats	2 tbsp pure maple syrup

Directions and Total Time: 50 minutes

Preheat the oven to 400°F. In a bowl, mix flour, salt, oats, and baking soda. Add in coconut milk and maple syrup and whisk until dough forms. Dust your hands with some flour and knead the dough into a ball. Shape the dough into a circle and place on a baking sheet.

Cut a deep cross on the dough and bake in the oven for 15 minutes at 450°F. Reduce the temperature to 400°F and bake further for 20-25 minutes or until a hollow sound is made when the bottom of the bread is tapped.

Black Bean & Quinoa Bowl with Avocado

Ingredients for 4 servings

1 cup brown quinoa, rinsed	3 tbsp tomato salsa
3 tbsp plant-based yogurt	¼ avocado, sliced
½ lime, juiced	2 radishes, shredded
2 tbsp chopped fresh cilantro	1 tbsp pepitas
1 (5 oz) can black beans	

Directions and Total Time: 25 minutes

Cook the quinoa with 2 cups of slightly salted water in a medium pot over medium heat or until the liquid absorbs, 15 minutes. Spoon the quinoa into serving bowls and fluff with a fork. In a small bowl, mix the yogurt, lime juice, cilantro, and salt. Divide this mixture on the quinoa and top with beans, salsa, avocado, radishes, and pepitas.

SALADS & ENTRÉES

Greek-Style Salad

Ingredients for 2 servings

10 cherry tomatoes, halved
1 cucumber, diced
½ cup green olives, halved
1 tsp Greek seasoning
2 tbsp extra-virgin olive oil
Salt and black pepper to taste
½ head iceberg lettuce, halved

Directions and Total Time: 10 minutes

Put the cherry tomatoes, cucumber, green olives, Greek seasoning, and a tablespoon of olive oil in a bowl. Add some salt and pepper and combine by tossing. Put wedges of lettuces on plates and add the mix on top. Drizzle the rest of the olive oil and add a bit of salt. Serve.

Radish-Cucumber Salad

Ingredients for 2 servings

¼ cup coconut milk
1 garlic clove, minced
1 lemon wedge, juiced
2 cucumbers, diced
4 radishes, sliced thin
Salt and black pepper to taste
2 tbsp chopped parsley

Directions and Total Time: 5 minutes

Combine the coconut milk, garlic, and lemon juice in a bowl. In a separate bowl, add the cucumbers and radishes, then sprinkle with salt and pepper. Put the resulting dressing on top of the veggies and stir until coated. Add some parsley on top and serve.

Minty Tofu Salad with Avocado

Ingredients for 2 servings

2 tbsp extra-virgin olive oil
1 tbsp lime juice
2 cucumbers, diced
2 avocados, diced
8 cherry tomatoes, halved
¼ cup crumbled tofu
¼ cup chopped fresh mint
Salt and black pepper to taste

Directions and Total Time: 5 minutes

Combine the olive oil and lime juice in a bowl. In a separate bowl, combine the cucumbers, avocados, and cherry tomatoes, then sprinkle with salt and pepper. Ladle the dressing over the cucumber mix and stir, making sure everything is well-coated. Toss in the tofu and mint, then shake the bowl.

German-Style Potato Salad

Ingredients for 4 servings

6 medium potatoes, scrubbed and chopped
2 celery sticks, chopped
¼ cup chopped parsley
1 tsp Dijon mustard
Salt and black pepper to taste
5 radishes, chopped
1 bell pepper, chopped
1 tbsp chopped chives

Directions and Total Time: 35 minutes

Bring about a quarter of a large pot of water to a boil. Add potatoes and continue boiling for 10 minutes. Add celery and boil for 10 minutes. Reserve 1 cup of cooking liquid. Drain the rest of the water. Set vegetables aside.

When cooled, transfer ½ cup potatoes to the blender. Pour in cooking liquid, then add parsley, mustard, salt, and pepper. Puree until no longer chunky. In a large bowl, combine potatoes and celery along with radishes, pepper, and chives. Top with the mustard dressing and toss to coat. Serve and enjoy.

Mediterranean Eggplant Salad

Ingredients for 2 servings

1 tsp olive oil
1 eggplant, diced
½ tsp ground cumin
½ tsp ground ginger
¼ tsp turmeric
¼ tsp ground nutmeg
Sea salt to taste
½ lemon, zested and juiced
2 lemon wedges
2 tbsp capers
1 tbsp chopped green olives
1 garlic clove, pressed
1 tsp mint, finely chopped
2 cups spinach, chopped
1 cucumber, cut into chunks
4 cherry tomatoes, halved

Directions and Total Time: 30 minutes

Saute eggplant in oil in a large skillet over medium heat. After 5 minutes, stir in cumin, ginger, turmeric, nutmeg, and salt. Continue cooking for 10 minutes or until the eggplant is very soft. Stir in lemon zest, lemon juice, capers, olives, garlic, and mint. Cook for another two minutes, stirring occasionally. Divide the spinach between the plates. Top with eggplant mixture, cucumber, and tomatoes. Garnish with a wedge of lemon to squeeze over the greens. Serve warm and enjoy.

Moroccan Garbanzo Bean Salad

Ingredients for 2 servings

1 tbsp olive oil
2 tbsp balsamic vinegar
1 tsp minced scallions
1 garlic clove, minced
1 tbsp basil, chopped
1 tbsp oregano, chopped
Salt to taste
1 (14-oz) can garbanzo beans
6 mushrooms, thinly sliced
1 zucchini, diced
2 carrots, diced

Directions and Total Time: 25 minutes

Whisk all the ingredients together in a large bowl, except for beans, mushrooms, zucchini and carrots, to make the dressing. Add all the veggies to a big bowl. Stir in the dressing and shake vigorously. Let it marinate for 15 minutes before serving.

Lettuce Wraps with Vegetables & Walnuts

Ingredients for 4 servings

1 cup walnuts, chopped
8 sun-dried tomatoes, diced
2 carrots, peeled and grated
1 celery stalk, thinly sliced
¼ cup chopped parsley
2 tsp taco seasoning
½ lime, zested and juiced
2 tsp olive oil
2 tsp maple syrup
Salt to taste
8 large lettuce leaves
2 spring onions, thinly sliced

Directions and Total Time: 25 minutes

Combine walnuts, tomatoes, carrots, celery, parsley, taco seasoning, lime juice, lime zest, oil, maple syrup, and salt in a large bowl. Spoon mixture among the lettuce leaves and garnish with spring onions. Serve and enjoy.

Italian Bean Salad

Ingredients for 4 servings

1 (16-oz) can mixed beans	1 tbsp Italian seasoning
1 lb cherry tomatoes, halved	1 tbsp apple cider vinegar
1 cup fresh parsley, chopped	1 tbsp maple syrup
6 pitted olives, sliced	1 tbsp extra-virgin olive oil
1 cucumber, sliced	Salt and black pepper to taste

Directions and Total Time: 20 minutes

Place beans, tomatoes, parsley, Italian seasoning, vinegar, maple syrup, salt, pepper, and olive oil in a large bowl and mix to combine. Top with olives and cucumber. Serve.

Lucky Quinoa Salad

Ingredients for 4 servings

1/3 cup quinoa, rinsed	3 tbsp olive oil
1 cup vegetable broth	2 tbsp apple cider vinegar
4 broccoli florets, steamed	2 tsp Dijon mustard
½ lb Brussels sprouts, shredded	Juice of half orange
2 scallions, diced	Salt and black pepper to taste
¼ cup sunflower seeds	1 tbsp pomegranate seeds
¾ cup dried cranberries	

Directions and Total Time: 25 minutes

Bring to a boil the quinoa and vegetable broth in a medium saucepan over high heat. Reduce the heat, cover, and simmer for 15 minutes until the water is absorbed. Remove and fluff the quinoa with a fork. Set aside to cool.

Combine the broccoli, Brussels sprouts, scallions, sunflower seeds, and cranberries in a medium mixing bowl, Add the cooled quinoa and mix well.

Whisk together the olive oil, vinegar, mustard, orange juice, salt, and pepper in a small bowl. Drizzle the resulting dressing over the salad and toss to coat. Refrigerate for 30 minutes. Top with pomegranate seeds and serve.

Quinoa Salad with Catalina Dressing

Ingredients for 4 servings

1 cup quinoa	2 (16-oz) cans chickpeas
2 English cucumbers, diced	½ cup sumac Catalina dressing
1 lb cherry tomatoes, halved	

Directions and Total Time: 20 minutes

Place the quinoa, 2 cups of salted water in a pot over medium heat and cook for 12-15 minutes. Allow to cool.

In a large bowl, combine the cucumbers, cherry tomatoes, and chickpeas. Add the quinoa to the cucumber mix, drizzle with the dressing, and stir well. Serve and enjoy!

Greek Fusilli Salad

Ingredients for 4 servings

½ cup raw cashews, soaked	1 tbsp fresh dill
4 oz cooked whole-grain fusilli	Salt and black pepper to taste
1 tbsp almond milk	¼ cup Kalamata olives
1 tbsp extra-virgin olive oil	¼ cup black olives, pitted
1 tbsp lemon juice	¼ cup sun-dried tomatoes
¼ cucumber, seeded and diced	¼ cup artichoke hearts, chopped
1 garlic clove	

Directions and Total Time: 25 minutes

Blend the soaked cashews, almond milk, olive oil, lemon juice, cucumber, garlic, dill, salt, and pepper in your food processor until smooth. Remove the cashew sauce to a bowl and set asisde. In a large mixing bowl, combine the fusilli, Kalamata olives, black olives, tomatoes, and artichoke hearts. Add the previously prepared cashew sauce and mix well to combine. Serve and enjoy!

Paradise Salad

Ingredients for 4 servings

1 mandarin orange, peeled and cut into segments	
2 tbsp toasted sesame seeds	1 grapefruit, peeled and cut
1 tbsp extra-virgin olive oil	into segments
8 cups kale, roughly torn	1 cup tahini dressing
¼ cup sunflower seeds	

Directions and Total Time: 20 minutes

Warm the olive oil in a pan over medium heat. Add the kale and cook for about 2 minutes, tossing once until charred lightly. Remove to a plate. Sprinkle the charred kale with the toasted sesame seeds, sunflower seeds, mandarin orange segments, and grapefruit segments. Pour the dressing over the salad. Serve and enjoy!

Corn & Asparagus Salad

Ingredients for 4 servings

2 heads romaine lettuce, halved lengthwise	
2 tbsp vegan cottage cheese	1 lb asparagus, trimmed
1 tsp garlic powder	16 cherry tomatoes, halved
2 bread slices	½ sliced red onion
1 cup corn kernels	½ cup Ranch dressing

Directions and Total Time: 30 minutes

Preheat air fryer to 400°F. Combine vegan cottage cheese and garlic in a bowl. Spread one side of each bread slice with half of the mixture and place them, spread-side up, in the frying basket. Grill for 2 minutes until toasted. Let cool completely before slicing into croutons. Set aside. Put the corn kernels in a baking dish in the air fryer. Grill for 4 minutes. Slice each asparagus into 3 pieces and Grill in the air fryer for 6-8 minutes until crisp-tender. Set aside. Put the lettuce halves, cut-side up, in the fryer and Grill for 3 minutes until golden brown. Divide the lettuce **halves** between serving plates and add the croutons, corn, asparagus, tomatoes, and red onion. Sprinkle each with Ranch dressing and serve right away.

Southern Bean Salad

Ingredients for 4 servings

¼ cup vegan salad dressing	2 cups frozen corn, thawed
1 tsp chili powder	1 cup cooked pearl barley
2 (14.5-oz) cans kidney beans	1 head torn Iceberg lettuce

Directions and Total Time: 15 minutes

Mix the salad dressing and chili powder in a bowl. Add in kidney beans, corn, barley, and lettuce. Serve.

Asian Edamame & Rice Salad

Ingredients for 4 servings

1 cup rice	2 tbsp cilantro, chopped
Salt to taste	1 tbsp sesame seeds
1 large sweet potato	½ cup pure orange juice
1 tsp olive oil	1 tbsp tamari
1 cup shelled edamame	1 tbsp rice vinegar
1 red bell pepper, chopped	2 tsp agave nectar
½ head red cabbage, shredded	2 tsp sesame oil
4 scallions, chopped	

Directions and Total Time: 65 minutes

Preheat the oven to 400°F. Place 2 cups of salted water in a pot over high heat. When the water comes to a boil, add the rice, reduce the heat, and cover. Simmer for 30 minutes. Peel sweet potatoes and dice vineagr into small cubes. Toss with olive oil, then arrange in a baking dish. Roast for 15-20 minutes while the rice is cooking. When the rice and potato are done cooking, set aside to cool slightly. Add the orange juice, tamari, rice vinegar, agave nectar, and sesame oil to a jar Cover and shake well. Assemble the salad by combining rice, sweet potato, edamame, bell pepper, red cabbage and scallions in a large bowl. Top with dressing and toss to coat. Garnish with cilantro and sesame seeds. Serve and enjoy.

Lentil Salad

Ingredients for 4 servings

2 tbsp olive oil	1 tbsp dried oregano
1 shallot, diced	1 tbsp balsamic vinegar
1 garlic clove, minced	¼ cup white wine vinegar
1 carrot, diced	Salt to taste
1 cup lentils	2 cups chopped mustard greens
1 tbsp dried basil	2 cups torn red leaf lettuce

Directions and Total Time: 60 minutes

Saute shallot and garlic in 1 teaspoon of oil in a large pot over medium heat. After 5 minutes, saute carrot until slightly cooked. Three minutes later, combine vegetables with lentils, basil, oregano, balsamic vinegar, and 2 cups of water. Bring the soup to a boil, then reduce the heat. Simmer uncovered for 20 to 30 minutes or until the lentils are soft but not mushy.

Mix together white wine vinegar, olive oil, and salt in a small bowl. Set aside. When the lentils are ready, drain all remaining liquid. Stir in about ¾ of the white wine vinegar dressing and mustard greens. Cook on low for 10 minutes, stirring occasionally. Toss red leaf lettuce with the rest of the dressing. Divide the lettuce among the plates, then spoon over the lentil mixture. Serve warm.

Easy Sushi Bowl

Ingredients for 1 serving

½ cup green beans	¼ cup fresh cilantro, chopped
¾ cup cooked brown rice	1 scallion, chopped
½ cup chopped spinach	¼ nori sheet
¼ cup sliced avocado	1 tbsp tamari
¼ cup shredded carrots	1 tbsp sesame seeds

Directions and Total Time: 15 minutes

Steam the green beans. Arrange the beans, rice, spinach, avocado, carrots, cilantro, and scallions in a bowl. Use scissors to cut the nori into small ribbons. Drizzle tamari over the bowl and garnish with nori and sesame seeds.

Curried Potato Samosas

Ingredients for 4 servings

4 small potatoes	2 tsp curry powder
1 tsp coconut oil	Salt and black pepper to taste
1 shallot, finely chopped	2 carrots, grated
2 garlic cloves, minced	¼ cup green peas
1 small piece ginger, grated	¼ cup parsley, chopped

Directions and Total Time: 60 minutes

Preheat the oven to 350°F. Poke the potatoes all around with a fork. Wrap each potato with foil and bake for 30 minutes. Add oil to a medium skillet of medium heat. Saute shallot for 5 minutes, then add garlic and ginger for another 3 minutes until all of the ingredients have softened. Stir in curry powder, salt, and pepper. Remove from the heat. When the potatoes are ready, remove the foil and slice it in half. When they are cool enough to handle, scoop out enough flesh while maintaining the stability of the skin. Add the flesh to the shallot mixture and carrots, peas, and parsley. Scoop the mixture back into the potato skins, then transfer to a baking dish. Bake at the same temperature for 10 minutes. Serve.

Green Salad with Almond Crunch

Ingredients for 4 servings

3 tbsp tahini	½ cup chopped almonds
2 tbsp Dijon mustard	6 radishes, finely sliced
3 tsp maple syrup	1 lb kale, roughly chopped
1 tbsp lemon juice	1 cored green apple, sliced
Salt to taste	

Directions and Total Time: 20 minutes

Preheat the oven to 325°F. Line a baking sheet with parchment paper. In a small bowl, combine 2 tablespoons tahini, mustard, 2 teaspoon maple syrup, lemon juice, and salt until well mixed. Set to the side. In a medium bowl, combine chopped almonds, salt and the rest of the tahini and maple syrup. Spread out the mixture onto the baking sheet and bake for 5 to 7 minutes. When the almond mixture is crunchy and just darker, let cool for 3 minutes. Toss radishes, kale, and apples in a large bowl with the dressing. Sprinkle over almond crunch. Serve.

Vegan-Style Caesar Salad

Ingredients for 4 servings

4 oz shaved vegan Parmesan cheese	
½ cup walnuts	1 tsp garlic powder
3 tbsp olive oil	1 tbsp capers, minced
½ lime, juiced	Salt and black pepper to taste
1 tbsp white miso paste	2 heads romaine lettuce, torn
1 tsp soy sauce	1 cup cherry tomatoes, halved
1 tsp Dijon mustard	2 oz whole-wheat croutons

Directions and Total Time: 20 minutes

Add walnuts, olive oil, lime juice, miso paste, soy sauce, mustard, garlic powder, capers, salt, pepper, and ½ cup water to a blender jar. Puree for about 2 minutes or until nearly smooth. Toss romaine and half of the dressing in a large bowl. Plate the salad for each portion, then top with tomatoes, Parmesan, and croutons. Have the rest of the dressing on the side. Serve and enjoy.

Daikon Radish Salad

Ingredients for 4 servings

1 peeled daikon radish, grated	Salt and black pepper to taste
1 carrot, shredded	2 tsp white wine vinegar
2 tbsp parsley, chopped	2 tbsp extra-virgin olive oil
1 scallion, chopped	2 tbsp chopped cashews

Directions and Total Time: 75 minutes

Whisk the olive oil, vinegar, salt, and pepper in a bowl. Add the daikon radish and carrot and stir to coat. Place covered in the fridge for 1 hour. Serve topped with chopped cashews, parsley and scallion.

Lebanese-Inspired Tabbouleh

Ingredients for 4 servings

1 cup whole-wheat couscous	1 tomato, diced
1 lime, zested and juiced	1 cup parsley, chopped
1 garlic clove, pressed	¼ cup fresh mint, chopped
Salt to taste	2 scallions, finely chopped
1 tbsp olive oil	4 tbsp pomegranate seeds
½ cucumber, diced	

Directions and Total Time: 20 minutes

Cover couscous in 1 cup boiling water in a medium bowl. Cover the bowl and set to the side. In a large bowl, stir lime zest, lime juice, garlic, salt, and olive oil. Add cucumber, tomato, parsley, mint, and scallions. Toss in the dressing until coated. Fluff the couscous with a fork, then toss into the salad until coated with dressing. Garnish with pomegranate seeds. Serve and enjoy.

Tijuana-Inspired Salad

Ingredients for 4 servings

1 lemon, juiced	1 (15-oz) can black beans
2 tbsp olive oil	1 cup grape tomatoes, halved
1 tbsp agave syrup	1 cup corn kernels
¼ tsp salt	1 avocado, diced
2 cups cooked quinoa	2 green onions, sliced
1 tbsp taco seasoning	12 tortilla chips, crushed
2 heads romaine lettuce, torn	

Directions and Total Time: 25 minutes

To make the vinaigrette, whisk lemon juice, olive oil, agave syrup, and salt in a small bowl. Set to the side. Combine quinoa and taco seasoning in a medium bowl. Toss lettuce and vinaigrette in a large bowl, then serve among four bowls. Top the lettuce with equal portions of quinoa, beans, tomatoes, corn, avocado, green onions, and crushed tortilla chips. Serve and enjoy.

Tri-Color Salad Bowl

Ingredients for 6 servings

1 cup baby bella mushrooms, sliced	
1 tbsp olive oil	½ cup vegetable broth
1 onion, chopped	2 cups spinach, chopped
12 diced sun-dried tomatoes	3 cups penne, cooked
6 garlic cloves, minced	1 (15-oz) can cannellini beans
Salt and black pepper to taste	3 tbsp vegan Parmesan cheese
¼ tsp red pepper flakes	2 tbsp chopped parsley

Directions and Total Time: 25 minutes

In a large skillet, heat oil over medium heat. Sauté onion, tomatoes, and mushrooms for about 5 minutes or until the onion is soft and the mushrooms have reduced. Stir in garlic, salt, black pepper, and red pepper flakes. Cook for 1 minute until aromatic. Pour in broth slowly and stir in spinach. Let simmer covered for 5 minutes to wilt the spinach. Stir in pasta and bean and heat through for about 2 minutes. Divide among 6 bowls. Top with Parmesan and chopped parsley. Serve warm and enjoy.

Fall Bowls

Ingredients for 4 servings

2 russet potatoes, cubed	1 tbsp tamari
2 tbsp olive oil	2 cups cooked chickpeas
Salt and black pepper to taste	3 tbsp vegan ranch dressing
2 cups broccoli florets	¼ cup sunflower seeds
4 cups grated purple cabbage	¼ cup thinly sliced scallions

Directions and Total Time: 35 minutes

Preheat the oven to 425°F. Use parchment paper to line a baking sheet. Toss potato and 1 tablespoon olive oil in a large bowl. Season with salt and pepper. Arrange the potatoes in a single layer on the baking sheet. Bake for 15 minutes. Using the same bowl, toss broccoli, cabbage, tamari, and 1 tablespoon of olive oil. Season with salt and pepper. After 15 minutes, toss the potatoes on the baking sheet. Arrange the broccoli-cabbage mixture over the potatoes and bake for 10 minutes when the potatoes are fork-tender. Toss and combine. Portion the chickpeas among 4 bowls, then add the vegetables over them. Drizzle with ranch and garnish with sunflower seeds and scallions. Serve warm and enjoy.

Tofu Caesar Salad with Pears

Ingredients for 4 servings

1 (14-oz) block tofu, cubed	½ tsp garlic powder
2 cups chopped ripe pears	½ tsp onion powder
2 minced green onions	½ cup vegan mayonnaise
¼ cup thinly sliced celery	½ head Iceberg lettuce, torn
1 tbsp chopped fresh parsley	Salt and black pepper to taste
¾ tsp dried dill	

Directions and Total Time: 20 minutes

Toss tofu, pears, onions, celery, parsley, dill, garlic powder, and onion powder in a large bowl. Gently stir in mayonnaise and season with salt and pepper. Serve on bed of lettuce in a salad platter and enjoy.

Pizza-Style Mushroom & Spinach Bowls

Ingredients for 4 servings

1 tbsp olive oil	5 oz baby spinach
1 carrot, sliced	2 cups cooked cannellini beans
½ red onion, thinly sliced	1 cup black olives, sliced
1 cup bella mushrooms, sliced	½ tsp Red pepper flakes
1 tsp Italian garlic seasoning	2 tbsp vegan Parmesan cheese
2 cups marinara sauce	1 tbsp chopped basil

Directions and Total Time: 15 minutes

In a large skillet, heat oil over medium heat. Stir in carrot, red onion, mushrooms, and Italian seasoning. Sauté for 3 to 5 minutes to soften the onion. Add garlic and sauté for another minute until aromatic. In each bowl, add ¼ cup marinara sauce, then a layer of spinach. Top with ¼ cup beans and ¼ of the vegetable mixture. Finish with the rest of the sauce and black olives. Top with red pepper flakes, Parmesan, and basil. Serve warm

Vegan Bacon & Avocado Salad

Ingredients for 4 servings

6 oz baby greens salad	1 peeled cucumber, diced
10 cherry tomatoes, halved	2 oz vegan bacon
1 avocado, diced	4 scallions, thinly sliced
1 cup corn kernels	4 tbsp vegan ranch dressing

Directions and Total Time: 25 minutes

Divide the baby greens among 4 bowls. Arrange each ingredient in a line across the greens: tomatoes, avocado, corn, cucumber, and vegan bacon. Top with scallions and ranch dressing. Serve and enjoy.

Hall of Fame Salad

Ingredients for 4 servings

1 lemon, juiced	1 cup corn kernels
2 tbsp olive oil	½ red onion, thinly sliced
1 tbsp maple syrup	2 cored Fuji apples, sliced
Salt to taste	½ cup chopped hazelnuts
5 oz package arugula	¼ cup raisins

Directions and Total Time: 20 minutes

Mix lemon juice, oil, maple syrup, and salt in a small bowl. Toss arugula, corn, red onion, and apples in a large bowl. Add dressing and toss. Serve salad among 4 plates. Sprinkle it with hazelnuts and raisins. Serve and enjoy.

Rich Multi-Grain Bowls

Ingredients for 2 servings

2 tsp olive oil	1 bunch spinach, chopped
1 cup cooked quinoa	1 tbsp tamari
1 (15-oz) can pink beans	Salt and black pepper to taste

Directions and Total Time: 15 minutes

Heat oil in a large skillet over medium heat. Stir in quinoa, beans, and spinach and continue stirring until the spinach is wilted. Cook for 3 to 5 minutes for everything to be heated through. Stir in tamari and season with salt and pepper. Divide between bowls. Serve warm and enjoy.

Arizona-Inspired Bean & Avocado Salad

Ingredients for 4 servings

1 head romaine lettuce, torn	¼ cup chopped fresh cilantro
1 (15-oz) can pinto beans	1 lime, juiced
1 cup grape tomatoes, halved	1 tbsp agave syrup
1 ½ cups corn kernels	1 tbsp olive oil
1 avocado, diced	Salt and black pepper to taste

Directions and Total Time: 20 minutes

Combine lettuce, beans, tomatoes, corn, avocado, and cilantro in a large bowl. Stir in lime juice, agave syrup, oil, salt, and pepper. Serve and enjoy.

Kidney Bean Salad

Ingredients for 6 servings

1 (15-oz) can kidney beans	Salt and black pepper to taste
1 cucumber, peeled and diced	3 tbsp extra-virgin olive oil
1 red onion, sliced	2 tsp lemon juice
4 radishes, diced	

Directions and Total Time: 15 minutes

To a large bowl, toss in all the ingredients together. Serve right away or refrigerate before serving.

Chickpea-Kale Salad Bowls with Pine Nuts

Ingredients for 4 servings

2 tbsp vegan green goddess dressing	
1 (15-oz) can chickpeas	1 pint grape tomatoes, halved
2 tbsp olive oil, divided	½ red onion, thinly sliced
1 tbsp ground coriander	½ cup chopped cilantro
1 tbsp ground cumin	¼ cup chopped parsley
Salt and black pepper to taste	¼ cup chopped mint
5 oz curly kale, chopped	2 tbsp toasted pine nuts
1 cup thinly sliced cucumber	

Directions and Total Time: 40 minutes

Preheat the oven to 425°F. Line a baking sheet with parchment paper. Toss chickpeas with 1 ½ tablespoon olive oil, coriander, cumin, salt, and pepper in a medium bowl. Arrange on the baking sheet in a single layer and roast for 20 minutes, tossing halfway through. When the chickpeas are brown and crisp, remove from the oven to cool for 5 minutes. While you are waiting on the chickpeas to cool, add kale and ½ tablespoon olive oil in a large bowl. Massage the oil into the kale for 2 minutes or until soft. Toss in cucumber, tomatoes, red onion, cilantro, parsley, and mint. To serve, portion the salad among 4 plates, then top with roasted chickpeas. Drizzle with dressing and garnish with toasted pine nuts. Serve.

Spring Lentil Salad

Ingredients for 4 servings

2 tbsp olive oil	1 tsp dried thyme
1 onion, chopped	1 (15-oz) can lentils
2 garlic cloves, minced	1 tbsp apple cider vinegar
½ red bell pepper, diced	Salt and black pepper to taste
½ zucchini, julienned	½ tsp red chili flakes
2 celery stalks, thinly sliced	5 oz mixed spring greens

Directions and Total Time: 20 minutes

In a medium skillet, heat oil over medium heat. Sauté onions for 3 minutes until softened. Add garlic and stir for 1 minute until aromatic. Stir in bell pepper, zucchini, celery and thyme. Cook for 3 to 5 minutes, stirring occasionally. When the pepper is tender, stir in lentils and vinegar. Season with salt, pepper, and chili flakes. Cook for 2 minutes, stirring occasionally. To serve, fill 4 bowls with greens and top with lentils. Serve warm.

Honolulu Tofu Bowls

Ingredients for 4 servings

1 red onion, sliced	5 oz baby spinach
1 red bell pepper, sliced	1 cup cooked quinoa
3 tsp olive oil	1 avocado, sliced
1 (14-oz) block tofu, cubed	2 tbsp chopped cilantro
1 sliced pineapple	1 tbsp coconut flakes
1 cup barbecue sauce	

Directions and Total Time: 30 minutes

Preheat the oven to 425°F. Line a baking sheet with parchment paper. In a medium bowl, toss onion and bell pepper with 2 teaspoons olive oil. Arrange the vegetables in a single layer on one side of the baking sheet and the tofu on the other side. Bake for 10 minutes, then toss with a spatula. Bake for another 10 minutes until the tofu is golden. While the tofu is baking, add 1 teaspoon oil in a large skillet over medium heat. Sauté the pineapple slices until it is caramelized and dark brown. Transfer the tofu to a bowl with barbecue sauce and toss until coated. To prepare the bowls, layer spinach, avocado, and quinoa among 4 bowls. Next, add vegetables, tofu, and pineapple. Top with cilantro and coconut flakes.

Power Green Salad

Ingredients for 4 servings

½ cup vegan green goddess dressing
8 asparagus spears, cut into 2-inch pieces

1 head Romaine lettuce	1 seedless cucumber, sliced
1 celery stick, finely sliced	1 zucchini, cut into ribbons
1 cored green apple, sliced	2 scallions, thinly sliced

Directions and Total Time: 20 minutes

Boil the asparagus for 1-2 minutes in boiling water, then drain, run under cold water to cool, then drain again. Divide the lettuce leaves between 4 plates. Top each with asparagus, celery, cucumber, zucchini, and apple. Drizzle with dressing and scatter with scallions.

Kale & Quinoa Salad with Avocado Dressing

Ingredients for 4 servings

1 avocado, peeled and pitted	8 kale leaves, chopped
1 tbsp lime juice	½ cup chopped snap beans
½ tsp ground coriander	1 cup cherry tomatoes, halved
1 garlic clove, minced	1 bell pepper, chopped
1 scallion, chopped	1 green onion, chopped
Salt to taste	2 cups cooked quinoa
¼ cup water	1 tbsp hummus

Directions and Total Time: 20 minutes

Add the avocado, lime juice, ground coriander, garlic, scallion, salt, and ¼ cup of water in a blender or food processor. Puree until the dressing is smooth. Add water a little bit at a time to thin it out if necessary. Check for seasoning. Prepare the salad by adding the kale, snap beans, cherry tomatoes, bell pepper, green onion, quinoa, and hummus in a large bowl. Toss with dressing until evenly coated. Divide the salad among the plates and garnish with a spoonful of hummus. Serve and enjoy.

Tricolor Quinoa Salad

Ingredients for 6 servings

3 tbsp olive oil	1 English cucumber
1 lemon, juiced	1 avocado, cubed
1 tsp garlic powder	1 red bell pepper, diced
½ tsp dried oregano	½ red onion, thinly sliced
1 bunch curly kale, chopped	10 sundried tomatoes, diced
2 cups cooked tricolor quinoa	½ cup slivered almonds

Directions and Total Time: 15 minutes

Whisk oil, lemon juice, garlic powder, and oregano in a small bowl. Pour the dressing over kale in a large bowl and massage until coated and soft. Toss in quinoa, cucumber, avocado, bell pepper, and red onion. Transfer to a serving bowl and top with tomatoes and almonds.

Kale & Tofu Bowls with Vegan Pesto

Ingredients for 4 servings

1 (14-oz) block tofu, cubed	½ cup shelled cooked edamame
1 tbsp olive oil	Salt and black pepper to taste
½ cup sliced red onions	1 cup vegan pesto
10 oz curly kale, chopped	2 cups cooked brown rice

Directions and Total Time: 30 minutes

Preheat the oven to 425°F. Arrange the tofu in a single layer on a parchment-lined baking sheet and bake for 10 minutes. Flip the tofu and bake for another 10 minutes until golden. In a large skillet, heat oil over medium heat. Sauté onions for 3 minutes until softened. Stir in kale and edamame and sauté for another 3 minutes. Continue stirring until wilted. Add salt and pepper to taste. Add tofu and pesto to a large bowl and toss to coat. Add rice to 4 bowls, then top with the kale mixture. Finish it off with the pesto tofu. Serve warm and enjoy.

Broccoli & Tempeh Salad with Cranberries

Ingredients for 4 servings

3 oz plant butter	Salt and black pepper to taste
¾ lb tempeh slices, cubed	2 oz almonds
1 lb broccoli florets	½ cup frozen cranberries

Directions and Total Time: 15 minutes

In a skillet, melt the plant butter over medium heat until no longer foaming, and fry the tempeh cubes until brown on all sides. Add the broccoli and stir-fry for 6 minutes. Season with salt and pepper. Turn the heat off. Stir in the almonds and cranberries to warm through. Serve.

Italian Salad with Roasted Veggies

Ingredients for 4 servings

1 ½ cups quartered mushrooms
1 cup cherry tomatoes
1 green onion, thinly sliced
1 tbsp allspice
10 oz green beans, thawed

2 cups fingerling potatoes
½ lb baby spinach
½ cup Italian dressing
¼ cup pepitas

Directions and Total Time: 35 minutes

Preheat air fryer to 380°F. Combine mushrooms, tomatoes, green onion, and allspice in a bowl. Set aside. Arrange the green beans on a baking pan, then put in the veggie mixture, and finally top with potatoes. Roast for 25 minutes until the potatoes are tender. Let cool completely before removing to a bowl; toss to combine. Stir in spinach, drizzle with Italian dressing, and scatter with pepitas; toss to combine. Serve right away.

Tofu-Beet Salad

Ingredients for 4 servings

2 tbsp plant butter
8 oz red beets
2 oz tofu, chopped into bits
½ red onion

1 cup vegan mayonnaise
1 small romaine lettuce, torn
Freshly chopped chives
Salt and black pepper to taste

Directions and Total Time: 50 minutes

Put beets in a pot, cover with water, and bring to a boil for 40 minutes. Melt plant butter in a non-stick pan over medium heat and fry tofu until browned. Set aside to cool. When the bits are ready, drain through a colander and allow cooling. Slip the skin off after and slice them. In a salad bowl, combine the beets, tofu, red onions, lettuce, salt, pepper, and mayonnaise and mix until the vegetables are adequately coated with the mayonnaise. Garnish with chives and serve.

Brussels Sprout & Roasted Chickpea Salad

Ingredients for 4 servings

1 lb Brussels sprouts, sliced
1 (15-oz) can chickpeas
2 tbsp olive oil
1 tbsp apple cider vinegar

Salt and black pepper to taste
1/3 cup sunflower seeds
2 tbsp vegan Parmesan cheese

Directions and Total Time: 30 minutes

Preheat the oven to 400°F. Prepare a baking sheet by lining it with parchment paper. Toss Brussels sprouts, chickpeas, oil, apple cider vinegar, salt, and pepper in a large bowl. Arrange on the baking sheet in a single layer and roast for 15 minutes. Stir in sunflower seeds and roast for 10 minutes. Top with Parmesan. Serve.

Picante Chickpea Salad

Ingredients for 2 servings

3 tbsp chipotle hot sauce
1 tsp garlic powder
1 (15.5-oz) can chickpeas
12 cherry tomatoes
2 cups torn romaine lettuce

1 cucumber, sliced
3 radishes, sliced
2 celery stalks, chopped
2 scallions, sliced
¼ cup Ranch dressing

Directions and Total Time: 20 minutes

Preheat air fryer to 360°F. Whisk chipotle hot sauce and garlic in a bowl. Add in chickpeas and toss to coat. Bake chickpeas and tomatoes, in a single layer, for 8-10 minutes until tomatoes are blistered. In the meantime, combine lettuce, cucumber, celery, radishes, and scallions in a bowl. Drizzle with Ranch dressing and toss to combine. Mix in Baked chickpeas and tomatoes and serve.

White Bean Falafel Salad

Ingredients for 4 servings

1 (15.5-oz) can white beans
½ sliced red onion
2 tbsp chopped cilantro
2 tbsp lemon juice
1 tsp garlic powder
1 tsp ground cumin

¼ cup chickpea flour
2 cups torn romaine lettuce
1 cup cherry tomatoes, halved
1 peeled cucumber, sliced
¼ cup Italian dressing

Directions and Total Time: 30 minutes

Preheat air fryer to 375°F. Using a fork, mash the white beans until smooth. Stir in ¼ cup of red onion, cilantro, lemon juice, garlic, cumin, and chickpea flour until well combined. Make 8 equal patties out of the mixture and Bake for 12 minutes until golden brown, turning once. Let cool slightly. Combine the lettuce, tomatoes, cucumber, and the remaining red onion in a bowl. Add in falafels and drizzle with Italian dressing; toss to combine.

Tofu Salad

Ingredients for 2 servings

4 tbsp olive oil
½ yellow bell pepper, diced
3 tomatoes, diced
½ cucumber, chopped
½ red onion, peeled and sliced

½ cup tofu cheese, cubed
10 Kalamata olives, pitted
½ tbsp red wine vinegar
2 tsp dried oregano
Salt and black pepper to taste

Directions and Total Time: 10 minutes

Pour the bell pepper, tomatoes, cucumber, red onion, tofu cheese, and olives into a salad bowl. Drizzle the red wine vinegar and olive oil over the vegetables. Season with salt, black pepper, and oregano, and toss the salad with two spoons. Share the salad into bowls and serve.

Dilly Green Squash Salad

Ingredients for 4 servings

2 tbsp plant butter
2 lb green squash, cubed
Salt and black pepper to taste
3 oz fennel, sliced
2 oz chopped green onions

1 cup vegan mayonnaise
2 tbsp chives, finely chopped
A pinch of mustard powder
Chopped dill to garnish

Directions and Total Time: 20 minutes

Put a pan over medium heat and melt plant butter. Fry in squash cubes until slightly softened but not browned, about 7 minutes. Allow the squash to cool. In a salad bowl, mix the cooled squash, fennel slices, green onions, vegan mayonnaise, chives, salt, pepper, and mustard powder. Garnish with dill and serve.

Peanut & Mango Rice Salad with Lime Dressing

Ingredients for 4 servings

1/3 cup grapeseed oil	3 tbsp fresh lime juice
3 ½ cups cooked brown rice	2 tsp agave nectar
½ cup chopped roasted peanuts	1 tsp grated fresh ginger
½ cup sliced mango	Salt and black pepper to taste
4 green onions, chopped	

Directions and Total Time: 15 minutes

In a bowl, mix the rice, peanuts, mango, and green onions. Set aside. In another bowl, whisk the lime juice, agave nectar, and ginger. Add oil, salt, and pepper and stir to combine. Pour over the rice bowl and toss to coat.

Bean & Tofu Pasta Salad

Ingredients for 4 servings

1 tbsp olive oil	2 large tomatoes, chopped
2 ½ cups bow tie pasta	1 (15 oz) can cannellini beans
1 medium zucchini, sliced	10 can green olives, sliced
2 garlic cloves, minced	½ cup crumbled tofu cheese

Directions and Total Time: 35 minutes

Cook the pasta until al dente, 10 minutes. Drain and set aside. Heat olive oil in a skillet and sauté zucchini and garlic for 4 minutes. Stir in tomatoes, beans, and olives. Cook until the tomatoes soften, 10 minutes. Mix in pasta. Allow warming for 1 minute. Stir in tofu cheese. Serve.

Dijon Kale Salad

Ingredients for 4 servings

2 tbsp olive oil	1 tbsp minced green onions
2 tbsp Dijon mustard	4 cups fresh kale, chopped
¼ cup fresh orange juice	1 peeled orange, segmented
1 tsp agave nectar	½ red onion, sliced paper-thin
2 tbsp minced fresh parsley	Salt and black pepper to taste

Directions and Total Time: 10 minutes

In a food processor, place the mustard, oil, orange juice, agave nectar, salt, pepper, parsley, and green onions. Blend until smooth. In a bowl, combine the kale, orange, and onion. Coat the salad with dressing. Serve and enjoy!

Spinach-Zucchini Salad

Ingredients for 2 servings

1 lemon, half zested and juiced, half cut into wedges

1 tsp olive oil	A pinch of salt
1 zucchini, chopped	2 tbsp capers
½ tsp ground cumin	1 tbsp chopped green olives
½ tsp ground ginger	1 garlic clove, pressed
¼ tsp turmeric	2 tbsp fresh mint, chopped
¼ tsp ground nutmeg	2 cups spinach, chopped

Directions and Total Time: 20 minutes

Warm olive oil in a skillet over medium heat. Place the zucchini and sauté for 10 minutes. Stir in cumin, ginger, turmeric, nutmeg, and salt. Pour in lemon zest, lemon juice, capers, garlic, and mint, cook for 2 minutes. Divide the spinach between serving plates and top with the zucchini mixture. Garnish with lemon wedges and olives.

Green Bean Salad with Roasted Mushrooms

Ingredients for 4 servings

1 lb cremini mushrooms, sliced	Salt and black pepper to taste
3 tbsp melted plant butter	Juice of 1 lemon
½ cup green beans	4 tbsp toasted hazelnuts

Directions and Total Time: 25 minutes

Preheat oven to 450°F. Arrange the mushrooms and green beans in a baking dish, drizzle the plant butter over, and sprinkle with salt and black pepper. Use your hands to rub the vegetables with the seasoning and roast in the oven for 20 minutes or until they are soft. Transfer the vegetables into a salad bowl, drizzle with the lemon juice, and toss the salad with hazelnuts. Serve immediately.

Farro & Bean Salad

Ingredients for 4 servings

4 cups watercress and arugula mix

2 tsp olive oil	1 red bell pepper, chopped
1 (14-oz) can black beans	2 scallions, chopped
1 cup corn kernels	4 large whole-grain tortillas
¼ cup fresh cilantro, chopped	1 tbsp oregano
Zest and juice of 1 lime	1 tsp cayenne pepper
3 tsp chili powder	¾ cup cooked faro
Salt and black pepper to taste	¼ cup chopped avocado
8 cherry tomatoes, halved	¼ cup mango salsa

Directions and Total Time: 20 minutes

Combine black beans, corn, cilantro, lime juice, lime zest, chili powder, salt, pepper, cherry tomatoes, bell peppers, and scallions in a bowl. Set aside. Brush the tortillas with olive oil and season with salt, pepper, oregano, and cayenne pepper. Slice into 8 pieces. Line with parchment paper a baking sheet. Arrange tortilla pieces and bake for 3-5 minutes until browned. On a serving platter, put the watercress and arugula mix, top with faro, bean mixture, avocado, and sprinkle with mango salsa all over to serve.

Couscous & Bean Salad

Ingredients for 4 servings

¼ cup olive oil	1 carrot, shredded
1 medium shallot, minced	½ cup chopped dried apricots
½ tsp ground coriander	¼ cup golden raisins
½ tsp turmeric	¼ cup chopped roasted cashews
¼ tsp ground cayenne	1 (15.5-oz) can white beans
1 cup couscous	2 tbsp minced cilantro leaves
2 cups vegetable broth	2 tbsp fresh lemon juice
1 yellow bell pepper, chopped	

Directions and Total Time: 15 minutes

Heat 1 tbsp of oil in a pot over medium heat. Place in shallot, coriander, turmeric, cayenne pepper, and couscous. Cook for 2 minutes, stirring often. Add in broth and salt. Bring to a boil. Turn the heat off and let sit covered for 5 minutes. Remove to a bowl and stir in bell pepper, carrot, apricots, raisins, cashews, beans, and cilantro. Set aside. In another bowl, whisk the remaining oil with lemon juice until blended. Pour over the salad and toss to combine. Serve immediately.

Hot Brussel Sprout Salad with Seeds & Pecans

Ingredients for 4 servings

½ cup olive oil
1 tbsp plant butter
1 lb Brussels sprouts, grated
1 lemon, juiced and zested
1 tsp chili paste

2 oz pecans
1 oz pumpkin seeds
1 oz sunflower seeds
½ tsp cumin powder

Directions and Total Time: 20 minutes

Put Brussels sprouts in a salad bowl. In a small bowl, mix lemon juice, zest, olive oil, salt, and pepper, and drizzle the dressing over the Brussels sprouts. Toss and allow the vegetable to marinate for 10 minutes. Melt plant butter in a pan. Stir in chili paste and toss the pecans, pumpkin seeds, sunflower seeds, cumin powder, and salt in the chili butter. Sauté on low heat for 3-4 minutes just to heat the nuts. Allow cooling. Pour the nuts and seeds mix in the salad bowl, toss, and serve.

Red Cabbage & Chickpea Salad with Avocado

Ingredients for 4 servings

1 yellow bell pepper, cut into sticks
¼ cup olive oil
1 carrot, shredded
1 cup shredded red cabbage
1 cup cherry tomatoes, halved
1 (15.5-oz) can chickpeas

¼ cup capers
1 avocado, sliced
1 ½ tbsp fresh lemon juice
Salt and black pepper to taste

Directions and Total Time: 15 minutes

Combine carrot, cabbage, tomatoes, bell pepper, chickpeas, capers, and avocado in a bowl. In another bowl, mix oil, lemon juice, salt, and pepper until thoroughly combined. Pour over the cabbage mixture and toss to coat.

Summer Avocado Salad

Ingredients for 4 servings

1/3 cup olive oil
1 garlic clove, chopped
1 red onion, sliced
½ tsp dried basil
Salt and black pepper to taste
¼ tsp pure date sugar

3 tbsp white wine vinegar
1 head Iceberg lettuce, torn
12 ripe grape tomatoes, halved
½ cup frozen peas, thawed
8 black olives, pitted
1 avocado, sliced

Directions and Total Time: 15 minutes

In a food processor, place the garlic, onion, oil, basil, salt, pepper, sugar, and vinegar. Blend until smooth. Set aside. Place the lettuce, tomatoes, peas, and olives on a nice serving plate. Top with avocado slices and drizzle the previously prepared dressing all over. Serve.

Raisin & Cashew Coleslaw with Haricots Verts

Ingredients for 4 servings

1/3 cup creamy peanut butter
3 cups haricots verts, chopped
2 carrots, sliced
3 cups shredded cabbage
1/3 cup golden raisins
¼ cup roasted cashew
1 garlic clove, minced

1 medium shallot, chopped
1 ½ tsp grated fresh ginger
2 tbsp soy sauce
2 tbsp fresh lemon juice
Salt to taste
⅛ tsp ground cayenne
¾ cup coconut milk

Directions and Total Time: 15 minutes

Place the haricots verts, carrots, and cabbage in a pot with water and steam for 5 minutes. Drain and transfer to a bowl. Add in raisins and cashew. Let cool. In a food processor, put the garlic, shallot, and ginger. Pulse until puréed. Add in peanut butter, soy sauce, lemon juice, salt, cayenne pepper. Blitz until smooth. Stir in coconut milk. Sprinkle the salad with the dressing and toss to coat.

Herby Lentil Salad

Ingredients for 4 servings

2 tsp olive oil
1 red onion, diced
1 garlic clove, minced
1 carrot, diced
1 cup lentils
1 tbsp dried basil

1 tbsp dried oregano
1 tbsp balsamic vinegar
2 cups water
Sea salt to taste
2 cups chopped Swiss chard
2 cups torn curly endive

Directions and Total Time: 40 minutes

In a bowl, mix the balsamic vinegar, olive oil, and salt. Set aside. Warm 1 tsp of oil in a pot over medium heat. Place the onion, garlic, and carrot and cook for 5 minutes. Mix in lentils, basil, oregano, balsamic vinegar, and water and bring to a boil. Lower the heat and simmer for 20 minutes. Mix in two-thirds of the dressing. Add in the Swiss chard and cook for 5 minutes on low. Let cool. Coat the endive with the remaining dressing. Transfer to a plate and top with lentil mixture to serve.

Cherry Millet & Bean Salad

Ingredients for 4 servings

¼ cup grapeseed oil
1 cup millet
1 (15.5-oz) can navy beans
1 celery stalk, finely chopped
1 carrot, shredded
3 green onions, minced

8 chopped kalamata olives
½ cup dried cherries
½ cup toasted pecans, chopped
½ cup minced fresh parsley
1 garlic clove, pressed
3 tbsp sherry vinegar

Directions and Total Time: 40 minutes

Cook the millet in salted water for 30 minutes. Remove to a bowl. Mix in beans, celery, carrot, green onions, olives, cherries, pecans, and parsley. In another bowl, whisk the garlic, grapeseed olil, vinegar, salt, and pepper until well mixed. Pour over the millet mixture and toss to coat.

Mustardy Collard & Tofu Salad

Ingredients for 2 servings

2 tbsp coconut oil
2 oz plant butter
¾ cup coconut cream
2 tbsp vegan mayonnaise
A pinch of mustard powder

1 garlic clove, minced
Salt and black pepper to taste
1 cup collards, rinsed
4 oz tofu cheese

Directions and Total Time: 10 minutes

In a small bowl, whisk the coconut whipping cream, vegan mayonnaise, mustard powder, coconut oil, garlic, salt, and black pepper until well mixed; set aside. Melt the plant butter in a large skillet over medium heat.

Sauté the collards until wilted and brownish. Season with salt and black pepper to taste. Transfer the collards to a salad bowl and pour the creamy dressing over. Mix the salad well and crumble the tofu cheese over. Serve.

Potato & Green Bean Salad

Ingredients for 4 servings

1 tbsp extra-virgin olive oil	2 carrots, sliced
Salt and black pepper to taste	1 tbsp lime juice
1 cup green beans, chopped	2 tsp dried dill
4 potatoes, quartered	1 cup cashew cream

Directions and Total Time: 25 minutes

Pour salted water in a pot over medium heat. Add in potatoes, bring to a boil and cook for 8 minutes. Put in carrots and green beans and cook for 8 minutes. Drain and put in a bowl. Mix in olive oil, lime juice, dill, cashew cream, salt, and pepper. Toss to coat. Serve cooled.

Spinach Salad a la Puttanesca with Seitan

Ingredients for 4 servings

3 cups baby spinach, cut into strips

4 tbsp olive oil	10 cherry tomatoes, halved
8 oz seitan, cut into strips	2 tbsp balsamic vinegar
2 garlic cloves, minced	2 tbsp torn fresh basil leaves
½ cup Kalamata olives, halved	2 tbsp minced fresh parsley
½ cup green olives, halved	1 cup pomegranate seeds
2 tbsp capers	

Directions and Total Time: 15 minutes

Heat half of the olive oil in a skillet over medium heat. Place the seitan and brown for 5 minutes on all sides. Add in garlic and cook for 30 seconds. Remove to a bowl and let cool. Stir in olives, capers, spinach, and tomatoes. Set aside. In another bowl, whisk the remaining oil, vinegar, salt, and pepper until well mixed. Pour this dressing over the seitan salad and toss to coat. Top with basil, parsley, and pomegranate seeds. Serve and enjoy!

Caramelized Onion & Daikon Salad

Ingredients for 4 servings

2 tsp olive oil	Salt to taste
1 lb daikon, peeled	1 tbsp rice vinegar
2 cups sliced sweet onions	

Directions and Total Time: 50 minutes

Place the daikon in a pot with salted water and cook 25 minutes, until tender. Drain and let cool. In a skillet over low heat, warm olive oil and add the onion. Sauté for 10-15 minutes until caramelized. Sprinkle with salt. Remove to a bowl. Chop the daikon into wedges and add to the onion bowl. Stir in the vinegar. Serve.

Carrot Salad

Ingredients for 4 servings

¼ cup olive oil	½ cup roasted walnuts
1 lb carrots, shredded	¼ cup chopped fresh parsley
2 oranges, chopped	2 tbsp fresh orange juice

2 tbsp fresh lime juice	Salt and black pepper to taste
2 tsp pure date sugar	

Directions and Total Time: 15 minutes

In a bowl, mix the carrots, oranges, walnuts, and parsley. Set aside. In another bowl, whisk the orange juice, lime juice, sugar, salt, pepper, and oil. Mix until blended. Pour over the carrot mixture and toss to coat. Adjust the seasoning. Serve and enjoy!

Asian Green Bean & Potato Salad

Ingredients for 4 servings

1 tbsp grapeseed oil	1 garlic clove, minced
1/3 cup peanut butter	½ tsp Asian chili paste
1 ½ lb baby potatoes, unpeeled	2 tbsp soy sauce
1 cup green beans	1 tbsp rice vinegar
½ cup shredded carrots	¾ cup coconut milk
4 green onions, chopped	3 tbsp chopped roasted peanuts

Directions and Total Time: 30 minutes

Place the potatoes in a pot with boiling salted water and cook for 20 minutes. Drain and let cool. Chop into chunks and place in a bowl. Stir in green beans, carrots, and green onions. Set aside.

Heat oil in a pot over medium heat. Place in garlic and cook for 30 seconds. Add in peanut butter, chili, soy sauce, vinegar, coconut milk. Cook for 5 minutes, stirring often. Pour over the potatoes and toss to coat. Serve garnished with peanuts.

Cannellini Bean & Veggie Salad

Ingredients for 2 servings

1 tbsp olive oil	A pinch of salt
2 tbsp balsamic vinegar	1 (14-oz) can cannellini beans
1 tsp minced fresh chives	1 green bell pepper, sliced
1 garlic clove, minced	1 zucchini, diced
1 tbsp fresh rosemary, minced	2 carrots, diced
1 tbsp fresh oregano, chopped	2 tbsp fresh basil, chopped

Directions and Total Time: 40 minutes

In a bowl, mix the olive oil, balsamic vinegar, chives, garlic, rosemary, oregano, and salt. Stir in the beans, bell pepper, zucchini, carrots, and basil. Serve.

Daily Fruit Salad

Ingredients for 6 servings

1 jicama, peeled and grated	Sea salt to taste
1 pineapple, peeled and sliced	1 ½ tbsp tahini
¼ cup non-dairy milk	Arugula for serving
2 tbsp fresh basil, chopped	Chopped cashews
1 large scallion, chopped	

Directions and Total Time: 15 minutes

Place jicama in a bowl. In a food processor, put the pineapple and enough milk. Blitz until puréed. Add in basil, scallions, tahini, and salt. Pour over the jicama and cover. Transfer to the fridge and marinate for 1 hour. Place a bed of arugula on a plate and top with the salad. Serve garnished with cashews.

Lebanese-Style Salad

Ingredients for 4 servings

1 tbsp olive oil	1 tomato, sliced
1 cup cooked bulgur	1 cup fresh parsley, chopped
Zest and juice of 1 lemon	¼ cup fresh mint, chopped
1 garlic clove, pressed	2 scallions, chopped
Sea salt to taste	4 tbsp sunflower seeds
½ cucumber, sliced	

Directions and Total Time: 25 minutes

In a bowl, mix the lemon juice, lemon zest, garlic, salt, and olive oil. Stir in cucumber, tomato, parsley, mint, and scallions. Toss to coat. Fluff the bulgur and stir it into the cucumber mix. Top with sunflower seeds and serve.

Savory Green Salad

Ingredients for 4 servings

¼ cup extra-virgin olive oil	6 radishes, sliced
1 large grapefruit	Juice of 1 lemon
2 cups coleslaw mix	2 tsp date syrup
2 cups green leaf lettuce, torn	1 tsp white wine vinegar
2 cups baby spinach	Sea salt and black pepper
1 bunch watercress	

Directions and Total Time: 10 minutes

Slice the grapefruit by cutting the ends, peeling all the white pith, and making an incise in the membrane to take out each segment. Transfer to a bowl. Stir in coleslaw, lettuce, spinach, watercress, and radishes. In a bowl, mix the lemon juice, date syrup, vinegar, salt, and pepper. Gently beat the olive oil until emulsified. Pour over the salad and toss to coat.

Quinoa & Tomato Salad with Sweet Onions

Ingredients for 4 servings

2 tbsp extra-virgin olive oil	Salt and black pepper to taste
1 ½ cups dry quinoa, drained	2 cups sliced sweet onions
2 ¼ cups water	2 tomatoes, sliced
1/3 cup white wine vinegar	4 cups shredded lettuce
1 tbsp chopped fresh dill	

Directions and Total Time: 25 minutes

Place the quinoa in a pot with salted water. Bring to a boil. Lower the heat and simmer covered for 15 minutes. Turn the heat off and let sit for 5 minutes. Using a fork, fluff the quinoa and set aside. In a small bowl, whisk the vinegar, olive oil, dill, salt, and pepper; set aside. In a serving plate, combine onions, tomatoes, quinoa, and lettuce. Pour in the dressing and toss to coat. Serve.

Green Bulgur Salad

Ingredients for 4 servings

1 avocado, peeled and pitted	8 large kale leaves, chopped
1 tbsp fresh lemon juice	½ cup chopped green beans
1 tbsp fresh dill	1 cup cherry tomatoes, halved
1 small garlic clove, pressed	1 bell pepper, chopped
1 scallion, chopped	2 scallions, chopped
Sea salt to taste	2 cups cooked bulgur

Directions and Total Time: 30 minutes

In a food processor, place the avocado, lemon juice, dill, garlic, scallion, salt, and ¼ cup water. Blend until smooth. Set aside the dressing. Put kale, green beans, cherry tomatoes, bell pepper, scallions, and bulgur in a serving bowl. Add in the dressing and toss to coat. Serve.

Italian Chickpea & Pasta Salad

Ingredients for 4 servings

½ cup olive oil	½ cup frozen peas, thawed
8 oz whole-wheat pasta	1 tbsp capers
1 (15.5-oz) can chickpeas	3 tsp dried chives
½ cup pitted black olives	¼ cup white wine vinegar
10 minced sun-dried tomatoes	½ tsp dried basil
1(6-oz) jar dill pickles, sliced	1 garlic clove, minced
2 roasted red peppers, diced	Salt and black pepper to taste

Directions and Total Time: 15 minutes

Cook the pasta in salted water for 8-10 minutes until al dente. Drain and remove to a bowl. Stir in chickpeas, olives, tomatoes, dill pickles, roasted peppers, peas, capers, and chives. In another bowl, whisk oil, vinegar, basil, garlic, sugar, salt, and pepper. Pour over the pasta and toss to coat. Serve and enjoy!

Radish Slaw with Tomatoes

Ingredients for 4 servings

¼ cup olive oil	2 ½ tbsp white wine vinegar
2 tomatoes, sliced	½ tsp chopped chervil
6 small red radishes, sliced	Salt and black pepper to taste

Directions and Total Time: 15 minutes

Mix tomatoes and radishes in a bowl. Set aside. In another bowl, whisk the vinegar, olive oil, chervil, salt, and pepper until mixed. Pour over the salad and toss to coat.

Celery & Chickpea Salad

Ingredients for 4 servings

1 (15.5-oz) can chickpeas	½ cup celery leaves, chopped
1 head fennel bulb, sliced	¼ cup vegan mayonnaise
½ cup sliced red onion	Salt and black pepper to taste

Directions and Total Time: 5 minutes

In a bowl, mash the chickpeas until chunky. Stir in fennel bulb, onion, celery, vegan mayonnaise, salt, and pepper.

Pear & Cucumber Rice Salad

Ingredients for 4 servings

¼ cup olive oil	1 pear, cored and diced
1 cup brown rice	½ cucumber, diced
¼ cup orange juice	¼ cup raisins

Directions and Total Time: 15 minutes

Place the rice in a pot with 2 cups of salted water. Bring to a boil, then lower the heat and simmer for 15 minutes. In a bowl, whisk together the olive oil, orange juice, salt, and pepper. Stir in the pear, cucumber, raisins, and cooked rice. Serve and enjoy!

Sesame Cabbage Salad

Ingredients for 6 servings

2 tbsp toasted sesame oil
4 cups shredded red cabbage
2 cups sliced napa cabbage
1 cup red radishes, sliced
¼ cup fresh orange juice

2 tbsp Chinese black vinegar
1 tbsp soy sauce
1 tsp grated fresh ginger
1 tbsp black sesame seeds

Directions and Total Time: 15 minutes

Mix the red cabbage, napa cabbage, and radishes in a bowl. In another bowl, whisk the orange juice, vinegar, soy sauce, sesame oil, and ginger. Pour over the slaw and toss to coat. Marinate covered in the fridge for 2 hours. Serve topped with sesame seeds.

Tomato & Cucumber Salad with Lentils

Ingredients for 4 servings

¾ cup olive oil
¼ cup white wine vinegar
2 tsp Dijon mustard
1 garlic clove
1 tbsp minced green onions
½ head romaine lettuce, torn
½ head iceberg lettuce, torn
1 (15.5-oz) can lentils, drained

2 ripe tomatoes, chopped
1 peeled cucumber, chopped
1 carrot, chopped
8 halved pitted kalamata olives
3 small red radishes, chopped
2 tbsp chopped fresh parsley
1 ripe avocado, chopped

Directions and Total Time: 15 minutes

Put the oil, vinegar, mustard, garlic, green onions, salt, and pepper in a food processor. Pulse until blended. Set aside. In a bowl, place the lettuces, lentils, tomatoes, cucumber, carrot, olives, radishes, parsley, and avocado. Pour enough dressing over the salad and toss to coat.

Philippino Salad

Ingredients for 4 servings

2 cups snow peas, sliced and blanched
¼ cup olive oil
½ tsp minced garlic
½ tsp grated fresh ginger
¼ tsp crushed red pepper
3 tbsp rice vinegar
1 tbsp soy sauce

3 papaya, chopped
1 large carrot, shredded
1 cucumber, peeled and sliced
3 cups torn romaine lettuce
½ cup chopped roasted almonds
Salt to taste

Directions and Total Time: 15 minutes

Combine the garlic, ginger, olive oil, red pepper, vinegar, 3 tbsp of water, salt, and soy sauce in a bowl. Set aside. In another bowl, add papaya, snow peas, cucumber slices, and carrot. Drizzle with the dressing and toss to coat. Place a bed of lettuce on a plate and top with the salad. Serve topped with almonds.

Potato Salad with Artichokes & Corn

Ingredients for 4 servings

1 (10-oz) package frozen artichoke hearts, cooked
1/3 cup olive oil
1 ½ lb potatoes, chopped
2 cups halved cherry tomatoes
½ cup sweet corn
3 green onions, minced

1 tbsp minced fresh parsley
2 tbsp fresh lemon juice
1 garlic clove, minced
Salt and black pepper to taste

Directions and Total Time: 30 minutes + cooling time

Place the potatoes in a pot with salted water and boil for 15 minutes. Drain and remove to a bowl. Cut the artichokes by quarts and mix into the potato bowl. Stir in tomatoes, corn, green onions, and parsley. Set aside. Whisk the oil, lemon juice, garlic, salt, and pepper in a bowl. Pour over the potatoes and toss to coat. Let sit for 20 minutes. Serve and enjoy!

Watercress & Eggplant Salad

Ingredients for 2 servings

1 lemon, half zested and juiced, half cut into wedges
1 tsp olive oil
1 eggplant, chopped
½ tsp ground cumin
½ tsp ground ginger
¼ tsp turmeric
¼ tsp ground nutmeg

Sea salt to taste
2 tbsp capers
1 tbsp chopped green olives
1 garlic clove, pressed
2 tbsp fresh mint, chopped
2 cups watercress, chopped

Directions and Total Time: 45 minutes

In a skillet over medium heat, warm the oil. Place the eggplant and cook for 5 minutes. Add in cumin, ginger, turmeric, nutmeg, and salt. Cook for another 10 minutes. Stir in lemon zest, lemon juice, capers, olives, garlic, and mint. Cook for 1-2 minutes more. Place some watercress on each plate and top with the eggplant mixture. Serve.

Jalapeño Veggie Relish

Ingredients for 6 servings

¼ cup sliced pimiento-stuffed green olives
1/3 cup olive oil
1 carrot, sliced
1 red bell pepper, sliced
1 cup cauliflower florets
2 celery stalks, chopped

½ cup chopped red onion
1 garlic clove, minced
1 jalapeño pepper, chopped
3 tbsp white wine vinegar

Directions and Total Time: 15 minutes

Combine the carrot, bell pepper, cauliflower, celery, and onion in a bowl. Add in salt and cold water. Cover and transfer to the fridge for 4-6 hours. Strain and wash the veggies. Remove to a bowl and mix in olives. Set aside. In another bowl, mix the garlic, jalapeño pepper, vinegar, and oil. Pour over the veggies and toss to coat. Let chill in the fridge and serve.

Greek Olive & Potato Salad

Ingredients for 4 servings

¼ cup olive oil
4 potatoes, chopped
Salt and black pepper to taste
2 tbsp apple cider vinegar
2 tbsp lemon juice

1 tsp dried dill
½ cucumber, chopped
¼ red onion, diced
6 chopped kalamata olives

Directions and Total Time: 30 minutes

In a pot with salted water, place the potatoes. Bring to a boil and cook for 20 minutes. Drain and let cool. Mix the olive oil, vinegar, lemon juice, and dill in a bowl. Add in cucumber, red onion, and olives. Toss to coat. Stir in the potatoes. Season with salt and pepper. Serve.

Balsamic Beet-Cucumber Salad

Ingredients for 2 servings

1 tsp olive oil
3 beets, peeled and sliced
1 cucumber, sliced

2 cups mixed greens
4 tbsp balsamic dressing
2 tbsp chopped almonds

Directions and Total Time: 40 minutes

Preheat oven to 390°F. In a bowl, stir the beets, oil, and salt. Toss to coat. Transfer to a baking dish and roast for 20 minutes, until golden brown. Once the beets are ready, divide between 2 plates and place a cucumber slice on each beet. Top with mixed greens. Pour over the dressing and garnish with almonds to serve.

Extravagant Quinoa Salad

Ingredients for 6 servings

1 cup canned mandarin oranges in juice, drained
1 cup diced yellow summer squash
3 tbsp olive oil
Juice of 1 ½ lemons
1 tsp garlic powder
½ tsp dried oregano
1 bunch baby spinach

2 cups cooked tricolor quinoa
1 red bell pepper, diced
½ red onion, sliced
½ cup dried cranberries
½ cup slivered almonds

Directions and Total Time: 15 minutes

Mix the oil, lemon juice, garlic powder, and oregano in a bowl. In another bowl, place the spinach and pour over the dressing, toss to coat. Stir in quinoa, oranges, squash, bell pepper, and red onion. Share into bowls and garnish with cranberries and almonds to serve.

Cabbage & Radish Ginger Slaw

Ingredients for 4 servings

2 tbsp chopped roasted hazelnuts
8 oz napa cabbage, cut crosswise into strips
2 tsp toasted sesame oil
1 cup grated carrots
1 cup sliced radishes
2 green onions, minced
2 tbsp chopped fresh parsley

2 tbsp rice vinegar
1 tbsp soy sauce
1 tsp grated fresh ginger
½ tsp dry mustard
Salt and black pepper to taste

Directions and Total Time: 15 minutes

Place the napa cabbage, carrot, radishes, green onions, and parsley in a bowl, stir to combine. In another bowl, mix vinegar, sesame oil, soy sauce, ginger, mustard, salt, and pepper. Pour over the slaw and toss to coat. Marinate covered in the fridge for 2 hours. Serve topped with hazelnuts.

Cabbage & Beet Slaw with Apples

Ingredients for 4 servings

2 tbsp olive oil
Juice of 1 lemon
½ beet, shredded

Sea salt to taste
2 apples, peeled and julienned
4 cups shredded red cabbage

Directions and Total Time: 10 minutes

Mix the olive oil, lemon juice, beet, and salt in a bowl. In another bowl, combine the apples and cabbage. Pour over the vinaigrette and toss to coat. Serve right away.

Simple Avocado Salad

Ingredients for 4 servings

3 tbsp sesame oil
2 medium avocados, sliced
2 tbsp soy sauce

1 tbsp mirin
2 tsp rice vinegar
2 tbsp toasted sesame seeds

Directions and Total Time: 15 minutes

Place the avocado in a bowl. Set aside. In another bowl, mix the oil, soy sauce, mirin, and vinegar. Pour over the avocado and toss to coat. Let sit for 10 minutes. Serve in bowls topped with sesame seeds.

Holiday Potato Salad

Ingredients for 4 servings

½ cup olive oil
1 ½ lb potatoes, chopped
4 portobello mushrooms, sliced
2 green onions, chopped

1 tbsp whole-wheat flour
2 tbsp pure date sugar
1/3 cup white wine vinegar
Salt and black pepper to taste

Directions and Total Time: 15 minutes

Place the potatoes in a pot with boiling salted water and cook for 20 minutes. Drain and remove to a bowl. Heat oil in a skillet over medium heat. Place the mushrooms and sauté for 5 minutes. Add the mushrooms to the potatoes. To the skillet, add in green onions and cook for 1 minute. Mix in flour, sugar, vinegar, ¼ cup of water, salt, and pepper. Bring to a boil and cook until creamy. Pour the resulting sauce over the potatoes and mushrooms and toss to coat. Serve immediately.

Cabbage Coleslaw with Radicchio

Ingredients for 2 servings

½ head white cabbage, shredded
¼ head radicchio, shredded
1 large carrot, shredded
¾ cup vegan mayonnaise
¼ cup soy milk

1 tbsp cider vinegar
½ tsp dry mustard
¼ tsp celery seeds
Salt and black pepper to taste

Directions and Total Time: 10 minutes

Combine cabbage, radicchio, and carrot in a bowl. In another bowl, whisk mayonnaise, soy milk, mustard, vinegar, celery seeds, salt, and pepper. Pour over the slaw and toss to coat. Serve immediately.

Veggie & Quinoa Salad

Ingredients for 4 servings

¼ cup olive oil
2 cups cooked quinoa
½ red onion, diced
1 red bell pepper, diced
1 orange bell pepper, diced
1 carrot, diced

2 tbsp rice vinegar
1 tbsp soy sauce
1 garlic clove, minced
1 tbsp grated fresh ginger
Salt and black pepper to taste

Directions and Total Time: 15 minutes

Combine the quinoa, onion, bell peppers, and carrots in a bowl. In another bowl, mix the olive oil, rice vinegar, soy sauce, garlic, ginger, salt, and pepper. Pour over the quinoa and toss to coat. Serve and enjoy!

Chickpea & Corn Salad

Ingredients for 4 servings

¼ cup olive oil
1 cup corn kernels
1 (15.5-oz) can chickpeas
1 celery stalk, sliced
2 green onions, minced
2 tbsp chopped fresh cilantro
2 tbsp white wine vinegar
½ tsp ground cumin
Salt and black pepper to taste

Directions and Total Time: 10 minutes

Combine the corn, chickpeas, celery, green onions, and cilantro in a bowl. Set aside. In another bowl, mix the oil, vinegar, cumin, salt, and pepper. Pour over the salad and toss to coat. Serve immediately.

Broccoli Rice Salad with Mango & Almonds

Ingredients for 4 servings

3 cups broccoli florets, blanched
1/3 cup roasted almonds, chopped
3 tbsp grapeseed oil
½ cup brown rice, rinsed
1 mango, chopped
1 small red bell pepper, diced
1 jalapeño, seeded and minced
1 tsp grated fresh ginger
2 tbsp fresh lemon juice

Directions and Total Time: 25 minutes

Place the rice in a bowl with salted water and cook for 18-20 minutes. Remove to a bowl. Stir in broccoli, mango, bell pepper, and chili. In another bowl, mix the ginger, lemon juice, and oil. Pour over the rice and toss to combine. Top with almonds to serve.

Faro & Chickpea Entrée

Ingredients for 4 servings

½ cup dried apricots, quartered
2 tbsp olive oil
½ cup chopped green onions
2 tsp minced fresh ginger
1 cup faro
¼ cup golden raisins
¼ tsp ground cumin
¼ tsp ground cayenne
1 tsp turmeric
1/3 cup pomegranate molasses
1 (15.5-oz) can chickpeas
¼ cup minced fresh cilantro

Directions and Total Time: 30 minutes

Heat oil in a pot over medium heat and sauté green onions, ginger, apricots, raisins, cumin, cayenne, turmeric, salt, and pepper for 2 minutes. Add in pomegranate molasses, faro, and 2 cups water. Bring to a boil, lower the heat, and simmer for 10 minutes. Stir in chickpeas and cilantro and cook for 10 minutes. Serve warm.

Pecan-Spinach Spinach Salad with Blackberries

Ingredients for 4 servings

¾ cup olive oil
10 oz baby spinach
1 cup raisins
1 cup fresh blackberries
¼ red onion, thinly sliced
½ cup chopped pecans
¼ cup balsamic vinegar
Salt and black pepper to taste

Directions and Total Time: 10 minutes

Combine the spinach, raisins, blackberries, red onion, and pecans in a bowl. In another bowl, mix vinegar, olive oil, salt, and pepper. Pour over the salad and toss to coat.

Spinach & Apple Salad with Walnuts

Ingredients for 4 servings

¼ cup tahini
2 tbsp Dijon mustard
3 tbsp maple syrup
1 tbsp lemon juice
½ cup finely chopped walnuts
2 tsp soy sauce
1 lb baby spinach
1 green apple, cored and sliced

Directions and Total Time: 20 minutes

Preheat oven to 360°F. Line with parchment paper a baking sheet. In a bowl, mix the tahini, mustard, 2 tbsp maple syrup, lemon juice, and salt. Set aside the dressing. In another bowl, combine the walnuts, soy sauce, and the remaining maple syrup. Spread evenly on the baking sheet and bake for 5 minutes, shaking once until crunchy. Allow cooling for 3 minutes. Combine the spinach and apples in a bowl. Pour over the dressing and toss to coat. Serve garnished with the walnut crunch.

Favorite Green Salad

Ingredients for 4 servings

1 head Iceberg lettuce
8 asparagus spears, chopped
2 seedless cucumbers, sliced
1 zucchini, cut into ribbons
1 carrot, cut into ribbons
1 avocado, sliced
½ cup vegan green dressing
2 scallions, thinly sliced

Directions and Total Time: 10 minutes

Share the lettuce into 4 bowls and add in some asparagus, cucumber, zucchini, carrot, and avocado. Sprinkle each bowl with 2 tbsp of dressing. Serve topped with scallions.

German Potato Salad

Ingredients for 4 servings

1 ½ lb small potatoes, unpeeled
2 celery stalks, sliced
¼ cup sweet pickle relish
3 tbsp minced green onions
¾ cup vegan mayonnaise
1 tbsp soy milk
1 tbsp white wine vinegar
1 tsp Dijon mustard
10 pitted black olives, sliced

Directions and Total Time: 25 minutes

Place the potatoes in a pot with boiling salted water and cook for 20 minutes. Drain and let cool. Once the potatoes are cooled, peel them and cut into small cubes. Remove to a bowl. Stir in celery, pickle relish, and green onions. In another bowl, mix the mayonnaise, soy milk, vinegar, mustard, salt, and pepper. Pour over the salad and toss to coat. Serve and enjoy!

Mexican Salad

Ingredients for 4 servings

2 heads romaine lettuce, torn
16 cherry tomatoes, halved
1 avocado, diced
1 cup corn kernels
1 cucumber, peeled and diced
4 oz soy chorizo
4 scallions, thinly sliced
Vegan ranch dressing

Directions and Total Time: 15 minutes

Place a bed of romaine lettuce in a serving bowl. Layer tomatoes, avocado, corn, cucumber, and soy chorizo. Serve topped with scallions and vegan ranch dressing.

Vegan-Style Caesar Salad

Ingredients for 4 servings

3 tbsp olive oil	1 tsp garlic powder
½ cup cashews	Salt and black pepper to taste
½ cup water	2 heads romaine lettuce, torn
Juice of ½ lime	2 tsp capers
1 tbsp white miso paste	1 cup cherry tomatoes, halved
1 tsp soy sauce	2 tbsp grated vegan Parmesan
1 tsp Dijon mustard	Whole-what bread croutons

Directions and Total Time: 10 minutes

In a blender, put cashews, water, olive oil, lime juice, miso paste, soy sauce, mustard, garlic powder, salt, and pepper. Blend until smooth. Mix the lettuce with half of the dressing in a bowl. Divide in individual bowls and add in capers, tomatoes, and plant-based Parmesan cheese. Serve topped with croutons.

Moroccan Salad with Pine Nuts

Ingredients for 4 servings

¼ cup olive oil	¼ cup capers
1 cup quinoa, rinsed	2 tbsp toasted pine nuts
1 (15.5-oz) can chickpeas	1 medium shallot, sliced
1 cup cherry tomatoes, halved	1 garlic clove, chopped
2 green onions, minced	1 tsp Dijon mustard
½ peeled cucumber, chopped	2 tbsp white wine vinegar

Directions and Total Time: 25 minutes

Boil salted water in a pot over medium heat. Add in quinoa, lower the heat and simmer for 15 minutes. Remove to a bowl. Stir in chickpeas, tomatoes, green onions, cucumber, capers, and pine nuts. Set aside. In a food processor, put the shallot, garlic, mustard, vinegar, oil, salt, and pepper. Pulse until blend. Pour over the salad and toss to coat. Serve immediately.

Black-Eyed Pea Salad with Baked Potatoes

Ingredients for 4 servings

¼ cup olive oil	1 (15.5-oz) can black-eyed peas
1 ½ lb potatoes, chopped	8 chopped sun-dried tomatoes
1 red onion, sliced	¼ cup green olives, halved
Salt and black pepper to taste	¼ cup chopped fresh parsley
3 tbsp white wine vinegar	

Directions and Total Time: 25 minutes

Preheat oven to 420°F. In a bowl, mix the potatoes, onion, and 1 tbsp of oil. Sprinkle with salt and pepper. Spread on a baking sheet and roast for 20 minutes. Remove to a bowl and let cool. In another bowl, combine the remaining oil, vinegar, salt, and pepper. Stir the peas, tomatoes, olives, and parsley into the potato bowl. Pour over the dressing and toss to coat. Serve.

Cherry & Carrot Salad

Ingredients for 4 servings

3 tbsp avocado oil	2 ½ cups toasted pecans
1 lb carrots, shredded	3 tbsp fresh lemon juice
1 cup sweetened dried cherries	Black pepper to taste

Directions and Total Time: 15 minutes

Combine the carrots, cherries, and pecans in a bowl. In another bowl, mix the lemon juice, avocado oil, and pepper. Pour over the salad and toss to coat. Serve.

Quesadillas Norteñas

Ingredients for 4 servings

1 cup grated plant-based cheddar cheese

1 tsp olive oil	1 (7 oz) can black beans
1 small onion, chopped	1 (7 oz) can sweet corn kernels
½ red bell pepper, chopped	4 whole-wheat tortillas
1 (7 oz) can chopped tomatoes	

Directions and Total Time: 35 minutes

Heat olive oil in a skillet and sauté onion and bell pepper for 3 minutes. Mix in tomatoes, black beans, sweet corn, and cook until the tomatoes soften, 10 minutes. Season with salt and black pepper.

Heat another medium skillet over medium heat and lay in one tortilla. Spread a quarter of the tomato mixture on top, scatter a quarter of the plant cheese on the sauce, and cover with another tortilla. Cook until the cheese melts. Flip and cook further for 2 minutes. Transfer to a plate and make one more piece using the remaining ingredients. Cut each tortilla set into quarters and serve.

Arugula Salad with Apples & Walnuts

Ingredients for 4 servings

2 tbsp olive oil	1 tbsp finely minced shallot
¼ cup chopped walnuts	2 tbsp champagne vinegar
10 oz arugula	Salt and black pepper to taste
1 apple, thinly sliced	¼ tsp English mustard

Directions and Total Time: 20 minutes

Preheat oven to 360°F. On a baking sheet, spread the walnuts and toast for 6 minutes. Let cool. In a bowl, combine the walnuts, arugula, and apple. In another bowl, mix the shallot, vinegar, olive oil, salt, pepper, and mustard. Pour over the salad and toss to coat. Serve.

Parsnip & Bean Salad with Pomegranate

Ingredients for 3 servings

2 tsp olive oil	3 cups chopped spinach
4 parsnips, sliced	1/3 cup pomegranate seeds
½ tsp ground cinnamon	1/3 cup sunflower seeds
Salt to taste	¼ cup raspberry vinaigrette
1 (15-oz) can cannellini beans	

Directions and Total Time: 40 minutes

Preheat oven to 390°F. In a bowl, combine the parsnips, olive oil, cinnamon, and salt. Spread on a baking tray and roast for 15 minutes. Flip the parsnips and add the beans. Roast for another 15 minutes. Allow cooling. Divide the spinach among plates and place the pomegranate seeds, sunflower seeds, and roasted parsnips and beans. Sprinkle with raspberry vinaigrette and serve.

SOUPS & STEWS

Bean & Carrot Soup

Ingredients for 4 servings

1 tsp olive oil	4 carrots, peeled and chopped
1 cup chopped onion	1 cup cooked cannellini beans
2 garlic cloves, minced	2 cups vegetable broth
1 celery stalk, chopped	Salt and black pepper to taste
1 tbsp minced fresh ginger	2 tbsp parsley, chopped

Directions and Total Time: 35 minutes

Saute olive oil, onion, garlic, celery and ginger in a large pot for 2-3 minutes. Add carrots and cook for about 3 minutes. Stir in beans, broth, 2 cups water, salt, and pepper. Reduce the heat and simmer for 20 minutes. Use an immersion blender or a regular blender to puree the soup. Ladle into bowls and garnish with parsley. Serve.

Creamy Coconut Green Soup

Ingredients for 4 servings

1 tsp coconut oil	1 cup baby spinach
2 green onions, diced	1 tbsp fresh mint, chopped
2 cups frozen peas	Salt and black pepper to taste
4 cups vegetable stock	¾ cup coconut milk
1 cup watercress, chopped	2 tbsp cilantro, chopped

Directions and Total Time: 20 minutes

Add coconut oil to a large pot over medium heat. When the oil is melted, add green onions and saute for 5 minutes. Stir in peas and stock. When the stock starts to boil, reduce the heat and stir in watercress, baby spinach, mint, salt, and pepper. Simmer covered for 5 minutes. Stir in coconut milk. Use an immersion blender or a regular blender to puree the soup. Ladle into bowls and garnish with cilantro. Serve warm and enjoy.

Split Pea & Tomato Soup

Ingredients for 6 servings

¼ cup white wine	4 cups vegetable stock
1 onion, chopped	1 large carrot, chopped
2 garlic cloves, minced	1 tbsp tamari
1 cup split peas	Salt and black pepper to taste
2 bay leaves	8 sun-dried tomatoes, diced
1 tbsp dried thyme	8 grape tomatoes, chopped
1 tbsp dried oregano	2 tbsp chopped chives

Directions and Total Time: 80 minutes

Saute wine, onion, and garlic in a large pot over medium heat. Stir occasionally for 5 minutes. Next, mix in peas, bay leaves, thyme, and oregano. Add stock and bring the soup to a boil. Reduce the heat and cover the pot. Cook for 40-50 minutes. Next, stir in the carrot and cook for another 15 minutes. When the carrot and the peas have softened, remove the bay leaves and transfer the soup to the blender jar. Puree the soup in batches if needed. Return the soup to the pot and mix in tamari, salt, pepper, and sun-dried tomatoes. Ladle the soup into bowls and garnish with grape tomatoes and chives. Serve warm.

Garden Green Soup

Ingredients for 4 servings

4 tbsp plant butter	3 tbsp minced mint leaves
1 cup fresh spinach, chopped	Salt and black pepper to taste
1 cup fresh kale, chopped	Juice from 1 lime
1 large avocado	1 cup collard greens, chopped
3 ½ cups coconut cream	2 garlic cloves, minced
4 cups vegetable broth	1 tsp green cardamom powder

Directions and Total Time: 20 minutes

Melt 2 tbsp of plant butter in a saucepan over medium heat and sauté spinach and kale for 5 minutes. Turn the heat off. Add the avocado, coconut cream, broth, salt, and pepper. Puree the ingredients with an immersion blender until smooth. Pour in the lime juice and set aside.

Melt the remaining plant butter in a pan and add the collard greens, garlic, and cardamom; sauté until the garlic is fragrant and has achieved a golden brown color, about 4 minutes. Fetch the soup into serving bowls and garnish with fried collards and mint. Serve warm.

Twisted Goulash Soup

Ingredients for 4 servings

½ tbsp crushed cardamom seeds

3 tbsp plant butter	¼ tsp red chili flakes
1 ½ cups tofu, crumbled	1 tbsp dried basil
1 white onion	Salt and black pepper to taste
2 garlic cloves	1 ½ cups diced tomatoes
8 oz diced butternut squash	4 cups vegetable broth
1 red bell pepper	1 ½ tsp red wine vinegar
1 tbsp paprika powder	2 tbsp chopped cilantro

Directions and Total Time: 25 minutes

Melt plant butter in a pot over medium heat and sauté onion and garlic for 3 minutes. Stir in tofu and cook for 3 minutes; add the butternut squash, bell pepper, paprika, red chili flakes, basil, cardamom seeds, salt, and pepper. Cook for 2 minutes. Pour in tomatoes and vegetable broth. Bring to a boil, reduce the heat and simmer for 10 minutes. Mix in red wine vinegar. Garnish with cilantro.

Creamy Broccoli Soup

Ingredients for 4 servings

3 oz plant butter	Salt and black pepper to taste
1 fennel bulb, chopped	1 garlic clove
10 oz broccoli, cut into florets	1 cup coconut cream cheese
3 cups vegetable stock	½ cup chopped fresh oregano

Directions and Total Time: 25 minutes

Put the fennel and broccoli into a pot, and cover with the vegetable stock. Bring the ingredients to a boil over medium heat until the vegetables are soft, about 10 minutes. Season the liquid with salt and black pepper, and drop in the garlic. Simmer the soup for 5 to 7 minutes and turn the heat off. Pour the coconut cream cheese, plant butter, and oregano into the soup; puree the ingredients with an immersion blender until completely smooth. Adjust the taste with salt and pepper. Serve.

Winter Soup

Ingredients for 6 servings

2 tbsp olive oil
1 cup chopped onion
3 garlic cloves, minced
1 tbsp thyme, fresh or dried
1 tsp hot paprika
5 cups vegetable broth
2 cups peeled beets, chopped
2 peeled sweet potatoes, cubed
1 cup peeled parsnips, diced
Salt and black pepper to taste
2 tbsp fresh mint, chopped
½ avocado, chopped
2 tbsp pumpkin seeds

Directions and Total Time: 50 minutes

Saute olive oil, onion, and garlic in a large pot. When the onions have softened after about 5 minutes, stir in thyme, paprika, beets, sweet potato, parsnips, broth, black pepper, and salt. Cover and simmer for at least 30 minutes or until the vegetables have softened. Next, add avocado. Use an immersion blender or a regular blender to puree the soup. Ladle into bowls and garnish with mint and pumpkin seeds. Serve warm and enjoy.

Miso Buckwheat & Bean Soup

Ingredients for 4 servings

½ cup buckwheat
4 cups vegetable broth
4 tbsp miso
1 cup cranberry beans, cooked
2 tbsp basil, finely chopped
2 scallions, thinly sliced

Directions and Total Time: 20 minutes

In a large pot of boiling water, add buckwheat and cook for 5 minutes while stirring occasionally. In a separate pot, heat the broth until just boiling. Remove from heat and stir in miso until dissolved. Drain the buckwheat and rinse under hot water. Transfer to the pot with the miso broth along with cranberry beans, basil, and scallions.

Holiday Jack Soup

Ingredients for 4 servings

1 lb butternut squash, peeled, seeded, and chopped
2 tbsp olive oil
Salt and black pepper to taste
1 onion, diced
4 cups vegetable stock
2 tsp ground sage
1 cup oat milk
1 tbsp plant-based butter
¼ cup toasted walnuts

Directions and Total Time: 45 minutes

Saute butternut squash in oil in a large saucepan over medium heat. Add salt and cook for about 10 minutes or until softened. Stir in onion and saute for another 5 minutes. Pour in stock and bring to a boil. Reduce the heat and simmer for 15 to 20 minutes. The squash will be fork-tender when ready. Stir in sage, butter, and oat milk. Use an immersion blender or a regular blender to puree the soup. Ladle into bowls and garnish with toasted walnuts and pepper. Serve warm and enjoy.

Peppery Pumpkin Soup

Ingredients for 6 servings

1 lb pumpkin
3 tbsp olive oil
Salt to taste
2 red bell peppers
1 onion
1 head garlic
2 cups vegetable broth
Zest and juice of 1 lime
1 tbsp tahini
½ tsp cayenne pepper
½ tsp ground coriander
½ tsp ground cumin
2 tbsp toasted pumpkin seeds

Directions and Total Time: 60 minutes

Preheat oven to 350°F. Cut the pumpkin in half lengthwise and scoop out the seeds. Pierce the flesh with a fork, then rub the flesh and skin with some oil. Season with salt. Place the pumpkin skin-side down in a large baking dish and cook for 20 minutes. Cut the peppers in half lengthwise and scoop out the seeds. Cut the onion in half and rub with oil. Cut the top of the garlic head and rub exposed areas with the remaining oil. Transfer to the baking dish after the pumpkin has baked for 20 minutes. Bake everything for another 20 minutes or until the squash and vegetables are tender.

When the pumpkin is cool enough to handle, scoop out the flesh and transfer to a blender jar. Give the peppers and onion a rough chop before adding to the blender. Squeeze the roasted garlic into the blender. Add broth, lime zest, lime juice, and tahini. Cover and puree until smooth. Add salt, cayenne, coriander, and cumin, then pulse until just combined. Pour into bowls and garnish with pumpkin seeds. Serve warm and enjoy.

Special Moong Dal Soup

Ingredients for 4 servings

1 cup red split moong dal beans
2 cups peeled and cubed sweet potatoes
1 tsp curry powder
1 tbsp coriander seeds
2 tbsp coconut oil
1 red onion, diced
1 tbsp minced fresh ginger
1 green chili, minced
1 sliced zucchini
Salt and black pepper to taste
4 cups vegetable stock
1 tsp toasted sesame oil
10 oz spinach, chopped
1 tbsp toasted sesame seeds

Directions and Total Time: 35 minutes

Bring beans, 2 cups water, and 1 teaspoon of curry powder to a boil in a large pot. Lower the heat and cover. Simmer for 10 minutes to soften the beans. Heat oil in another large pot over medium heat. Saute onion, ginger, and green chili for 5 minutes. When soft, add sweet potato and cook for another 10 minutes. Stir in zucchini and cook for another 5 minutes. Season with curry powder, pepper, and salt. Pour in stock and bring to a boil. Reduce the heat and cover. Simmer for 20 to 30 minutes. When the sweet potato is tender, add the beans to the soup along with salt, sesame oil, coriander seeds, and spinach. Stir and simmer to wilt the spinach. Ladle into bowls and garnish with toasted sesame seeds. Serve.

Tomato & Spinach Soup with Quinoa

Ingredients for 6 servings

3 tbsp olive oil
1 onion, chopped
1 celery stalk, chopped
2 garlic cloves, minced
1 (15-oz) can diced tomatoes
3 cups vegetable broth
Salt and black pepper to taste
1 lb quinoa
1 (5-oz) package baby spinach

Directions and Total Time: 30 minutes

In a large stockpot, add oil over medium heat. Stir in onion and sauté for 3 minutes. When the onions are soft, stir in garlic and celery and cook for another minute. Pour in tomatoes with juice, broth, and 4 cups of water. Season with salt and pepper and bring to a boil. Cover and reduce the heat to simmer. Remove the lid and stir in quinoa. Cook for 9 minutes. Remove the pot from the heat and stir in spinach until wilted. Serve warm.

Zuppa di Pomodoro e Ceci

Ingredients for 2 servings

2 cups chopped cavolo nero (curly kale)	
2 tsp olive oil	½ tsp dried oregano
½ chopped onion	½ tsp dried sage
2 garlic cloves, minced	1 tbsp balsamic vinegar
1 cup mushrooms, chopped	1 (19-oz) can diced tomatoes
Salt to taste	1 (14-oz) can chickpeas
1 tbsp dried basil	2 cups water

Directions and Total Time: 30 minutes

Heat oil in a large pot and saute onion, garlic, mushrooms, and a pinch of salt. After 7 to 8 minutes or when the vegetables have softened, stir in basil, sage, and oregano. Pour in vinegar and scrape any browned bits from the bottom of the pan. Stir in tomatoes, chickpeas, and water. Next, add the cavolo nero and salt. Cover the pot and simmer the soup for 10 - 15 minutes. The soup is ready when the cavolo nero is soft. Serve warm.

Red Lentil Daal

Ingredients for 4 servings

1 cup red lentils	1 vegetable stock cube
1 red bell pepper, diced	½ lemon, juiced
1 onion, chopped	1 tbsp korma curry paste
3 garlic cloves, minced	Salt to taste
1 tsp minced fresh ginger	¼ tsp cayenne pepper

Directions and Total Time: 30 minutes

Fill a large pot with 5 cups of water. Stir in all of the ingredients and cover. Over medium heat, bring to a boil. Reduce the heat to low and simmer for 15 to 20 minutes. Stir occasionally. The lentils will be soft and the daal will have thickened. Serve warm and enjoy.

Crockpot Mexican Chili

Ingredients for 4 servings

1 cup black beans, soaked	3 tbsp Tajín seasoning
1 onion, chopped	4 cups vegetable broth
1 celery stalk, chopped	1 (28-oz) can diced tomatoes
3 garlic cloves, minced	Salt to taste
1 green bell pepper, diced	2 tbsp chopped cilantro
1 ½ cups frozen corn kernels	2 tbsp vegan sour cream

Directions and Total Time: 8 hours 5 minutes

In a crockpot, add beans, onion, celery, garlic, bell pepper, corn, Tajín, broth, tomatoes, and salt. Stir, cover, and cook on low for 8 hours. When done, ladle into bowls and garnish with cilantro and sour cream. Serve warm.

Vegan Chili Sin Carne

Ingredients for 4 servings

1 onion, diced	2 tbsp canned sweet corn
2 garlic cloves, minced	2 tsp chipotle chili powder
2 tbsp olive oil	½ tsp ground cumin
1 (28-oz) can tomatoes	Salt to taste
1 tbsp tomato paste	2 tbsp fresh cilantro, chopped
1 (14-oz) can kidney beans	

Directions and Total Time: 30 minutes

Heat oil in a large pot, then saute onion and garlic for 5 minutes. Next, stir in tomatoes, tomato paste, beans, chipotle powder, sweet corn, cumin, chipotle chili powder, and salt. Simmer for a minimum of 10 minutes. Ladle into bowls and garnish with cilantro. Serve warm.

Effortless Green Gazpacho

Ingredients for 4 servings

1 peeled avocado, cubed	Salt to taste
2 peeled cucumbers, diced	½ tsp sherry vinegar
2 tbsp chopped cilantro	1 tbsp mint leaves
1 lime, juiced	

Directions and Total Time: 20 minutes

Place the avocado, cucumber, 1 cup of water, cilantro, lime juice, sherry vinegar, and salt in your food processor and puree until smooth. Garnish with mint leaves.

Thai-Spiced Coconut Soup

Ingredients for 4 servings

1 ½ cups vegetable broth	1 (15-oz) can coconut milk
2 garlic cloves, minced	1 lemon, juiced
1 tbsp minced fresh ginger	2 tbsp chopped Thai basil
1 celery stick, chopped	½ tsp Thai green curry paste
1 cup Bella mushrooms, sliced	1 tbsp chopped cilantro

Directions and Total Time: 15 minutes

In a large pot, heat ½ cup broth over medium heat. Sauté garlic and ginger for 1 minute until aromatic. Stir in celery, mushrooms, and the rest of the broth. Let it come to a boil, then reduce to low. Stir in coconut milk, lemon juice, basil, curry paste, and cilantro. Simmer for 5 minutes to heat through. Serve warm and enjoy.

Halloween Soup

Ingredients for 4 servings

2 lb pumpkin, peeled, seeded, and cubed	
1 peeled potato, cubed	½ lemon, juiced
1 onion, chopped	2 tbsp maple syrup
3 garlic cloves, minced	½ tsp ground nutmeg
4 cups vegetable broth	Salt and black pepper to taste

Directions and Total Time: 30 minutes

Add pumpkin, potato, onion, garlic, and broth in a large pot over medium heat. Bring to a boil, reduce the heat and cook for 15 minutes until the pumpkin is fork-tender. Stir in the rest of the ingredients. Transfer the soup to a blender and puree until smooth. Serve.

Butternut Squash Massaman Curry

Ingredients for 4 servings

1 ½ lb butternut squash, peeled, seeded, and cubed
1 tbsp olive oil   Salt to taste
1 onion, chopped   ½ lemon, juiced
1 green bell pepper, chopped   2 tbsp chopped cilantro
1 (15-oz) can coconut milk   4 cups cooked brown rice
4 tsp massaman curry paste

Directions and Total Time: 30 minutes

In a large skillet, heat oil over medium heat. Sauté onion and bell pepper for 5 minutes until softened. Stir in squash, coconut milk, and curry paste. Bring to a boil, then reduce the heat to low. Simmer and cover. Cook for 10 minutes until the squash is fork-tender. Stir in salt and lime juice. Adjust the seasoning and heat with salt and curry paste as needed. Add rice to 4 plates and spoon the curry over the rice. Garnish with cilantro. Serve warm.

Crockpot Zuppa Toscana

Ingredients for 4 servings

1 cup cannellini beans, soaked   3 fresh rosemary sprigs
1 shallot, chopped   2 bay leaves
3 garlic cloves, minced   Salt and black pepper to taste
2 carrots, sliced   ¼ tsp red pepper flakes
2 celery stalks, thinly sliced   1 (14-oz) can diced tomatoes
6 cups vegetable broth   10 oz spinach, chopped

Directions and Total Time: 8 hours 10 minutes

In a crockpot, add beans, shallot, garlic, carrots, celery, broth, rosemary, and bay leaves. Stir, cover, and cook on low for 8 hours. Remove the cover and add salt, black pepper, red pepper flakes, and tomatoes with juice. Stir, cover, and cook on high for 30 minutes. Remove the bay leaves and rosemary sprigs. Stir in spinach, cover, and let sit for 5 minutes. When it is wilted, ladle the soup into bowls. Serve warm and enjoy.

Orzo Zuppa Minestrone

Ingredients for 4 servings

1 tsp olive oil   ¼ cup canned tomato paste
1 white onion, chopped   3 ½ cups canned diced tomatoes
1 carrot, peeled and chopped   1 vegetable bouillon cube
4 garlic cloves, minced   2 cups kidney beans, soaked
1 tsp thyme   1 cup green beans, chopped
1 tbsp Italian seasoning   4 oz whole-grain orzo

Directions and Total Time: 45 minutes

Heat the oil in a pot over medium heat. Stir-fry the onion for 4 minutes or until softened. Stir in the carrot, garlic, and Italian seasoning for another 2-3 minutes. Add the tomato paste and continue to stir for 1 minute. Add the diced tomatoes, thyme, 4 cups of water, bouillon cube, and kidney beans and stir until combined. Pour the green beans. Bring to a gentle boil and continue cooking for 25 minutes, or until the veggies are tender. In the meantime, cook the orzo according to the package directions. Drain, rinse, and set aside. Stir in the cooked orzo. Serve.

French-Style Bean Bisque

Ingredients for 4 servings

1 tbsp olive oil   1 (16-oz) can navy beans
½ cup diced celery   1 tbsp white miso paste
½ white onion, diced   ½ cup chopped parsley
2 garlic cloves, minced   ½ cup nutritional yeast
1 (28-oz) can plum tomatoes   Salt and black pepper to taste
2 cups vegetable broth

Directions and Total Time: 20 minutes

In a saucepan with a lid over medium heat, heat the olive oil. Add the celery, onion, and garlic and sauté until fragrant, 3-4 minutes.

Pour the tomatoes, broth, navy beans, and miso paste and simmer for 10 minutes with the lid on but sligthly open. Remove from the heat and add ¼ cup of parsley.

Transfer the soup to a blender, and pulse until smooth

Add in the nutritional yeast and remaining parsley. Season with salt and pepper and serve.

Minty Green Split Pea Soup

Ingredients for 4 servings

2 tbsp olive oil   2 cups green split peas, rinsed
1 large yellow onion, diced   1 cup soy milk
2 garlic cloves, minced   1 tbsp lemon juice
Sea salt to taste   1 tbsp chopped mint
4 cups vegetable broth   ½ tsp red chili flakes

Directions and Total Time: 25 minutes

Heat the oil in a large saucepan with a lid over medium heat. Stir in the onion and garlic until soft and translucent, 3 minutes. Pour salt, broth, and split peas and simmer, with the lid on, for 15 minutes or until the peas are cooked, but not mushy. Combine half the soup, soy milk, and lemon juice in a blender and blend until smooth. Remove the soup to the pot and stir well. Serve garnished with mint and red chili flakes.

Pumpkin Squash Cream Soup

Ingredients for 4 servings

2 tbsp olive oil   10 oz pumpkin squash
4 tbsp plant butter   Juice of 1 lime
2 red onions, cut into wedges   ¾ cup vegan mayonnaise
2 garlic cloves, skinned   1 tbsp toasted pumpkin seeds
10 oz pumpkin, cubed

Directions and Total Time: 55 minutes

Preheat oven to 400 F. Place the onions, garlic, and pumpkin on a baking sheet and drizzle with olive oil. Season with salt and pepper. Roast for 30 minutes or until the vegetables are golden brown and fragrant. Remove the vegetables from the oven and transfer them to a pot. Add 2 cups of water, bring the ingredients to boil over medium heat for 15 minutes. Turn the heat off. Add in plant butter and puree until smooth. Stir in lime juice and vegan mayonnaise. Spoon into serving bowls and garnish with pumpkin seeds to serve.

Curried Bean & Veggie Soup

Ingredients for 4 servings

2 tsp olive oil	2 cubed sweet potatoes
1 cup canned cannellini beans	1 cup sliced zucchini
2 tsp curry powder	Salt and black pepper to taste
1 red onion, diced	1 bunch spinach, chopped
1 tbsp minced fresh ginger	Toasted sesame seeds

Directions and Total Time: 55 minutes

Mix the beans with 1 tsp of curry powder until well combined. Warm the oil in a pot over medium heat. Place the onion and ginger and cook for 5 minutes until soft. Add in sweet potatoes and cook for 10 minutes. Put in zucchini and cook for 5 minutes. Season with the remaining curry, pepper, and salt. Pour in 4 cups of water and bring to a boil. Lower the heat and simmer for 25 minutes. Stir in beans and spinach. Cook until the spinach wilts. Garnish with sesame seeds to serve.

Golden Beet & Potato Soup

Ingredients for 6 servings

2 tbsp olive oil	1 yellow bell pepper, chopped
1 onion, chopped	1 Yukon Gold potato, diced
1 carrot, chopped	6 cups vegetable broth
1 celery stalk, chopped	1 tsp dried thyme
2 garlic cloves, minced	Salt and black pepper to taste
1 peeled golden beet, diced	1 tbsp lemon juice

Directions and Total Time: 55 minutes

Heat the oil in a pot over medium heat. Place the onion, carrot, celery, and garlic. Cook for 5 minutes or until softened. Stir in beet, bell pepper, and potato, cook uncovered for 1 minute. Pour in the broth and thyme. Season with salt and pepper. Cook for 45 minutes until the vegetables are tender. Serve sprinkled with lemon juice.

Dilly Cauliflower Soup

Ingredients for 4 servings

1 head cauliflower, cut into florets	
2 tbsp coconut oil	1 tsp cumin powder
5 oz plant butter	¼ tsp nutmeg powder
½ lb celery root, trimmed	3 ½ cups vegetable stock
1 garlic clove	Juice from 1 lemon
1 medium white onion	¼ cup coconut cream
¼ cup fresh dill, chopped	

Directions and Total Time: 26 minutes

Set a pot over medium heat, add the coconut oil and allow heating until no longer shimmering.
Add the celery root, garlic clove, and onion; sauté the vegetables until fragrant and soft, about 5 minutes. Stir in the dill, cumin, and nutmeg, and fry further for 1 minute. Mix in the cauliflower florets and vegetable stock. Bring the soup to a boil for 12 to 15 minutes or until the cauliflower is soft. Turn the heat off. Add the plant butter and lemon juice. Puree the ingredients with an immersion blender until smooth. Mix in coconut whipping cream. Season the soup with salt and pepper.

African Lentil Soup

Ingredients for 4 servings

3 ¼ cups vegetable broth	½ tsp cumin
1 cup brown lentils, rinsed	Salt to taste
2 shallots, thinly sliced	2 tbsp lemon juice
2 garlic cloves, minced	2 tbsp chopped cilantro

Directions and Total Time: 30 minutes

Bring the broth to a boil in a pot over high heat. Pour in the lentils, two-thirds of the shallots, garlic, cumin, and salt. Reduce the heat and simmer for 15 minutes.

In a another skillet, over medium heat, caramelize the remaining shallots with a few splashes of water, stirring frequently to keep the onions from sticking to the pan. Cook until soft and brown, 15 minutes.

Pour the lemon juice into the soup and use an immersion blender to blend the soup until smooth. Serve the soup in bowls topped with caramelized onions and cilantro.

Basil Mushroom Soup

Ingredients for 4 servings

15 oz mixed mushrooms, chopped	
5 oz shiitake mushrooms, chopped	
1 vegetable stock cube, crushed	
4 oz unsalted plant butter	½ tsp dried rosemary
1 small onion, finely chopped	1 tbsp plain vinegar
1 clove garlic, minced	1 cup coconut cream
½ lb celery root, chopped	4 leaves basil, chopped

Directions and Total Time: 40 minutes

Place a saucepan over medium heat, add the plant butter to melt, then sauté the onion, garlic, mushrooms, and celery root in the butter until golden brown and fragrant, about 6 minutes. Fetch out some mushrooms and reserve for garnishing. Add the rosemary, 3 cups of water, stock cube, and vinegar. Stir the mixture and bring it to a boil for 6 minutes. After, reduce the heat and simmer the soup for 15 minutes or until the celery is soft. Mix in the coconut cream and puree the ingredients using an immersion blender. Simmer for 2 minutes. Spoon the soup into serving bowls, garnish with the reserved mushrooms and basil. Serve and enjoy!

Asian-Style Mushroom Soup

Ingredients for 4 servings

2 tbsp olive oil	2 tbsp soy sauce
4 green onions, chopped	4 cups vegetable broth
1 carrot, chopped	Salt and black pepper to taste
8 oz shiitake mushrooms, sliced	2 tbsp parsley, chopped
3 tbsp rice wine	

Directions and Total Time: 25 minutes

Heat the oil in a pot over medium heat. Place the green onions and carrot and cook for 5 minutes. Stir in mushrooms, rice wine, soy sauce, broth, salt, and pepper. Bring to a boil, then lower the heat and simmer for 15 minutes. Top with parsley and serve warm.

Spicy Seitan Soup with Tortilla Strips

Ingredients for 4 servings

2 tbsp olive oil	4 cups vegetable broth
1 (14.5-oz) can diced tomatoes	8 oz seitan, cut into strips
1 (4-oz) can green chiles, minced	Salt and black pepper to taste
1 cup canned sweet corn	¼ cup chopped fresh cilantro
1 red onion, chopped	3 tbsp fresh lime juice
2 garlic cloves, minced	4 corn tortillas, cut into strips
2 jalapeño peppers, sliced	1 ripe avocado, chopped

Directions and Total Time: 40 minutes

Preheat oven to 350°F. Heat the oil in a pot over medium heat. Place sweet corn, garlic, jalapeño, and onion and cook for 5 minutes. Stir in broth, seitan, tomatoes, canned chiles, salt, and pepper. Bring to a boil, then lower the heat and simmer for 20 minutes. Stir in cilantro and lime juice. Arrange the tortilla strips on a baking sheet and bake for 8 minutes until crisp. Top with tortilla strips and avocado.

Bean & Spinach Soup

Ingredients for 4 servings

1 (15.5-oz) can cannellini beans, drained

2 tbsp olive oil	5 cups vegetable broth
1 medium onion, chopped	¼ tsp crushed red pepper
2 large garlic cloves, minced	Salt and black pepper to taste
1 carrot, chopped	3 cups chopped baby spinach

Directions and Total Time: 40 minutes

Heat oil in a pot over medium heat. Place in carrot, onion, and garlic and cook for 3 minutes. Put in beans, broth, red pepper, salt, and black pepper and stir. Bring to a boil, then lower the heat and simmer for 25 minutes. Stir in baby spinach and cook for 5 minutes until the spinach wilts. Serve warm and enjoy!

Tomato Bean Soup

Ingredients for 5 servings

2 tsp olive oil	1 tbsp dried basil
1 onion, chopped	½ tbsp dried oregano
2 garlic cloves, minced	1 (19-oz) can diced tomatoes
1 cup mushrooms, chopped	1 (14-oz) can kidney beans
Sea salt to taste	2 cups chopped mustard greens

Directions and Total Time: 30 minutes

Heat the oil in a pot over medium heat. Place in the onion, garlic, mushrooms, and salt and cook for 5 minutes. Stir in basil and oregano, tomatoes, and beans. Pour in 5 cups of water and stir. Simmer for 20 minutes. Add in mustard greens and cook for 5 minutes until greens soften. Serve immediately.

Zucchini Cream Soup with Walnuts

Ingredients for 4 servings

2 tsp olive oil	3 tsp ground sage
3 zucchinis, chopped	3 tbsp nutritional yeast
Salt and black pepper to taste	1 cup non-dairy milk
1 onion, diced	¼ cup toasted walnuts
4 cups vegetable stock	

Directions and Total Time: 45 minutes

Heat the oil in a skillet and place zucchini, onion, salt, and pepper; cook for 5 minutes. Pour in vegetable stock and bring to a boil. Lower the heat and simmer for 15 minutes. Stir in sage, nutritional yeast, and milk. Purée the soup with a blender until smooth. Serve garnished with toasted walnuts and pepper.

Za´atar Chickpea Soup with Veggies

Ingredients for 5 servings

2 tbsp olive oil	2 tsp smoked paprika
1 onion, chopped	1 tsp ground cumin
1 carrot, chopped	1 tsp za'atar spice
1 celery stalk, chopped	¼ tsp ground cayenne pepper
1 eggplant, chopped	6 cups vegetable broth
1 (28-oz) can diced tomatoes	4 oz whole-wheat vermicelli
2 tbsp tomato paste	2 tbsp minced cilantro
1 (15.5-oz) can chickpeas	

Directions and Total Time: 35 minutes

Heat the oil in a pot over medium heat. Place onion, carrot, and celery and cook for 5 minutes. Add the eggplant, tomatoes, tomato paste, chickpeas, paprika, cumin, za´atar spice, and cayenne pepper. Stir in broth and salt. Bring to a boil, then lower the heat and simmer for 15 minutes. Add in vermicelli and cook for another 5 minutes. Serve topped with chopped cilantro.

Vegetable Lentil Soup

Ingredients for 4 servings

2 tbsp olive oil	¼ tsp crushed red pepper
1 onion, chopped	1 bay leaf
2 garlic cloves, minced	Salt to taste
4 cups vegetable broth	4 cups chopped spinach
2 russet potatoes, cubed	1 cup green lentils, rinsed
½ tsp dried oregano	

Directions and Total Time: 55 minutes

Warm the oil in a pot over medium heat. Place the onion and garlic and cook covered for 5 minutes. Stir in broth, potatoes, oregano, red pepper, bay leaf, lentils, and salt. Bring to a boil, then lower the heat and simmer uncovered for 30 minutes. Add in spinach and cook for another 5 minutes. Discard the bay leaf and serve immediately.

Cilantro Ramen Soup

Ingredients for 4 servings

7 oz Japanese buckwheat noodles

4 tbsp sesame paste	2 tbsp fresh cilantro, chopped
1 cup canned pinto beans	2 scallions, thinly sliced

Directions and Total Time: 25 minutes

In boiling salted water, add in the noodles and cook for 5 minutes over low heat. Remove a cup of the noodle water to a bowl and add in the sesame paste; stir until it has dissolved. Pour the sesame mix in the pot with the noodles, add in pinto beans, and stir until everything is hot. Serve topped with cilantro and scallions in bowls.

Spicy Pumpkin Soup

Ingredients for 6 servings

3 tbsp olive oil
1 (2-pound) pumpkin, sliced
1 tsp salt
2 red bell peppers
1 onion, halved
1 head garlic

6 cups water
Zest and juice of 1 lime
¼ tsp cayenne pepper
½ tsp ground coriander
½ tsp ground cumin

Directions and Total Time: 55 minutes

Preheat oven to 350 F. Brush the pumpkin slices with oil and sprinkle with salt. Arrange the slices skin-side-down and on a greased baking dish and bake for 20 minutes. Brush the onion with oil. Cut the top of the garlic head and brush with oil. When the pumpkin is ready, add bell peppers, onion, and garlic, and bake for another 10 minutes. Allow cooling.

Take out the flesh from the pumpkin skin and transfer to a food processor. Cut the pepper roughly, peel and cut the onion, and remove the cloves from the garlic head. Transfer to the food processor and pour in the water, lime zest, and lime juice. Blend the soup until smooth. Sprinkle with salt, cayenne, coriander, and cumin. Serve.

Mint Coconut Soup with Arugula

Ingredients for 4 servings

1 tsp coconut oil
1 onion, diced
2 cups green beans
4 cups water

1 cup arugula, chopped
1 tbsp fresh mint, chopped
Salt and black pepper to taste
¾ cup coconut milk

Directions and Total Time: 30 minutes

Place a pot over medium heat and heat the coconut oil. Add in the onion and sauté for 5 minutes. Pour in green beans and water. Bring to a boil, lower the heat and stir in arugula, mint, salt, and pepper. Simmer for 10 minutes. Stir in coconut milk. Transfer to a food processor and blitz the soup until smooth. Serve and enjoy!

Power Green Bisque

Ingredients for 6 servings

3 tbsp olive oil
1 red onion, chopped
2 carrots, chopped
1 potato, peeled and chopped
1 zucchini, sliced
1 ripe tomato, quartered

2 garlic cloves, crushed
½ tsp dried rosemary
Salt and black pepper to taste
6 cups vegetable broth
1 tbsp minced fresh parsley

Directions and Total Time: 25 minutes

Preheat oven to 400°F. Arrange the onion, carrots, potato, zucchini, tomato, and garlic on a greased baking dish. Sprinkle with oil, rosemary, salt, and pepper. Cover with foil and roast for 30 minutes. Uncover and turn them. Roast for another 10 minutes.

Transfer the veggies into a pot and pour in the broth. Bring to a boil, lower the heat and simmer for 5 minutes. Transfer to a food processor and blend the soup until smooth. Serve topped with parsley.

Sweet Potato & White Bean Soup

Ingredients for 6 servings

3 tbsp olive oil
1 onion, chopped
2 carrots, chopped
1 sweet potato, chopped
1 yellow bell pepper, chopped
2 garlic cloves, minced
4 tomatoes, chopped

6 cups vegetable broth
1 bay leaf
Salt to taste
1 tsp ground cayenne pepper
1 (15.5-oz) can white beans
1/3 cup whole-wheat pasta
¼ tsp turmeric

Directions and Total Time: 50 minutes

Heat the oil in a pot over medium heat. Place onion, carrots, sweet potato, bell pepper, and garlic. Cook for 5 minutes. Add in tomatoes, broth, bay leaf, salt, and cayenne pepper. Stir and bring to a boil. Lower the heat and simmer for 10 minutes. Put in white beans and simmer for 15 more minutes. Cook the pasta in a pot with boiling salted water and turmeric for 8-10 minutes, until pasta is al dente. Strain and transfer to the soup. Discard the bay leaf. Spoon into a bowl and serve.

Authentic Tomato Soup

Ingredients for 4 servings

3 tbsp olive oil
2 lb tomatoes, halved
2 tsp garlic powder
1 tbsp balsamic vinegar

Salt and black pepper to taste
4 shallots, chopped
2 cups vegetable broth
½ cup basil leaves, chopped

Directions and Total Time: 60 minutes

Preheat oven to 450 F. In a bowl, mix tomatoes, garlic, 2 tbsp of oil, vinegar, salt, and pepper. Arrange the tomatoes onto a baking dish. Bake for 30 minutes until the tomatoes get dark brown color. Take out from the oven.

Heat the remaining oil in a pot over medium heat. Place the shallots and cook for 3 minutes, stirring often. Add in roasted tomatoes and broth. Bring to a boil, then lower the heat and simmer for 10 minutes. Transfer to a food processor and blitz the soup until smooth. Serve topped with basil.

Bangkok-Style Tofu Soup

Ingredients for 4 servings

1 cup shiitake mushrooms, sliced
1 tbsp canola oil
1 onion, chopped
2 tbsp minced fresh ginger
2 tbsp soy sauce
1 tbsp pure date sugar
1 tsp chili paste

2 cups light vegetable broth
8 oz extra-firm tofu, chopped
2 (13.5-oz) cans coconut milk
1 tbsp fresh lime juice
3 tbsp chopped fresh cilantro

Directions and Total Time: 30 minutes

Heat the oil in a pot over medium heat. Place in onion and ginger and sauté for 3 minutes until softened. Add in soy sauce, mushrooms, sugar, and chili paste. Stir in broth. Bring to a boil, then lower the heat and simmer for 15 minutes. Strain the liquid and discard solids. Return the broth to the pot. Stir in tofu, coconut milk, and lime juice. Cook for 5 minutes. Garnish with cilantro.

Pinto Bean & Corn Soup

Ingredients for 4 servings

2 tbsp olive oil
1 red onion, chopped
1 red bell pepper, chopped
1 carrot, chopped
2 garlic cloves, minced
1 tsp ground cumin
1 tsp dried oregano
1 (14.5-oz) can diced tomatoes

1 (15.5-oz) can pinto beans
4 cups vegetable broth
2 cups corn kernels
1 tsp fresh lemon juice
Salt and black pepper to taste
2 stalks green onions, chopped
Tabasco sauce for garnish

Directions and Total Time: 55 minutes

Heat the oil in a pot over medium heat. Place in onion, bell pepper, carrot, and garlic. Sauté for 5 minutes. Add in cumin, oregano, tomatoes, beans, salt, pepper, and broth. Bring to a boil, then lower the heat and simmer for 15 minutes. In a food processor, transfer 1/3 of the soup and blend until smooth. Return to the pot and stir in the corn. Cook for 10 minutes. Drizzle with lemon juice and garnish with green onions and hot sauce.

Herby Mushroom & Bell Pepper Soup

Ingredients for 6 servings

1 cup cremini mushrooms, quartered
1 cup white mushrooms, quartered
3 tbsp olive oil
1 onion, chopped
1 large carrot, chopped
1 lb mixed bell peppers, diced

6 cups vegetable broth
¼ cup chopped fresh parsley
1 tsp minced fresh thyme
Salt and black pepper to taste

Directions and Total Time: 45 minutes

Heat the oil in a pot over medium heat. Place onion, carrot, and mushrooms and cook for 5 minutes. Add in bell peppers and broth and stir. Bring to a boil, lower the heat, and simmer for 20 minutes. Adjust the seasoning with salt and black pepper. Serve in soup bowls topped with parsley and thyme.

Pressure Cooker Potato Coconut Soup

Ingredients for 5 servings

1 tbsp olive oil
3 green onions, chopped
4 garlic cloves, minced
6 russet potatoes, chopped

½ (13.5-oz) can coconut milk
5 cups vegetable broth
Salt and black pepper to taste

Directions and Total Time: 25 minutes

Set your pressure cooker to Sauté. Place in green onions, garlic, and olive oil. Cook for 3 minutes until softened. Add in potatoes, coconut milk, broth, pepper and salt. Lock the lid in place, set time to 6 minutes on High. Once ready, perform a natural pressure release for 10 minutes. Allow cooling for a few minutes. Using an immersion blender, blitz the soup until smooth. Serve and enjoy!

Vegetable & Black-Eyed Pea Soup

Ingredients for 6 servings

2 carrots, chopped
1 onion, chopped

2 cups canned black-eyed peas
1 tbsp soy sauce

3 tsp dried thyme
1 tsp onion powder
½ tsp garlic powder

Salt and black pepper to taste
9 chopped pitted black olives

Directions and Total Time: 45 minutes

Place carrots, onion, black-eyed peas, 3 cups of water, soy sauce, thyme, onion powder, garlic powder, salt, and pepper in a pot. Bring to a boil, then reduce the heat to low. Cook for 20 minutes. Allow cooling for a few minutes. Transfer to a food processor and blend until smooth. Stir in black olives. Serve and enjoy!

Chili Lentil Soup with Collard Greens

Ingredients for 2 servings

1 tsp olive oil
1 onion, chopped
6 garlic cloves, minced
1 tsp chili powder
½ tsp ground cinnamon

Salt to taste
1 cup yellow lentils
1 cup canned diced tomatoes
1 celery stalk, chopped
2 cups chopped collard greens

Directions and Total Time: 35 minutes

Heat oil in a pot over medium heat. Place onion and garlic and cook for 5 minutes. Stir in chili powder, celery, cinnamon, and salt. Pour in lentils, tomatoes and juices, and 2 cups of water. Bring to a boil, then lower the heat and simmer for 15 minutes. Stir in collard greens. Cook for an additional 5 minutes. Serve warm and enjoy!

Rice & Bean Soup with Spinach

Ingredients for 6 servings

2 tbsp olive oil
6 cups baby spinach
1 onion, chopped
2 garlic cloves, minced
1 (15.5-oz) can black-eyed peas

6 cups vegetable broth
Salt and black pepper to taste
½ cup brown rice
1 tbsp Tabasco sauce

Directions and Total Time: 45 minutes

Heat the olive oil in a pot over medium heat. Place the onion and garlic and sauté for 3 minutes until softened. Pour in broth and season with salt and pepper. Bring to a boil, then lower the heat and stir in rice. Simmer for 15 minutes. Stir in peas and spinach and cook for another 5 minutes. Serve topped with Tabasco sauce.

Sweet Potato & Mustard Green Soup

Ingredients for 6 servings

2 tbsp olive oil
1 red onion, chopped
1 leek, chopped
2 garlic cloves, minced
6 cups vegetable broth

1 lb red potatoes, chopped
1 lb sweet potatoes, diced
¼ tsp crushed red pepper
1 bunch mustard greens, torn

Directions and Total Time: 30 minutes

Heat the oil in a pot over medium heat. Place onion, leek, and garlic and sauté for 5 minutes. Pour in broth, potatoes, and red pepper. Bring to a boil, then lower the heat and season with salt and pepper. Simmer for 15 minutes. Add in mustard greens, cook for 5 minutes until the greens are tender. Serve and enjoy!

Winter Soup

Ingredients for 6 servings

2 tsp olive oil
1 chopped onion
3 garlic cloves, minced
1 tbsp thyme
2 tsp paprika
2 cups peeled daikon, cubed

2 cups red potatoes, cubed
2 peeled cups parsnips, cubed
½ tsp sea salt
1 cup fresh mint, chopped
2 tbsp balsamic vinegar
2 tbsp pumpkin seeds

Directions and Total Time: 40 minutes

Heat the olive oil in a pot over medium heat. Place onion and garlic. Sauté for 3 minutes. Add in thyme, paprika, daikon, red potato, parsnips, 3 cups of water, and salt. Bring to a boil and cook for 30 minutes. Remove the soup to a food processor and add in balsamic vinegar; purée until smooth. Top with mint and pumpkin seeds.

Broccoli Soup with Ginger

Ingredients for 4 servings

1 head broccoli, chopped into florets
2 tsp olive oil
1 onion, chopped
1 tbsp minced fresh ginger
2 carrots, chopped

1 cup coconut milk
3 cups vegetable broth
½ tsp turmeric
Salt and black pepper to taste

Directions and Total Time: 50 minutes

In a pot over medium heat, place the onion, ginger, and olive oil, cook for 4 minutes. Add in carrots, broccoli, broth, turmeric, pepper, and salt. Bring to a boil and cook for 15 minutes. Transfer the soup to a food processor and blend until smooth. Stir in coconut milk and serve.

Leek Soup with Cauliflower

Ingredients for 4 servings

1 head cauliflower, cut into florets
2 tbsp olive oil
3 leeks, thinly sliced
4 cups vegetable stock

Salt and black pepper to taste
3 tbsp chopped fresh chives

Directions and Total Time: 25 minutes

Heat the oil in a pot over medium heat. Place the leeks and sauté for 5 minutes. Add in cauliflower, vegetable stock, salt, and pepper and cook for 10 minutes. Blend the soup until purée in a food processor. Top with chives.

Cream of Mushroom Soup

Ingredients for 2 servings

2 tsp olive oil
1 onion, chopped
2 cups chopped mushrooms
Salt and black pepper to taste

2 tbsp whole-wheat flour
1 tsp dried rosemary
4 cups vegetable broth
1 cup coconut cream

Directions and Total Time: 20 minutes

In a pot over medium heat, warm the oil. Place the onion, mushrooms, and salt and cook for 5 minutes. Stir in the flour and cook for another 1-2 minutes. Add in rosemary, vegetable broth, coconut cream, and pepper. Lower the heat and simmer for 10 minutes. Serve.

Autumn Squash Soup

Ingredients for 5 servings

1 (2-lb) butternut squash, peeled and cubed
1 red bell pepper, chopped
1 large onion, chopped
3 garlic cloves, minced

4 cups vegetable broth
1 cup coconut cream

Directions and Total Time: 30 minutes

Place the squash, bell pepper, onion, garlic, and broth in a pot. Bring to a boil. Lower the heat and simmer for 20 minutes. Stir in coconut cream, salt, and pepper. Transfer to a food processor purée the soup until smooth. Serve.

Spinach Soup with Vermicelli

Ingredients for 6 servings

1 tbsp olive oil
1 onion, chopped
4 garlic cloves, minced
1 (14.5-oz) can diced tomatoes

6 cups vegetable broth
8 oz vermicelli
1 (5-oz) package baby spinach

Directions and Total Time: 20 minutes

Preparing the Ingredients

Warm the oil in a pot over medium heat. Place in onion and garlic and cook for 3 minutes. Stir in tomatoes, broth, salt, and pepper. Bring to a boil, then lower the heat and simmer for 5 minutes. Pour in vermicelli and spinach and cook for another 5 minutes. Serve warm.

Cream of Pomodoro Soup

Ingredients for 5 servings

2 tbsp olive oil
1 (28-oz) can tomatoes
1 tsp smoked paprika
2 cups vegetable broth

2 tsp dried herbs
1 red onion, chopped
1 cup non-dairy milk
Salt and black pepper to taste

Directions and Total Time: 15 minutes

Place the tomatoes, olive oil, paprika, broth, dried herbs, onion, milk, salt, and pepper in a pot. Bring to a boil and cook for 10 minutes. Transfer to a food processor and blend the soup until smooth.

Mushroom, Brussel Sprout & Tofu Soup

Ingredients for 4 servings

1 cup shredded Brussels sprouts
½-inch piece fresh ginger, minced
2 tsp olive oil
7 oz firm tofu, cubed
1 cup sliced mushrooms
1 garlic clove, minced
Salt to taste

2 tbsp apple cider vinegar
2 tbsp soy sauce
1 tsp pure date sugar
¼ tsp red pepper flakes
1 scallion, chopped

Directions and Total Time: 40 minutes

Heat the oil in a skillet over medium heat. Place mushrooms, Brussels sprouts, garlic, ginger, and salt. Sauté for 7-8 minutes until the veggies are soft. Pour in 4 cups of water, vinegar, soy sauce, sugar, pepper flakes, and tofu. Bring to a boil, then lower the heat and simmer for 5-10 minutes. Top with scallions and serve.

Kale Soup with Potatoes

Ingredients for 4 servings

2 tbsp olive oil	¼ tsp ground cayenne pepper
1/3 cup plant butter	⅛ tsp ground nutmeg
1 onion, chopped	Salt and black pepper to taste
1 ½ lb potatoes, chopped	4 cups kale
4 cups vegetable broth	

Directions and Total Time: 45 minutes

Heat the oil in a pot over medium heat. Place in the onion and sauté for 5 minutes. Pour in potatoes and broth and cook for 20 minutes. Stir in butter, cayenne pepper, nutmeg, salt, and pepper. Add in kale and cook 5 minutes until wilted. Serve and enjoy!

Bean & Rice Noodle Soup

Ingredients for 6 servings

2 carrots, chopped	8 oz brown rice noodles
2 celery stalks, chopped	1 (15-oz) can pinto beans
6 cups vegetable broth	1 tsp dried herbs

Directions and Total Time: 10 minutes

Place a pot over medium heat and add carrots, celery, and vegetable broth. Bring to a boil. Add in noodles, beans, dried herbs, salt, and pepper. Reduce the heat and simmer for 5 minutes. Serve warm and enjoy!

Rice Soup with Veggies

Ingredients for 6 servings

3 tbsp olive oil	½ red bell pepper, chopped
2 carrots, chopped	4 unpeeled potatoes, quartered
1 onion, chopped	6 cups vegetable broth
1 celery stalk, chopped	½ cup brown rice, rinsed
2 garlic cloves, minced	½ cup frozen green peas
2 cups chopped cabbage	2 tbsp chopped parsley

Directions and Total Time: 40 minutes

Heat the olive oil in a medium pot over medium heat. Place carrots, onion, celery, and garlic. Cook for 5 minutes. Add in cabbage, bell pepper, potatoes, and broth. Bring to a boil, lower the heat, and add the brown rice, salt, and pepper. Simmer uncovered for 25 minutes until vegetables are tender. Stir in peas and cook for 5 minutes. Top with parsley and serve warm.

Traditional Ribollita

Ingredients for 6 servings

3 tbsp olive oil	6 cups vegetable broth
2 celery stalks, chopped	1 (14.5-oz) can diced tomatoes
2 carrots, chopped	2 bay leaves
3 shallots, chopped	Salt and black pepper to taste
3 garlic cloves, minced	2 (15.5-oz) cans white beans
½ cup brown rice	¼ cup chopped basil

Directions and Total Time: 1 hour 25 minutes

Heat oil in a pot over medium heat. Place celery, carrots, shallots, and garlic and cook for 5 minutes. Add in brown rice, broth, tomatoes, bay leaves, salt, and pepper.

Bring to a boil, then lower the heat and simmer uncovered for 20 minutes. Stir in beans and basil and cook for 5 minutes. Discard bay leaves and spoon into bowls. Sprinkle with chopped basil. Serve warm and enjoy!

Zuppa di Pomodoro e Pasta

Ingredients for 4 servings

¼ cup olive oil	4 cups vegetable broth
4 cups cubed bread	2 tbsp minced parsley
2 garlic cloves, minced	Salt and black pepper to taste
8 oz whole-wheat pasta	2 tbsp basil leaves, chopped
1 (28-oz) can diced tomatoes	

Directions and Total Time: 30 minutes

Preheat oven to 400°F. Arrange the bread cubes on a baking tray and toast for 10 minutes, shaking them once. Heat olive oil in a pot over medium heat. Place the garlic and cook for 1 minute until softened. Add in pasta, tomatoes, broth, parsley, salt, and pepper. Bring to a boil, then lower the heat and simmer for 10 minutes. Share the toasted bread into soup bowls and spoon in the soup all over. Sprinkle with basil. Serve and enjoy!

Tofu Soup with Mushrooms

Ingredients for 4 servings

4 cups water	¼ cup chopped green onions
2 tbsp soy sauce	3 tbsp tahini
4 white mushrooms, sliced	6 oz extra-firm tofu, diced

Directions and Total Time: 20 minutes

Pour the water and soy sauce into a pot over medium heat and bring the mixture to a boil. Add in mushrooms and green onions. Lower the heat and simmer for 10 minutes. In a bowl, combine ½ cup of hot soup with tahini. Pour the mixture into the pot and simmer 2 minutes more, but not boil. Stir in tofu. Serve warm.

Easy Sunday Soup

Ingredients for 5 servings

2 tbsp vegetable oil	1 yellow summer squash, sliced
1 onion, chopped	2 ripe tomatoes, diced
1 carrot, chopped	Salt and black pepper to taste
2 garlic cloves, minced	5 cups vegetable broth
3 small new potatoes, sliced	2 cups chopped kale
1 zucchini, sliced	¼ cup basil leaves, chopped

Directions and Total Time: 45 minutes

Heat the vegetable oil in a pot over medium heat. Place onion, carrot, and garlic and cook covered for 5 minutes. Add in potatoes, zucchini, yellow squash, tomatoes, salt, and pepper. Cook for 5 minutes. Stir in broth and bring to a boil. Lower the heat and simmer for 30 minutes. Stir in kale and basil. Spoon the soup into bowls. Serve.

Hot Coconut Soup with Potatoes

Ingredients for 6 servings

3 tbsp olive oil	1 garlic clove, minced
1 onion, chopped	1 tbsp hot powder

1 lb carrots, chopped
2 potatoes, chopped
6 cups vegetable broth
Salt and black pepper to taste

1 (13.5-oz) can coconut milk
1 tbsp minced fresh parsley
Chopped roasted cashews

Directions and Total Time: 25 minutes

Heat the oil in a pot over medium heat. Place in onion and garlic and cook for 3 minutes. Add in hot powder, cook for 30 seconds. Stir in carrots, potatoes, broth, and salt. Bring to a boil, lower the heat and simmer for 15 minutes. With an immersion blender, blitz the soup until smooth. Sprinkle with salt and pepper. Mix in coconut milk and cook until hot. Garnish with parsley and chopped cashews to serve.

Country Bean Soup

Ingredients for 4 servings

2 tsp olive oil
1 carrot, chopped
1 onion, chopped
2 garlic cloves, minced
1 tbsp rosemary, chopped

2 tbsp apple cider vinegar
1 cup dried white beans
¼ tsp salt
2 tbsp nutritional yeast

Directions and Total Time: 30 minutes

Heat the oil in a pot over medium heat. Place carrots, onion, and garlic and cook for 5 minutes. Pour in vinegar to deglaze the pot. Stir in 5 cups water and beans and bring to a boil. Lower the heat and simmer for 45 minutes until the beans are soft. Add in salt and nutritional yeast and stir. Serve topped with chopped rosemary.

Apple & Pumpkin Curry

Ingredients for 4 servings

1 tsp olive oil
1 onion, chopped
1-inch piece fresh ginger, diced
1 apple, cored and chopped
1 tsp curry powder
½ tsp pumpkin pie spice

½ tsp smoked paprika
¼ tsp red pepper flakes
3 cups canned pumpkin purée
Salt and black pepper to taste
½ cup almond milk
4 tbsp nutritional yeast

Directions and Total Time: 25 minutes

Warm the olive oil in a pot over medium heat. Place in the onion, ginger, and apple and cook for 5 minutes. Add in curry powder, pumpkin pie spice, paprika, and pepper flakes. Stir in 4 cups water, pumpkin, salt, and pepper. Cook for 10 minutes. Puree with an immersion blender until smooth. Pour in milk and nutritional yeast. Serve.

Spring Onion & Broccoli Soup

Ingredients for 6 servings

2 tbsp olive oil
3 spring onions, chopped
6 cups vegetable broth
3 potatoes, chopped
2 cups broccoli florets, chopped

2 garlic cloves, minced
1 cup soy milk
Salt and black pepper to taste
1 tbsp minced chives

Directions and Total Time: 35 minutes

Heat the oil in a pot over medium heat. Place in spring onions and garlic and sauté for 5 minutes until translucent.

Add in broth, potatoes, and broccoli. Bring to a boil, then lower the heat and simmer for 20 minutes. Mix in soy milk, salt, and pepper. Cook for 5 more minutes. Serve topped with chives.

Celery & Mushroom Stock

Ingredients for 6 servings

5 dried porcini mushrooms, soaked and liquid reserved
8 oz Cremini mushrooms, chopped
1 tbsp olive oil
1 onion, unpeeled and quartered
1 carrot, coarsely chopped
1 celery rib with leaves, chopped

1 onion, chopped
½ cup chopped fresh parsley
Salt and black pepper to taste
5 cups water

Directions and Total Time: 1 hour 15 minutes

Warm the oil in a pot over medium heat. Place in quartered onion, carrot, celery, and cremini mushrooms. Cook for 5 minutes until softened. Add in the dried mushrooms and reserved liquid, onion, salt, pepper, and water. Bring to a boil and simmer for 1 hour. Let cool for a few minutes, then pour over a strainer into a pot. Divide between glass mason jars and allow cooling completely. Seal and store in the fridge for up to 5 days or 1 month in the freezer.

Acorn Squash Soup with Pumpkin Seeds

Ingredients for 4 servings

1 tbsp canola oil
½ cup toasted pumpkin seeds
1 tbsp chopped ginger paste
1 onion, chopped
1 celery stalk, chopped
4 cups vegetable broth

1 acorn squash, chopped
1 tbsp soy sauce
¼ tsp ground allspice
Salt and black pepper to taste
1 cup soy milk

Directions and Total Time: 30 minutes

Heat the oil in a pot over medium heat. Place in onion and celery and sauté for 5 minutes until tender. Add in broth and squash, bring to a boil. Lower the heat and simmer for 20 minutes. Stir in soy sauce, ginger paste, allspice, salt, and pepper. Transfer to a food processor and blend the soup until smooth. Return to the pot. Mix in soy milk and cook until hot. Garnish with pumpkin seeds.

Walnut & Lentil Soup

Ingredients for 4 servings

2 tbsp olive oil
3 shallots, chopped
3 cups vegetable broth
2 garlic cloves, minced
4 cups fresh spinach

½ cup lentils
1 tsp minced fresh sage
¼ tsp ground allspice
Salt and black pepper to taste
¼ cup walnuts, chopped

Directions and Total Time: 30 minutes

Heat the olive oil in a pot over medium heat. Place in the shallots and garlic and sauté for 3 minutes until translucent. Add in the vegetable broth, lentils, sage, allspice, salt, and pepper. Bring to a boil, lower the heat, and simmer for 15 minutes. Add the spinach and cook for another 5 minutes until the spinach wilts. Sprinkle with walnuts. Serve warm and enjoy!

Creamy Artichoke Soup with Almonds

Ingredients for 4 servings

2 (10-oz) packages artichoke hearts

1 tbsp olive oil	Salt to taste
1/3 cup plant butter	⅛ tsp ground cayenne pepper
2 medium shallots, chopped	1 cup plain coconut cream
3 cups vegetable broth	1 tbsp snipped fresh chives
1 tsp fresh lemon juice	2 tbsp sliced toasted almonds

Directions and Total Time: 30 minutes

Heat the oil in a pot over medium heat. Place in shallots and sauté until softened, about 3 minutes. Add in artichokes, broth, lemon juice, and salt. Bring to a boil, lower the heat, and simmer for 10 minutes. Stir in butter and cayenne pepper. Transfer to a food processor and blend until purée. Return to the pot. Mix in the coconut cream and simmer for 5 minutes. Serve warm topped with chives and almonds. Enjoy!

Chana Dal Soba Soup

Ingredients for 6 servings

4 oz soba noodles, broken into thirds

2 tbsp olive oil	1 (28-oz) can diced tomatoes
1 onion, chopped	1 cup Chana dal, rinsed
1 carrot, sliced	1 tsp dried thyme
2 garlic cloves, minced	6 cups vegetable broth

Directions and Total Time: 30 minutes

Warm the oil in a pot over medium heat. Place in onion, carrot, and garlic and sauté for 5 minutes. Add in tomatoes, chana dal, thyme, and broth. Bring to a boil, then lower the heat and season with salt and pepper. Simmer for 15 minutes. Stir in soba noodles, cook 5 minutes more. Serve immediately.

Lime-Mushroom Curry Soup

Ingredients for 4 servings

½ cup sliced shiitake mushrooms

1 tbsp coconut oil	1 (8-oz) can tomato sauce
1 red onion, sliced	2 tbsp cilantro, chopped
1 carrot, chopped	Juice from 1 lime
2 garlic cloves, minced	Salt to taste
1 (13.5-oz) can coconut milk	2 tbsp red curry paste
4 cups vegetable stock	

Directions and Total Time: 15 minutes

Melt coconut oil in a pot over medium heat. Place in onion, garlic, carrot, and mushrooms and sauté for 5 minutes. Pour in coconut milk, vegetable stock, tomato sauce, cilantro, lime juice, salt, and curry paste. Cook until heated through. Serve and enjoy!

White Bean & Carrot Soup

Ingredients for 4 servings

2 tsp olive oil	4 cups vegetable broth
1 leek, chopped	2 (15-oz) cans white beans
4 garlic cloves, minced	2 tbsp lemon juice
2 carrots, peeled and chopped	2 cups green beans
1 tbsp dried herbs	

Directions and Total Time: 20 minutes

Heat the oil in a pot over medium heat. Place in leek, garlic, carrots, pepper, and salt. Cook for 5 minutes until fragrant. Season with dried herbs. Stir in broth, green beans, and white beans, reduce the heat and simmer for 10 minutes. Stir in lemon juice and serve.

Tomato Soup with Parmesan Croutons

Ingredients for 6 servings

2 oz grated plant-based Parmesan cheese

3 oz plant butter	4 cloves garlic, peeled only
3 tbsp olive oil	1 small white onion, diced
3 tbsp flax seed powder	1 small red bell pepper, diced
1 ¼ cups almond flour	1 cup coconut cream
2 tsp baking powder	½ tsp dried rosemary
5 tbsp psyllium husk powder	2 tbsp chopped fresh basil
2 tsp plain vinegar	Salt and black pepper to taste
2 lb fresh ripe tomatoes	2 tbsp basil leaves, chopped

Directions and Total Time: 1 hour 25 minutes

In a medium bowl, mix the flax seed powder with 9 tbsp of water and set aside to soak for 5 minutes. Preheat oven to 350°F and line a baking sheet with parchment paper. In another bowl, combine almond flour, baking powder, psyllium husk powder, and salt. When the vegan "flax egg" is ready, mix in 1 ¼ cups boiling water and plain vinegar. Add in the flour mixture and whisk for 30 seconds. Form 8 flat pieces out of the dough. Place the flattened dough on the baking sheet while leaving enough room between each to allow rising.

Bake for 40 minutes. Remove the croutons to cool and break them into halves. Mix the plant butter with plant-based Parmesan cheese and spread the mixture in the inner parts of the croutons. Increase the oven's temperature to 450°F and bake the croutons further for 5 minutes or until golden brown and crispier.

In a baking pan, put tomatoes, garlic, onion, red bell pepper, and drizzle with olive oil. Roast in the oven for 25 minutes and after broil for 3 to 4 minutes until some of the tomatoes are slightly charred. Transfer to a blender and add coconut cream, rosemary, basil, salt, and pepper. Puree until smooth and creamy. Pour the soup into serving bowls, drop some croutons on top, and garnish with chopped basil leaves. Serve and enjoy!

Citrus Butternut Squash Soup

Ingredients for 6 servings

2 tbsp olive oil	1 potato, peeled and chopped
1 onion, chopped	1 lb butternut squash, cubed
1 celery stalk, chopped	6 cups vegetable broth
½ tsp ground allspice	2 tbsp fresh orange juice

Directions and Total Time: 30 minutes

Heat the oil in a pot over medium heat. Place in onion and celery and sauté for 5 minutes until tender. Add in allspice, potato, squash, and broth. Cook for 20 minutes. Stir in orange juice. Using an immersion blender, blitz the soup until purée. Return to the pot and heat.

Sopa Norteña

Ingredients for 4 servings

3 tbsp olive oil	1 (4-oz) can hot chilies
1 onion, chopped	1 tsp ground cumin
3 garlic cloves, chopped	½ tsp dried oregano
1 cup sweet corn	4 cups vegetable broth
1 (14.5-oz) can diced tomatoes	Salt and black pepper to taste
1 (15.5-oz) can black beans	¼ cup chopped cilantro

Directions and Total Time: 30 minutes

Warm the olive oil in a pot over medium heat. Place in the onion and garlic and sauté for 3 minutes. Add in sweet corn, tomatoes, beans, chilies, cumin, oregano, broth, salt, and pepper. Reduce the heat and simmer for 15 minutes. Garnish with cilantro to serve.

Parsley Rice Soup with Green Beans

Ingredients for 4 servings

2 tbsp olive oil	½ cup brown rice
1 medium onion, minced	1 cup green beans, chopped
2 garlic cloves minced	2 tbsp chopped parsley

Directions and Total Time: 50 minutes

Heat oil in a pot over medium heat. Place in onion and garlic and sauté for 3 minutes. Add in rice, 4 cups water, salt, and pepper. Bring to a boil, lower the heat, and simmer for 15 minutes. Stir in beans and cook for 10 minutes. Top with parsley. Serve warm and enjoy!

Garbanzo & Spinach Soup

Ingredients for 4 servings

2 tbsp olive oil	1 cup spinach, chopped
1 onion, chopped	4 cups vegetable stock
1 green bell pepper, diced	¼ tsp ground cumin
1 carrot, peeled and diced	Sea salt to taste
4 garlic cloves, minced	¼ cup chopped cilantro
1 (15-oz) can garbanzo beans	

Directions and Total Time: 25 minutes

Heat the oil in a pot over medium heat. Place in onion, garlic, bell pepper, and carrot and sauté for 5 minutes until tender. Stir in garbanzo beans, spinach, vegetable stock, cumin, and salt. Cook for 10 minutes. Mash the garbanzo using a potato masher, leaving some chunks. Sprinkle with cilantro. Serve and enjoy!

Rice & Bean Soup with Sun-Dried Tomatoes

Ingredients for 6 servings

2 tbsp olive oil	12 sun-dried tomatoes, diced
3 garlic cloves, minced	6 cups vegetable broth
1 tbsp chili powder	Salt and black pepper to taste
1 tsp dried oregano	½ cup brown rice
3 (15.5-oz) cans kidney beans	1 tbsp chopped cilantro
1 habanero pepper, chopped	

Directions and Total Time: 40 minutes

Heat the oil in a pot over medium heat. Place in garlic and sauté for 1 minute. Add in chili powder, oregano, beans, habanero, tomatoes, broth, rice, salt, and pepper.

Cook for 30 minutes. Put the rice in a pot with boiling salted water and cook for 5 minutes. Spoon the soup in individual bowls and garnish with cilantro to serve.

Parsnip & Fennel Bisque

Ingredients for 6 servings

3 tbsp olive oil	2 garlic cloves, minced
2 green onions, chopped	½ tsp dried thyme
½ fennel bulb, sliced	¼ tsp dried marjoram
2 large carrots, shredded	6 cups vegetable broth
2 parsnips, shredded	1 cup soy milk
1 potato, chopped	1 tbsp minced fresh parsley

Directions and Total Time: 30 minutes

Heat the olive oil in a pot over medium heat. Place in green onions, fennel, carrots, parsnips, potato, and garlic. Sauté for 5 minutes until softened. Add in thyme, marjoram, and broth. Bring to a boil, lower the heat. Simmer for 20 minutes. Transfer to a blender and pulse the soup until smooth. Return to the pot and mix in soy milk. Sprinkle with parsley. Serve and enjoy!

Cilantro Black Bean Soup

Ingredients for 4 servings

2 tbsp olive oil	2 tomatoes, chopped
1 onion, chopped	4 cups vegetable broth
1 celery stalk, chopped	1 (15.5-oz) can black beans
2 medium carrots, chopped	1 tsp dried thyme
1 green bell pepper, chopped	¼ tsp cayenne pepper
2 garlic cloves, minced	1 tbsp minced cilantro

Directions and Total Time: 50 minutes

Heat the olive oil in a pot over medium heat. Place in onion, celery, carrots, bell pepper, garlic, and tomatoes. Sauté for 5 minutes, stirring often until softened. Stir in broth, beans, thyme, salt, and cayenne. Bring to a boil, then lower the heat and simmer for 15 minutes. Transfer the soup to a food processor and pulse until smooth. Serve in soup bowls garnished with cilantro. Enjoy!

Korean-Style Bean Chili

Ingredients for 4 servings

2 tsp sesame oil	1 (14.5-oz) can diced tomatoes
1 cup green onions, chopped	2 cups vegetable broth
3 cloves garlic, minced	2 tbsp red miso paste
1 lb yellow squash, chopped	2 tbsp water
2 cups shredded napa cabbage	1 tbsp hot sauce
1 (14.5-oz) can red beans	2 tsp tamari sauce

Directions and Total Time: 35 minutes

Heat the sesame oil in a pot over medium heat. Place in green onion, garlic and yellow squash, and cook for 5 minutes. Stir in cabbage, beans, tomatoes, and broth.

Bring to a boil, then lower the heat and simmer covered for 15 minutes. Mix the miso paste with hot water in a bowl. Remove the pot from heat and stir in the miso, tamari, and hot sauces. Adjust the seasoning and serve.

Carrot & Spinach Gnocchi Soup

Ingredients for 4 servings

1 tsp olive oil	1 cup gnocchi
1 cup green bell peppers	¾ cup non-dairy milk
Salt and black pepper to taste	¼ cup nutritional yeast
2 garlic cloves, minced	2 cups chopped fresh spinach
2 carrots, chopped	8 pitted black olives, chopped
3 cups vegetable broth	1 cup croutons

Directions and Total Time: 25 minutes

Heat the oil in a pot over medium heat. Place in bell peppers, garlic, carrots, pepper, and salt and cook for 5 minutes. Stir in broth. Bring to a boil. Put in gnocchi, cook for 10 minutes. Add in spinach and cook for another 5 minutes. Stir in milk, nutritional yeast, and olives. Serve warm in bowls topped with croutons. Enjoy!

Green Coconut Soup

Ingredients for 4 servings

2 tbsp coconut oil	1 (13.5-oz) can coconut milk
1 ½ cups vegetable broth	Juice of ½ lime
2 garlic cloves, minced	2 tbsp chopped basil
1 onion, chopped	1 tbsp chopped cilantro
1 tbsp minced fresh ginger	4 lime wedges
1 green bell pepper, sliced	

Directions and Total Time: 15 minutes

Warm the coconut oil in a medium pot over medium heat. Place in onion, garlic, and ginger and sauté for 3 minutes. Add in bell peppers and broth. Bring to a boil, then lower the heat and simmer. Stir in coconut milk, lime juice, and chopped cilantro. Simmer for 5 minutes. Serve garnished with basil and lime. Enjoy!

Swiss Chard & Zucchini Lentil Soup

Ingredients for 4 servings

2 tbsp olive oil	1 (14.5-oz) can diced tomatoes
1 onion, chopped	1 cup red lentils, rinsed
1 zucchini, chopped	4 cups vegetable broth
1 garlic clove, minced	3 cups chopped Swiss chard
1 tbsp hot paprika	

Directions and Total Time: 30 minutes

Heat the oil in a pot over medium heat. Place in onion, zucchini, and garlic and sauté for 5 minutes until tender. Add in paprika, tomatoes, lentils, broth, salt, and pepper. Bring to a boil, then lower the heat and simmer for 15 minutes, stirring often. Add in the Swiss chard and cook for another 3-5 minutes. Serve immediately.

Home-Style Minestrone Soup

Ingredients for 4 servings

2 tbsp olive oil	1 cup green peas
1 onion, chopped	½ cup orzo
1 carrot, chopped	1 (15-oz) can diced tomatoes
1 stalk celery, chopped	2 tsp Italian seasoning
2 garlic cloves, minced	Salt and black pepper to taste
4 cups vegetable stock	

Directions and Total Time: 20 minutes

Heat the oil in a pot over medium heat. Place in onion, garlic, carrot, and celery and sauté for 5 minutes until tender. Stir in vegetable stock, green peas, orzo, tomatoes, salt, pepper, and Italian seasoning. Cook for 10 minutes.

Dilly Rice Soup with Vegetables

Ingredients for 6 servings

3 tbsp olive oil	½ cup brown rice
1 onion, chopped	7 cups vegetable broth
1 carrot, chopped	1 tsp dried dill weed
1 celery stalk, chopped	Salt and black pepper to taste
1 cup wild mushrooms, sliced	

Directions and Total Time: 30 minutes

Heat the olive oil in a pot over medium heat. Place in onion, carrot, and celery and sauté for 5 minutes. Add in mushrooms, rice, broth, dill weed, salt, and pepper. Bring to a boil, then lower the heat, and simmer uncovered for 20 minutes. Serve and enjoy!

Rutabaga Soup with Turnips

Ingredients for 5 servings

2 tbsp olive oil	1 turnip chopped
1 onion, diced	1 red potato, chopped
3 garlic cloves, minced	5 cups vegetable stock
1 carrot, chopped	2 tsp dried thyme
1 rutabaga, chopped	

Directions and Total Time: 30 minutes

Heat the oil in a pot over medium heat. Place the onion and garlic and sauté for 3 minutes until translucent. Stir in carrot, rutabaga, turnip, potato, vegetable stock, salt, pepper, and thyme. Simmer for 10 minutes. In a food processor, put the soup and blend until purée. Serve.

Summer Vegetable Soup

Ingredients for 4 servings

2 tbsp olive oil	4 green onions, chopped
2 lb tomatoes, chopped	2 garlic cloves, minced
1 cucumber, peeled, chopped	2 tbsp white wine vinegar
1 green bell pepper, chopped	Salt to taste
1 slice whole-wheat bread	2 tbsp minced fresh parsley

Directions and Total Time: 15 minutes

In a food processor, place half of the tomatoes, cucumber, bell pepper, 1 cup cold of water, bread, green onions, and garlic. Blitz until smooth. Pour in oil, salt, and vinegar and pulse until combined. Transfer to a bowl and combine with remaining tomatoes. Close the lid and let chill in the fridge for 1-2 hours. Garnish with parsley.

Bell Pepper & Butternut Squash Soup

Ingredients for 4 servings

2 tbsp olive oil	1 red bell pepper, chopped
½ cup plant butter	4 cups vegetable broth
1 onion, chopped	Salt and black pepper to taste
½ lb butternut squash, cubed	¼ cup toasted pumpkin seeds

Directions and Total Time: 30 minutes

Heat oil in a pot over medium heat. Place in onion, squash, and bell pepper. Sauté for 5 minutes until soft. Stir in broth, butter, salt, and pepper. Bring to a boil, then lower the heat, and simmer for 20 minutes. Blend the soup with an immersion blender. Top with seeds.

Fresh Gazpacho

Ingredients for 4 servings

3 tbsp olive oil	2 lb plum tomatoes, chopped
2 garlic cloves, crushed	1 (14.5-oz) can diced tomatoes
Salt and black pepper to taste	1 cup tomato juice
2 cucumbers	2 tbsp chopped dill
2 tsp lemon juice	

Directions and Total Time: 15 minutes

Put the garlic, olive oil, and salt and pulse in a food processor until paste-like consistency forms. Add in 1 cucumber, chopped tomatoes, canned tomatoes, and lemon juice. Blitz until smooth. Put tomato juice, salt, and pepper. Mix until smooth. Cover and let chill in the fridge before serving. Enjoy topped with dill.

Zucchini Velouté with Green Beans

Ingredients for 6 servings

3 tbsp olive oil	3 medium zucchini, sliced
1 onion, chopped	½ tsp dried marjoram
1 garlic clove, minced	½ cup plain almond milk
2 cups green beans	2 tbsp minced jarred pimiento
4 cups vegetable broth	

Directions and Total Time: 30 minutes

Heat oil in a pot and sauté onion and garlic for 5 minutes. Add in green beans and broth. Cook for 10 minutes. Stir in zucchini and cook for 10 minutes. Blitz with an immersion blender until smooth. Mix in almond milk and cook again until hot. Top with pimiento and marjoram.

Corn & Potato Chowder with Mushrooms

Ingredients for 4 servings

2 tbsp olive oil	4 cups vegetable stock
1 onion, chopped	2 cups canned corn
1 cup chopped fennel bulb	2 cups cubed red potatoes
2 carrots, chopped	1 cup almond milk
1 cup mushrooms, chopped	½ tsp chili paste
¼ cup whole-wheat flour	Salt and black pepper to taste

Directions and Total Time: 30 minutes

Heat the oil in a pot over medium heat. Place in onion, fennel, carrots, and mushrooms. Sauté for 5 minutes until tender. Stir in flour. Pour in vegetable stock. Lower the heat. Add in corn, potatoes, almond milk, and chili paste. Simmer for 20 minutes. Sprinkle with salt and pepper.

Cabbage & Pumpkin Soup

Ingredients for 4 servings

2 tsp olive oil	1 onion, chopped
3 cups pumpkin, chopped	1 garlic clove, minced

2 cups water	1 tsp paprika
1 (15-oz) can black-eyed peas	1 tbsp red pepper flakes
2 tbsp lime juice	3 cups shredded cabbage
1 tbsp pure date sugar	1 cup mushrooms, chopped

Directions and Total Time: 30 minutes

Warm the oil in a pot over medium heat. Place in pumpkin, onion, garlic, and salt. Cook for 5 minutes. Stir in water, peas, lime juice, sugar, paprika, and pepper flakes. Bring to a boil and cook for 15 minutes. Add in cabbage and mushrooms and cook for 5 minutes. Allow cooling before serving.

Tomato & Celery Rice Soup

Ingredients for 6 servings

3 tbsp olive oil	1 (14.5-oz) can diced tomatoes
1 onion, chopped	2 cups tomato juice
1 medium carrot, chopped	2 bay leaves
1 celery stalk, chopped	½ tsp ground cumin
1 lb potatoes, chopped	Salt and black pepper to taste
½ cup long-grain brown rice	1 tbsp minced fresh parsley

Directions and Total Time: 40 minutes

Heat oil in a pot and sauté onion, carrot, and celery for 10 minutes. Add potatoes, rice, tomatoes, tomato juices, bay leaves, cumin, 6 cups water, salt, and pepper. Bring to a boil, then lower the heat and simmer uncovered for 20 minutes. Discard the bay leaves. Scatter with parsley.

Spicy Basil Gazpacho

Ingredients for 4 servings

2 tbsp olive oil	2 garlic cloves, minced
2 cups water	Juice of 1 lemon
1 red onion, chopped	2 tbsp chopped fresh basil
6 tomatoes, chopped	½ tsp chili pepper
1 red bell pepper, diced	

Directions and Total Time: 15 minutes

In a food processor, place the olive oil, half of the onion, half of the tomato, half of the bell pepper, garlic, lemon juice, basil, water, and chili pepper. Season with salt and pepper. Blitz until smooth. Transfer to a bowl and add reserved onion, tomatoes, and bell pepper. Let chill in the fridge before serving.

Chickpea Chili

Ingredients for 4 servings

2 tsp olive oil	1 (28-oz) can tomatoes
1 onion, chopped	1 tbsp tomato paste
1 cup vegetable broth	1 (14-oz) can chickpeas
2 garlic cloves, minced	1 tsp chili powder
1 potato, cubed	Salt and black pepper to taste
1 carrot, chopped	¼ cup parsley leaves, chopped

Directions and Total Time: 30 minutes

Heat oil in a pot over medium heat. Place in onion and garlic and sauté for 3 minutes. Add in potato, carrot, tomatoes, broth, tomato paste, chickpeas, and chili; season. Simmer for 20 minutes. Garnish with parsley.

Tomato Bean Chili with Brown Rice

Ingredients for 6 servings

30 oz canned roasted tomatoes and peppers
3 tbsp olive oil
1 onion, chopped
4 garlic cloves, minced
1 (15-oz) can kidney beans
½ cup brown rice
2 cups vegetable stock
3 tbsp chili powder
1 tsp sea salt

Directions and Total Time: 30 minutes

Heat the oil in a pot over medium heat. Place onion and garlic and cook for 3 minutes until fragrant. Stir in beans, rice, tomatoes and peppers, stock, chili powder, and salt. Cook for 20 minutes. Serve and enjoy!

Basil Soup with Rotini

Ingredients for 4 servings

1 tbsp olive oil
1 medium onion, chopped
1 celery rib, minced
3 garlic cloves, minced
3 cups diced fresh tomatoes
2 tbsp tomato paste
3 cups vegetable broth
2 bay leaves
½ cup rotini pasta
2 tbsp chopped fresh basil

Directions and Total Time: 25 minutes

Heat oil in a pot and sauté onion, celery, and garlic for 5 minutes. Add in tomatoes, tomato paste, broth, and bay leaves. Bring to a boil and add the rotini. Cook for 10 minutes. Discard bay leaves. Garnish with basil.

Garbanzo & Pumpkin Chili with Kale

Ingredients for 6 servings

¾ cup garbanzo beans, soaked
1 (28-oz) can diced tomatoes
2 cups chopped pumpkin
2 tbsp chili powder
1 tsp onion powder
½ tsp garlic powder
3 cups kale, chopped
½ tsp salt

Directions and Total Time: 60 minutes

In a saucepan over medium heat, place garbanzo, tomatoes, pumpkin, 5 cups of water, salt, chili, onion, and garlic powders. Bring to a boil. Reduce the heat and simmer for 50 minutes. Stir in kale and cook for 5 minutes until the kale wilts. Serve warm and enjoy!

Italian-Style Slow-Cooked Lentil & Potato Stew

Ingredients for 4 servings

2 tbsp olive oil
1 carrot, cubed
2 russet potatoes, cubed
1 celery stalk, thinly sliced
1 onion, chopped
2 garlic cloves, minced
1 cup dried lentils
3 cups vegetable broth
1 cup canned tomatoes, diced
1 bay leaf
2 tsp Italian seasoning
Salt to taste
5 baby spinach

Directions and Total Time: 8 hours 15 minutes

Add the olive oil, carrot, potatoes, celery, onion, garlic, lentils, broth, tomatoes with liquid, bay leaf, Italian seasoning, and salt to your slow cooker pot. Stir to combine. Cover and cook on low for 8 hours. Remove the lid and take out the bay leaf. Stir in spinach and let it warm through until wilted. Serve warm and enjoy!

Grandma´s Succotash Stew

Ingredients for 4 servings

1 (16-oz) package frozen succotash
2 tbsp olive oil
1 cup canned chickpeas
1 onion, chopped
2 russet potatoes, chopped
2 carrots, sliced
1 (14.5-oz) can diced tomatoes
2 cups vegetable broth
2 tbsp soy sauce
1 tsp dry mustard
½ tsp dried thyme
½ tsp ground allspice
¼ tsp ground cayenne pepper
Salt and black pepper to taste

Directions and Total Time: 30 minutes

Heat the olive oil in a saucepan over medium heat. Place in onion and sauté for 3 minutes. Stir in chickpeas, potatoes, carrots, tomatoes, succotash, broth, soy sauce, mustard, thyme, allspice, and cayenne pepper. Sprinkle with salt and pepper. Bring to a boil, then lower the heat and simmer for 20 minutes. Serve hot and enjoy!

Nicaraguan Lentil Stew

Ingredients for 4 servings

2 tbsp olive oil
1 onion, chopped
1 carrot, sliced
2 garlic cloves, minced
1 sweet potato, chopped
¼ tsp crushed red pepper
1 cup red lentils, rinsed
1 (14.5-oz) can diced tomatoes
1 tsp hot curry powder
1 tsp chopped thyme
¼ tsp ground allspice
Salt and black pepper to taste
1 cup water
1 (13.5-oz) can coconut milk

Directions and Total Time: 50 minutes

Warm oil in a pot and sauté onion and carrot for 5 minutes, stirring occasionally until softened. Add in garlic, sweet potato, and crushed red pepper. Put in red lentils, tomatoes, curry powder, allspice, salt, and black pepper, stir to combine. Pour in water and simmer for 30 minutes until the vegetables are tender. Stir in coconut milk and simmer for 10 minutes. Serve topped with thyme.

Turnip & Pearl Barley Stew

Ingredients for 6 servings

3 tbsp olive oil
1 onion, chopped
2 garlic cloves, minced
2 turnips, chopped
4 potatoes, chopped
1 cup pearl barley
1 (28-oz) can diced tomatoes
3 tsp dried mixed herbs
Salt and black pepper to taste

Directions and Total Time: 30 minutes

Warm the oil in a pot over medium heat. Add onion and garlic and sauté for 3 minutes until fragrant. Stir in turnips, potatoes, barley, tomatoes, 3 cups of water, salt, pepper, and herbs. Cook for 20 minutes. Serve warm.

Turmeric Spinach Stew

Ingredients for 6 servings

3 tbsp olive oil
3 potatoes, cubed
2 carrots, sliced
4 shallots, chopped
2 garlic cloves, minced
1 tbsp ground turmeric
1 tsp ground ginger
1 ½ cups vegetable broth
4 cups shredded spinach
Salt to taste

Directions and Total Time: 30 minutes

Cook the potatoes in salted water over medium heat, about 15 minutes. Drain and reserve. Heat the oil in a saucepan over medium heat. Place in carrots and shallots and cook for 5 minutes. Stir in garlic, turmeric, ginger, and salt. Cook for 1 minute more. Add in cooked potatoes and broth. Bring to a boil, then lower the heat. Stir in the spinach and cook for 3 minutes until wilted.

Eggplant & Green Pea Stew

Ingredients for 5 servings

2 tbsp canola oil	2 cups vegetable broth
1 onion, chopped	1 (14.5-oz) can diced tomatoes
2 garlic cloves, minced	2 tbsp soy sauce
2 fresh hot chilies, minced	½ tsp ground turmeric
1 tbsp grated fresh ginger	1 (13.5-oz) can coconut milk
1 russet potato, chopped	1 tbsp tamarind paste
1 medium eggplant, chopped	2 tbsp fresh lime juice
8 oz green peas	3 tbsp minced fresh cilantro
2 cups cauliflower florets	2 tbsp minced scallions

Directions and Total Time: 40 minutes

Warm oil in a pot over medium heat. Place onion, garlic, chilies, and ginger and cook for 5 minutes. Stir in potato, eggplant, green peas, cauliflower, broth, tomatoes, soy sauce, and turmeric. Cook for 20 minutes. Lower the heat and pour in coconut milk, tamarind, salt, and pepper. Simmer for 5 minutes. Mix in lime juice. Top with cilantro and scallions to serve. Enjoy!

Spicy Tamarind Bean Stew

Ingredients for 4 servings

1 (4-oz) can mild chopped green chilies	
2 tbsp olive oil	1 cup vegetable broth
1 onion, chopped	2 tbsp chili powder
2 potatoes, chopped	1 tsp ground coriander
2 (15-oz) cans cannellini beans	½ tsp ground cumin
1 (28-oz) can diced tomatoes	Salt and black pepper to taste
2 tbsp tamarind paste	1 cup frozen peas, thawed
¼ cup pure agave syrup	

Directions and Total Time: 40 minutes

Heat the oil in a pot over medium heat. Place in the onion and sauté for 3 minutes until translucent. Stir in potatoes, beans, tomatoes, and chilies. Cook for 5 minutes more. In a bowl, whisk the tamarind paste with agave syrup and broth. Pour the mixture into the pot. Stir in chili powder, coriander, cumin, salt, and pepper. Bring to a boil, then lower the heat and simmer for 20 minutes until the potatoes are tender. Add in peas and cook for another 5 minutes. Serve warm and enjoy!

Eggplant & Chickpea Stew with Mushrooms

Ingredients for 4 servings

2 tbsp olive oil	1 cup mushrooms, sliced
1 onion, chopped	2 garlic cloves, minced
1 eggplant, chopped	1 (15.5-oz) cans chickpeas
2 medium carrots, sliced	1 (28-oz) can diced tomatoes
1 red potato, chopped	1 tbsp minced parsley

½ tsp dried oregano	½ cup vegetable broth
½ tsp dried basil	Salt and black pepper to taste
1 tbsp soy sauce	

Directions and Total Time: 30 minutes

Heat the oil in a pot over medium heat. Place in onion, garlic, eggplant, and carrots and sauté for 5 minutes. Lower the heat and stir in potato, mushrooms, chickpeas, tomatoes, oregano, basil, soy sauce, salt, pepper, and broth. Simmer for 15 minutes. Sprinkle with parsley.

Effortless Veggie Stew

Ingredients for 4 servings

2 tbsp olive oil	1 yellow summer squash, sliced
3 shallots, chopped	1 lb plum tomatoes, chopped
1 carrot, sliced	Salt and black pepper to taste
½ cup dry white wine	3 cups fresh corn kernels
3 new potatoes, cubed	1 cup green beans
1 red bell pepper, chopped	¼ cup fresh basil
1 ½ cups vegetable broth	¼ cup chopped fresh parsley
2 zucchini, sliced	

Directions and Total Time: 35 minutes

Heat oil in a pot over medium heat. Place shallots and carrot and cook for 5 minutes. Pour in white wine, potatoes, bell pepper, and broth. Bring to a boil, lower the heat, and simmer for 5 minutes. Stir in zucchini, yellow squash and tomatoes. Sprinkle with salt and pepper. Simmer for 20 more minutes. Put in corn, green beans, basil, and parsley. Simmer an additional 5 minutes.

Potato & Kale Stew

Ingredients for 4 servings

2 tbsp olive oil	1 tsp paprika
1/3 cup chunky almond butter	¼ tsp red pepper flakes
1 onion, diced	Salt to taste
2 peeled potatoes, chopped	2 cups kale, chopped

Directions and Total Time: 30 minutes

Warm the olive oil in a saucepan over medium heat and cook the onion for 3 minutes. Add in potatoes, almond butter, paprika, pepper flakes, 4 cups water, and salt; stir. Bring to a boil and simmer 20 for minutes. Add in the kale and cook for 5 minutes. Serve warm and enjoy!

Classic Lentil Stew

Ingredients for 4 servings

2 tsp olive oil	1 tbsp paprika
2 carrots, chopped	2 garlic cloves, sliced
1 onion, chopped	1 (28-oz) can diced tomatoes
Salt and black pepper to taste	1 cup lentils, rinsed

Directions and Total Time: 25 minutes

Heat the oil in a pot over medium heat. Place in carrots, onion, paprika, and garlic. Sauté for 5 minutes until tender. Stir in 4 cups of water, tomatoes, and lentils. Bring to a boil, then lower the heat and simmer for 20 minutes. Sprinkle with salt and pepper. Serve warm.

Kale & Pea Rice Sew

Ingredients for 6 servings

2 tsp olive oil	1 cup brown rice
1 cups bell peppers	2 cups vegetable broth
Salt and black pepper to taste	4 tbsp balsamic vinegar
1 onion, chopped	1 cup frozen peas, thawed
2 garlic cloves, minced	1 cup non-dairy milk
1 tbsp dried herbs	2 cups chopped kale

Directions and Total Time: 30 minutes

Heat the oil in a pot over medium heat. Place in bell peppers, onion, garlic, and salt and cook for 5 minutes until tender. Put in dried herbs, brown rice, broth, vinegar, and pepper. Bring to a boil, then lower the heat and simmer for 20 minutes. Stir in peas, milk, and kale until the kale wilts. Serve warm and enjoy!

Spanish Veggie & Chickpea Stew

Ingredients for 4 servings

2 tbsp olive oil	2 cups winter squash, chopped
1 onion, chopped	1 russet potato, cubed
2 carrots, chopped	1 ½ cups vegetable broth
½ tsp ground cumin	1 (15.5-oz) can chickpeas
½ tsp ground ginger	1 tsp lemon zest
½ tsp paprika	Salt and black pepper to taste
½ tsp saffron	½ cup pitted green olives
1 (14.5-oz) can diced tomatoes	1 tbsp minced cilantro
½ head broccoli, cut into florets	½ cup toasted slivered almonds

Directions and Total Time: 30 minutes

Heat the olive oil in a pot over medium heat. Place onions and carrots and sauté for 5 minutes until tender. Add in cumin, ginger, paprika, salt, pepper, and saffron and cook for 30 seconds. Stir in tomatoes, broccoli, squash, potato, chickpeas, and broth. Bring to a boil, then lower the heat, and simmer for 20 minutes. Add in the olives and lemon zest, stir, and simmer for 2-3 minutes. Garnish with cilantro and almonds to serve.

Elegant Kidney Bean Stew

Ingredients for 4 servings

2 tbsp olive oil	2 russet potatoes, chopped
3 cups cooked red kidney beans	1 (14.5-oz) can diced tomatoes
1 yellow onion, chopped	1 (4-oz) can diced green chiles
2 carrots, sliced	1 ½ cups vegetable broth
3 garlic cloves, minced	Salt and black pepper to taste
1 tsp grated fresh ginger	3 cups eggplants, chopped
½ tsp ground cumin	¼ cup chopped roasted peanuts
1 tsp ras el hanout	

Directions and Total Time: 40 minutes

Heat the olive oil in a pot over medium heat. Place the onion, garlic, ginger, and carrots and sauté for 5 minutes until tender. Stir in cumin, ras el hanout, potatoes, beans, tomatoes, chiles, and broth. Season with salt and pepper. Bring to a boil, then lower the heat, and simmer for 20 minutes. Add in the eggplants, stir, and cook for 10 minutes. Serve warm garnished with peanuts.

Root-Veggie Medley Stew with Seitan

Ingredients for 4 servings

2 tbsp olive oil	1 head savoy cabbage, chopped
8 oz seitan, cubed	1 (14.5-oz) can diced tomatoes
1 leek, chopped	1 (15.5-oz) can white beans
2 garlic cloves, minced	2 cups vegetable broth
1 russet potato, chopped	½ cup dry white wine
1 carrot, chopped	½ tsp dried thyme
1 parsnip, chopped	½ cup crumbled angel hair pasta
1 cup butternut squash, cubed	

Directions and Total Time: 65 minutes

Heat the olive oil in a pot over medium heat. Place in seitan and cook for 3 minutes. Sprinkle with salt and pepper. Add in the leek and garlic and cook for another 3 minutes until softened. Stir in potato, carrot, parsnip, and squash and cook for 10 minutes. Add in cabbage, tomatoes, white beans, broth, wine, thyme, salt, and pepper. Bring to a boil, lower the heat and simmer for 15 minutes. Put in pasta and cook for 5 minutes. Serve.

African-Style Veggie Stew

Ingredients for 4 servings

3 peeled russet potatoes, cubed	1 tsp ground cumin
2 tbsp olive oil	1 tsp ras el hanout seasoning
6 carrots, sliced	Salt to taste
1 onion, chopped	1 ½ cups vegetable broth
4 garlic cloves, minced	4 cups shredded green cabbage
1 tbsp ground turmeric	1 tbsp cilantro, finely chopped

Directions and Total Time: 20 minutes

Boil water in a pot of over medium heat. Add potatoes and cook for 10 minutes. Drain the potatoes in a colander and set to the side. While waiting for the potatoes to cook, heat a large skillet with oil over medium heat. Sauté carrots and onions for 5 minutes. Stir in garlic, turmeric, cumin, ras el hanout, and salt. Sauté for 1 minute or until aromatic. Stir in the potatoes and 1 cup of broth. Bring to a boil then reduce the heat. Top with cabbage and cover the skillet. Simmer for 3 minutes. Stir the cabbage into the potatoes. Pour the rest of the broth over the vegetables and return the lid over the skillet. Simmer for 5 minutes, stirring occasionally. When the cabbage is wilted, garnish with cilantro. Serve warm.

One-Pot Habanero Pinto Beans

Ingredients for 6 servings

1 tsp olive oil	½ cup vegetable broth
2 red bell peppers, diced	1 tsp ground cumin
1 habanero pepper, minced	1 tsp chili powder
2 (14.5-oz) cans pinto beans	Salt and black pepper to taste

Directions and Total Time: 20 minutes

Heat the oil in a pot over medium heat. Place in bell and habanero peppers, sauté for 5 minutes until tender. Add in beans, broth, cumin, chili powder, salt, and pepper. Bring to a boil, then simmer for 10 minutes. Serve.

SNACKS & SIDES

Walnut-Topped Brussels Sprout Leaves

Ingredients for 2 servings

1 cup Brussels sprout leaves
½ tbsp extra-virgin olive oil
Salt and black pepper to taste
½ tsp lemon zest
1 tbsp walnuts, chopped

Directions and Total Time: 25 minutes

Turn the oven on to 375°F. Lay parchment paper or a silicone mat on a cookie sheet and set aside. Put the Brussels sprout leaves in a bowl with the olive oil and lemon zest and toss. Add some salt and pepper and toss again. Bake in the oven for 12 minutes. Scatter with lemon zest and walnuts and serve.

Picante Cauliflower

Ingredients for 2 servings

½ cauliflower head, cut into florets
1 tbsp extra-virgin olive oil
1 tsp garlic powder
Salt and black pepper to taste
1 tbsp plant-based butter
¼ cup hot sauce
1 tsp cilantro, chopped

Directions and Total Time: 35 minutes

Turn the oven on to 400°F. Lay a silicone mat or parchment paper on a cookie sheet and set aside. Pour some olive oil over the cauliflower, then sprinkle in the garlic powder. Add some salt and pepper, then toss. Place the cauliflower on one side of the cookie sheet and cook for 15 minutes. Use a metal spoon to flip all the pieces, then cook for an additional 10 minutes. On medium heat, put the plant-based butter and hot sauce in a pan and stir until the butter melts and is mixed into the sauce. Use a cooking brush to rub the sauce on the cauliflower, then cook for another 5 minutes. Serve hot, topped with cilantro. Enjoy!

Mediterranean Kale

Ingredients for 2 servings

1 tbsp extra-virgin olive oil
1 garlic clove, minced
1 shallot, thinly sliced
2 cups kale, chopped
¼ lime, juiced
1 tbsp capers, chopped
Salt and black pepper to taste

Directions and Total Time: 10 minutes

Pour the olive oil into a skillet and turn the burner on medium. Toss the garlic and shallot in and cook for a minute. Stir regularly. Place the kale, lime juice, and capers in the skillet and cook for another 3-4 minutes, allowing the kale to wilt. Add more salt and pepper and stir. Place in equal amounts on 2 plates. Serve.

Hot Roasted Hazelnuts

Ingredients for 4 servings

1 tsp ground cumin
1 tsp cayenne pepper
Salt and black pepper to taste
2 cups hazelnuts
1 tbsp extra-virgin olive oil

Directions and Total Time: 10 minutes

Combine the cumin, cayenne pepper, salt, and pepper in a bowl. Put a skillet on the stove and turn on medium heat. Toss the hazelnuts in the dry skillet and roast for 5 minutes. After roasting, mix with the seasoning mix, then pour in olive oil and stir, coating the nuts well. After lining a cooking sheet with parchment paper or silicone mat, put the nuts on top, and allow to chill. Serve.

Thyme Roasted Asparagus

Ingredients for 2 servings

½ cup grated plant-based Parmesan cheese
1 bunch of asparagus
2 tbsp extra-virgin olive oil
¼ cup bread crumbs
½ tsp garlic powder
Salt and black pepper to taste
½ tsp dried thyme

Directions and Total Time: 20 minutes

Turn the oven on to 425°F. Snap the ends off the asparagus and put it in a large sealable bag. Add the olive oil and shake to coat. Open the bag and toss in the bread crumbs, plant-based Parmesan cheese, and garlic powder. Last, add some thyme, salt, and pepper, then close the bag and shake until the asparagus is well-coated. Place the asparagus in one layer on the cookie sheet and cook for 8-10 minutes.

Mushroom Nori Roll Bites

Ingredients for 4 servings

2 tbsp peanut butter
2 tbsp soy sauce
4 nori sheets
1 mushroom, sliced
½ chili garlic salt
1 tbsp pickled ginger
½ cup grated carrots
1 tsp chopped cilantro

Directions and Total Time: 25 minutes

Preheat the oven to 350°F. Whisk together peanut butter and soy sauce until smooth. Prepare a sheet of nori with the rough side up and the long way. Smear a thin line of the peanut mixture on the far side of the nori from one side to the other. Arrange a line of mushroom slices, ginger, garlic salt, cilantro, and carrots on the closest end. Roll the vegetables inside the nori. The tahini mixture will seal the roll. Continue this process for the remaining 3 rolls. Arrange the rolls on a baking sheet and bake for 8-10 minutes. The rolls will be just browned and crispy. Cool for a few minutes until you can slice them into 3 smaller rolls. Serve warm and enjoy.

Curried Kale & Lentil Dip

Ingredients for 6 servings

1 to 2 leaves kale, rinsed and stemmed
1 (14-oz) can lentils
1 lemon, zested and juiced
1 tbsp tahini
1 tsp curry powder
1 tsp ground cumin
1 tsp smoked paprika
Salt to taste

Directions and Total Time: 30 minutes

All ingredients to a blender and blend until smooth. Adjust the seasoning and serve. Enjoy!

Chipotle Baked Broccoli with Almonds

Ingredients for 2 servings

½ broccoli head, cut into florets
2 tbsp grated plant-based Parmesan cheese
2 tbsp extra-virgin olive oil   Salt to taste
1 tsp chipotle powder   2 tbsp sliced almonds
½ tsp garlic powder   2 lemon wedges

Directions and Total Time: 30 minutes

Turn the oven on to 400°F. Add the broccoli, olive oil, chipotle powder, and garlic powder to a bowl and toss. Add some salt and toss again. Put the broccoli in one layer on a parchment-lined cookie sheet and bake for 20 minutes. Take it out and stir the broccoli, then put the sliced almonds with the broccoli and stir again. Cook for an additional 5 minutes. Take it out, squirt the lemon wedges on top, and and cover with plant-based Parmesan.

Curried Roasted Cauliflower

Ingredients for 2 servings

½ cauliflower head, cut into florets
1 tbsp extra-virgin olive oil   ¼ tsp red curry paste
Salt and black pepper to taste   1 garlic clove, minced
½ cup coconut milk   1 tbsp chopped chervil
2 tbsp almond butter

Directions and Total Time: 30 minutes

Turn the oven on to 400°F. Put the cauliflower on one side on a parchment-lined cookie sheet, then pour some olive oil over all of it. Add some salt and pepper as well. Cook for 20 minutes. As the cauliflower is roasting, pour the coconut milk, almond butter, curry paste, and garlic into a blender, then blend until creamy. When the cauliflower is cooked, put equal amounts on 2 plates and drizzle some peanut sauce all over. Top with chervil.

Crispy Smoky Roasted Chickpeas

Ingredients for 2 servings

1 (14-oz) can chickpeas   1 tsp smoked paprika
2 tbsp shoyu soy sauce   1 tsp onion powder
½ tsp ginger powder   ½ tsp garlic powder

Directions and Total Time: 35 minutes

Preheat the oven to 400°F. Combine all of the ingredients in a large bowl. Arrange them in a single layer on a baking sheet. Bake for 10 minutes, then stir the chickpeas with a spatula. Bake for another 10-15 minutes until the chickpeas are toasty. Serve warm and enjoy.

Bean Tacos with Red Cabbage Slaw

Ingredients for 6 servings

1 cup white button mushrooms, stemmed and diced
3 cups sliced purple cabbage   1 tbsp olive oil
¼ cup vegan mayonnaise   Salt and black pepper to taste
½ lemon, juiced   6 corn tortillas
¼ cup chopped parsley   3 tbsp chipotle sauce
1 (15-oz) can red beans   1 tbsp sesame seeds
1 green onion, thinly sliced

Directions and Total Time: 35 minutes

Preheat the oven to 400°F. Lightly spray a baking sheet with cooking oil. Add cabbage, mayonnaise, lemon juice, parsley, and salt in a large bowl. Toss to coat. In a separate bowl, mix beans, mushrooms, onion, oil, salt, and pepper. Transfer to the baking sheet and spread out evenly. Bake for 20 minutes, tossing with a spatula halfway through. Arrange the tortillas over the bean and mushroom mixture. Bake for 2 more minutes, then place the tortillas on a plate. To prepare the tacos, spread a spoonful of the mixture on the tortilla, then top with the slaw. Drizzle with chipotle sauce. Top with sesame seeds.

Mini Bean Sprout Wraps

Ingredients for 4 servings

1 cup bean sprouts   ½ tsp cayenne pepper
½ cup cilantro, chopped   Salt and black pepper to taste
1 garlic clove, minced   1 lime, zested and juiced
2 tbsp ground almonds   2 tbsp ground flaxseed
2 tbsp flaked coconut   2 wraps corn wraps
1 tbsp coconut oil

Directions and Total Time: 10 minutes +chilling time

Combine all of the ingredients except the corn wraps into a food processor. Pulse until mixed. Slowly add 1-2 tbsp of water so that it all comes together. Spread half of the mixture on each wrap, then roll it. Refrigerate for 30 minutes. When ready to serve, slice each roll into 8 smaller pieces. Serve and enjoy.

Tomatoes Provençal

Ingredients for 2 servings

½ cup shaved plant-based Parmesan cheese
1 large tomato, cut into 4 slices   1 tsp parsley, chopped
1 tsp herbs de Provence

Directions and Total Time: minutes

Turn the oven on to 400°F. Lay a silicone mat or parchment paper on a cookie sheet and set aside. Place the tomatoes in one layer on the cookie sheet and toss the herbs de Provence on top. Add some parmesan and parsley, then cook for 10 minutes.

Mexican Bean Spread

Ingredients for 6 servings

1 cup torn romaine lettuce   ¼ tsp jalapeño powder
1 (15-oz) can black beans   2 avocados, mashed
Salt and black pepper to taste   1 cup salsa
1 cup vegan sour cream   2 tbsp chives, chopped
2 tsp taco seasoning   Tortilla chips, for serving

Directions and Total Time: 25 minutes

Mash beans, salt, and pepper in a medium bowl. Spread it evenly on the bottom of a 1-quart serving dish. Combine sour cream, jalapeno powder, and taco seasoning in a small bowl. Spread that layer over the bean mixture. Next, spread on the avocado, then the salsa. Top with romaine and chives. Serve with tortilla chips and enjoy.

Roasted Vegetable Pitas

Ingredients for 6 servings

1 ½ cups raw cashews, soaked overnight
1 cup baby Bella mushrooms, sliced
1 lime, juiced   10 oz spinach, chopped
1 tsp garlic powder   6 whole-wheat pita breads
1 tsp shallot powder   6 tsp olive oil
½ tsp porcini powder   3 tbsp vegan Parmesan cheese
Salt to taste   ½ tsp red pepper flakes

Directions and Total Time: 25 minutes

Preheat the oven to 350°F. Line 2 baking sheets with parchment paper. Add cashews, 1 ½ cups of water, lime juice, garlic, shallot, porcini powder, and salt in a blender jar. Puree until smooth. Transfer the mixture to a large bowl. Stir in spinach until well combined. Brush some olive oil on the pita breads, then arrange them on the baking sheets. Spread ½ cup of the spinach mixture on each pita, then a layer of mushrooms. Bake for 15 minutes until the pita edges start to become golden. Season with Parmesan and red pepper flakes. Serve.

Cabbage Pancakes with Hot Sauce

Ingredients for 4 servings

2 cups shredded green cabbage
¼ cup creamy peanut butter   1 ¼ cups vegetable broth
4 tsp tamari   3 green onions, thinly sliced
1 tsp sriracha sauce   2 garlic cloves, minced
1 cup all-purpose flour   Salt and black pepper to taste
1 tbsp baking powder   1 tbsp olive oil

Directions and Total Time: 25 minutes

Whisk peanut butter, ¼ cup water, 2 teaspoons tamari, and sriracha in a small bowl until well blended. Set aside. Stir flour, baking powder, broth, and 2 teaspoons tamari in a large bowl. Fold in cabbage, green onions, garlic, salt, and pepper until just combined. In a medium skillet, heat olive oil over medium heat. Pour ½ cup of the batter into the skillet. Look for bubbles in the middle of the pancake. Flip the pancake, then gently press down with the spatula. Cook for another 1 to 2 minutes. Repeat the process with the rest of the batter and add more oil as needed to prevent sticking. To serve, cut the pancakes into quarters. Serve with peanut sauce for dipping.

Hot Butter Bean Dip

Ingredients for 6 servings

1 (14-oz) can butter beans   1 tsp ground cumin
1 lime, zested and juiced   ¼ tsp chili powder
1 tbsp soy sauce   1 cup tortilla chips
¼ cup fresh cilantro, chopped

Directions and Total Time: 15 minutes

Puree the butter beans, lime zest, lime juice, and soy sauce in a food processor. Slowly add ¼ cup water while it is blending until smooth and the desired consistency. Stir in cilantro, cumin, and chili powder. Transfer to a serving bowl. Serve with tortillas and enjoy!

Swiss Chard & Chickpea Burritos

Ingredients for 6 servings

3 tbsp olive oil   1 bunch Swiss chard, chopped
1 shallot, chopped   4 whole-wheat tortillas
2 garlic cloves, minced   2 cups cooked brown rice
1 (15-oz) can chickpeas   2 avocados, sliced
2 tsp paprika   ½ cup vegan sour cream
1 tsp chipotle powder   ½ cup salsa
Salt and black pepper to taste

Directions and Total Time: 30 minutes

In a large skillet, heat 1 tablespoon of oil over medium heat. Stir in shallot and sauté until soft, about 3 minutes. Stir in garlic and cook for another minute or until aromatic. Next, stir in chickpeas, paprika, chipotle powder, salt, and pepper. Continue stirring for 3 minutes, then add chard and cook for another 3 minutes until wilted. To build the burrito, lay a tortilla on a flat work surface. Add ¼ cup rice, ¼ cup chard mixture, avocado slices, and 1 tablespoon sour cream on the half closest to you. Start folding the tortilla over the mixture and roll away from you. Fold in the sides and continue until the burrito is completely rolled up. Repeat the process for the rest of the tortillas and filling. In a large skillet, heat 1 teaspoon of oil over medium-low heat. Transfer the burrito to the skillet, seam-side down. Add weight to it to keep it in place. Cook for 2 minutes, then carefully flip the burrito. Cook for another 2 minutes or until the tortilla is crisp and golden. Repeat the process for the remaining burritos. Serve with salsa and enjoy.

Traditional Hummus

Ingredients for 6 servings

1 tbsp olive oil   Salt to taste
1 (14-oz) can chickpeas   1 tsp ground cumin
1 tbsp tahini   1 tbsp parsley, chopped
1 lemon, zested and juiced   ¼ tsp paprika
2 garlic cloves, minced   Toasted pitas for serving

Directions and Total Time: 15 minutes

Puree olive oil, chickpeas, tahini, lemon zest, lemon juice, garlic, salt, and cumin in the food processor. Slowly pour ¼ cup water while it is blending until it reaches the desired consistency. Transfer the hummus to a serving bowl. Garnish with parsley and paprika. Serve with pitas.

Herb Sweet Potato Fries

Ingredients for 2 servings

1 medium sweet potato   ¼ tsp dried basil
1 tsp olive oil   ¼ tsp dried oregano
Garlic salt to taste   ¼ tsp dried rosemary

Directions and Total Time: 55 minutes

Preheat the oven to 350°F. Peel the sweet potato then cut into fries. Use your hands to rub the oil and seasonings on the fries. Arrange in a single layer on a large baking sheet. Bake for 15-20 minutes, then flip the fries. Bake for another 15-25 minutes or until the fries are soft.

Rosemary Potato Wedges

Ingredients for 4 servings

3 potatoes, cut into wedges	1 tsp nutritional yeast
8 garlic cloves, peeled	Salt to taste
2 tsp olive oil	2 tbsp chopped rosemary

Directions and Total Time: 35 minutes

Preheat the oven to 350°F. Toss the potato wedges in a large bowl with garlic cloves, oil, nutritional yeast, and salt. Arrange on a rectangular baking sheet and bake for 20-25 minutes. When the potatoes are soft and golden, sprinkle with rosemary. Serve warm and enjoy.

Chili-Garlic Flatbreads

Ingredients for 2 servings

1 tsp olive oil	2 whole-grain round flatbreads
¼ tsp chili garlic salt	

Directions and Total Time: 10 minutes

Combine oil and chili garlic salt in a small bowl. Brush the oil mixture on the flatbreads and broil on high for 5 minutes. Serve hot and enjoy.

Kale & Beet Chips

Ingredients for 2 servings

4 cups curly kale, torn	1 tbsp olive oil
1 beet, thinly sliced	Sea salt to taste
2 tbsp apple cider vinegar	

Directions and Total Time: 15 minutes

Preheat oven to 350°F. Line a baking sheet with parchment paper. Toss kale, beet, vinegar, and olive oil in a bowl. Massage the kale with the mixture until soft and dark green. Arrange the vegetables in a single layer on the baking sheet. Bake for 20 to 25 minutes or until crisp. Season with sea salt and cool completely. Serve when cooled or store in an airtight container for up to 5 days.

Pumpkin & Cavolo Nero Hash

Ingredients for 4 servings

4 cups cavolo nero (kale), chopped	
2 tbsp olive oil	1 tsp smoked paprika
1 onion, chopped	1 tsp dried rosemary
2 garlic cloves, minced	½ cup vegetable broth
2 cups pumpkin cubes	Salt and black pepper to taste

Directions and Total Time: 40 minutes

In a large skillet, heat oil over medium heat. Sauté onion for 3 minutes until soft. Stir in garlic and sauté for another minute until aromatic. Next, mix in pumpkin, smoked paprika, and rosemary. Cook for 5 minutes until the pumpkin starts to brown on the edges. Stir in broth slowly. Cover the skillet and simmer for 7 minutes. Remove the lid and top the pumpkin with cavolo nero. Return the lid and simmer until the kale is wilted, or about 2 minutes. Season with salt and pepper and simmer uncovered for 5 minutes. When the liquid has cooked off and the pumpkin is fork-tender, it is ready.

Great Northern Bean Quesadillas with Spinach

Ingredients for 4 servings

1 (15-oz) can great northern beans	
¼ cup vegetable broth	Salt and black pepper to taste
3 tbsp olive oil	1 cup chopped spinach
½ lemon, juiced	4 whole-wheat tortillas
2 garlic cloves, minced	¼ cup vegan barbecue sauce
½ tsp dried oregano	

Directions and Total Time: 25 minutes

Add beans, broth, 1 ½ tablespoons olive oil, lemon juice, garlic, oregano, salt, and pepper in a blender jar. Puree until smooth, about 1 minute. Set aside. Toss spinach and 1 tablespoon of olive oil in a bowl until coated. In a large skillet, heat ½ tablespoon olive oil over medium heat. Spread ¼ of the bean mixture over half of the tortilla, then cover with ¼ cup of spinach. Fold the tortilla in half over the mixture, then press down. Cook for 2 minutes on each side. Transfer to a plate when golden. Repeat with the remaining tortillas. To serve, cut each tortilla into quarters and plate with BBQ sauce on the side or drizzled on top. Serve warm and enjoy.

Easy-Peasy Shepherd's Pie

Ingredients for 6 servings

1 ½ lb cooked potatoes, mashed	1 (15-oz) can lentils
1 tbsp cornstarch	1 ½ cups mushrooms, diced
1 cup vegetable broth	1 tbsp tomato purée
2 tsp olive oil	1 ½ tsp dried thyme
½ cup chopped onions	Salt and black pepper to taste
2 garlic cloves, minced	

Directions and Total Time: 40 minutes

Preheat the oven to 425°F. Whisk broth and cornstarch in a small bowl. Set aside. In an oven-safe skillet, heat oil over medium heat. Sauté onion for 3 minutes until softened. Sauté garlic for 1 minute until aromatic. Stir in lentils, mushrooms, tomato puree, thyme, salt, and pepper. Cook for 2 minutes, then slowly pour in the slurry. Remove from heat after 3 to 5 minutes when the mixture has thickened. Cover the lentil mixture completely with the potatoes. Bake for 18 to 20 minutes until the pie is bubbling. Serve warm and enjoy!

Asian-Inspired Rice

Ingredients for 4 servings

1 tsp sesame oil	Salt to taste
1 cup vegetable broth	½ lime, juiced
1 cup jasmine rice	¾ cup shelled edamame
½ cup full-fat coconut milk	1 red chili, minced
2 tsp minced fresh ginger	

Directions and Total Time: 20 minutes

In a saucepan, add oil, broth, rice, coconut milk, ginger, and salt over medium heat. Stir, then cover. Bring to a boil, reduce the heat. Simmer for 15 minutes until all of the liquid is absorbed. Remove and sit for 5 minutes. Fluff with a fork. Stir in lime juice, edamame, and red chili.

Chipotle Lentil Tortillas

Ingredients for 6 servings

1 ½ cups torn romaine lettuce	12 corn tortillas
2 tomatoes, chopped	4 tbsp vegan sour cream
2 (15-oz) cans lentils	1 cup shredded carrot
1 ½ cups chunky mild salsa	6 scallions, thinly sliced
1 tbsp taco seasoning	2 tbsp hot sauce
½ tsp chipotle powder	

Directions and Total Time: 15 minutes

Add lentils, salsa, taco seasoning and chipotle powder to a large skillet over medium heat. Bring to a boil. Reduce the heat and simmer for 5 to 8 minutes to reduce the liquid by half. Spread a layer of the lentil mixture on each tortilla, then top with lettuce, tomatoes, and sour cream. Next, add carrots, scallions, and hot sauce. Serve.

Black Bean & Quinoa Nachos

Ingredients for 4 servings

½ cup shredded purple cabbage	
½ cup salsa	Tortilla chips
¼ cup quinoa	¾ cup canned black beans
1 tsp tamari sauce	½ cup vegan cheddar shreds
½ tsp ancho chili powder	½ cup chopped tomatoes
½ tsp cumin	¼ cup vegan sour cream
½ tsp garlic powder	2 scallions, chopped

Directions and Total Time: 25 minutes

Over medium heat, stir together salsa, quinoa, ½ cup water, tamari sauce, ancho chili powder, cumin, and garlic powder in a medium saucepan. Cover and bring to a boil. Keep the pan covered and reduce the heat. Simmer for 15 minutes until all of the liquid is absorbed. Remove from heat and let it sit for 5 minutes. Fluff with a fork. To build the nachos, arrange a layer of chips on a platter. Top the chips with beans, quinoa, cheese shreds, tomato, and cabbage. Repeat the order for another layer. Drizzle with sour cream and garnish with scallions. Serve.

Curry Bean Hummus

Ingredients for 6 servings

1 (15-oz) can cannellini beans	½ tsp dried oregano
2 tbsp toasted sesame oil	½ tsp ground cumin
1 tsp garlic powder	Salt and black pepper to taste
½ tsp curry powder	2 tbsp olive oil for drizzling

Directions and Total Time: 10 minutes

Add all of the ingredients except the olive oil to a blender jar. Blend until smooth, adding up to 2 tablespoons of water to adjust the consistency. To serve, pour the hummus into a bowl, then drizzle with oil. Serve a.

Sundried Tomato & Bean Bruschetta

Ingredients for 4 servings

1 (15-oz) can cannellini beans	2 tbsp olive oil
5 sundried tomatoes, chopped	¼ cup chopped fresh basil
1 garlic clove, minced	Salt and black pepper to taste
¼ cup chopped Sicilian olives	1 sliced baguette, toasted

Directions and Total Time: 20 minutes

Combine all ingredients except the baguette in a large bowl until well mixed. To serve, place a heaping spoonful on top of each toasted bread slice and arrange on an appetizer plate. Serve and enjoy.

BBQ Roasted Cauliflower

Ingredients for 4 servings

1 head cauliflower, cut into florets	
2 tbsp olive oil	2 tbsp cornstarch
¾ cup sucanat	4 cups cooked brown rice
1/3 cup white wine vinegar	2 scallions, chopped
1 tbsp ketchup	2 tbsp white sesame seeds
¼ cup tamari sauce	

Directions and Total Time: 30 minutes

Preheat the oven to 450°F. Line a baking sheet with parchment paper. Toss cauliflower and oil in a large bowl. Arrange in a single layer on the baking sheet and roast for 15 minutes. Toss the cauliflower and roast for another 10 minutes until golden and tender. While the cauliflower is in the oven, add sucanat, 2/3 cup water, vinegar, and ketchup in a large skillet over medium heat. Bring to a boil, then reduce the heat and simmer. Whisk tamari and cornstarch in a small bowl. Stir slowly in the skillet until combined. Cook for 2 to 4 minutes until the sauce has thickened. Mix the roasted cauliflower in the skillet with the sauce and stir until coated. Portion out rice among 4 bowls, then spoon cauliflower over the rice. Top with scallions and sesame seeds. Serve warm.

Nutty Lentil Spread

Ingredients for 6 servings

1 tbsp olive oil	1 tsp dried oregano
1 onion, chopped	½ cup vegan mayonnaise
1 (15-oz) can lentils	Salt to taste
½ cup chopped walnuts	12 Kalamata olives, sliced

Directions and Total Time: 10 minutes

Warm the olive oil in a skillet over medium heat. Sauté the onion for 3 minutes to soften. Add onion, lentils, walnuts, mayonnaise, oregano, and salt to a blender jar. Puree until smooth. Be sure to scrape down the sides. Pour into a serving dish and top with olives. Serve.

Baked Turnip Chips

Ingredients for 2 servings

2 peeled turnips, sliced	½ tsp garlic powder
1 tbsp vegetable oil	¼ tsp salt
1 tbsp vegan Parmesan cheese	1 tsp paprika

Directions and Total Time: 30 minutes

Preheat the oven to 400°F. Line a baking sheet with parchment paper. Combine all of the ingredients in a large bowl until well coated. Arrange the slices in a single layer on the baking sheet. Bake for 15 minutes, then flip the slices. Bake for another 10 minutes until golden and the edges start to curl up. Serve and enjoy.

Spicy Veggie Tostadas

Ingredients for 4 servings

½ cup diced white button mushrooms
10 oz chopped broccoli florets   1 tsp onion powder
1 (15-oz) cannellini beans   4 corn tortillas
½ cup halved grape tomatoes   Sriracha sauce
2 tbsp olive oil   2 tbsp vegan sour cream
2 tsp soy sauce   2 tbsp chopped cilantro
1 tsp garlic powder

Directions and Total Time: 30 minutes

Preheat the oven to 425°F. Line a baking sheet with parchment paper. Toss broccoli, beans, tomatoes, mushrooms, 1 tablespoon olive oil, soy sauce, garlic powder, and onion powder in a large bowl. Arrange the vegetable mixture in a single layer on the baking sheet. Bake for 10 minutes, toss the mixture, then bake for another 5 to 10 minutes until the broccoli is fork-tender and the beans start to split. While the vegetables are baking, add 1 tablespoon oil to a medium skillet over medium heat. Fry both sides of each tortilla until golden. Divide the tortillas among 4 plates. Scoop the broccoli mixture onto each tortilla, gently pressing the beans into the tortilla. Top with sriracha, sour cream, and cilantro. Serve warm and enjoy.

Avocado-Quinoa Collard Wraps with Coleslaw

Ingredients for 4 servings

4 large collard green leaves   2 radishes, sliced
¼ cup hummus   ½ cup julienned carrots
½ cup cooked quinoa   ½ cup sprouts
1 avocado, sliced   ½ cup shredded cabbage

Directions and Total Time: 20 minutes

Cut the stems from each collard leaf. Lay the leaves on a flat work surface with the stem side pointing away from you. Spread 1 tablespoon of hummus down the center of each leaf, then 2 tablespoons of quinoa. Continue with some avocado slices, 2 slices of radishes, 2 tablespoons of carrots, 2 tablespoons of cabbage, and some of sprouts. Fold the sides of the leaf toward the middle, then fold the bottom part of the leaf over the filling. Roll the leaf until completely rolled and secure with two toothpicks. Cut in half on the diagonal. Repeat the process for the rest of the leaves and filling. Serve.

Carrot Noodles with Spinach

Ingredients for 2 servings

¼ cup vegan butter   5 oz spinach, sliced
1 chopped shallot   ¼ cup chopped parsley
1 lb carrots, spiralizer   Salt and black pepper to taste

Directions and Total Time: 20 minutes

Melt butter in a large skillet over medium heat. Sauté shallot for 3 minutes until softened. Stir in carrot and cook for 3 minutes. When the edges start to brown, sauté the spinach for 2 minutes to wilt. Turn off the heat and stir in parsley, salt, and pepper. Serve warm and enjoy.

Vegan Mac "n" Cheese

Ingredients for 4 servings

½ cup diced red bell pepper   2 garlic cloves, minced
1 carrot, cubed   ½ lime, juiced
1 peeled sweet potato, cubed   1 tbsp Dijon mustard
Salt to taste   ¼ tsp turmeric
2 tbsp olive oil   1 lb cooked elbow macaroni
½ garlic powder

Directions and Total Time: 25 minutes

Place a large saucepot over medium heat and add 1 ¾ cups of water, sweet potato, and carrot. Cover and bring to a boil. Cook for 10 minutes until soft but not falling apart. Remove from the heat but do not drain. Heat 1 tablespoon of oil in a medium skillet over medium heat. Sauté garlic powder and bell pepper for 3 minutes to soften the pepper. Stir in garlic and sauté for 1 minute until aromatic. Add the vegetables from the saucepot along with the mixture from the skillet to a blender jar. Pour in the rest of the olive oil, lime juice, mustard, turmeric, and salt. Blend slowly and gradually increase speed until smooth. Transfer the sauce to a serving dish with the cooked pasta. Toss and serve warm. Enjoy!

Tofu Hot Dogs

Ingredients for 6 servings

1 (14-oz) tofu block   ½ tsp shallot powder
1 head romaine lettuce, torn   Salt to taste
1 cup hot sauce   6 vegan hot dog buns, toasted
2 tbsp vegan butter   2 tbsp vegan ranch dressing
1 tbsp cane sugar   2 tbsp chives, thinly sliced
½ tsp garlic powder

Directions and Total Time: 25 minutes

Preheat the oven to 425°F. Line a baking sheet with parchment paper. Slice the tofu horizontally into 2 thin strips. Cut each strip crosswise into 6 pieces. There will be 12 total pieces. Arrange the tofu in a single layer on the baking sheet and bake for 10 minutes. Flip the tofu and bake for another 10 minutes until golden and crisp.

While the tofu is baking, in a medium saucepan, combine hot sauce, butter, sugar, garlic powder, shallot powder, and salt over medium heat. When it just comes to a boil, reduce the heat and simmer until the butter has melted and the sugar has completely dissolved. Remove the resulting sauce from the heat. After the tofu is taken out of the oven, drizzle half of the sauce over the tofu and toss with care to coat. To make the sandwich, add romaine lettuce to a bun and add 2 pieces of tofu next to it. Drizzle with the rest of the sauce and some ranch dressing. Garnish with chives. Serve warm and enjoy.

Cauliflower Fajitas

Ingredients for 4 servings

1 head cauliflower, cut into florets
½ cup corn kernels   1 tbsp Tajín seasoning
4 garlic cloves, sliced   2 scallions, thinly sliced
2 tbsp avocado oil

Directions and Total Time: 30 minutes

Preheat the oven to 425°F. Line a baking sheet with parchment paper. Toss cauliflower, corn, garlic, oil, and Tajin seasoning in a large bowl. Arrange the cauliflower mixture on the baking sheet and bake for 15 minutes. Toss the cauliflower and bake for another 10 minutes until golden. Transfer to a serving dish and garnish with scallions. Serve warm and enjoy.

Pad Thai Noodles with Tofu

Ingredients for 4 servings

1 cup chopped cauliflower florets
1 (14-oz) block tofu, cubed
½ cup vegetable broth
3 tbsp dark-brown sugar
3 tbsp creamy peanut butter
2 tbsp soy sauce
1 lime, juiced and zested

2 tsp sriracha sauce
4 oz rice noodles
1 cup chopped broccoli florets
1/3 cup crushed peanuts
2 scallions, thinly sliced
2 tbsp chopped chives

Directions and Total Time: 25 minutes

Preheat the oven to 425°F. Line a baking sheet with parchment paper. Arrange the tofu in a single layer on the baking sheet. Bake for 10 minutes and toss with a spatula. Bake for another 10 minutes until golden. While the tofu is baking, whisk broth, sugar, peanut butter, soy sauce, lime juice, lime zest, and sriracha in a small bowl. Cook the rice noodles according to the package directions. In the last 2 minutes of boiling the noodles, add the broccoli and cauliflower. Drain the pot with a colander and return the noodles and vegetables to the pot. Stir in peanut butter sauce and tofu until coated. Spoon the pad thai into 4 bowls. Garnish with crushed peanuts, chives, and scallions. Serve warm and enjoy.

Rosemary Potato Mash

Ingredients for 4 servings

3 lb Yukon gold potatoes, peeled and cubed
Salt and black pepper to taste   ¼ cup almond milk
¼ cup vegan butter

Directions and Total Time: 30 minutes

In a large stockpot, add potatoes and enough water to cover them. Salt the water and turn the heat to medium-high. Bring the water to a boil and cook the potatoes for 12-18 minutes. When the potatoes are fork-tender, drain in a colander and return to the pot. Add butter and milk to the potatoes, then mash them to the desired consistency. Season with salt and pepper. Serve warm.

Tofu Muffins

Ingredients for 6 servings

1 cup diced white button mushrooms
1 (14-oz) block tofu
½ cup vegetable broth
2 tbsp olive oil
1 tbsp cornstarch
1 tsp onion powder
1 tsp garlic powder

½ tsp ground turmeric
Salt to taste
1 chopped shallot
½ red bell pepper, chopped
1 tsp dried rosemary

Directions and Total Time: 30 minutes

Preheat the oven to 425°F. Lightly spray nonstick cooking spray on a 12-cup muffin tin. Add tofu, broth, oil, cornstarch, onion powder, garlic powder, turmeric, and salt to a blender jar. Blend until smooth. Pour into a large bowl and add shallot, bell pepper, mushrooms, and rosemary. Stir to combine. Scoop ¼ cup of the mixture into each muffin cup. Bake for 20 to 25 minutes until a toothpick in the middle comes out clean. Serve warm.

Primavera Spaghetti Squash

Ingredients for 4 servings

4 lb halved spaghetti squash, seeded
2 cups chopped broccoli florets
3 tbsp olive oil
1 onion, chopped
1 celery stalk, chopped
½ cup green olives, sliced
1 cup halved grape tomatoes
3 garlic cloves, minced

1 tsp dried oregano
Salt and black pepper to taste
1 tbsp pine nuts
2 tbsp vegan Parmesan cheese
½ tsp red pepper flakes

Directions and Total Time: 50 minutes

Preheat the oven to 400°F. Line a baking sheet with parchment paper. Brush 1 tablespoon oil on the rims and inside of the squash. Place cut-side down on the baking sheet and bake for 35 to 45 minutes. When the flesh is fork-tender, set the squash aside to cool for 10 to 15 minutes. In a large skillet, heat 1 tablespoon of oil over medium heat. Sauté onion, garlic, broccoli, and celery for 3 minutes until softened. Stir in olives and tomatoes. Cook for 3 to 5 minutes until the tomatoes have shrunk and the broccoli is fork-tender. Remove from heat. Scrape the strands gently from the squash lengthwise for the longest noodles. Add the noodles to the skillet and gently stir along with 1 tablespoon oil, oregano, salt, and pepper. Portion among 4 bowls. Top with pine nuts, Parmesan, and red pepper flakes. Serve warm and enjoy.

Spinach & Tofu Stuffed Portobellos

Ingredients for 4 servings

1 tbsp olive oil
1 leek, chopped
3 garlic cloves, minced
1 (14-oz) block tofu, crumbled
5 oz baby spinach
2 tsp Italian seasoning

1 tsp onion powder
½ tsp garlic powder
½ tsp ground nutmeg
1 tomato, chopped
Salt and black pepper to taste
4 portobello mushroom caps

Directions and Total Time: 35 minutes

Preheat the oven to 450°F. Lightly spray a baking sheet with cooking oil. Heat oil in a large skillet over medium heat. Sauté leeks for 3 minutes until softened. Sauté garlic for 1 minute until aromatic. Add tofu and spinach to the skillet. Cook for 3 minutes to wilt the spinach. Stir in Italian seasoning, onion powder, garlic powder, nutmeg, tomato, salt, and pepper. Arrange the mushroom caps on the baking sheet with the top side down. Stuff the mushroom caps with the tofu mixture and bake for 15 to 20 minutes. The stuffing will be golden. Serve warm.

Veggie & Quinoa Fajitas

Ingredients for 4 servings

½ cup blanched almonds
2 tbsp fajita seasoning
1 tbsp olive oil
2 green onions, chopped
1 cup Bella mushrooms, diced

1 cup cooked quinoa
5 oz baby spinach
12 corn tortillas
2 tbsp vegan sour cream
2 tbsp salsa

Directions and Total Time: 45 minutes

Preheat the oven to 425°F. Line a baking sheet with parchment paper. Add almonds, ¾ cup water, and fajita seasoning to a blender jar. Blend for 2 minutes until smooth. Warm the oil in a large skillet over medium heat. Sauté green onions and mushrooms for 3 to 5 minutes until mushrooms reduce in size. Stir in quinoa and spinach to wilt the spinach. After 3 minutes, reduce the heat and stir in the almond mixture. Remove from the heat. Arrange the tortillas on the baking sheet. They can overlap. Bake for 2 minutes, then transfer to a large plate.

Take one of the tortillas and place on a flat work surface. Add 2 heaping tablespoons to the part of the tortilla closest to you. Tuck in the sides and roll the tortilla away from you. Transfer the fajita to the baking sheet and place seam-side down. Continue rolling the rest of the fajitas. Lightly spray with cooking oil. Bake for 18 minutes until golden. Top with sour cream and salsa. Serve warm.

Picante Zucchini Boats with Chickpeas & Kale

Ingredients for 4 servings

1 (15-oz) can chickpeas, half mashed and a half left whole
½ cup cayenne-based hot sauce
2 large green zucchinis
2 cups chopped baby kale
1 tbsp vegan butter, melted
¼ tsp garlic powder

¼ tsp shallot powder
Salt to taste
2 tbsp vegan ranch
2 tbsp chopped parsley

Directions and Total Time: 30 minutes

Preheat the oven to 450°F. Cut the zucchini lengthwise and scoop out some of the flesh from each half. Leave about ¼"-thick wall for the shell. Combine mashed chickpeas, whole chickpeas, kale, cayenne hot sauce, butter, garlic, shallot powder, and salt in a large bowl. Spoon the mixture into the zucchini shells, then place on a parchment-lined baking sheet. Bake for 15 to 20 minutes until the zucchini is fork-tender. Drizzle with ranch and top with parsley. Serve.

Green Chili Guacamole

Ingredients for 4 servings

2 avocados, diced
1 Roma tomato, chopped
1 green chili, minced
2 minced spring onions

½ lime, juiced
2 tbsp chopped cilantro
Salt and black pepper to taste
Tortilla chips for serving

Directions and Total Time: 20 minutes

Put the avocados, tomato, green chili, spring onions, lime juice, salt, pepper, and cilantro in a large bowl. Crush with a fork until well combined. Serve with tortilla chips.

Cornbread Zucchini Muffins

Ingredients for 6 servings

1 cup almond milk
1 tbsp apple cider vinegar
1 cup ground yellow cornmeal
¾ cup all-purpose flour
¼ cup sucanat

2 tsp baking soda
Salt to taste
¼ cup coconut oil
3 cups grated green zucchini

Directions and Total Time: 30 minutes

Preheat the oven to 400°F. Lightly spray nonstick cooking spray on a 12-cup muffin tin or use muffin liners.
Whisk milk and vinegar in a small bowl. Whisk cornmeal, flour, sucanat, baking soda, and salt to a large bowl. Stir in milk mixture and coconut oil until combined. Fold in zucchini. Add ¼ cup of the batter to each muffin cup. Bake for 20 to 22 minutes or until golden. Serve warm.

Fall Squash Risotto

Ingredients for 4 servings

1 lb acorn squash, peeled, seeded, and cubed
1 cup brown rice
1 leek, chopped
4 garlic cloves, minced
1 tsp dried thyme
¼ tsp ground nutmeg

3 cups vegetable broth
¼ cup yellow mustard
Salt and black pepper to taste
2 tbsp olive oil
2 tbsp parsley, chopped

Directions and Total Time: 30 minutes

Warm the olive oil in a saucepan over medium heat. Sauté the leek and garlic for 3 minutes until softened. Add the squash, brown rice, thyme, and nutmeg and stir for 1-3 more minutes. Add the broth and cook until the liquid absorbs, stirring periodically, about 20 minutes. Stir in mustard, salt, and pepper. Top with parsley and serve.

Mouth-Watering Mushroom Noodles

Ingredients for 6 servings

2 cups white button mushrooms, sliced
8 oz rice noodles
3 tbsp toasted sesame oil
1 sliced red onion
1 green bell pepper, sliced

2 tbsp chili-garlic sauce
2 tbsp soy sauce
½ lime, juiced
1 cup chopped cilantro

Directions and Total Time: 25 minutes

Cook the pasta according to the directions. Drain in a colander and return to the pot. Toss with 1 tablespoon sesame oil, then set aside. Heat 1 tablespoon sesame oil in a large skillet over medium heat. Sauté onion and bell pepper for 5 minutes until softened. Add another tablespoon of sesame oil and sauté the mushrooms for 5 minutes. When the mushrooms have reduced in size, stir in chili garlic sauce, soy sauce, and lime juice. Cook for 2 minutes. When the mixture is heated through, toss in noodles and cilantro until well coated. Serve warm.

Home-Style Taro Chips

Ingredients for 2 servings

1 tbsp olive oil
1 cup thinly sliced taro

Salt to taste
½ cup hummus

Directions and Total Time: 20 minutes

Preheat air fryer to 325°F. Put the sliced taro in the greased frying basket, spread the pieces out, and drizzle with olive oil. Air Fry for 10-12 minutes, shaking the basket twice. Sprinkle with salt and serve with hummus.

Chipotle Mushroom Taquitos

Ingredients for 6 servings

2 portobello mushroom caps, sliced	
2 tbsp soy sauce	1 yellow bell pepper, sliced
1 tbsp olive oil	1 red bell pepper, sliced
2 limes, juiced	1 jalapeño pepper, sliced
2 tbsp chopped fresh cilantro	1 onion, sliced
1 tsp ground cumin	12 flour tortillas, warmed
1 tsp garlic powder	½ head lettuce, torn
1 tsp onion powder	½ cup guacamole
1 tsp chipotle powder	3 tbsp vegan sour cream

Directions and Total Time: 20 minutes

Whisk together the soy sauce, oil, lime juice, cilantro, cumin, garlic powder, onion powder, and chipotle powder in a medium bowl. Stir in the mushrooms and let sit for at least 10 minutes. After that, toss the bell peppers, jalapeño pepper, and onions with the mushroom until coated with the marinade. In a large skillet, add the vegetables and marinade over medium heat. Cook for 8 minutes stirring occasionally. When the vegetables are tender and the liquid has been absorbed, transfer to a serving dish with lettuce, guacamole, and sour cream on the side. Serve warm with tortillas and enjoy.

Tex-Mex Stuffed Avocado

Ingredients for 4 servings

2 halved avocados, pitted	1 garlic clove, minced
1 (15-oz) can black beans	1 tsp olive oil
1 cup corn kernels	Salt and black pepper to taste
½ cup diced tomatoes	¼ tsp smoked paprika
½ lime, juiced	1 tbsp chopped cilantro

Directions and Total Time: 20 minutes

Remove some flesh from the avocado, leaving about ¼ to ½-inch wall for stability. Transfer the avocado flesh to a large mixing bowl. Combine with the rest of the ingredients until thoroughly mixed. Divide the mixture among the avocado shells. Serve and enjoy.

Orange-Glazed Carrots

Ingredients for 3 servings

3 carrots, cut into spears	1 tsp maple syrup
1 tbsp orange juice	½ tsp dried rosemary
2 tsp balsamic vinegar	¼ tsp salt
1 tsp avocado oil	¼ tsp lemon zest

Directions and Total Time: 25 minutes

Preheat air fryer to 390°F. Put the carrots in a baking pan. Add the orange juice, balsamic vinegar, oil, maple syrup, rosemary, salt, and zest. Stir well. Roast for 15-18 minutes, shaking them once or twice until the carrots are bright orange, glazed, and tender. Serve hot and enjoy!

Lentil Sloppy Joes

Ingredients for 4 servings

2 tsp hot sauce	1 (7-oz) can tomato sauce
2 tbsp olive oil	1 tbsp dark-brown sugar
1 onion, chopped	1 tbsp red pepper flakes
½ green bell pepper, chopped	1 tsp ground cumin
1 garlic clove, minced	½ tsp ground fennel seeds
1 (15-oz) can lentils	4 hamburger buns, toasted

Directions and Total Time: 25 minutes

Warm the olive oil in a large skillet over medium heat. Sauté the onion and bell pepper for 3 minutes until onion is softened. Reduce the heat to medium and sauté garlic for 1 minute until aromatic. Stir in lentils and heat through for 2 minutes. Stir in tomato sauce, hot sauce, sugar, red pepper flakes, cumin and fennel seeds. Cover and simmer for 10 minutes. Add salt and pepper. Portion the sloppy joes between the buns. Serve warm and enjoy.

Meatless Lentil Alla Bolognese

Ingredients for 4 servings

1 tbsp olive oil	2 tsp dried rosemary
1 onion, chopped	Salt to taste
2 carrots, peeled and grated	1 tsp red pepper flakes
4 garlic cloves, minced	3 cups tomato sauce
1 (15-oz) can lentils	16 oz cooked fusilli pasta
1 tbsp dark-brown sugar	

Directions and Total Time: 25 minutes

Warm the olive oil in a large pan over medium heat. Sauté the onion and carrots for 5 minutes until softened. Sauté garlic for 1 minute until aromatic. Stir in lentils, sugar, rosemary, salt, and pepper flakes. Next, add tomato sauce and simmer for 5 minutes. When everything is heated through, ladle the sauce over the cooked pasta. Serve.

Pesto Brown Rice with Lima Beans

Ingredients for 2 servings

1 cup lima beans	6 cherry tomatoes, halved
1 cup vegan pesto sauce	3 cups cooked brown rice

Directions and Total Time: 10 minutes

Heat the pesto sauce, beans and cherry tomatoes in a skillet over medium-low heat for 4-5 minutes, until heated through. Stir in the rice until well mixed and serve.

Thyme Roasted Potatoes

Ingredients for 4 servings

1 ½ lb baby red potatoes, halved	1 tbsp minced fresh thyme
2 tbsp olive oil	Salt and black pepper to taste
3 garlic cloves, minced	

Directions and Total Time: 35 minutes

Preheat the oven to 425°F. Combine all of the ingredients in a large bowl until well coated. Arrange the potatoes in a single layer on a parchment-lined baking sheet and bake for 15 minutes. Toss the potatoes with a spatula and bake for another 15 minutes until golden. Serve warm.

Crispy Mushrooms

Ingredients for 4 servings

2 portobello mushroom caps, cut into ¼-inch-thick strips
3 tbsp olive oil
2 tsp shoyu sauce
Salt and black pepper to taste
2 tbsp rosemary, chopped

Directions and Total Time: 30 minutes

Preheat the oven to 375°F. Line a baking sheet with parchment paper. Toss mushrooms, oil, shoyu sauce, salt, and pepper in a medium bowl until coated. Arrange on the baking sheet in a single layer. Bake for 15 minutes, then toss the mushrooms with a spatula. Bake for another 10 to 15 minutes until the mushrooms are darkened and reduced in size. Top with rosemary. Serve warm.

Five Spice Fries

Ingredients for 2 servings

1 Yukon Gold potato, cut into fries
1 tbsp coconut oil
1 tsp coconut sugar
1 tsp garlic powder
½ tsp Chinese five-spice
Salt to taste
¼ tsp turmeric
¼ tsp paprika

Directions and Total Time: 30 minutes

Preheat air fryer to 390°F. Toss the potato pieces with coconut oil, sugar, garlic, Chinese five-spice, salt, turmeric, and paprika in a bowl and stir well. Place in the greased frying basket and Air Fry for 18-25 minutes, tossing twice, until softened and golden. Serve warm.

Curried Veggie Samosas

Ingredients for 4 servings

4 cooked potatoes, mashed
¼ cup peas
2 tsp coconut oil
3 garlic cloves, minced
1 ½ tbsp lemon juice
1 ½ tsp cumin powder
1 tsp onion powder
1 tsp ground coriander
Salt to taste
½ tsp curry powder
¼ tsp cayenne powder
10 rice paper wrappers
1 cup cilantro chutney

Directions and Total Time: 30 minutes

Preheat air fryer to 390°F. In a bowl, place the mashed potatoes. Add the peas, oil, garlic, lemon juice, cumin, onion powder, coriander, salt, curry powder, and cayenne. Stir well. Fill a bowl with water. Soak a rice paper wrapper in the water for a few seconds. Lay it on a flat surface. Place ¼ cup of the potato filling in the center of the wrapper and roll like a burrito or spring roll. Repeat the process until you run out of ingredients. Place the "samosas" inside the greased frying basket, separating them. Air Fry for 8-10 minutes or until hot and crispy around the edges. Let cool for a few minutes. Enjoy with the cilantro chutney.

Toasted Choco-Nuts

Ingredients for 2 servings

2 cups almonds
2 tsp maple syrup
2 tbsp cacao powder

Directions and Total Time: 10 minutes

Preheat air fryer to 350°F. Distribute the almonds in a single layer in the frying basket and Bake for 3 minutes. Shake the basket and Bake for another 1 minute until golden brown. Remove them to a bowl. Drizzle with maple syrup and toss. Sprinkle with cacao powder and toss until well coated. Let cool completely. Store in a container at room temperature for up to 2 weeks or in the fridge for up to a month.

Garam Masala Cauliflower Pakoras

Ingredients for 4 servings

½ cup finely chopped cauliflower
2/3 cup chickpea flour
1 tbsp cornstarch
Salt to taste
2 tsp cumin powder
½ tsp coriander powder
½ tsp turmeric
1 tsp garam masala
⅛ tsp baking soda
⅛ tsp cayenne powder
1 ½ cups minced onion
½ cup chopped cilantro
¼ cup lime juice

Directions and Total Time: 30 minutes

Preheat your air fryer to 350°F. Combine the flour, cornstarch, salt, cumin, coriander, turmeric, garam masala, baking soda, and cayenne in a bowl. Stir well. Stir in the onion, cilantro, cauliflower, and lime juice to the flour mix. Using your hands, stir the mix, massaging the flour and spices into the vegetables. Form the mixture into balls and place them in the greased frying basket. Spray the tops of the pakoras in the air fryer with oil and Air Fry for 15-18 minutes, turning once until crispy.

No-Guilty Spring Rolls

Ingredients for 6 servings

2 cups shiitake mushrooms, thinly sliced
4 cups green cabbage, chopped
4 tsp sesame oil
6 garlic cloves, minced
1 tbsp grated ginger
1 cup grated carrots
Salt to taste
16 rice paper wraps
½ tsp ground cumin
½ tsp ground coriander

Directions and Total Time: 20 minutes

Warm the sesame oil in a pan over medium heat. Add garlic, ginger, mushrooms, cabbage, carrots, cumin, coriander, and salt and stir-fry for 3-4 minutes or until the cabbage is wilted. Remove from heat. Get a piece of rice paper, wet with water, and lay it on a flat, non-absorbent surface. Place ¼ cup of the filling in the middle, then fold the bottom over the filling and fold the sides in. Roll up to make a mini burrito. Repeat until you have the number of spring rolls you want. Preheat air fryer to 390°F. Place the spring rolls in the greased frying basket. Spray the top of each spring roll with oil and Air Fry for 8-10 minutes or until crispy and golden.

Garlic-Parmesan Popcorn

Ingredients for 2 servings

¼ cup popcorn kernels
1 tbsp lemon juice
1 tsp garlic powder
2 tsp grated vegan Parmesan

Directions and Total Time: 15 minutes

Preheat air fryer to 400°F. Line the basket with aluminum foil. Put in the popcorn kernels in a single layer. Grill for 6-8 minutes until they stop popping. Remove them into a bowl. Drizzle with lemon juice and toss until well coated. Sprinkle with garlic powder and grated Parmesan and toss to coat. Drizzle with more lemon juice. Serve.

Caraway Seed Pretzel Sticks

Ingredients for 4 servings

½ pizza dough	1 tsp baking soda
Flour, for dusting	2 tbsp caraway seeds

Directions and Total Time: 30 minutes

Preheat air fryer to 400°F. Roll out the dough, on parchment paper, into a rectangle, then cut it into 8 strips. Whisk the baking soda and 1 cup of hot water until well dissolved in a bowl. Submerge each strip, shake off any excess, and stretch another 1 to 2 inches. Scatter with caraway seeds and let rise for 10 minutes in the frying basket. Grease with cooking spray and Air Fry for 8 minutes until golden brown, turning once. Serve.

Cheesy Potato Skins

Ingredients for 4 servings

2 russet potatoes, halved lengthwise
½ cup Alfredo sauce   1 tbsp grated vegan Parmesan
2 scallions, chopped

Directions and Total Time: 50 minutes

Preheat air fryer to 400°F. Wrap each potato, cut-side down with parchment paper, and Roast for 30 minutes. Carefully scoop out the potato flesh, leaving ¼-inch meat, and place it in a bowl. Stir in Alfredo sauce, scallions, and Parmesan cheese until well combined. Fill each potato skin with the cheese mixture and Grill for 3-4 minutes until crispy. Serve right away.

Rich Spinach Chips

Ingredients for 4 servings

10 oz spinach	Salt and black pepper to taste
2 tbsp lemon juice	½ tsp garlic powder
2 tbsp olive oil	½ tsp onion powder

Directions and Total Time: 20 minutes

Preheat air fryer to 350°F. Place the spinach in a bowl, and drizzle with lemon juice and olive oil and massage with your hands. Scatter with salt, pepper, garlic, and onion and gently toss to coat well. Arrange the leaves in a single layer and Bake for 3 minutes, shake and Bake for another 1-3 minutes until brown. Let cool completely.

Spicy Roasted Cauliflower

Ingredients for 4 servings

½ head cauliflower, cut into florets	
¼ cup chopped red onion	3 tbsp enchilada sauce
¾ cup chickpea flour	2 tbsp lime juice
2 tsp allspice	½ cup almond milk

Directions and Total Time: 30 minutes

Preheat oven to 360°F. Beat the chickpea flour, allspice, 2 tbsp of hot sauce, 1 tbsp of lime juice, and milk in a shallow bowl. Add in cauliflower florets and toss until completely coated. Bake for 15 minutes until browned and crispy, turning once. Whisk 1 tbsp of enchilada sauce, red onion, and 1 tbsp of lime juice until well combined. Drizzle over the cauliflower. Serve and enjoy!

Crispy Samosa Rolls

Ingredients for 4 servings

2/3 cup canned peas	1 tsp curry powder
4 scallions, finely sliced	1 tsp Garam masala
2 cups grated potatoes	¼ cup chickpea flour
2 tbsp lemon juice	1 tbsp tahini
1 tsp ground ginger	8 rice paper wrappers

Directions and Total Time: 30 minutes

Preheat air fryer to 350°F. Mix the peas, scallions, potatoes, lemon juice, ginger, curry powder, Garam masala, and chickpea flour in a bowl. In another bowl, whisk tahini and 1/3 cup of water until combined. Set aside on a plate. Submerge the rice wrappers, one by one, into the tahini mixture until they begin to soften and set aside on a plate. Fill each wrap with 1/3 cup of the veggie mixture and wrap them into a roll. Bake for 15 minutes until golden brown and crispy, turning once.

Balsamic Stuffed Mushrooms

Ingredients for 4 servings

¼ cup chopped roasted red peppers
10 oz spinach, chopped   1 tsp garlic powder
3 scallions, chopped   1 tbsp balsamic vinegar
¼ cup chickpea flour   12 portobello mushroom caps
1 tbsp grated vegan Parmesan   ½ lemon

Directions and Total Time: 30 minutes

Preheat air fryer to 360°F. To a bowl, add the spinach. Add the scallions, red pepper, chickpea flour, vegan Parmesan cheese, garlic, and balsamic vinegar and stir until well combined. Fill each mushroom cap with the spinach mixture until covering the tops, pressing down slightly. Bake for 12 minutes until crispy. Drizzle with lemon juice before serving. Enjoy!

Turkish Mutabal (Eggplant Dip)

Ingredients for 2 servings

1 medium eggplant	1 tsp garlic powder
2 tbsp tahini	¼ tsp sumac
2 tbsp lemon juice	1 tsp chopped parsley

Directions and Total Time: 40 minutes

Preheat air fryer to 400°F. Place the eggplant in a pan and roast for 30 minutes, turning once. Let cool for 5-10 minutes. Scoop out the flesh and place it in a bowl. Squeeze any excess water; discard the water. Mix the flesh, tahini, lemon juice, garlic, and sumac until well combined. Scatter with parsley and serve.

Quick-To-Make Quesadillas

Ingredients for 4 servings

1 ½ cups cherry tomatoes, halved
12 oz vegan goat cheese
2 tbsp vinegar
1 tbsp taco seasoning
1 ripe avocado, pitted
4 scallions, finely sliced
2 tbsp lemon juice
4 flour tortillas
¼ cup hot sauce
½ cup Alfredo sauce

Directions and Total Time: 30 minutes

Preheat air fryer to 400°F. Slice goat cheese into 4 pieces. Set aside. In a bowl, whisk vinegar and taco seasoning until combined. Submerge each slice into the vinegar and Air Fry for 12 minutes until crisp, turning once. Let cool slightly before cutting into ½-inch thick strips.

Using a fork, mash the avocado in a bowl. Stir in scallions and lemon juice and set aside. Lay one tortilla on a flat surface, cut from one edge to the center, then spread ¼ of the avocado mixture on one quadrant, 1 tbsp of hot sauce on the next quadrant, and finally 2 tbsp of Alfredo sauce on the other half. Top the non-sauce half with ¼ of cherry tomatoes and ¼ of goat cheese strips. To fold, start with the avocado quadrant, folding each over the next one until you create a stacked triangle. Repeat the process with the remaining tortillas. Air Fry for 5 minutes until crispy, turning once. Serve warm.

Black Bean Fajitas

Ingredients for 2 servings

1 (15.5-oz) black beans
1 tbsp fajita seasoning
2 tbsp lime juice
2 flour tortillas
¼ cup salsa
2 scallions, thinly sliced
1 tbsp hot sauce

Directions and Total Time: 20 minutes

Preheat air fryer to 400°F. Using a fork, mash the beans until smooth. Stir in fajita seasoning and lime juice. Set aside. Place tortillas on a flat surface, spread half of the salsa on each tortilla, scatter with scallions, and top with the bean mixture. Drizzle with the hot sauce. For the burritos, fold in the sides of the tortilla, then fold up the bottom, and finally roll up. Grill for 10 minutes until crispy, turning once. Serve warm and enjoy!

Green Dip with Pine Nuts

Ingredients for 3 servings

10 oz canned artichokes, chopped
2 scallions, finely chopped
½ cup pine nuts
½ cup almond milk
3 tbsp lemon juice
2 tsp grated vegan Parmesan
2 tsp tapioca flour
10 oz spinach, chopped
1 tsp allspice

Directions and Total Time: 30 minutes

Preheat air fryer to 360°F. Arrange spinach, artichokes, and scallions in a pan. Set aside. In a food processor, blitz the pine nuts, milk, lemon juice, Parmesan cheese, flour, and allspice on high until smooth. Pour it over the veggies and Bake for 20 minutes, stirring every 5 minutes.

Easy Zucchini Lasagna Roll-Ups

Ingredients for 2 servings

2 medium zucchini
2 tbsp lemon juice
1 ½ cups vegan ricotta cheese
1 tbsp allspice
2 cups marinara sauce
½ cup grated vegan mozzarella

Directions and Total Time: 40 minutes

Preheat oven to 400°F. Cut the ends of each zucchini, then slice into ¼-inch thick pieces and drizzle with lemon juice. Roast for 5 minutes until slightly tender. Let cool slightly. Combine vegan ricotta cheese and allspice in a bowl; set aside. Spread 2 tbsp of marinara sauce on the bottom of a baking pan. Spoon 1-2 tbsp of the ricotta mixture onto each slice, roll up each slice and place them spiral-side up in the pan. Scatter with the remaining ricotta mixture and drizzle with marinara sauce. Top with vegan mozzarella and Bake at 360°F for 20 minutes until the cheese is bubbly and golden brown. Serve warm.

Provence French Fries

Ingredients for 4 servings

2 russet potatoes
1 tbsp olive oil
1 tbsp herbs de Provence

Directions and Total Time: 25 minutes

Preheat air fryer to 400°F. Slice the potatoes lengthwise into ½-inch thick strips. In a bowl, whisk the olive oil and herbs de Provence. Toss in the potatoes to coat. Arrange them in a single and Air Fry for 18-20 minutes, shaking once, until crispy. Serve warm and enjoy!

Burritos Enmolados with Tofu

Ingredients for 2 servings

1 ½ cups shredded red cabbage
4 tbsp lime juice
2 tbsp mole hot sauce
½ tsp ground cumin
16 oz super-firm tofu
2 scallions, finely sliced
1 ½ tbsp vegan mayonnaise
2 tbsp chopped cilantro
4 corn tortillas

Directions and Total Time: 30 minutes

Preheat air fryer to 400°F. Whisk 2 tbsp of lime juice, 1 tbsp of mole sauce and cumin until smooth. Set aside. Slice tofu into 4 pieces. Submerge the slices into the sauce and arrange them in a single layer. Drizzle with half of the sauce and Air Fry for 6 minutes. Turn the slices, drizzle with the remaining sauce, and Air Fry for another 6 minutes. Let cool slightly before cutting into ½-inch strips. Combine red cabbage, scallions, mayonnaise, cilantro, 2 tbsp of lime juice, and 1 tbsp of hot sauce. Set aside. Air Fry corn tortillas for 2-3 minutes in a single layer. For the tacos, fill each tortilla with ¼ of slaw and top each with ¼ of tofu strips. Serve immediately.

Original Grilled Cheese Sandwiches

Ingredients for 2 servings

¼ cup sliced roasted red peppers
¼ cup Alfredo sauce
4 bread slices
¼ cup vegan mozzarella
3 tbsp sliced red onions

Directions and Total Time: 15 minutes

Preheat air fryer to 400°F. Lay 2 bread slices on a flat surface, spread some Alfredo sauce on one side, and place them in the frying basket. Scatter with mozzarella cheese, roasted peppers, and red onion. Drizzle with the remaining Alfredo sauce and top with the remaining bread slices. Grill for 4 minutes, turn the sandwiches, and Grill for 3 more minutes until toasted. Serve warm.

Sriracha Spring Rolls

Ingredients for 4 servings

2 tbsp nut butter	4 scallions, sliced
2 tbsp lime juice	16 oz coleslaw mix
1 tbsp sriracha hot sauce	8 spring roll wrappers

Directions and Total Time: 30 minutes

Preheat air fryer to 350°F. Whisk the nut butter, lime juice, and hot sauce in a bowl. Stir in scallions and coleslaw until well coated. Lay the wrappers face up, and fill each with 1/8 cup of filling onto the corner. Then fold up over the filling, pushing back to compact it, and finally fold the sides. Grease them with cooking spray and Bake for 17 minutes until golden brown and crispy, turning once. Serve warm and enjoy!

Chickpea Cakes

Ingredients for 4 servings

1 (14-oz) can chickpeas	½ tsp cayenne pepper
½ red bell pepper, chopped	2 tbsp lemon juice
3 scallions, chopped	2 tbsp vegan mayonnaise
¼ tsp garlic powder	1 cup chickpea flour

Directions and Total Time: 25 minutes

Preheat air fryer to 400°F. Using a fork, mash the chickpeas. Combine them with bell pepper, scallions, garlic, cayenne pepper, lemon juice, and mayonnaise until well mixed in a bowl. Mix in chickpea flour until fully incorporated. Make 6 equal patties out of the mixture and Air Fry for 13-15 minutes until browned and crispy, turning once. Serve immediately and enjoy!

Crunchy Green Beans

Ingredients for 4 servings

1 tbsp tahini	1 tsp allspice
1 tbsp lemon juice	1 lb green beans, trimmed

Directions and Total Time: 15 minutes

Preheat air fryer to 400°F. Whisk tahini, lemon juice, 1 tbsp of water, and allspice in a bowl. Put in the green beans and toss to coat. Roast for 5 minutes until golden brown and cooked. Serve immediately.

Avocado-Sweet Potato Bites

Ingredients for 2 servings

2 sweet potatoes, cut lengthwise into slices	
Salt and black pepper to taste	1 tomato, chopped
2 avocados, peeled and pitted	1 tsp chopped cilantro
½ tsp hot sauce	

Directions and Total Time: 20 minutes

Preheat the oven to 450°F. Line a baking sheet with parchment paper. Arrange the sweet potato in a single layer on the baking sheet, spraying both sides lightly with cooking oil. Season with salt and pepper. Bake for 6 minutes and flip the slice. Bake for 6 minutes until golden. In a small bowl, mash avocado with salt and pepper. Top the sweet potatoes with the avocado mash. Drizzle with hot sauce. Top with tomatoes and cilantro.

Pizza-Style Hot Avocado Tortillas

Ingredients for 2 servings

¼ cup thinly sliced sundried tomatoes	
2 flour tortillas	½ tsp garlic powder
1 pitted avocado, peeled	¼ cup chopped fresh basil
½ lime, juiced	¼ tsp red pepper flakes
Salt and black pepper to taste	

Directions and Total Time: 15 minutes

Preheat the oven to 370°F. Arrange the tortillas on a parchment-lined baking sheet and lightly spray with cooking oil. Bake for 5 minutes, then flip the tortillas. Lightly spray again and bake for 3 minutes until golden and just crisp. Mash avocado together with lime juice, garlic powder, salt, and pepper in a medium bowl. Spread the avocado mixture over each tortilla. Top with tomatoes, basil, and red pepper flakes. Serve and enjoy.

Savory Eggplant Fries

Ingredients for 4 servings

1 eggplant, sliced	2 tsp onion powder
2 ½ tbsp shoyu	4 tsp olive oil
2 tsp garlic powder	2 tbsp fresh basil, chopped

Directions and Total Time: 20 minutes

Preheat air fryer to 390°F. Place the eggplant slices in a bowl and sprinkle the shoyu, garlic, onion, and oil on top. Coat the eggplant evenly. Place the eggplant in a single layer in the greased frying basket and Air Fry for 5 minutes. Remove and put the eggplant in the bowl again. Toss the eggplant slices to coat evenly with the remaining liquid and put back in the fryer. Roast for another 3 minutes. Remove the basket and flip the pieces over to ensure even cooking. Roast for another 5 minutes or until the eggplant is golden and tender. Top with basil.

Thyme Sweet Potato Chips

Ingredients for 2 servings

1 sweet potato, unpeeled, thinly sliced	
1 tbsp olive oil	Salt to taste
¼ tsp dried thyme	

Directions and Total Time: 20 minutes

Preheat air fryer to 390°F. Spread the sweet potato slices in the greased basket and brush with olive oil. Air Fry for 6 minutes. Remove the basket, shake, and sprinkle with thyme and salt. Cook for 6 more minutes or until lightly browned. Serve warm and enjoy!

Yellow Onion Rings

Ingredients for 3 servings

½ sweet yellow onion	Salt and black pepper to taste
½ cup cream of tartar	¾ tsp garlic powder
¾ cup flour	½ tsp dried oregano
1 tbsp cornstarch	1 cup bread crumbs

Directions and Total Time: 30 minutes

Preheat air fryer to 390°F. Cut the onion into ½-inch slices. Separate the onion slices into rings. Place the cream of tartar in a bowl and set aside. In another bowl, combine the flour, cornstarch, salt, pepper, and garlic. Stir well and set aside. In a separate bowl, combine the breadcrumbs with oregano and salt. Dip the rings into the cream of tartar, dredge in flour, dip into the cream again, and then coat into the crumb mixture. Put the greased frying basket without overlapping. Spritz them with cooking oil and Air Fry for 13-16 minutes, shaking once or twice until the rings are crunchy and browned.

Korean Brussels Sprouts

Ingredients for 4 servings

1 lb trimmed Brussels sprouts	1 ½ tsp soy sauce
1 ½ tbsp maple syrup	2 garlic cloves, minced
1 ½ tsp white miso	1 tsp grated fresh ginger
1 tsp toasted sesame oil	½ tsp Gochugaru chili flakes

Directions and Total Time: 20 minutes

Preheat air fryer to 390°F. Place the Brussels sprouts in the greased basket, spray with oil and Air Fry for 10-14 minutes, tossing once, until crispy, tender, and golden. In a bowl, combine maple syrup and miso. Whisk until smooth. Add the sesame oil, soy sauce, garlic, ginger, and Gochugaru flakes. Stir well. When the Brussels sprouts are done, add them to the bowl and toss with the sauce.

Cholula Onion Rings

Ingredients for 4 servings

1 large Vidalia onion	2 tbsp Cholula hot sauce
½ cup chickpea flour	1 tsp allspice
1/3 cup almond milk	2/3 cup bread crumbs
2 tbsp lemon juice	

Directions and Total Time: 30 minutes

Preheat air fryer to 380°F. Cut ½-inch off the top of the onion's root, then cut into ½-inch thick rings. Set aside. Combine the chickpea flour, milk, lemon juice, hot sauce, and allspice in a bowl. In another bowl, add in breadcrumbs. Submerge each ring into the flour batter until well coated, then dip into the breadcrumbs, and Air Fry for 14 minutes until brown and crispy, turning once.

Healthy Seed Crackers

Ingredients for 6 servings

¼ cup plant butter, melted	1/3 cup sesame seeds
1/3 cup sesame seed flour	1/3 cup chia seeds
1/3 cup pumpkin seeds	1 tbsp psyllium husk powder
1/3 cup sunflower seeds	1 tsp salt

Directions and Total Time: 60 minutes

Preheat oven to 300°F. Combine the sesame seed flour with pumpkin seeds, sunflower seeds, sesame seeds, chia seeds, psyllium husk powder, and salt. Pour in the plant butter and 1 cup of boiling water and mix the ingredients until a dough forms with a gel-like consistency. Line a baking sheet with parchment paper and place the dough on the sheet. Cover the dough with another parchment paper and, with a rolling pin, flatten the dough into the baking sheet. Remove the parchment paper on top.

Tuck the baking sheet in the oven and bake for 45 minutes. Allow the crackers to cool and dry in the oven, about 10 minutes. After, remove the sheet and break the crackers into small pieces. Serve and enjoy!

Cannellini Dip

Ingredients for 2 servings

1 (16-oz) can cannellini beans	1 tsp dried thyme
1 lemon, juced and zested	¼ cup olive oil
2 garlic cloves	4 whole wheat pita bread

Directions and Total Time: 20 minutes

Place the beans, lemon juice, lemon zest, garlic, thyme, and olive oil in your food processor and blend until smooth. Refrigerate. Serve with pita bread.

Kalamata Tapenade

Ingredients for 2 servings

½ cup kalamata olives	1 tbsp extra-virgin olive oil
1 tbsp capers	1 tbsp lemon juice
2 tbsp chopped parsley	Sea salt to taste
1 tbsp red onion, diced	

Directions and Total Time: 15 minutes

Put the olives, capers, parsley, olive oil, red onion, and lemon juice in a blender and pulse until the mixture is thick and chunky. Season with salt and lemon juice. Keep in the refrigerator for up to 5 days.

Avocado Purée with Sauerkraut

Ingredients for 2 servings

¼ cup sauerkraut, chopped	½ tsp sesame seeds
1 medium avocado, mashed	½ tsp ground flaxseed
Salt and black pepper to taste	

Directions and Total Time: 15 minutes

Combine the sauerkraut, ground flaxseed, and mashed avocado in a bowl. Season with salt and pepper. Sprinkle with sesame seeds before serving.

Authentic Falafel Pitas

Ingredients for 4 servings

2 (16-oz) cans chickpeas	Salt to taste
8 garlic cloves	4 tbsp whole-grain flour
¾ cup fresh parsley	3 whole-grain pitas
1 tbsp cumin	1 Persian cucumber, sliced
½ tbsp smoked paprika	2 tomatoes, sliced
½ lime, zested	1/3 cup tahini sauce

Directions and Total Time: 15 minutes

Preheat the oven to 370°F. Blend together the chickpeas, garlic, parsley, cumin, paprika, lime zest, and salt in your food processor until the mixture resembles breadcrumbs. Sift the flour 1 tablespoon at a time and mix until the mixture becomes a dough. Shape it into small patties. Arrange the patties on a parchment-lined baking sheet and bake them for 18-20 minutes until golden brown, turning once. Split the top of the pitas and fill them with falafel patties, cucumber and tomato slices. Drizzle tahini sauce on top and close the pitas. Serve and enjoy!

Spiced Aishi Baladi (Egyptian Pita)

Ingredients for 4 servings

2 whole-grain pitas, cut into triangles
½ cup almonds, chopped   ½ tsp cumin
1 tbsp sesame seeds   ½ tsp ground coriander
1 tbsp dried thyme   ½ tsp cayenne pepper
½ tsp fennel seeds   2 tbsp extra-virgin olive oil

Directions and Total Time: 15 minutes

Place a skillet over medium heat and add the almonds and sesame seeds. Toast for 4 minutes or until they start to brown. Add the thyme, fennel seeds, cumin, coriander, and cayenne pepper and toast for 1 minute more. Remove the skillet from the heat and transfer the mixture to a food processor. Blitz until grainy consistency forms. Serve with pita and a small dish of olive oil for dipping.

Vegetarian Meal with Tahini Dip

Ingredients for 4 servings

2 ½ cups seedless red grapes   1 tsp sea salt
1 tbsp olive oil   1 cup cherry tomatoes
2 tbsp dried rosemary   1 cucumber, sliced
½ cup tahini   1 tbsp red onion, diced
½ cup water   1 cup black olives, pitted

Directions and Total Time: 40 minutes

Preheat oven to 420°F. Place the grapes in a baking dish and sprinkle with olive oil and rosemary; toss to coat. Roast the grapes for 25 minutes, stirring halfway through cooking. Place the tahini, water, and salt in a small bowl and whisk well. Serve the roasted grapes, tomatoes, cucumber slices, red onion, and olives with the tahini dip.

Colorful Veggie Lettuce Roll-Ups

Ingredients for 2 servings

¼ cup roasted red pepper spread
¼ red bell pepper, cut into strips
¼ green bell pepper, cut into thin strips
4 large round lettuce leaves   ½ carrot, cut into sticks
1 cup shredded cabbage   ½ cucumber, cut into sticks

Directions and Total Time: 20 minutes

Spread the roasted red pepper spread over the center of the lettuce leaves. Divide the cabbage, carrot, bell peppers, and cucumber between the lettuce leaves. Roll up, folding the ends to secure tightly. Serve and enjoy!

Roasted Lentil Dip

Ingredients for 4 servings

1 (16-oz) can red lentils   2 tbsp extra-virgin olive oil
4 oz roasted red peppers   1 tbsp tahini
¼ tsp red chili flakes   1 garlic clove
Juice of 1 lemon   Sea salt to taste

Directions and Total Time: 20 minutes

Blitz the lentils, roasted red peppers, lemon juice, olive oil, tahini, and garlic in your food processor until smooth. Adjust the seasoning with salt. Top with red chili flakes.

Mushroom Gyros

Ingredients for 4 servings

2 cups sliced portobello mushrooms
2 tbsp olive oil   ¼ tsp ground cloves
2/3 cup sliced green onions   2/3 cup hummus
1 ½ tbsp apple cider vinegar   4 whole-flatbreads
1 ½ tbsp soy sauce   2 cups chopped lettuce
2 tsp ground cumin   1 cucumber, seeded and diced
1 tsp ground coriander   3 radishes, sliced
1 tsp paprika

Directions and Total Time: 25 minutes

Warm the olive oil in a saucepan over medium heat. Add the mushrooms and green onions and cook for about 5 minutes until the mushrooms are browned. Pour in the vinegar, soy sauce, cumin, coriander, paprika, and cloves and stir for 1 minute. Deglaze the pan with 3 tbsp of water, stirring to scrape up the browned bits from the bottom, then cook, covered, for another 8 minutes.

Spread the hummus on the flatbreads. Layer half of each flatbread with the cooked mushrooms, chopped lettuce, cucumber, and radishes. Fold the flatbreads in half over the fillings. Serve and enjoy!

Hot Houmous & Carrot Tortillas

Ingredients for 2 servings

2/3 cup Hummus   2 cups baby spinach
2 whole-grain tortilla wraps   ½ tsp cayenne pepper
1 carrot, cut into matchsticks ½ tsp paprika

Directions and Total Time: 15 minutes

Spread one side of each tortilla with half of the hummus. Scatter over the carrot sticks and baby spinach. Sprinkle with paprika and cayenne pepper. Roll up tightly and cut in half. Serve and enjoy!

Tamari Hazelnuts

Ingredients for 1 serving

1 tsp toasted sesame oil   2 tbsp tamari sauce
½ cup raw hazelnuts

Directions and Total Time: 10 minutes

Heat a skillet over medium heat. Place in hazelnuts and toast for 7-8 minutes, moving continually with a spatula. Stir in tamari sauce and sesame oil to coat. Remove and allow the tamari mixture to dry on the hazelnuts. Serve.

Oven-Roasted Baby Potatoes

Ingredients for 4 servings

2 lb baby potatoes
2 tbsp extra-virgin olive oil
4 garlic cloves, minced
1 tbsp dried oregano
Salt and black pepper to taste

Directions and Total Time: 25 minutes

Preheat the oven to 370°F. Place the baby potatoes, olive oil, garlic, oregano, salt, pepper, and lemon juice in a bowl and toss until well-coated. Remove the mixture to a parchment-lined baking tray. Roast for 20 minutes, shaking every 5 minutes, until fork-tender and slightly charred. Serve warm.

Fried Cauliflower with Parsnip Purée

Ingredients for 6 servings

½ cup grated plant-based mozzarella cheese
1 lb peeled parsnips, quartered   30 oz cauliflower florets
½ cup almond milk   A pinch of nutmeg
½ cup breadcrumbs   1 tsp cumin powder
3 tbsp melted plant butter   2 tbsp sesame oil
¼ cup coconut flour   1 cup coconut cream
¼ tsp cayenne pepper

Directions and Total Time: 35 minutes

Preheat oven to 425°F and line a baking sheet with parchment paper. In a small bowl, combine almond milk, coconut flour, and cayenne pepper. In another bowl, mix salt, breadcrumbs, and plant-based mozzarella cheese. Dip each cauliflower floret into the milk mixture, coating properly, and then into the cheese mixture. Place the breaded cauliflower on the baking sheet and bake in the oven for 30 minutes, turning once after 15 minutes.

Make slightly salted water in a saucepan and add the parsnips. Bring to boil over medium heat for 15 minutes or until the parsnips are fork-tender. Drain and transfer to a bowl. Add in melted plant butter, cumin powder, nutmeg, and coconut cream. Puree the ingredients using an immersion blender until smooth. Spoon the parsnip mash into serving plates and drizzle with some sesame oil. Serve with the baked cauliflower when ready.

Hearty Squash Nachos

Ingredients for 4 servings

1 ½ cups coconut oil
1 large yellow squash
1 tbsp taco seasoning
Salt to taste

Directions and Total Time: 26 minutes

With a mandolin slicer, cut the squash into thin, round slices and place in a colander. Sprinkle the squash with a lot of salt and allow sitting for 5 minutes. After, press the water out of the squash and pat dry with a paper towel. Pour the coconut oil into a deep skillet and heat the oil over medium heat. Carefully add the squash slices in the oil, about 20 pieces at a time, and fry until crispy and golden brown. Use a slotted spoon to remove the squash onto a paper towel-lined plate. Sprinkle the slices with taco seasoning and serve.

Sticky Maple Popcorns

Ingredients for 4 servings

1 tsp plant butter, melted
½ cup popcorn kernels
¼ tsp cinnamon powder
½ tsp pure maple syrup
Salt to taste

Directions and Total Time: 15 minutes

Pour the popcorn kernels into a large pot and set over medium heat. Cover the lid and let the kernels pop completely. Shake the pot a few times to ensure even popping, 10 minutes. In a small bowl, mix the cinnamon powder, maple syrup, butter, and salt. When the popcorn is ready, turn the heat off, and toss in the cinnamon mixture until well distributed. Pour the popcorn into serving bowls, allow cooling, and enjoy.

Lemony Pistachio Dip

Ingredients for 4 servings

½ cup olive oil
3 tbsp coconut cream
¼ cup water
Juice of half a lemon
½ tsp smoked paprika
½ tsp cayenne pepper
½ tsp salt
3 oz toasted pistachios

Directions and Total Time: 10 minutes

Pour the pistachios, coconut cream, water, lemon juice, paprika, cayenne pepper, and salt. Puree the ingredients at high speed until smooth. Add the olive oil and puree a little further. Manage the consistency of the dip by adding more oil or water. Spoon the dip into little bowls and serve with julienned celery and carrots.

Baked Chili Eggplant with Almonds

Ingredients for 4 servings

2 tbsp plant butter
2 large eggplants
Salt and black pepper to taste
1 tsp red chili flakes
4 oz raw ground almonds

Directions and Total Time: 30 minutes

Preheat oven to 400°F. Cut off the head of the eggplants and slice the body into 2-inch rounds. Season with salt and black pepper and arrange on a parchment paper-lined baking sheet. Drop thin slices of the plant butter on each eggplant slice, sprinkle with red chili flakes, and bake in the oven for 20 minutes. Slide the baking sheet out and sprinkle with the almonds. Roast further for 5 minutes or until golden brown. Serve and enjoy!

Sweet Brussels Sprouts

Ingredients for 4 servings

1 lb Brussels sprouts, quartered
2 tbsp olive oil
1 tsp maple syrup
1 tbsp balsamic vinegar

Directions and Total Time: 20 minutes

Preheat air fryer to 400°F. Whisk the olive oil, maple syrup, and balsamic vinegar in a bowl. Put in Brussels sprouts and toss to coat. Place them, cut-side up, in a single layer, and Roast for 10 minutes until crispy. Serve.

Roasted Garlic with Coconut-Broccoli Mash

Ingredients for 4 servings

1 head broccoli, cut into florets
2 tbsp olive oil + for garnish   ¼ tsp dried thyme
4 oz plant butter   Juice and zest of half a lemon
½ head garlic   4 tbsp coconut cream
1 tsp salt

Directions and Total Time: 45 minutes

Preheat oven to 400°F. Use a knife to cut a ¼ inch off the top of the garlic cloves, drizzle with olive oil, and wrap in aluminum foil. Place on a baking sheet and roast for 30 minutes. Remove and set aside when ready.

Pour the broccoli into a pot, add 3 cups of water, and 1 teaspoon of salt. Bring to a boil until tender, about 7 minutes. Drain and transfer the broccoli to a bowl. Add the plant butter, thyme, lemon juice and zest, coconut cream, and olive oil. Use an immersion blender to puree the ingredients until smooth and nice. Spoon the mash into serving bowls and garnish with some olive oil. Serve.

Curried Mushroom Cauli "Risotto"

Ingredients for 4 servings

8 oz baby Bella mushrooms, stemmed and sliced
2 tbsp toasted sesame oil   Salt and black pepper to taste
1 large cauliflower head   ½ tsp curry powder
1 onion, chopped   1 tsp freshly chopped parsley
3 garlic cloves, minced   2 scallions, thinly sliced

Directions and Total Time: 15 minutes

Use a knife to cut the entire cauliflower head into 6 pieces and transfer to a food processor. With the grater attachment, shred the cauliflower into a rice-like consistency. Heat half of the sesame oil in a large skillet over medium heat and then add the onion and mushrooms. Sauté for 5 minutes or until the mushrooms are soft. Add the garlic and sauté for 2 minutes or until fragrant. Pour in the cauliflower and cook until the rice has slightly softened, about 10 minutes.

Season with salt, black pepper, and curry powder and mix the ingredients until well combined. After, turn the heat off and stir in the parsley and scallions. Dish the cauli rice into serving plates and serve warm.

Garlicky Baked Baby Potatoes

Ingredients for 4 servings

2 tbsp grated plant-based Parmesan cheese
4 tbsp plant butter, melted   Salt and black pepper to taste
4 garlic cloves, minced   1 ½ lb baby potatoes
3 tbsp chopped chives

Directions and Total Time: 40 minutes

Preheat the oven to 400°F. In a bowl, mix the butter, garlic, chives, salt, pepper, and plant Parmesan cheese. Toss the potatoes in the butter mixture until coated. Spread the mixture into a baking sheet, cover with foil, and roast for 30 minutes. Remove the potatoes from the oven and toss in the remaining butter mixture. Serve.

Crispy Onion Rings with Kale Dip

Ingredients for 4 servings

1 tbsp flaxseed meal + 3 tbsp water
½ cup grated plant-based Parmesan cheese
2 tbsp olive oil   2 tbsp dried cilantro
1 onion, sliced into rings   1 tbsp dried oregano
2 tsp garlic powder   Salt and black pepper to taste
½ tbsp sweet paprika powder   1 cup vegan mayonnaise
2 oz chopped kale   4 tbsp coconut cream
1 cup almond flour   Juice of ½ a lemon

Directions and Total Time: 35 minutes

Preheat oven to 400°F. In a bowl, mix the flaxseed meal and water and leave the mixture to thicken and fully absorb for 5 minutes. In another bowl, combine almond flour, plant-based Parmesan cheese, half of the garlic powder, sweet paprika, and salt. Line a baking sheet with parchment paper in readiness for the rings. When the vegan "flax egg" is ready, dip in the onion rings one after another and then into the almond flour mixture. Place the rings on the baking sheet and grease with cooking spray. Bake for 15-20 minutes or until golden brown and crispy. Remove the onion rings into a serving bowl.

Put kale in a food processor. Add in olive oil, cilantro, oregano, remaining garlic powder, salt, black pepper, vegan mayonnaise, coconut cream, and lemon juice; puree until nice and smooth. Allow the dip to sit for about 10 minutes for the flavors to develop. After, serve the dip with the crispy onion rings.

Lentil & Bean Tacos

Ingredients for 6 servings

¼ cup chopped red onion   ½ cup diced tomato
1 (15-oz) can red kidney beans ¼ cup chopped cilantro
1(15-oz) can red lentils   ¼ cup lime juice
2 tbsp taco seasoning   12 corn tortillas
1 tbsp hot sauce

Directions and Total Time: 35 minutes

Preheat air fryer to 360°F. Using a fork, mash the beans and lentils in a bowl. Mix in taco seasoning, hot sauce, red onion, tomato, cilantro, and lime juice. Fill each tortilla with 2 tbsp of bean mixture, keeping the filling close to one side, and roll them. Bake for 20 minutes until crispy. Serve right away.

Picante Mixed Nuts

Ingredients for 4 servings

1 tbsp plant butter, melted   ¼ tsp garlic powder
1 cup mixed nuts   ¼ tsp onion powder
¼ tsp hot sauce

Directions and Total Time: 35 minutes

Preheat the oven to 350°F and line a baking sheet with baking paper. In a medium bowl, mix the nuts, butter, hot sauce, garlic powder, and onion powder. Spread the mixture on the baking sheet and toast in the oven for 10 minutes. Remove the sheet, allow cooling, and serve.

Spiced Nut Mix

Ingredients for 4 servings

1 tbsp coconut oil	1 tsp cumin powder
8 oz walnuts and pecans	1 tsp paprika powder
1 tsp salt	

Directions and Total Time: 10 minutes

In a bowl, mix walnuts, pecans, salt, coconut oil, cumin powder, and paprika powder until the nuts are well coated with spice and oil. Pour the mixture into a pan and toast while stirring continually. Once the nuts are fragrant and brown, transfer to a bowl. Allow cooling and serve with chilled berry juice.

Spinach Fritters with Avocado Hummus

Ingredients for 4 servings

1 tbsp olive oil	¼ cup sesame paste
½ cup melted plant butter	Juice from ½ lemon
½ cup baby spinach	1 garlic clove, minced
½ tsp plain vinegar	½ tsp coriander powder
3 large avocados, chopped	Salt and black pepper to taste
¼ cup pumpkin seeds	½ cup chopped parsley

Directions and Total Time: 30 minutes

Preheat the oven to 300°F. Put the spinach in a bowl and toss with olive oil, vinegar, and salt. Place in a parchment paper-lined baking sheet and bake until the leaves are crispy but not burned, about 15 minutes. Place the chopped avocado into the bowl of a food processor. Add in parsley, plant butter, pumpkin seeds, sesame paste, lemon juice, garlic, coriander powder, salt, and black pepper. Puree until smooth. Spoon the hummus into a bowl and serve with spinach chips.

Kale Carrot "Noodles"

Ingredients for 4 servings

4 tbsp plant butter	1 garlic clove, minced
2 large carrots	1 cup chopped kale
¼ cup vegetable broth	Salt and black pepper to taste

Directions and Total Time: 15 minutes

Peel the carrots with a slicer and run both through a spiralizer to form noodles. Pour the vegetable broth into a saucepan and add the carrot noodles. Simmer (over low heat) the carrots for 3 minutes. Strain through a colander and set the vegetables aside. Place a large skillet over medium heat and melt the plant butter. Add the garlic and sauté until softened and put in the kale; cook until wilted. Pour the carrots into the pan, season with salt and black pepper, and stir-fry for 3 to 4 minutes. Spoon the vegetables into a bowl and serve with pan-grilled tofu.

"Cheesy" Broccoli Tots

Ingredients for 4 servings

1 head broccoli, cut into florets
2 cups grated plant-based Parmesan cheese

2/3 cup toasted almond flour	1 tbsp flaxseed powder
2 garlic cloves, minced	Salt to taste

Directions and Total Time: 30 minutes

Preheat the oven to 350°F and line a baking sheet with parchment paper. In a small bowl, mix the flaxseed powder with the 3 tbsp water and allow thickening for 5 minutes to make the vegan "flax egg". Place the broccoli in a safe microwave bowl, sprinkle with 2 tbsp of water, and steam in the microwave for 1 minute or until softened. Transfer the broccoli to a food processor and add the vegan "flax egg," almond flour, garlic, plant cheese, and salt. Blend until coarsely smooth.

Pour the mixture into a bowl and form 2-inch oblong balls from the mixture. Place the tots on the baking sheet and bake in the oven for 15 to 20 minutes or until firm and compacted. Remove the tots from the oven and serve warm with tomato dipping sauce.

Simple Pumpkin Noodles

Ingredients for 4 servings

¼ cup plant butter	1 bunch kale, sliced
½ cup chopped onion	¼ cup chopped fresh parsley
1 lb pumpkin, spiralized	Salt and black pepper to taste

Directions and Total Time: 15 minutes

Melt butter in a skillet over medium heat. Place the onion and cook for 3 minutes. Add in pumpkin and cook for another 7-8 minutes. Stir in kale and cook for another 2 minutes until the kale wilts. Sprinkle with parsley, salt, and pepper, and serve.

Veggie Sandwich

Ingredients for 2 servings

1 tsp olive oil, divided	¼ cucumber, sliced
¼ cup vegan mayonnaise	½ cup lettuce, chopped
2 slices whole-grain bread	½ tomato, sliced

Directions and Total Time: 15 minutes

Spread the mayonnaise over a bread slice, top with the cucumber, lettuce, and tomato and finish with the other slice. Heat the oil in a skillet over medium heat. Place the sandwich and grill for 3 minutes, then flip over and cook for a further 3 minutes. Cut the sandwich in half.

Broccoli & Mushroom Faux "Risotto"

Ingredients for 4 servings

1 cup cremini mushrooms, chopped
¾ cup grated plant-based Parmesan cheese

1 small red onion, chopped	1 large head broccoli, grated
1 cup coconut cream	¾ cup white wine
2 garlic cloves, minced	4 oz plant butter

Directions and Total Time: 25 minutes

Place a pot over medium heat, add, and melt the plant butter. Sauté the mushrooms in the pot until golden, about 5 minutes. Add the garlic and onions and cook for 3 minutes or until fragrant and soft. Mix in the broccoli, 1 cup water, and half of the white wine. Season with salt and black pepper and simmer the ingredients (uncovered) for 8 to 10 minutes or until the broccoli is soft.

Mix in the coconut whipping cream and simmer until most of the cream has evaporated. Turn the heat off and stir in the Parmesan cheese until well incorporated. Dish the risotto and serve warm as itself or with grilled tofu.

Zucchini & Tofu Skewers

Ingredients for 4 servings

1 (14 oz) block tofu, cubed
1 zucchini, cut into rounds
2 tbsp lemon juice
1 tsp smoked paprika
1 tbsp olive oil
1 tsp cumin powder
1 tsp garlic powder
Salt and black pepper to taste

Directions and Total Time: 10 minutes

Preheat a grill to medium heat. Meanwhile, thread the tofu and zucchini alternately on the wooden skewers.

In a small bowl, whisk the olive oil, lemon juice, paprika, cumin powder, and garlic powder. Brush the skewers all around with the mixture and place on the grill grate. Cook on both sides until golden brown, 5 minutes. Season with salt and pepper and serve afterward.

Stuffed Cabbage Rolls

Ingredients for 4 servings

3 cloves garlic, minced, divided
¼ cup coconut oil, divided
1 large white onion, chopped
1 cup crumbled soy chorizo
1 cup cauliflower rice
1 can tomato sauce
1 tsp dried oregano
1 tsp dried basil
8 full green cabbage leaves

Directions and Total Time: 35 minutes

Heat half of the coconut oil in a saucepan over medium heat. Add half of the onion, half of the garlic, and all of the soy chorizo. Sauté for 5 minutes or until the chorizo has browned further, and the onion softened. Stir in the cauli rice, season with salt and black pepper, and cook for 3 to 4 minutes. Turn the heat off and set the pot aside. Heat the remaining oil in a saucepan over medium heat, add, and sauté the remaining onion and garlic until fragrant and soft. Pour in the tomato sauce, and season with salt, black pepper, oregano, and basil. Add ¼ cup water and simmer the sauce for 10 minutes.

While the sauce cooks, lay the cabbage leaves on a flat surface and spoon the soy chorizo mixture into the middle of each leaf. Roll the leaves to secure the filling. Place the cabbage rolls in the tomato sauce and cook further for 10 minutes. Serve the cabbage rolls with sauce over mashed broccoli or with mixed seed bread.

Serrano Pepper Nut Sandwiches

Ingredients for 4 servings

2 tbsp canola oil for frying
¾ cup chopped walnuts
¾ cup chopped cashews
1 medium carrot, grated
1 small onion, chopped
1 garlic clove, minced
1 serrano pepper, minced
¾ cup old-fashioned oats
¾ cup breadcrumbs
2 tbsp minced fresh cilantro
½ tsp ground coriander
Salt and black pepper to taste
2 tsp fresh lime juice
4 sandwich rolls
Lettuce leaves for garnish

Directions and Total Time: 20 minutes

Pulse walnuts, cashews, carrot, onion, garlic, serrano pepper, oats, breadcrumbs, cilantro, coriander, lime juice, salt, and pepper in a food processor until well mixed. Remove and form into 4 burgers. Warm the canola oil in a skillet over medium heat. Cook the burgers for 5 minutes per side, until golden brown. Serve in sandwich rolls with lettuce and a dressing of your choice.

Hot Cabbage Sauté with Sesame Seeds

Ingredients for 4 servings

1 head green cabbage, shredded
1 tbsp toasted sesame oil
½ tbsp olive oil
1 tbsp hot sauce
2 tbsp soy sauce
½ tbsp pure date sugar
2 carrots, julienned
3 green onions, thinly sliced
2 garlic cloves, minced
1 tbsp fresh grated ginger
Salt and black pepper to taste
1 tbsp sesame seeds

Directions and Total Time: 15 minutes

In a small bowl, mix the soy sauce, sesame oil, hot sauce, and date sugar. Heat the olive oil in a large skillet and sauté the cabbage, carrots, green onion, garlic, salt, pepper, and ginger until softened, 5 minutes. Toss in the prepared sauce. Cook for 1 to 2 minutes. Dish the food and garnish it with sesame seeds. Serve and enjoy!

Cajun Sweet Potato Chips

Ingredients for 4 servings

2 sweet potatoes, peeled and sliced
2 tbsp melted plant butter
1 tbsp Cajun seasoning

Directions and Total Time: 55 minutes

Preheat the oven to 400°F and line a baking sheet with parchment paper. In a medium bowl, add the sweet potatoes, plant butter, and Cajun seasoning. Toss well. Spread the chips on the baking sheet, making sure not to overlap, and bake in the oven for 50 minutes to 1 hour or until crispy. Remove the sheet and pour the chips into a large bowl. Allow cooling and enjoy.

Bell Pepper & Carrot Sushi

Ingredients for 4 servings rolls

2 tbsp almond butter
2 tbsp tamari
4 standard nori sheets
1 green bell pepper, sliced
1 tbsp pickled ginger
½ cup grated carrots

Directions and Total Time: 15 minutes

Preheat oven to 350°F. Whisk the almond butter and tamari until smooth and thick. Place a nori sheet on a flat surface with the rough side facing up. Spoon a bit of the tamari mixture at the other side of the nori sheet, and spread on all sides. Put bell pepper slices, carrots, and ginger in a layer at the other end of the sheet. Fold up in the tahini direction to seal. Repeat the process with the remaining sheets. Arrange on a baking tray and bake for about 10 minutes until browned and crispy. Allow cooling for a few minutes before slicing into 4 pieces.

Mushroom Traybake with Herbs

Ingredients for 4 servings

2 cups chopped cremini mushrooms
1 bread loaf, cubed   ½ cup carrots, diced
2 tbsp plant butter   ½ tsp dried marjoram
1 large onion, diced   1 cup vegetable broth
1 cup celery, diced   ¼ cup chopped fresh parsley

Directions and Total Time: 85 minutes

Melt the butter in a large skillet and sauté onion, celery, mushrooms, and carrots for 5 minutes. Mix in marjoram, salt, and pepper. Pour in the vegetable broth and mix in parsley and bread. Cook until the broth reduces by half, 10 minutes. Pour the mixture into a baking dish and cover with foil. Bake in the oven at 375°F for 30 minutes. Uncover and bake further for 30 minutes or until golden brown on top, and the liquid absorbs. Remove the dish from the oven and serve the stuffing.

Spinach & Quinoa Stuffed Tomatoes

Ingredients for 4 servings

¾ cup quinoa   3 garlic cloves, minced
1 tbsp olive oil   1 cup chopped spinach
8 medium tomatoes   1 (7 oz) can chickpeas, drained
1 ½ cups water   ½ cup chopped fresh basil
1 small onion, diced

Directions and Total Time: 50 minutes

Preheat the oven to 400°F. Cut off the heads of tomatoes and use a paring knife to scoop the inner pulp of the tomatoes. Season with some olive oil, salt, and black pepper. Add the quinoa and water to a medium pot, season with salt, and cook until the quinoa is tender and the water absorbs, 10 to 15 minutes. Fluff and set aside. Heat the remaining olive oil in a skillet and sauté the onion and garlic for 30 seconds. Mix in the spinach and cook until wilted, 2 minutes. Stir in the basil, chickpeas, and quinoa; allow warming for 2 minutes. Spoon the mixture into the tomatoes, place the tomatoes into the baking dish and bake in the oven for 20 minutes or until the tomatoes soften. Serve and enjoy!

Hummus Quesadillas with Tomato Salsa

Ingredients for 4 servings

1 (15.5-oz) can garbanzo beans, mashed
8 flour tortilla wraps
1 tsp chili powder   1 cup tomato salsa
2 tbsp canola oil   ½ cup minced red onion

Directions and Total Time: 15 minutes

Warm the canola oil in a pot over medium heat. Place in mashed garbanzo and chili powder, cook for 5 minutes, stirring often. Set aside. Heat a pan over medium heat. Put one tortilla in the pan and top with ¼ each of the garbanzo spread, tomato salsa, and onion. Cover with other tortillas and cook for 2 minutes, flip the quesadilla and cook for another 2 minutes until crispy. Repeat the process with the remaining tortillas. Slice and serve.

Seitan Bites

Ingredients for 4 servings

¼ cup chopped mixed bell peppers
Olive oil for brushing   1 tbsp almond flour
1 tbsp flaxseed powder   1 tsp garlic powder
1 lb seitan, crumbled   1 tsp onion powder
Salt and black pepper to taste   1 tbsp vegan mayonnaise

Directions and Total Time: 25 minutes

Preheat the oven to 400°F and line a baking sheet with parchment paper. In a bowl, mix flaxseed powder with 3 tbsp water and allow thickening for 5 minutes. Add in seitan, bell peppers, salt, pepper, almond flour, garlic powder, onion powder, and vegan mayonnaise. Mix and form 1-inch balls from the mixture. Arrange on the baking sheet, brush with cooking spray, and bake in the oven for 15 to 20 minutes or until brown and compacted. Remove from the oven and serve.

Basil-Tomato Bruschetta

Ingredients for 6 servings

1 tbsp olive oil   1 whole-wheat baguette, sliced
3 tomatoes, chopped   Garlic salt to taste
¼ cup chopped fresh basil   Balsamic vinegar for garnish

Directions and Total Time: 20 minutes

Preheat oven to 420°F. Mix the tomatoes, basil, and olive in a bowl. Set aside. Arrange baguette slices on a baking sheet and toast for 6 minutes on both sides until brown. Sprinkle with the garlic salt and top with the tomato mixture. Drizzle with balsamic vinegar and serve.

Avocado & Soy Chorizo Tacos

Ingredients for 4 servings

2 tbsp olive oil   4 large lettuce leaves
8 oz soy chorizo   2 ripe avocados, sliced
4 soft flour tortillas   1 tomato, sliced
¼ cup vegan mayonnaise

Directions and Total Time: 20 minutes

Warm the oil in a skillet over medium heat. Place the soy chorizo and cook for 6 minutes on all sides until browned. Set aside. Spread mayonnaise over tortillas and top with lettuce leaves and tomato siles. Cover with avocado slices and finish with soy chorizo. Roll up the tortillas and serve immediately.

Coconut-Banana Cream Filled Strawberries

Ingredients for 4 servings

12 strawberries   ¼ tsp banana extract
1 tbsp coconut flakes   2 tbsp maple syrup
¼ cup cashew cream

Directions and Total Time: 10 minutes

Use a teaspoon to scoop out some strawberry pulp to create a hole within. In a bowl, mix the cashew cream, banana extract, and maple syrup. Spoon the mixture into the strawberries and garnish with coconut flakes. Serve.

Baked Tomato Chips with Pepitas

Ingredients for 6 servings

¼ cup olive oil
5 tomatoes, sliced
½ cup pepita seeds
1 tbsp nutritional yeast
Salt and black pepper to taste
1 tsp garlic puree

Directions and Total Time: 15 minutes

Preheat oven to 400°F. Over the sliced tomatoes, drizzle olive oil. In a food processor, add pepitas, nutritional yeast, garlic, salt, and pepper. Pulse until the desired consistency is attained. Toss in tomato slices to coat. Set the tomato slices on a baking pan. Bake for 10 minutes.

Energy Chocolate & Walnut Bars

Ingredients for 4 servings

2 tbsp dark chocolate chips
1 tbsp cocoa powder
2 tbsp melted coconut oil
1 cup walnuts
3 tbsp sunflower seeds
1 ½ tsp vanilla extract
¼ tsp cinnamon powder
2 tbsp toasted almond meal
2 tsp pure maple syrup

Directions and Total Time: 60 minutes

In a food processor, add the walnuts, sunflower seeds, chocolate chips, cocoa powder, vanilla extract, cinnamon powder, coconut oil, almond meal, maple syrup, and blitz a few times until combined. Line a flat baking sheet with plastic wrap, pour the mixture onto the sheet and place another plastic wrap on top. Use a rolling pin to flatten the batter and then remove the top plastic wrap. Freeze the snack until firm, 1 hour. Remove from the freezer, cut into 1 ½-inch sized bars and enjoy immediately.

Carrot & Beet Stir-Fry

Ingredients for 4 servings

2 peeled beets, cut into wedges
2 tbsp plant butter
3 small carrots, cut crosswise
1 red onion, cut into wedges
½ tsp dried oregano
1/8 tsp salt

Directions and Total Time: 20 minutes

Steam the beets and carrots in a safe microwave bowl until softened, 6 minutes. Meanwhile, melt the butter in a large skillet and sauté the onion until softened, 3 minutes. Stir in the carrots, beets, oregano, and salt. Mix well and cook for 5 minutes. Serve warm.

Yummy Tofu-Avocado Wraps

Ingredients for 4 servings

1 lb tofu, cut into strips
3 cups torn romaine lettuce
3 ripe Roma tomatoes, diced
10 sliced pitted green olives
6 tbsp olive oil
1 tbsp soy sauce
¼ cup apple cider vinegar
1 tsp yellow mustard
1 large carrot, shredded
1 medium avocado, chopped
1/3 cup minced red onion
4 whole-grain flour tortillas

Directions and Total Time: 25 minutes

Heat 2 tbsp of olive oil in a skillet over medium heat. Place the tofu, cook for 10 minutes until golden brown. Drizzle with soy sauce. Let cool.

In a bowl, whisk the vinegar, mustard, salt, pepper, and the remaining oil. In another bowl, mix the lettuce, tomatoes, carrot, avocado, onion, and olives. Pour the dressing over the salad and toss to coat. Lay out a tortilla on a clean flat surface and spoon ¼ of the salad, some tofu, and then roll-up. Cut in half. Repeat the process with the remaining tortillas. Serve and enjoy!

Simple Roasted Asparagus

Ingredients for 4 servings

1 lb asparagus, trimmed
1 tbsp lemon juice
2 tbsp plant butter
2 garlic cloves, minced
1 tsp Dijon mustard

Directions and Total Time: 35 minutes

Melt the butter in a skillet and sauté the asparagus until softened with some crunch, 7 minutes. Mix in the garlic and cook until fragrant, 30 seconds. In a small bowl, quickly whisk the mustard, lemon juice and pour the mixture over the asparagus. Cook for 2 minutes. Serve.

Stuffed Bell Peppers with Tofu

Ingredients for 4 servings

1 cup red and yellow bell peppers
1 cup grated plant-based Parmesan cheese
1 oz tofu, chopped
1 cup coconut cream cheese
1 tbsp chili paste, mild
2 tbsp melted plant butter

Directions and Total Time: 25 minutes

Preheat oven to 400°F. Use a knife to cut the bell peppers into two (lengthwise) and remove the core.

In a bowl, mix tofu, coconut cream cheese, chili paste, and melted butter until smooth. Spoon the cheese mixture into the bell peppers and use the back of the spoon to level the filling in the peppers. Grease a baking sheet with cooking spray and arrange the stuffed peppers on the sheet. Sprinkle the plant-based Parmesan cheese on top and bake the peppers for 15-20 minutes until the peppers are golden brown and the cheese melted. Remove onto a serving platter and serve warm.

Mini Mushroom Tarts

Ingredients for 4 servings

12 thin bread slices
12 oz mushrooms, chopped
1 tbsp olive oil
2 spring onions, chopped
2 garlic cloves, minced
¼ cup chopped fresh cilantro
1 tsp dried thyme
1 tbsp soy sauce

Directions and Total Time: 20 minutes

Preheat oven to 390°F. Using a small round tin, make circles from the bread slices. Coat the circles with oil and press at the bottom of a muffin tin. Bake for 10 minutes, until toasted. Heat 1 tbsp of oil in a skillet over medium heat. Place in spring onions, garlic, and mushrooms and cook for 5 minutes, until tender. Add in cilantro, thyme, and soy sauce and cook for 2-3 minutes more, until liquid has absorbed. Divide the mixture between the muffin cups and bake for 3-5 minutes. Serve.

Grilled Veggies with Romesco Dip

Ingredients for 4 servings

½ cup olive oil + 2 tbsp for brushing
1 (12-oz) jar roasted peppers, drained
1 bunch asparagus, trimmed   1 tbsp tomato paste
2 slices toasted bread, chopped   Salt and black pepper to taste
½ cup toasted almonds   1 green bell pepper, julienned
1 garlic clove, minced   ½ tsp sweet paprika
1 tbsp red wine vinegar   1 yellow bell pepper, julienned
1 tsp crushed red chili flakes

Directions and Total Time: 35 minutes

In your food processor, place the roasted peppers, almonds, garlic, vinegar, toasted bread, paprika, and tomato paste; pulse, pouring slowly ½ cup of olive oil until the desired consistency is reached. Season with salt and black pepper and set aside. Heat a grill pan over medium heat. Toss the vegetables in the remaining olive oil, season with chili flakes, salt, and pepper, and cook in the pan for 3-5 minutes per side. Serve with the dip.

Basil Brussel Sprout Bake with Cranberries

Ingredients for 4 servings

1 white onion, chopped   ½ cup dried cranberries
3 tbsp olive oil   1 lemon, juiced
1 lb Brussels sprouts, halved 1 tbsp chopped fresh basil

Directions and Total Time: 50 minutes

Preheat the oven to 425°F. Spread the Brussels sprouts on a roasting sheet, drizzle with olive oil, and season with salt and black pepper. Mix the seasoning onto the vegetables and roast in the oven until light brown and tender, 20 to 25 minutes. Transfer the Brussels sprouts to a large salad bowl and mix in the onion, cranberries, lemon juice, and basil. Serve immediately.

Minty String Beans

Ingredients for 4 servings

2 tbsp chopped mint leaves   1 cup string beans, trimmed
¼ tsp red chili flakes   Salt to taste
1 tbsp sesame oil   2 tbsp pure tahini

Directions and Total Time: 10 minutes

Pour the string beans into a safe microwave dish, sprinkle with 1 tbsp of water, and steam in the microwave until softened, 1 minute. Heat the sesame oil in a large skillet and toss in the string beans and chili flakes until well coated. Season with salt and mix in the tahini and mint leaves. Cook for 1-2 minutes and turn the heat off. Serve.

Sprout Wraps with Hazelnuts

Ingredients for 6 servings

1 tbsp coconut oil   1 tsp cayenne pepper
½ cup fresh parsley, chopped   Salt and black pepper to taste
1 cup sprouts   Zest and juice of 1 lime
1 garlic clove, pressed   2 tbsp ground flaxseed
2 tbsp ground hazelnuts   2 tbsp water
2 tbsp flaked coconut   2 whole-wheat wraps

Directions and Total Time: 60 minutes

Pulse parsley, sprouts, garlic, hazelnuts, coconut flakes, coconut oil, cayenne, salt, pepper, lime juice, lime zest, flaxseed, and water in a food processor until well blended. Divide the mixture between the wraps and roll-up. Let chill in the fridge for 30 minutes. Slice and serve.

Rice Vermicelli & Veggies Stuffed Lettuce Rolls

Ingredients for 4 servings

½ red bell pepper, cut into strips
2 tbsp sesame oil   3 oz rice vermicelli
2 green onions   6 soft green leaf lettuce leaves
2 tbsp soy sauce   1 medium carrot, shredded
2 tbsp balsamic vinegar   ½ cucumber, sliced lengthwise
1 tsp pure date sugar   1 cup fresh cilantro leaves
⅛ tsp crushed red pepper

Directions and Total Time: 15 minutes

Separate the white part of the green onions, chop and transfer to a bowl. Stir in soy sauce, balsamic vinegar, date sugar, red pepper, and 3 tbsp water. Set aside. Slice the green part diagonally and set aside. Submerge the vermicelli in a bowl with hot water for 4 minutes. Drain and mix in the sesame oil. Allow cooling. Put the lettuce leaves on a flat surface. Divide vermicelli between each leaf in the middle, add green onion slices, carrot, cucumber, bell pepper, and cilantro. Roll the leaves up from the smaller edges. Arrange the rolls seam facing down on a plate. Serve with the dipping sauce.

Daikon Strips with Guacamole

Ingredients for 4 servings

Juice of 1 lime   1 garlic clove, minced
1 avocado, cubed   ¼ cup chopped cilantro
½ red onion, sliced   1 daikon, cut into matchsticks

Directions and Total Time: 15 minutes

Place the avocado in a bowl and squeeze the lime juice. Sprinkle with salt. Mash the avocado using a fork, stir in onion, garlic, and cilantro. Serve with daikon slices.

Vegan-Style Mac & Cheese

Ingredients for 4 servings

2 cups plant-based cheddar cheese, grated
2 tbsp olive oil   Salt and black pepper to taste
8 oz elbow macaroni   ¼ cup flour
½ tsp dry mustard powder   2 tbsp parsley, chopped
2 cups almond milk

Directions and Total Time: 35 minutes

Cook elbow macaroni in boiling water for 8-10 minutes until al dente. Drain. Heat olive oil in a skillet over medium heat. Place flour, mustard powder, salt, and pepper and stir for about 3-5 minutes. Gradually pour in almond milk while stirring constantly with a spatula for another 5 minutes until the mixture is smooth. Turn off the heat and mix in cheddar cheese. When the cheese is melted, fold in macaroni and toss to coat. Top with parsley.

Green Bean & Mushroom Wontons

Ingredients for 12 servings

4 green beans, chopped crosswise
3 tbsp toasted sesame oil   1 tsp soy sauce
2 tbsp olive oil   1 tbsp fresh lime juice
12 vegan wonton wrappers   1 medium carrot, shredded
12 shiitake mushrooms, sliced   Toasted sesame seeds

Directions and Total Time: 20 minutes

Preheat oven to 360°F. Coat the wonton with some sesame oil and arrange on a baking sheet. Bake for 5 minutes until golden brown and crispy. Set aside.

Warm the olive oil in a skillet over medium heat. Place the mushrooms and stir-fry for 5 minutes until softened. Add in green beans and soy sauce and cook for 2-3 minutes; reserve. In a bowl, whisk the lime juice and the remaining sesame oil. Stir in carrot and mushroom mixture. Divide the mixture between the wontons and sprinkle with sesame seeds. Serve and enjoy!

Tofu Sandwiches with Sunflower Seeds

Ingredients for 4 servings

1 lb extra-firm tofu, crumbled   ½ cup vegan mayonnaise
1 medium carrot, chopped   8 slices whole-grain bread
1 celery stalk, chopped   4 slices ripe tomato
3 green onions, minced   4 lettuce leaves
¼ cup shelled sunflower seeds

Directions and Total Time: 15 minutes

Place the tofu in a bowl. Stir in carrot, celery, green onions, and sunflower seeds. Mix in mayonnaise, salt, and pepper. Toast the bread slices. Spread the tofu mixture onto 4 bread slices. Layer a tomato slice and lettuce leaf. Top each sandwich with a bread slice and cut diagonally.

Smoky Tangy Potato Chips

Ingredients for 4 servings

1 tsp canola oil   ¼ tsp onion powder
1 lb potato, peeled and sliced   ¼ tsp chili powder
1 tsp smoked paprika   ⅛ tsp ground mustard
½ tsp garlic powder   ⅛ tsp liquid smoke
1 tbsp tarragon   Salt to taste

Directions and Total Time: 40 minutes

Preheat oven to 390°F. Combine the paprika, garlic powder, tarragon, onion powder, chili powder, salt, and mustard in a bowl. Mix the potatoes, canola oil, liquid smoke, and tarragon mixture in another bowl; toss to coat. Spread the potatoes on a lined with parchment paper baking tray and bake for 30 minutes, flipping once halfway through cooking until golden. Serve and enjoy!

Mixed Seed Cookies

Ingredients for 4 servings

¼ cup plant butter, melted   1/3 cup chia seeds
1/3 cup coconut flour   1/3 cup pumpkin seeds
1/3 cup sesame seeds   Salt to taste
1/3 cup sunflower seeds

Directions and Total Time: 50 minutes

Preheat an oven to 300°F and line a baking sheet with parchment paper. In a bowl, mix the coconut flour, sesame seeds, sunflower seeds, chia seeds, pumpkin seeds, and salt. Add the plant butter, 1 cup of boiling water, and mix until well combined. Spread the mixture on the baking sheet and bake in the oven until the batter is firm, 45 minutes. Remove the crackers and allow cooling for 10 minutes. Break the crackers into pieces and serve.

Roasted Butternut Squash with Maple Glaze

Ingredients for 4 servings

2 tbsp olive oil   ¼ cup pure maple syrup
1 butternut squash, cubed   1 tsp red chili flakes
4 garlic cloves, minced   1 tsp coriander seeds

Directions and Total Time: 40 minutes

Preheat the oven to 375°F. In a medium bowl, toss the squash with olive oil, garlic, maple syrup, salt, black pepper, red chili flakes, and coriander seeds. Spread the mixture on a baking sheet and roast in the oven for 25 to 30 minutes or until the potatoes soften and golden brown. Remove from the oven, plate, and serve.

Fall Pumpkin Cookies

Ingredients for 6 servings

3 tbsp melted coconut oil   1 cup whole-wheat flour
1 (2-lb) pumpkin, sliced   2 tsp baking powder
1 tbsp maple syrup

Directions and Total Time: 70 minutes

Preheat oven to 360°F. Place the pumpkin in a greased tray and bake for 45 minutes until tender. Let cool before mashing it. Mix the mashed pumpkin, 1 ½ tbsp of coconut oil, and maple syrup in a bowl. Combine the flour and baking powder in another bowl. Fold in the pumpkin mixture and whisk with a fork until smooth.

Divide the mixture into balls. Arrange spaced out on a lined with a wax paper baking sheet; flatten the balls until a cookie shape is formed. Brush with the remaining melted coconut oil. Bake for 10 minutes until they rise and become gold. Serve and enjoy!

Roasted Red Pepper & Pecan Crostini

Ingredients for 16 servings

2 tbsp olive oil   1 tbsp soy sauce
2 jarred roasted red peppers   2 tbsp chopped green onions
1 cup unsalted pecans   ¼ cup nutritional yeast
¼ cup water   2 tbsp balsamic vinegar

Directions and Total Time: 15 minutes

Cut 1 red pepper and set aside. Slice the remaining pepper into strips, reserve for garnish. Pulse the pecans in a food processor until a fine powder forms. Pour in water, chopped red pepper, and soy sauce. Pulse until smooth. Put in green onions, yeast, vinegar, and oil. Blend until well mixed. Spread mixture onto toasted bread slices topped with pepper strips. Serve and enjoy!

Easy-Peasy Primavera Lettuce Rolls

Ingredients for 4 servings

1 tbsp olive oil
2 oz rice noodles
2 tbsp Thai basil, chopped
2 tbsp cilantro, chopped
1 garlic clove, minced
1 tbsp minced fresh ginger

Juice of ½ lime
2 tbsp soy sauce
1 avocado, sliced
2 carrots, peeled and julienned
8 leaves butter lettuce

Directions and Total Time: 20 minutes

In a bowl, place the noodles in hot water and let them sit for 4 minutes. Drain and mix with olive oil. Allow cooling. Combine the basil, cilantro, garlic, ginger, lime juice, and soy sauce in another bowl. Add in cooked noodles, avocado, and carrots. Divide the mixture between the lettuce leaves. Fold in and secure with toothpicks. Serve.

Mexican Salsa with Tortilla Chips

Ingredients for 4 servings

3 large heirloom tomatoes, chopped
¼ cup olive oil
1 green onion, finely chopped
½ bunch parsley, chopped
2 garlic cloves, minced

1 Jalapeño pepper, minced
Juice of 1 lime
Salt to taste
Whole-grain tortilla chips

Directions and Total Time: 15 minutes

Combine the tomatoes, green onion, parsley, garlic, jalapeño pepper, lime juice, olive oil, and salt in a medium bowl. Let it rest for 10 minutes at room temperature. Serve with tortilla chips and enjoy!

Delicious Glazed Carrots

Ingredients for 4 servings

1 tbsp lemon juice
2 tbsp plant butter
1 lb baby carrots

2 tbsp pure maple syrup
½ tsp black pepper
¼ cup chopped fresh parsley

Directions and Total Time: 15 minutes

Boil some water in a medium pot. Cook the carrots until tender, 5 to 6 minutes. Drain the carrots. Melt the butter in a large skillet and mix in the maple syrup and lemon juice. Toss in the carrots, season with black pepper, and toss in the parsley. Serve and enjoy!

Tofu Mix Stuffed Bell Peppers

Ingredients for 4 servings

4 bell peppers, top removed
2 tbsp olive oil
1 onion, chopped
2 garlic cloves, minced

1 (14-oz) block tofu, crumbled
1 (5-oz) package baby spinach
2 tsp Italian seasoning
Salt and black pepper to taste

Directions and Total Time: 35 minutes

Preheat oven to 450°F. Heat the oil in a skillet over medium heat. Cook the onion and garlic for 3 minutes. Put in tofu and spinach and cook for 3 minutes until the spinach wilts. Stir in Italian seasoning, salt, and pepper. Fill the bell peppers with the spinach mixture and arrange them on a greased baking sheet. Bake for 25 minutes.

Tempeh & Walnut Balls

Ingredients for 6 servings

8 oz tempeh, cut into pieces
1 (2-oz) jar chopped pimientos
¼ cup nutritional yeast

¼ cup vegan mayonnaise
2 tbsp soy sauce
¾ cup chopped walnuts

Directions and Total Time: 35 minutes

Place the tempeh in a pot with boiling water and cook for 30 minutes. Let cool. In a blender, put the tempeh, pimientos, yeast, mayo, and soy sauce. Pulse until smooth. Remove to a bowl and let chill in the fridge for 2 hours. Heat a skillet over medium heat. Add the walnuts and toast for 2-3 minutes, shaking constantly. Remove to a large plate and leave to cool. Mold the tempeh mixture into a ball and roll on the walnuts' plate. Serve chilled.

Mushrooms Stuffed with Swiss Chard & Pecans

Ingredients for 4 servings

8 oz white mushrooms, stems chopped and reserved
2 tbsp olive oil
1 garlic clove, minced
1 cup cooked Swiss chard

1 cup finely chopped pecans
½ cup breadcrumbs
Salt and black pepper to taste

Directions and Total Time: 20 minutes

Preheat oven to 390°F. Warm oil in a skillet over medium heat, add the mushroom stems and garlic and sauté for 3 minutes. Mix in chard, pecans, breadcrumbs, salt, and pepper. Cook for another 2 minutes, stirring occasionally. Divide the resulting mixture between the mushroom caps and arrange on a greased baking dish. Bake for 15 minutes, until golden. Serve immediately.

Pecan & Chickpea Balls

Ingredients for 6 servings

¼ cup plant butter, melted
1 (15.5-oz) can chickpeas
½ cup chopped pecans
¼ cup minced green onions
1 garlic clove, minced

3 tbsp whole-wheat flour
3 tbsp breadcrumbs
4 tbsp hot sauce
¼ tsp salt
⅛ tsp ground cayenne pepper

Directions and Total Time: 35 minutes

Preheat oven to 350°F. In a food processor, put the chickpeas, pecans, green onions, garlic, flour, breadcrumbs, 2 tbsp hot sauce, salt, and cayenne pepper. Pulse until chunky texture is formed. Shape the mixture into 1-inch balls. Arrange on a greased baking pan. Bake for 25-30 minutes, turning halfway through. In a bowl, whisk the remaining hot sauce with plant butter. Remove the balls to a serving plate and pour the hot butter all over.

Mango-Tofu Pitas

Ingredients for 4 servings

¼ cup chopped mango chutney
4 whole-wheat pitas, halved
1 lb extra-firm tofu, crumbled
½ cup vegan mayonnaise
2 tsp Dijon mustard
1 tbsp curry powder

Salt to taste
⅛ tsp ground cayenne
¾ cup shredded carrots
1 fennel bulb, sliced
¼ cup minced red onion
4 lettuce leaves

Directions and Total Time: 15 minutes

In a bowl, place tofu, mayonnaise, chutney, mustard, curry powder, salt, and cayenne pepper and stir to combine. Mix in the carrots, fennel, and onion. Let sit in the fridge for 20 minutes. Cover the pieces of the pita bread with lettuce leaves and scoop some of the tofu mixture in. Serve immediately.

Mushroom & Kale Burritos with Avocado

Ingredients for 2 servings

2 portobello mushroom caps, sliced
1 avocado, pitted and peeled
1 red bell pepper, cut into strips
1 ½ tbsp toasted sesame oil
3 tbsp soy sauce

3 tbsp fresh lemon juice
2 whole-grain flour tortillas
2 cups kale, chopped
1 ripe tomato, chopped

Directions and Total Time: 15 minutes

Whisk soy sauce, 2 tbsp of lemon juice, and oil in a bowl. Toss in portobello strips and marinate for 45 minutes. Drain and set aside. Using a fork, mash the avocado with the remaining lemon juice. Spread the avocado mash over tortillas and top with kale, mushrooms, bell pepper strips, and tomato. Sprinkle with salt and pepper. Fold the outside edges over the filling to make burritos. Cut in half and transfer to a serving platter. Enjoy!

Tomato & White Bean Bake

Ingredients for 4 servings

1 (14-oz) can white beans
2 tbsp soy sauce
1 tbsp nutritional yeast
1 tsp smoked paprika

1 tsp onion powder
½ tsp garlic powder
10 cherry tomatoes, halved

Directions and Total Time: 30 minutes

Preheat oven to 390°F. Mix the beans, soy sauce, yeast, paprika, onion powder, and garlic powder in a greased baking sheet and bake for 20-25 minutes, stirring once. Arrange the tomato halves on top and bake for 5-8 minutes. Serve and enjoy!

Stuffed Tomato Bites

Ingredients for 6 servings

6 tomatoes, whole
2 cucumbers, chopped
Juice of 1 lemon

½ red bell pepper, minced
2 green onions, finely minced
Salt to taste

Directions and Total Time: 15 minutes

Remove the tops of the tomatoes. Using a tablespoon, scoop out the seeds and pulp. Arrange them on a platter. Combine the cucumbers, lemon juice, bell pepper, green onions, and salt in a bowl. Stir to combine. Divide the mixture between the tomatoes and serve.

Roasted Hazelnut Snack

Ingredients for 6 servings

2 tbsp extra-virgin olive oil
1 lb raw hazelnuts
3 tbsp tamari sauce

1 tbsp nutritional yeast
2 tsp chili powder

Directions and Total Time: 20 minutes

Preheat oven to 390°F. Combine the hazelnuts, tamari, and oil in a bowl. Toss to coat. Spread the mixture on a parchment-lined baking pan and roast in the oven for about 15 minutes until browned. Let cool for e few minutes. Sprinkle with yeast and chili powder. Serve.

Salty Seed Bars

Ingredients for 6 servings

1 tsp vegan Worcestershire sauce
¾ cup pumpkin seeds
½ cup sunflower seeds
½ cup sesame seeds
¼ cup poppy seeds

1 tsp minced garlic
1 tsp tamari sauce
½ tsp ground cayenne pepper
½ tsp dried oregano

Directions and Total Time: 55 minutes

Preheat oven to 320°F. Line with parchment paper a baking sheet. Mix the pumpkin seeds, sunflower seeds, sesame seeds, poppy seeds, garlic, tamari, Worcestershire sauce, cayenne, oregano, and ½ cup water in a bowl.

Spread on the baking sheet and bake for 25 minutes. Turn the seeds and bake for another 20-25 minutes. Allow cooling before slicing into bars.

Carrot & Arugula Hummus Gyros

Ingredients for 4 servings

4 whole-wheat pitas, halved
1 garlic clove, chopped
¾ cup tahini
2 tbsp fresh lemon juice
⅛ tsp ground cayenne

Salt to taste
1 (15.5-oz) can chickpeas
2 medium carrots, grated
1 large ripe tomato, sliced
2 cups arugula

Directions and Total Time: 15 minutes

In a food processor, add in garlic, tahini, lemon juice, salt, cayenne pepper, and ¼ cup of water. Pulse until smooth. In a bowl, mash the chickpeas with a fork.

Stir in carrots and tahini mixture; reserve. Spread the hummus over the pitas and top with a tomato slice and arugula. Serve and enjoy!

Black Olive & Dill Pickle Phyllo

Ingredients for 6 servings

1 sheet puff pastry, thawed
18 pitted black olives, quartered
2 tbsp olive oil
2 medium onions, thinly sliced

1 garlic clove, minced
1 tsp chopped fresh rosemary
Salt and black pepper to taste
1 tbsp chopped dill pickles

Directions and Total Time: 25 minutes

Warm the oil in a skillet over medium heat. Place in onions, garlic, rosemary, salt, and pepper and sauté for 5 minutes. Add in dill pickles, stir and set aside.

Preheat oven to 390°F. Roll out the pastry and, using a small bowl, cut into 3-inch circles. Arrange the circles on a greased baking sheet and top with onion mixture. Scatter the olives over. Bake for 15 minutes until golden.

LUNCH

Mustard Chickpea Patties

Ingredients for 6 servings

1 red bell pepper	Juice of ½ lemon
1 (19-oz) can chickpeas	1 tsp dried thyme
1 cup ground almonds	½ tsp dried tarragon
2 tsp yellow mustard	1 cup spinach
2 tsp maple syrup	1 ½ cups rolled oats
1 garlic clove, pressed	

Directions and Total Time: 50 minutes

Preheat the oven to 350°F. Prep a baking sheet by lining it with parchment paper. Cut the red pepper in half lengthwise. Remove stem and seeds. Place the pepper on the baking sheet cut side up. Roast for 10 minutes. While the pepper is cooking, add chickpeas, almonds, mustard, maple syrup, garlic, lemon juice, thyme, tarragon and spinach in the food processor. Pulse to mix, but not pureed. Transfer the roasted pepper as well as oats to the food processor. Pulse to chop. Divide into 12 portions and shape into patties. Place a new sheet of parchment on the baking sheet and arrange the patties on the sheet. Bake for about 30 minutes or until the outside is golden.

Garam Masala Chickpea Wraps

Ingredients for 3 servings

1 tbsp sesame oil	1 cup diced cucumber
1 lime, juiced and zested	1 red bell pepper, diced
1 tbsp garam masala	½ cup fresh cilantro, chopped
Salt to taste	3 whole-grain wraps
1 (14-oz) can chickpeas	2 cups shredded lettuce

Directions and Total Time: 20 minutes

Whisk the sesame oil, lime zest, lime juice, garam masala, and salt in a medium bowl to a creamy, thick consistency. Slowly add 3-4 tablespoons of water to thin out the tahini sauce. Stir in chickpeas, cucumber, bell pepper, and cilantro. Divide the chickpea salad between the three wraps. Top with lettuce. Roll it up. Serve and enjoy.

Cilantro Sweet Potato Burgers

Ingredients for 4 servings

1 cup cooked brown rice	¼ cup cilantro, finely chopped
1 cup grated sweet potato	1 tsp chili powder
½ cup diced onion	½ cup ground almonds
Salt to taste	1 tsp olive oil

Directions and Total Time: 35 minutes

In a large bowl, combine rice, sweet potato, onion, and salt. Sit for about 5 minutes to draw out the moisture from the vegetables. Mix in cilantro, chili powder, and almonds until the batter becomes sticky. Slowly add water if necessary. Divide the mixture into 4 portions and shape into patties. In a large skillet over medium heat, add oil. When the oil starts to shimmer, place the patties in the skillet. Cook for 7-10 minutes. Flip the patties and cook for another 5-7 minutes. Serve warm

Dijon Burgers

Ingredients for 6 servings

1 tbsp soy sauce	¼ tsp cayenne pepper
1 tbsp white wine vinegar	2 tbsp cilantro, chopped
2 tsp Dijon mustard	Salt and black pepper to taste
2 garlic cloves, minced	1 cup millet
1 tsp dried thyme	2 carrots, grated
½ tsp dried oregano	2 tbsp parsley, chopped
½ tsp dried sage	3 tbsp olive oil
½ tsp smoked paprika	1 cup arugula

Directions and Total Time: 45 minutes

Mix together soy sauce, white wine vinegar, and mustard in a medium bowl until it comes together in a thick consistency. Slowly add 1 to 2 tablespoons of water to thin out the dressing. Whisk until smooth, then add the garlic, thyme, oregano, sage, smoked paprika, cayenne pepper, cilantro, salt, and black pepper. Stir well. Set the resulting dressing aside. Add the millet, 2 cups of water, and salt in a medium pot over high heat. Bring to a boil and cook for 2-3 minutes. Reduce the heat, cover, and simmer the millet for 15 minutes. Do not stir. Millet should be soft with no more liquid in the pan when it is done. Add cooked millet to a large bowl along with carrots, parsley, and the dressing that was made. Combine until it comes together. Measure ¼-cup portions and shape into patties. Add 1 teaspoon olive oil to a large skillet. Cook each patty for 5 minutes on one side, then flip. Cook for 5 more minutes. Serve warm with arugula.

Cumin Lentil Patties

Ingredients for 6 servings

1 cup lentils	½ tsp ground cumin
3 carrots, grated	½ tsp garlic powder
1 shallot, diced	½ tsp tabasco sauce
¾ cup almond flour	Salt and black pepper to taste
½ tsp smoked paprika	

Directions and Total Time: 45 minutes

In a medium pot, add lentils and 3 cups of water. When the water comes to a boil, reduce the heat and simmer for 15 minutes. Toss carrots and shallots in a large bowl along with flour, paprika, cumin, garlic, tabasco, salt, and pepper. When the lentils are cooked and soft, drain extra water then transfer to the bowl. Mash the ingredients slightly. Divide into 12 portions and shape into patties. Add oil to a large skillet over medium heat. Pan-fry the patties for 15 minutes, flipping once. Serve warm.

Sharma Bowl

Ingredients for 2 servings

½ cup brown mushrooms, sliced	
1 tsp coconut oil	¼ cup canned coconut milk
½ red onion, thinly sliced	1 tsp miso paste
Salt to taste	¾ cup cooked quinoa
2 asparagus, chopped	3 pitted black olives
2 grape tomatoes, halved	1 cup baby spinach
2 tbsp fresh mint, chopped	1 tbsp ½ red chili, finely sliced

Directions and Total Time: 30 minutes

Warm the coconut oil in a skillet over medium heat. Add and sauté the onion for 3-5 minutes until translucent. Stir in mushrooms, asparagus until softened. Next, add tomatoes and cook for another 10 minutes. Season with salt. While the vegetables are cooking, whisk mint, coconut milk, and miso paste in a medium bowl. When the tomatoes are just soft, pour the sauce into the skillet and remove from the heat. Divide the quinoa between 2 plates. Spoon the vegetables over the quinoa, then top with spinach and black olives. Garnish with red chili.

Chili Black Bean Burritos

Ingredients for 6 servings

1 tsp olive oil	2 tsp chili powder
1 red onion, diced	1 tsp ground cumin
2 garlic cloves, minced	Salt to taste
1 zucchini, chopped	1 (14-oz) can black beans
1 bell pepper, diced	6 corn tortillas
1 tomato, diced	

Directions and Total Time: 55 minutes

Preheat the oven to 325°F. Heat the olive oil in a large skillet over medium heat. Saute onion for about 5 minutes until soft. Next, add garlic and saute until fragrant. Stir in zucchini and bell pepper for another 5 minutes. Then add the tomato and heat through for about 1-2 minutes. Mix in chili powder, cumin, salt, and black beans. Scoop some of the black bean mixture in the middle of each tortilla. Fold in the sides and roll into the burrito. Place each roll seam side down in a baking dish. Cover the burritos with any excess juices from the skillet. Bake in the oven for 20-30 minutes. Serve warm and enjoy.

Sicilian-Style Vegan Pasta

Ingredients for 1 serving

½ cup cooked cannellini beans	
½ cup whole-grain pasta	¼ cup thinly sliced zucchini
Salt to taste	½ cup spinach
1 tsp olive oil	1 tbsp balsamic vinegar
¼ cup sliced mushrooms	3 black Sicilian olives, chopped

Directions and Total Time: 30 minutes

Cook pasta in a pot of boiling water and salt according to the package directions. While the pasta is cooking, heat oil in a large skillet and saute mushrooms and zucchini for about 7 to 8 minutes. Stir in beans and heat for 2 minutes. Next, add the spinach and cook until it just wilts. Drizzle with vinegar. Mix the pasta with the bean mixture. Garnish with olives. Serve warm and enjoy.

Spaghetti Squash in Lemon-Mint Sauce

Ingredients for 3 servings

1 cup cherry tomatoes, diced	1 spaghetti squash
3 tbsp olive oil	Salt and to taste
1 lemon, zested and juiced	1 cup chopped bell pepper
2 tbsp mint, minced	½ tsp dried basil
1 garlic clove, pressed	½ tsp ground fennel

Directions and Total Time: 50 minutes

Whisk olive oil and lemon juice, then mix in the mint, lemon zest, and garlic. Reserve until ready to use. Bring a large pot of water to a boil. Cut the squash in half lengthwise and remove seeds. Carefully place the squash in the boiling water along with salt. Boil for 30 minutes. Remove the squash carefully from the hot water and let cool. Reserve half of the squash for another dish. Scrape out the flesh and transfer the "noodles" to a strainer. Let drain for about 10 minutes, tossing about halfway through. In a large bowl, add cooked spaghetti squash and mint-lime dressing. Toss to coat. Add cherry tomatoes and bell pepper. Garnish with basil and fennel.

Thai Curry Noodle Bowl

Ingredients for 2 servings

1 cup snap peas, trimmed and halved	
8 oz soba noodles	2 tbsp cashews, chopped
1 cup chopped spinach	1 tbsp grated fresh ginger
1 carrot, julienned	2 tbsp peanut butter
1 bell pepper, thinly sliced	2 tbsp rice vinegar
1 chopped green onion	3 tbsp soy sauce
1 avocado, thinly sliced	1 tsp toasted sesame oil

Directions and Total Time: 25 minutes

Add noodles to a medium pot of boiling water. Reduce the heat to keep a low boil for 6 to 7 minutes. Stir to prevent sticking. Drain in a colander and rinse with cold water. While the noodles are cooking, squeeze the grated ginger and keep its juice in a small bowl. Whisk the peanut butter, rice vinegar, 2 tbsp of soy sauce, and sesame oil. Slowly add 2-3 tablespoons of water for desired consistency. Reserve. Prepare the bowl by placing spinach first. Top with noodles and drizzle the remaining soy sauce. Add the vegetables, then top with the dressing. Garnish with sliced avocado and cashews.

Favorite Lentil Sliders

Ingredients for 4 servings

4 tsp olive oil	2 tsp allspice
½ cup chopped onions	8 vegan slider buns
3 garlic cloves, minced	1 tbsp Dijon mustard
1 (15-oz) can lentils	1 tbsp ketchup
1 tbsp soy sauce	12 pickle slices
½ cup vegan breadcrumbs	

Directions and Total Time: 35 minutes

Preheat oven to 425°F. In a large skillet, heat 2 teaspoons of oil over medium heat. Sauté onion for 3 minutes until softened. Stir in garlic and sauté for 1 minute until aromatic. In a large bowl, add the onion mixture along with lentils, soy sauce, breadcrumbs, and allspice. Mash until it becomes a dough consistency. Scoop a heaping ¼ cup serving and shape into a patty. Arrange the patties on a parchment-lined baking sheet. Brush with 2 teaspoons oil and bake for 10 minutes. Flip the patties and bake for another 10 minutes until browned. Place the patties on buns and top with mustard, ketchup, and pickles. Serve.

Granny-Way Shepherds Pie

Ingredients for 6 servings

1 cup lentils	½ cup peas
6 peeled potatoes, chopped	½ tsp dried thyme
¼ cup coconut milk	½ tsp ground coriander
1 tbsp coconut oil	1 tbsp white wine
1 onion, diced	Salt and black pepper to taste
1 tsp olive oil	2 tbsp whole-grain flour
2 carrots, diced	

Directions and Total Time: 90 minutes

Add 3 cups of water along with the lentils in a medium pot. Bring to a boil, then reduce the heat and simmer for 15 minutes. In a large pot, add potatoes and cover with salted water. Cook for about 20 minutes. Reserve ½ cup of cooking liquid and drain the rest. Mash the potatoes then stir in coconut milk and oil. Season with salt. Preheat the oven to 350°F. Drain the lentils in a colander and pour into a baking dish. Use the lentil pot to saute onions in olive oil over medium heat.

After about 5 minutes, stir in carrots and cook for 5 more minutes. When the carrots are softened, add peas, thyme, coriander, and white wine. Stir to combine. Transfer to the dish with the lentils. Stir in pepper, salt, and flour. Add ½ cup of water and continue stirring until the flour is dissolved. Cover the lentil mixture with the mashed potatoes. Bake for 20-30 minutes until the top of the shepard's pie is golden. Serve warm and enjoy.

Couscous & Veggie Stir-Fry

Ingredients for 4 servings

1 head broccoli, cut into florets	
1 cup trimmed snow peas, halved	2 cups chopped bok choy
1 cup couscous	2 scallions, chopped
Salt to taste	1 tsp toasted sesame oil
2 tsp olive oil	1 tbsp soy sauce
1 cup shelled edamame beans	2 tbsp sesame seeds

Directions and Total Time: 20 minutes

Add couscous, 2 cups water, and salt to a medium pot. Bring the water to a boil, then cover. Remove from the heat and let the couscous steep for 5 to 8 minutes. In a large skillet, saute broccoli in olive oil on high heat. Season with a pinch of salt and cook until softened. Stir in the rest of the vegetables. The bok choy needs about a minute to wilt. Add two tablespoons of water to create steam to finish off the dish. Drizzle with sesame oil and soy sauce and toss to coat. Remove the skillet from the heat. Plate a scoop of couscous, then top with the stir-fry vegetables. Garnish with sesame seeds and add extra soy sauce and sesame oil to taste. Serve warm and enjoy.

Olive & Walnut Zoodles

Ingredients for 4 servings

2 tbsp olive oil	Salt to taste
2 zucchini, sliced into noodles	2 tbsp parsley, chopped
1 orange, zested and juiced	10 black olives, chopped
1 garlic clove, minced	¼ cup walnuts, chopped

Directions and Total Time: 15 minutes

Heat the olive oil in a large wok over high heat. Stir fry zucchini for about 2 minutes. Whisk orange zest, orange juice, garlic, and salt in a bowl. Toss the noodles in the orange sauce. Top with parsley, olives, and walnuts.

Brussels Sprouts & Cabbage with Mayo Sauce

Ingredients for 4 servings

1 lb Brussels sprouts, sliced	1 tsp lemon juice
¼ cup vegan mayonnaise	2 tbsp olive oil
2 tbsp Dijon mustard	Salt and black pepper to taste
¼ tsp pure maple syrup	2 cups sliced green cabbage

Directions and Total Time: 20 minutes

Whisk mayonnaise, mustard, maple syrup, and lemon juice in a small bowl. Set to the side. Over medium heat, add oil to a large skillet. Sear the Brussels sprouts for two minutes on each side. Season with salt and pepper. Reduce the heat, then add the cabbage for 2-4 minutes. When the cabbage is tender, serve among 4 plates and top with maple syrup sauce. Serve hot and enjoy.

Vegan Brown Butter Asparagus & Beans

Ingredients for 4 servings

¼ cup vegan butter	Salt and black pepper to taste
3 garlic cloves, thinly sliced	2 tbsp vegan Parmesan cheese
1 lb asparagus, each cut into 3	2 tbsp sliced almonds
1 (15-oz) can cannellini beans	

Directions and Total Time: 15 minutes

In a large skillet, melt butter over medium heat until it begins to brown, or about 3 - 5 minutes. Reduce the heat and stir in garlic. Sauté for 30 seconds or until aromatic. Stir in asparagus and sauté for 3 minutes stirring frequently. Next, add cannellini beans and cook for 2 minutes. Season with salt and pepper. Garnish with Parmesan and almonds. Serve warm and enjoy.

Vegetarian Paella

Ingredients for 4 servings

1 cup canned artichokes, quartered	
1 lemon, cut into wedges for garnish	
2 tbsp olive oil	½ cup green beans, chopped
1 onion, chopped	1 tbsp Spanish paprika
1 red bell pepper, 2 sliced	1 tsp ground turmeric
3 garlic cloves, minced	Salt to taste
1 tomato, diced	2 cups cooked brown rice
1 cup frozen peas, thawed	2 tbsp chopped parsley

Directions and Total Time: 25 minutes

In a large skillet, heat oil over medium heat. Sauté onion and bell pepper for 3 to 5 minutes until softened. Sauté garlic for 1 minute until aromatic. Stir in tomato, peas, green beans, artichokes, paprika, turmeric, and salt.

Heat through for 4 minutes, stirring occasionally. Stir in rice until completely mixed. Transfer to a serving dish and garnish with parsley and lemon wedges. Serve warm.

Las Vegas-Inspired Burgers

Ingredients for 6 servings

2 tbsp flax meal	½ tsp red pepper flakes
2 (15-oz) cans black beans	Salt and black pepper to taste
1 cup vegan breadcrumbs	2 tbsp olive oil
2 tbsp tamari	2 ripe avocados, mashed
1 tsp garlic powder	6 vegan hamburger buns
1 tsp ground cumin	1 cup salsa

Directions and Total Time: 25 minutes

Whisk flax meal and ¼ cup water in a small bowl. Set to the side to thicken. In a large bowl, mash 1 can of beans. Stir in the second can of beans, breadcrumbs, tamari, the flax-meal mixture, garlic powder, cumin, red pepper flakes, salt, and pepper until well combined while keeping the second can of beans whole. On a flat surface, pour the mixture out and shape into a log. Cut into 6 equal patty portions. In a large skillet, heat olive oil over medium heat. Arrange the patties in the skillet and cook for 3 minutes. Flip the patties and cook for another 3 minutes until brown and crisp. While the patties are cooking, season the mashed avocado with salt and pepper. To build the burger, layer the burger on top of the bottom bun, then spread 2 tablespoons of salsa on the burger. Dollop ¼ cup avocado mash, then top with the bun top. Serve warm and enjoy.

Pinto Bean & Potato Bake

Ingredients for 4 servings

2 russet potatoes, cubed

1 (15-oz) can pinto beans	1 tsp red pepper flakes
1 red bell pepper, diced	1 tsp ground cumin
1 onion, diced	Salt and black pepper to taste
3 tbsp olive oil	2 tbsp vegan sour cream
1 tsp chili garlic powder	1 tbsp chopped cilantro

Directions and Total Time: 30 minutes

Preheat the oven to 425°F. Line a baking sheet with parchment paper. Mix potatoes, beans, bell pepper, onion, oil, chili garlic powder, red pepper flakes, cumin, salt, and black pepper in a large bowl until well combined. Arrange the mixture in a single layer on the baking sheet. Bake for 10 minutes, toss with a spatula, then bake for another 10 minutes until the potatoes are golden and fork-tender. Garnish with sour cream and cilantro. Serve.

Famous Swedish Balls The Vegan Way

Ingredients for 4 servings

2 cups portobello mushrooms, diced
1 (15-oz) can chickpeas, mashed

¼ cup applesauce	½ tsp garlic powder
1 tbsp olive oil	¼ tsp paprika
2 chopped green onions	¼ tsp caraway seeds
3 garlic cloves, minced	¼ tsp fennel seeds
1½ cups vegan breadcrumbs	Salt to taste
¼ cup chopped fresh parsley	2 pinches cayenne pepper
2 tbsp soy sauce	2 cups mushroom gravy
½ tsp shallot powder	2 tbsp minced parsley

Directions and Total Time: 45 minutes

Preheat the oven to 400°F. Line a baking sheet with parchment paper. In a large skillet, heat oil over medium heat. Sauté mushrooms and green onions for 5 minutes until soft. Stir in garlic and sauté for 1 minute until aromatic. In a large bowl, combine chickpeas, breadcrumbs, parsley, applesauce, soy sauce, shallot powder, garlic powder, paprika, caraway seeds, fennel seeds, salt, and cayenne pepper until well mixed. Measure a heaping tablespoon of the mixture and roll into a ball in your hands. Arrange the balls on the baking sheet and bake for 15 minutes. Use tongs to turn the balls and bake for another 10 minutes until browned. While the Swedish balls are baking, warm the gravy in a medium saucepan. When the balls are done, transfer them to the saucepan and coat with the gravy. Garnish with parsley.

Brown Rice Stir-Fry with Vegetables

Ingredients for 4 servings

1 cup cremini mushrooms, chopped

¾ cup vegetable broth	2 tbsp olive oil
2 tbsp soy sauce	¼ tsp cayenne powder
1 tbsp ketchup	2 green onions, sliced
1 tbsp minced fresh ginger	3 cups broccoli florets
3 garlic cloves, minced	1 red bell pepper, diced
2 tsp cornstarch	4 cups cooked brown rice

Directions and Total Time: 20 minutes

Whisk broth, soy sauce, ketchup, ginger, garlic, and cornstarch in a small bowl. Set to the side. Heat oil in a large skillet over medium heat. Sauté cayenne, green onions, broccoli, bell pepper, and mushrooms for 6 to 8 minutes until softened and the broccoli is bright green. Whisk the broth mixture again and add to the vegetables. Stir, then reduce the heat to medium. Stir occasionally for 2 minutes for the sauce to thicken. Portion out the rice among 4 bowls and top with veggies. Serve warm.

Avocado Spaghetti Carbonara

Ingredients for 6 servings

12 diced sun-dried tomatoes	1 tsp onion powder
1 lb spaghetti	½ tsp garlic powder
1 cup green peas	Salt and black pepper to taste
1 avocado, peeled and pitted	4 oz vegan bacon, chopped
1 ¾ cups vegetable broth	3 tbsp vegan Parmesan
¼ cup olive oil	1 tsp red pepper flakes
½ lemon, juiced	

Directions and Total Time: 25 minutes

Prepare the spaghetti according to the directions on the package. In the last 2 minutes of the cook time, add peas and tomatoes to the water and pasta. Drain everything in a colander and set to the side. In a blender jar, add avocado, broth, olive oil, lemon juice, onion powder, garlic powder, salt, and pepper. Blend for 1 to 2 minutes until smooth and creamy. In a serving dish, combine pasta, bacon, vegetables, and avocado-cream sauce. Top with Parmesan and red pepper flakes. Serve warm.

Spinach & Tofu Benedict Florentine

Ingredients for 4 servings

4 vegan English muffins, toasted
1 (14-oz) block tofu	1 tsp lime juice
1 tsp olive oil	1 tsp Sriracha sauce
10 oz baby spinach	½ tsp ground turmeric
1 cup vegan mayonnaise	¼ tsp black pepper
3 tbsp vegan butter, melted	2 tbsp chopped chives

Directions and Total Time: 30 minutes

Preheat the oven to 425°F. Line a baking sheet with parchment paper. Slice the tofu horizontally into 4 thin strips. Cut each strip crosswise into 4 pieces. There will be 16 total pieces. Arrange the tofu in a single layer on the baking sheet and bake for 10 minutes. Flip the tofu and bake for another 10 minutes until golden and crisp. While the tofu is baking, in a large skillet, heat oil over medium heat. Add spinach and sauté for 2 minutes until wilted. Add mayonnaise, butter, lime juice, sriracha sauce, turmeric, and pepper to a small saucepan. Heat on medium-low heat to warm through. Place an open, toasted English muffin on a plate. Layer some spinach, then 2 pieces of tofu. Top with the sauce and garnish with chives. Repeat for the rest of the English muffins.

Oven-Baked Lentil Kofta Bake

Ingredients for 4 servings

2 tsp olive oil	½ lemon, juiced
1 (15-oz) can lentils	1 tsp ground cumin
¼ cup flax meal	½ tsp tomato purée
3 garlic cloves, minced	2 tbsp parsley, chopped
1 shallot, finely chopped	Salt and black pepper to taste
½ cup chopped parsley	

Directions and Total Time: 40 minutes

Preheat the oven to 425°F. Line a baking sheet with parchment paper. Mix all of the ingredients in a large bowl and mash into a dough consistency. Scoop 1 heaping tablespoon of dough and shape into a ball. Arrange on the baking sheet and gently press into a disk. Repeat this process until all of the dough is used. Brush tops with olive oil and bake for 10 minutes. Flip the falafel and bake for another 10 minutes until crisp. Serve warm.

Sesame Soy Roasted Broccoli

Ingredients for 4 servings

1 head broccoli, cut into florets
1 tbsp soy sauce	1 tbsp sesame seeds
2 tbsp sesame oil	

Directions and Total Time: 20 minutes

Preheat the oven to 425°F. Line a baking sheet with parchment paper. Toss broccoli, oil, and soy sauce in a large bowl until well coated. Arrange the florets on the baking sheet and roast for 10 minutes. Toss the florets with a spatula and roast for another 5 minutes until just browning on the edges. Transfer to a serving bowl and sprinkle with sesame seeds. Serve warm and enjoy.

Tofu Scramble with Mushrooms & Kale

Ingredients for 4 servings

1 cup sliced white button mushrooms
1 (14-oz) block tofu	1 tbsp olive oil
2 tbsp vegan butter, melted	½ cup diced onion
¼ cup vegetable broth	½ cup diced red bell pepper
1 tsp garlic powder	1 cup kale, chopped
½ tsp ground turmeric	5 oz baby spinach
Salt and black pepper to taste	2 scallions, thinly sliced

Directions and Total Time: 25 minutes

Divide tofu into 4 equal portions. Crumble one piece of tofu into a blender jar and set the other 3 to the side. Put butter, broth, salt, garlic powder, turmeric, and pepper in the blender jar. Puree until smooth. In a medium skillet, heat oil over medium heat. Sauté onion, bell pepper, and mushrooms for 3 to 5 minutes until softened. Crumble the rest of the tofu into the skillet and stir to combine. Sauté for 2 minutes, stirring occasionally. Pour in the sauce from the blender and stir to combine. Stir in spinach and kale and cook for 3 minutes or until wilted. Simmer for 5 minutes stirring halfway through. Sprinkle with sliced scallions. Serve warm and enjoy.

Amazing Parmesan Cornmeal

Ingredients for 6 servings

1 cup soy milk	2 tbsp vegan butter
1 cup yellow cornmeal	1 tsp ground black pepper
1 cup vegan Parmesan cheese	

Directions and Total Time: 30 minutes

In a large saucepan, add soy milk and 3 cups of salted water over medium heat. Bring to a boil, then whisk in cornmeal continuously. Cook for 3 to 5 minutes, constantly whisking to avoid lumps and sticking. Reduce the heat to low and cover. Simmer for 25 minutes. Whisk every 5 minutes to prevent lumps and to stick. When the cornmeal is cooked and creamy, stir in Parmesan and butter. Season with black pepper. Serve hot and enjoy.

Farfalle with White Sauce

Ingredients for 4 servings

4 cups cauliflower florets	½ cup cashew pieces
1 medium onion, chopped	2 large garlic cloves, peeled
8 oz farfalle pasta	2 tbsp fresh lemon juice
2 tbsp chives scallions, minced	Salt and black pepper to taste

Directions and Total Time: 30 minutes

Preheat your air fryer to 390°F. Put the cauliflower in the fryer basket, spray with oil, and Bake for 8 minutes. Remove the basket, stir, and add the onion. Roast for 10 minutes or until the cauliflower is golden and the onions soft. Cook the farfalle pasta according to the package directions. Set aside. Put the roasted cauliflower and onions along with the cashews, 1 ½ of cups of water, garlic, lemon juice, salt, and pepper in a blender. Blend until creamy. Pour a large portion of the sauce on top of the warm pasta and add the minced scallions. Serve.

Lentil Burritos with Cilantro Chutney

Ingredients for 4 servings

1 cup cilantro chutney	Salt to taste
1 lb cooked potatoes, mashed	½ tsp turmeric
2 tsp sunflower oil	¼ tsp cayenne powder
3 garlic cloves, minced	4 large flour tortillas
1 ½ tbsp fresh lime juice	1 cup cooked lentils
1 ½ tsp cumin powder	½ cup finely chopped cabbage
1 tsp onion powder	¼ cup minced red onions
1 tsp coriander powder	

Directions and Total Time: 30 minutes

Preheat air fryer to 390°F. Place the mashed potatoes, sunflower oil, garlic, lime, cumin, onion powder, coriander, salt, turmeric, and cayenne in a large bowl. Stir well until combined. Lay the tortillas out flat on the counter. In the middle of each, distribute the potato filling. Add some of the lentils, cabbage, and red onions on top of the potatoes. Close the wraps by folding the bottom of the tortillas up and over the filling, then folding the sides in, then rolling the bottom up to form a burrito. Place the wraps in the greased frying basket, seam side down. Air Fry for 6-8 minutes, flipping once until golden and crispy. Serve topped with cilantro chutney.

Grilled Cheese Sandwich

Ingredients for 1 serving

2 sprouted bread slices	1 garlic clove, minced
1 tsp sunflower oil	2 tbsp kimchi
2 Halloumi cheese slices	1 cup Iceberg lettuce, torn
1 tsp mellow white miso	

Directions and Total Time: 15 minutes

Preheat your air fryer to 390°F. Brush the outside of the bread with sunflower oil. Put the sliced Halloumi cheese, oiled sides facing out inside and close the sandwich. Put the sandwich in the frying basket and Air Fry for 12 minutes, flipping once until golden and crispy on the outside. On a plate, open the sandwich and spread the miso and garlic clove over the inside of one slice. Top with the kimchi and lettuce. Close the sandwich and cut it in half. Serve immediately and enjoy!

Golden Fried Tofu

Ingredients for 4 servings

1 (15-oz) package tofu, cubed	¼ tsp onion powder
¼ cup flour	Salt and black pepper to taste
¼ cup cornstarch	2 tbsp cilantro, chopped
1 tsp garlic powder	

Directions and Total Time: 20 minutes

Preheat air fryer to 390°F. Combine the flour, cornstarch, salt, garlic, onion powder, and black pepper in a bowl. Stir well. Place the tofu cubes in the flour mix. Toss to coat. Spray the tofu with oil and place them in a single layer in the greased frying basket. Air Fry for 14-16 minutes, flipping the pieces once until golden and crunchy. Top with freshly chopped cilantro and serve immediately.

Creamy Cauliflower Alfredo Rigatoni

Ingredients for 6 servings

4 cups cauliflower florets	Salt and black pepper to taste
1 ½ cups almond milk	1 tsp garlic powder
¼ cup silken tofu	1 lb cooked rigatoni pasta
½ lemon, juiced	3 tbsp vegan Parmesan cheese
2 tbsp Dijon mustard	2 tbsp chopped parsley
1 ½ tsp shallot powder	2 tsp truffle oil

Directions and Total Time: 20 minutes

Steam cauliflower for 10 to 12 minutes. When it is fork-tender, place in a blender jar. Add milk, tofu, lemon juice, mustard, shallot powder, salt, garlic powder, and pepper. Puree for 1 to 2 minutes until smooth. In a large bowl, add pasta and pour over the sauce. Toss to coat. Portion out the pasta among 6 bowls. Top with Parmesan, parsley, and truffle oil. Serve warm and enjoy.

Tofu Piccata

Ingredients for 4 servings

1 (14-oz) block tofu, drained	1 tbsp whole-wheat flour
1 tbsp olive oil	1 ½ lemons, juiced
2 shallots, chopped	2 tbsp vegan butter
3 garlic cloves, minced	2 tbsp capers
Salt and black pepper to taste	1 tbsp dry vermouth
1 cup vegetable broth	

Directions and Total Time: 30 minutes

Preheat the oven to 425°F. Line a baking sheet with parchment paper. Cut tofu horizontally into 3 thin strips, then cut each strip in half crosswise. Take each piece and cut on the diagonal to make 12 triangles. Arrange the tofu in a single layer on the baking sheet and bake for 10 minutes. Flip the triangles and bake for another 10 minutes until golden. While the tofu is baking, heat oil over medium heat in a large skillet. Stir in shallots and sauté for 3 minutes to soften. Sauté garlic for 1 minute until aromatic. Season with salt and pepper and slowly pour in broth. Reduce the heat and let it simmer. Whisk flour and ¼ cup water in a small bowl. Add the slurry to the skillet and stir. When the sauce starts to thicken, stir in lemon juice, butter, capers, and vermouth until the butter has completely melted. Dip the tofu in the piccata sauce until coated. Arrange on a serving platter, then drizzle with the rest of the piccata sauce. Serve warm.

Avocado & Vegan Bacon Sandwiches

Ingredients for 4 servings

½ cup vegan mayonnaise	8 tomato slices
4 bread slices, toasted	2 cups lettuce, torn
1 peeled avocado, sliced	1 tsp chili sauce
4 vegan bacon slices	Salt and black pepper to taste

Directions and Total Time: 20 minutes

Spread the mayonnaise on the bread slices and drizzle with chili sauce. Add the lettuce and tomato and arrange the avocado on top. Season with salt and pepper to taste and top with vegan bacon. Serve and enjoy!

Tofu & Spinach Lasagna

Ingredients for 4 servings

½ cup shredded plant-based mozzarella cheese
8 oz lasagne noodles
1 tbsp olive oil
2 cups crumbled tofu
2 cups fresh spinach
2 tbsp cornstarch

1 tsp onion powder
Salt and black pepper to taste
2 garlic cloves, minced
2 cups marinara sauce

Directions and Total Time: 30 minutes

Cook the noodles until a little firmer than al dente. Drain and set aside. While the noodles are cooking, make the filling. In a big pan over medium heat, add the olive oil, tofu, and spinach. Stir-fry for a minute, add the cornstarch, onion powder, salt, pepper, and garlic. Stir until the spinach wilts. Remove from heat.

Preheat oven to 390°F. Pour a thin layer of marinara sauce in a baking pan. Layer 2-3 lasagne noodles on top of the marinara sauce. Top with a little more sauce and some of the tofu mix. Add another 2-3 noodles on top, then another layer of sauce, then another layer of tofu. Finish with a layer of noodles and a final layer of sauce. Sprinkle with mozzarella on top. Bake for 15 minutes or until the noodle edges are browned and the cheese is melted. Serve.

Kale & Lentils with Crispy Onions

Ingredients for 4 servings

2 cups cooked red lentils
1 onion, cut into rings
½ cup kale, steamed
3 garlic cloves, minced

½ lemon, juiced and zested
2 tsp cornstarch
1 tsp dried oregano
Salt and black pepper to taste

Directions and Total Time: 40 minutes

Preheat air fryer to 390°F. Put the onion rings in the greased frying basket; do not overlap. Spray with oil and season with salt. Air Fry for 14-16 minutes, stirring twice until crispy and crunchy. Place the kale and lentils into a pan over medium heat and stir until heated through. Remove and add the garlic, lemon juice, cornstarch, salt, zest, oregano and black pepper. Stir well and pour in bowls. Top with the crisp onion rings and serve.

Black Bean Stuffed Potato Boats

Ingredients for 4 servings

4 russets potatoes
1 cup chipotle vegan mayonnaise
1 cup canned black beans
2 tomatoes, chopped

1 scallion, chopped
1/3 cup chopped cilantro
1 poblano chile, minced
1 avocado, diced

Directions and Total Time: 55 minutes

Preheat your air fryer to 390°F. Clean the potatoes, poke with a fork, and spray with oil. Put in the air fryer basket and Bake in the air fryer for 30 minutes or until softened. Heat the beans in a pan over medium heat. Put the potatoes on a plate and cut them across the top. Open them with a fork so you can stuff them. Top each potato with chipotle mayonnaise, beans, tomatoes, scallions, cilantro, poblano chile, and avocado. Serve immediately.

Zucchini Tamale Pie

Ingredients for 4 servings

1 cup canned diced tomatoes with juice
1 zucchini, diced
3 tbsp safflower oil
1 cup cooked pinto beans
3 garlic cloves, minced
1 tbsp corn masa flour
1 tsp dried oregano
½ tsp ground cumin

1 tsp onion powder
Salt to taste
½ tsp red chili flakes
½ cup ground cornmeal
1 tsp nutritional yeast
2 tbsp chopped cilantro
½ tsp lime zest

Directions and Total Time: 45 minutes

Warm 2 tbsp of the oil in a skillet over medium heat and sauté the zucchini for 3 minutes or until they begin to brown. Add the beans, tomatoes, garlic, flour, oregano, cumin, onion powder, salt, and chili flakes. Cook over medium heat, stirring often, about 5 minutes until the mix is thick and no liquid remains. Remove from heat. Spray a baking pan with oil and pour the mix inside. Smooth out the top and set aside. In a pot over high heat, add the cornmeal, 1 ½ cups of water, and salt. Whisk constantly as the mix begins to boil. Once it boils, reduce the heat to low. Add the yeast and oil and continue to cook, stirring often, 10 minutes or until the mix is thick and hard to stir. Remove from heat. Preheat your air fryer to 325°F. Add the cilantro and lime zest into the cornmeal mix and thoroughly combine. Using a rubber spatula, spread it evenly over the filling in the baking pan to form a crust topping. Put in the frying basket and Bake for 20 minutes or until the top is golden. Let it cool for 5 to 10 minutes, then cut and serve. Enjoy!

Pinto Bean Casserole

Ingredients for 2 servings

1 (15-oz) can pinto beans
¼ cup tomato sauce
2 tbsp cornstarch
2 garlic cloves, minced

½ tsp dried oregano
½ tsp cumin
1 tsp smoked paprika
Salt and black pepper to taste

Directions and Total Time: 15 minutes

Preheat air fryer to 390°F. Stir the beans, tomato sauce, cornstarch, garlic, oregano, cumin, smoked paprika, salt, and pepper in a bowl until combined. Spray a baking pan with oil and pour the bean mix in. Bake in the fryer for 4 minutes. Remove, stir, and Bake for 4 minutes or until the mix is thick and heated through. Serve hot.

Tortilla Pizza Margherita

Ingredients for 1 serving

1/3 cup grated plant-based mozzarella cheese
1 flour tortilla
¼ cup tomato sauce

3 basil leaves

Directions and Total Time: 15 minutes

Preheat oven to 350°F. Put the tortilla in a greased baking sheet and pour the sauce in the center. Spread across the whole tortilla. Sprinkle with cheese and bake for 8-10 minutes or until crisp. Remove and top with basil leaves.

Cheddar-Bean Flautas

Ingredients for 4 servings

1 cup shredded cheddar cheese
8 corn tortillas   1 cup guacamole
1 (15-oz) can refried beans

Directions and Total Time: 15 minutes

Preheat air fryer to 390°F. Wet the tortillas with water. Spray the frying basket with oil and stack the tortillas inside. Air Fry for 1 minute. Remove to a flat surface, laying them out individually. Scoop an equal amount of beans in a line down the center of each tortilla. Top with cheddar cheese. Roll the tortilla sides over the filling and put seam-side down in the greased frying basket. Air Fry for 7 minutes or until the tortillas are golden and crispy. Serve immediately topped with guacamole.

Baked Meat-Free Burgers

Ingredients for 3 servings

¾ cup canned red kidney beans   1 tbsp balsamic vinegar
¼ cup roasted red peppers   ½ tsp ground coriander
1 tbsp hot sauce   3 tbsp aquafaba

Directions and Total Time: 30 minutes

Preheat oven to 360°F. In a food processor, blitz the beans, red peppers, hot sauce, balsamic vinegar, and ¼ cup of water until smooth. Remove to a bowl. Add ground coriander and aquafaba and toss until well combined. Make 3 patties out of the mixture and bake for 16 minutes until golden brown, turning once. Serve.

Balsamic Lentil Patties

Ingredients for 4 servings

1 (15.5-oz) can lentils   1 tbsp allspice
¼ cup canned diced tomatoes   1 tsp liquid smoke
2 tbsp balsamic vinegar   2 tbsp aquafaba
2 tbsp hot sauce

Directions and Total Time: 25 minutes

Preheat air fryer to 360°F. Using a fork, mash the lentils in a bowl. Stir in tomatoes and their juice, balsamic vinegar, hot sauce, allspice, liquid smoke, and aquafaba with hands. Make 4 patties out of the mixture. Bake them for 15 minutes until crispy, turning once. Serve.

Thyme Meatless Patties

Ingredients for 3 servings

½ cup oat flour   1 tsp maple syrup
1 tsp allspice   ½ tsp liquid smoke
½ tsp ground thyme   1 tsp balsamic vinegar

Directions and Total Time: 25 minutes

Preheat air fryer to 400°F. Mix the oat flour, allspice, thyme, maple syrup, liquid smoke, balsamic vinegar, and water in a medium bowl. Make 6 patties out of the mixture. Place them onto a parchment paper and flatten them to ½-inch thick. Grease the patties with cooking spray and Grill for 12 minutes until crispy, turning once.

Bok Choy & Tofu Stir-Fry

Ingredients for 4 servings

2 ½ cups baby bok choy   1 tbsp plain vinegar
1 tbsp sesame oil   2 garlic cloves, minced
5 oz plant butter   1 tsp chili flakes
2 cups tofu, cubed   1 tbsp fresh ginger, grated
1 tsp garlic powder   3 green onions, sliced
1 tsp onion powder   1 cup vegan mayonnaise

Directions and Total Time: 45 minutes

Melt half of the butter in a wok over medium heat, add the bok choy, and stir-fry until softened. Season with salt, black pepper, garlic powder, onion powder, and plain vinegar. Sauté for 2 minutes; set aside. Melt the remaining butter in the wok, add and sauté garlic, chili flakes, and ginger until fragrant. Put the tofu in the wok and cook until browned on all sides. Add the green onions and bok choy, heat for 2 minutes, and add the sesame oil. Stir in vegan mayonnaise, cook for 1 minute, and serve.

Bagels with Avocado & Tomatoes

Ingredients for 2 servings

2/3 cup all-purpose flour   1 ripe avocado
½ tsp active dry yeast   1 tbsp lemon juice
1/3 cup Greek yogurt   2 tbsp chopped red onions
8 cherry tomatoes   Black pepper to taste

Directions and Total Time: 35 minutes

Preheat your air fryer to 400°F. Beat the flour, dry yeast, and Greek yogurt until you get a smooth dough, adding more flour if necessary. Make 2 equal balls out of the mixture. Using a rolling pin, roll each ball into a 9-inch long strip. Form a ring with each strip and press the ends together to create 2 bagels. In a bowl with hot water, soak the bagels for 1 minute. Shake excess water and let rise for 15 minutes in the fryer. After, Bake for 5 minutes, turn the bagels, top with tomatoes, and Bake for another 5 minutes. Cut avocado in half, discard the pit and remove the flesh into a bowl. Mash with a fork and stir in lemon juice and onions. Once the bagels are ready, let cool slightly and cut them in half. Spread on each half some guacamole, top with 2 slices of Baked tomatoes, and sprinkle with pepper. Serve immediately.

Tex-Mex Stuffed Sweet Potatoes

Ingredients for 2 servings

2 medium sweet potatoes   1 tsp taco seasoning
1 (15.5-oz) can black beans   2 tbsp lime juice
2 scallions, finely sliced   ¼ cup Ranch dressing
1 tbsp hot sauce

Directions and Total Time: 40 minutes

Preheat your air fryer to 400°F. Add the sweet potatoes to the fryer basket and Roast for 30 minutes. Toss the beans, scallions, hot sauce, taco seasoning, and lime juice. Set aside. Once the potatoes are ready, cut them lengthwise, 2/3 through. Spoon ¼ of the bean mixture into each half and drizzle Ranch dressing before serving.

Veggie & Tofu Scramble Bowls

Ingredients for 2 servings

1 russet potato, cubed	½ tsp garlic powder
1 bell pepper, cut into strips	½ tsp onion powder
½ tofu, cubed	¼ tsp ground turmeric
1 tbsp nutritional yeast	1 tbsp apple cider vinegar

Directions and Total Time: 25 minutes

Preheat your air fryer to 400°F. Put in potato cubes and bell pepper strips and Air Fry for 10 minutes. Combine the tofu, nutritional yeast, garlic, onion, turmeric, and apple vinegar in a small pan. Fit a trivet in the fryer, lay the pan on top, and Air Fry for 5 more minutes until potatoes are tender. Share the potatoes and bell peppers into 2 bowls and top each with the tofu scramble. Serve immediately. Enjoy!

Sweet & Spicy Vegetable Stir-Fry

Ingredients for 2 servings

½ pineapple, cut into chunks	5 oz cauliflower florets
¼ cup Tabasco sauce	1 carrot, thinly sliced
¼ cup lime juice	1 cup frozen peas, thawed
2 tsp allspice	2 scallions, chopped

Directions and Total Time: 45 minutes

Preheat air fryer to 400°F. Whisk Tabasco sauce, lime juice, and allspice in a bowl. Then toss in cauliflower, pineapple, and carrots until coated. Strain the remaining sauce; reserve it. Air Fry the veggies for 12 minutes, shake, and Air Fry for 10-12 more minutes until cooked. Once the veggies are ready, remove to a bowl. Meanwhile, combine peas, scallions, and reserved sauce until coated. Transfer to a pan and Air Fry them for 3 minutes. Remove them to the bowl and serve right away.

Pizza Margherita with Spinach

Ingredients for 4 servings

½ cup pizza sauce	1 pizza dough
1 tsp dried oregano	1 cup baby spinach
1 tsp garlic powder	½ cup vegan mozzarella

Directions and Total Time: 50 minutes

Preheat air fryer to 400°F. Whisk pizza sauce, oregano, and garlic in a bowl. Set aside. Form 4 balls with the pizza dough and roll out each into a 6-inch round pizza. Lay one crust in the basket, spread ¼ of the sauce, then scatter with ¼ of spinach and finally top with vegan mozzarella cheese. Grill for 8 minutes until golden brown and the crust is crispy. Repeat the process with the remaining crusts. Serve immediately and enjoy!

Cheesy Eggplant Lasagna

Ingredients for 4 servings

¾ cup chickpea flour	1 ½ cups panko bread crumbs
½ cup oat milk	1 eggplant, sliced
3 tbsp lemon juice	2 cups jarred tomato sauce
1 tbsp chili sauce	½ cup vegan ricotta cheese
2 tsp allspice	1/3 cup vegan mozzarella

Directions and Total Time: 40 minutes

Preheat air fryer to 400°F. Whisk chickpea flour, milk, lemon juice, chili sauce, and allspice until smooth. Set aside. On a plate, put the breadcrumbs. Submerge each eggplant slice into the batter, shaking off any excess, and dip into the breadcrumbs until well coated. Bake for 10 minutes, turning once. Let cool slightly. Spread 2 tbsp of tomato sauce at the bottom of a baking pan. Lay a single layer of eggplant slices, scatter with vegan ricotta and top with tomato sauce. Repeat the process until no ingredients are left. Scatter with mozzarella cheese on top and Bake at 350°F for 10 minutes until the eggplants are cooked and the cheese golden brown. Serve immediately.

Quinoa Green Pizza

Ingredients for 2 servings

¾ cup quinoa flour	1/3 cup vegan ricotta cheese
½ tsp dried basil	2/3 cup broccoli florets
½ tsp dried oregano	½ tsp garlic powder
1 tbsp apple cider vinegar	

Directions and Total Time: 25 minutes

Preheat air fryer to 350°F. Whisk quinoa flour, basil, oregano, apple cider vinegar, and ½ cup of water until smooth. Set aside. Cut 2 pieces of parchment paper. Place the quinoa mixture on one paper, top with another piece, and flatten to create a crust. Discard the top piece of paper. Bake for 5 minutes, turn and discard the other piece of paper. Spread the ricotta cheese over the crust, scatter with broccoli, and sprinkle with garlic. Grill at 400°F for 5 minutes until golden brown. Serve warm.

Coconut Mini Tarts

Ingredients for 2 servings

¼ cup almond butter	½ cup oat flour
1 tbsp coconut sugar	2 tbsp strawberry jam
2 tbsp coconut yogurt	

Directions and Total Time: 25 minutes

Preheat air fryer to 350°F. Use 2 pieces of parchment paper, each 8-inches long. Draw a rectangle on one piece. Beat the almond butter, coconut sugar, and coconut yogurt in a shallow bowl until well combined. Mix in oat flour until you get a dough. Put the dough onto the undrawing paper and cover it with the other one, rectangle-side up. Using a rolling pin, roll out until you get a rectangle. Discard top paper. Cut it into 4 equal rectangles. Spread on 2 rectangles, 1 tbsp of strawberry jam each, then top with the remaining rectangles. Using a fork, press all edges to seal them. Bake for 8 minutes.

Vegetarian Stuffed Bell Peppers

Ingredients for 3 servings

1 cup mushrooms, chopped	2 tbsp dried parsley
1 tbsp allspice	2 tbsp hot sauce
¾ cup vegan Alfredo sauce	Salt and black pepper to taste
½ cup canned diced tomatoes	3 large bell peppers
1 cup cooked rice	

Directions and Total Time: 40 minutes

Preheat oven to 375°F. Whisk mushrooms, allspice and 1 cup of boiling water until smooth. Stir in Alfredo sauce, tomatoes, rice, parsley, hot sauce, salt, and black pepper. Set aside. Cut the top of each bell pepper, take out the core and seeds without breaking the pepper. Fill each pepper with the rice mixture and cover them with aluminum foil, folding the edges. Roast for 30 minutes until tender. Let cool before unwrapping. Serve warm.

Effortless Mac `n´ Cheese

Ingredients for 4 servings

1 cup coconut cream cheese	1 tbsp grated vegan Parmesan
1 cup almond milk	16 oz cooked elbow macaroni
½ cup vegan mozzarella	

Directions and Total Time: 15 minutes

Preheat your air fryer to 400°F. Whisk the coconut cream cheese, milk, mozzarella cheese, and Parmesan cheese until smooth in a bowl. Stir in the macaroni and pour into a baking dish. Cover with foil and Bake in the air fryer for 6 minutes. Remove foil and Bake until cooked through and bubbly, 3-5 minutes. Serve warm and enjoy!

Mushroom Bolognese Casserole

Ingredients for 4 servings

1 cup canned diced tomatoes	¾ tsp dried oregano
2 garlic cloves, minced	1 cup chopped mushrooms
1 tsp onion powder	16 oz cooked spaghetti
¾ tsp dried basil	

Directions and Total Time: 20 minutes

Preheat air fryer to 400°F. Whisk the tomatoes and their juices, garlic, onion powder, basil, oregano, and mushrooms in a baking pan. Cover with aluminum foil and Bake for 6 minutes. Slide out the pan and add the cooked spaghetti; stir to coat. Cover with aluminum foil and Bake for 3 minutes until heated through and bubbly.

Pineapple & Veggie Souvlaki

Ingredients for 4 servings

1 (15-oz) can pineapple rings in pineapple juice
8 whole mushrooms, quartered

1 red bell pepper, seeded	1 tsp ground nutmeg
2 tbsp apple cider vinegar	14 oz tofu cheese
2 tbsp hot sauce	1/3 cup vegan butter, softened
1 tbsp allspice	1 red onion, peeled

Directions and Total Time: 35 minutes

Preheat your grill to 400°F. Whisk the vegan butter, pineapple juice, apple vinegar, hot sauce, allspice, and nutmeg until smooth. Slice the tofu into 16 cubes, then the bell pepper into 16 chunks, and finally red onion into 8 wedges, separating each wedge into 2 pieces. Cut pineapple ring into quarters. Place veggie cubes and tofu into the butter bowl and toss to coat. Thread the veggies, tofu, and pineapple onto 8 skewers, alternating 16 pieces on each skewer. Grill for 15 minutes until golden brown.

Vegan Buddha Bowls

Ingredients for 2 servings

12 oz broccoli florets	16 oz super-firm tofu, cubed
½ cup quinoa	1 tsp lemon juice
1 peeled sweet potato, cubed	2 tsp olive oil
¾ cup bread crumbs	Salt to taste
¼ cup chickpea flour	2 scallions, thinly sliced
¼ cup hot sauce	1 tbsp sesame seeds

Directions and Total Time: 45 minutes

Preheat your air fryer to 400°F. Add quinoa and 1 cup of boiling water in a baking pan, cover it with aluminum foil, and Air Fry for 10 minutes. Set aside covered. Put the sweet potatoes in the air fryer basket and Air Fry for 2 minutes. Add in broccoli and Air Fry for 5 more minutes. Shake up and cook for another 3 minutes. Set the veggies aside. On a plate, put the breadcrumbs.

In a bowl, whisk chickpea flour and hot sauce. Toss in tofu cubes until coated and dip them in the breadcrumbs. Air Fry for 10 minutes until crispy. Share quinoa and fried veggies into 2 bowls. Top with crispy tofu and drizzle with lemon juice, olive oil and salt to taste. Scatter with scallions and sesame seeds before serving. Enjoy!

Curried Cauliflower

Ingredients for 2 servings

12 oz cauliflower florets	1 tbsp curry powder
1 cup canned diced tomatoes	1 tsp ground ginger
2 cups almond milk	½ tsp ground cumin
2 tbsp lime juice	16 oz vegan cheddar, cubed
1 tbsp allspice	¼ cup chopped cilantro

Directions and Total Time: 30 minutes

Preheat your air fryer to 375°F. Combine the tomatoes and their juices, milk, lime juice, allspice, curry powder, ginger, and cumin in a baking pan. Toss in cauliflower and cheddar cheese until coated. Roast for 15 minutes, stir well, and Roast for another 10 minutes until bubbly. Scatter with cilantro. Serve and enjoy!

Bean Alfredo with Cherry Tomatoes & Zucchini

Ingredients for 2 servings

1 (16-oz) can cooked white cannellini beans, drained

2 zucchini, spiralized	¼ cup nutritional yeast
16 cherry tomatoes, halved	1 cup nondairy milk
1 garlic clove	¼ cup vegan Parmesan cheese
2 tbsp chopped fresh parsley	¼ tsp red chili flakes

Directions and Total Time: 20 minutes

In a food processor, mix in the beans, garlic, parsley, nutritional yeast, and milk. Blend until smooth. Remove the bean sauce to a medium saucepan over low heat.

Meanwhile, gently sauté the zucchini noodles and cherry tomatoes in a large skillet over medium heat for 5 minutes, until the vegetables are soft and less crunchy.

Divide the zucchini noodles between 2 plates, top with the Alfredo sauce, and sprinkle with 2 tbsp of vegan Parmesan cheese and chili flakes to serve.

Portobello & Eggplant Ciabatta

Ingredients for 4 servings

1 cup Portobello mushrooms, sliced
1 small eggplant, sliced   2 tbsp olive oil
1 orange bell pepper, sliced   2 cups arugula
½ yellow onion, sliced   4 whole-grain ciabatta buns
2 garlic cloves, minced   ¾ cup tomato sauce
1 tbsp Italian seasoning

Directions and Total Time: 30 minutes

Preheat the oven to 420°F. In a large bowl, mix well the eggplant, mushrooms, bell pepper, onion, Italian seasoning, garlic, and olive oil.

Roast the vegetables on for 20 minutes, flipping the eggplant halfway through, until cooked. Cut open the buns and spread the tomato sauce on the inside of both halves of each bun. Lay ¼ of the grilled veggies on the lower half of the bun, scatter some arugula, and put the top half of the bun on to finish the sandwich. Serve.

Mushroom & Lentil Döner Kebab

Ingredients for 4 servings

1 tbsp lemon juice   ¼ tsp ground cinnamon
1 tbsp tomato puree   ¼ tsp ground fennel seeds
2 tbsp soy sauce   4 large romaine lettuce leaves
1 (16-oz) can brown lentils ½ cup diced cucumber
½ cup mushrooms, sliced   ½ cup diced tomatoes
2 tsp ground cumin   4 tbsp Kalamata olives
1 tsp ground coriander   ½ cup vegan Tzatziki
1 tsp paprika

Directions and Total Time: 10 minutes

Stir together the lemon juice, tomato puree, and soy sauce until well combined in a bowl. Stir in the lentils, mushrooms, cumin, coriander, paprika, cinnamon, and ground fennel seeds, until the lentils are evenly coated.

In a skillet, gently warm the lentil mixture over medium heat for 5 minutes, or until warmed through. Transfer ¼ of the lentil mixture to each of the 4 large romaine lettuce leaves. Top each lettuce wrap with the cucumber, tomatoes, and olives, then drizzle the vegan Tzatziki over the filling before rolling the lettuce leaf. Serve.

Thyme Tofu Casserole

Ingredients for 4 servings

14 oz extra-firm tofu   ½ tsp garlic powder
1 tbsp sesame oil   1 tsp chopped thyme
1 tbsp soy sauce   2 tbsp cornstarch

Directions and Total Time: 30 minutes

Preheat oven to 400°F. Whisk together the sesame oil, soy sauce, garlic powder, thyme, and 1 tbsp of cornstarch in a medium mixing bowl until smooth.

Slice the tofu block in half lengthwise and then cut each rectangle into about 16 cubes. Toss the tofu in the sauce and stir well to combine. Stir in the remaining cornstarch. Lay the tofu cubes on a baking sheet in a single layer and cook in the oven for 25 minutes, flipping once. Serve.

Garbanzo Bean & Avocado Sandwiches

Ingredients for 3 servings

1 (16-oz) can garbanzo beans   Salt and black pepper to taste
1 avocado   6 whole-grain bread slices
2 tsp apple cider vinegar   1 cup baby spinach
1 garlic clove, minced   ½ cucumber, sliced
2 tbsp dried parsley   ¼ cup broccoli sprouts
2 tbsp chopped red onions

Directions and Total Time: 25 minutes

Mash the garbanzo beans and avocado together with a fork in a medium bowl. Pour in the vinegar, garlic, and parsley and stir well. Season with salt and pepper. Spread the garbanzo bean mash on 3 slices of bread. Top each with half of the spinach, broccoli sprouts, red onions, and cucumber. Close the sandwiches with the other 3 slices of bread and enjoy.

Goddess Pita Pizza

Ingredients for 2 servings

2 tsp extra-virgin olive oil   ¼ cup tomato sauce
¼ red bell pepper, cut into strips 2 whole-wheat pitas
¼ zucchini, cut into thin slices ¼ cup sun-dried tomatoes
¼ cup diced mushrooms   6 black olives
¼ cup diced red onions   ¼ cup nutritional yeast

Directions and Total Time: 15 minutes

Preheat oven to 350°F. Warm the olive oil in a skillet over medium heat. Sauté the bell pepper, zucchini, mushrooms, and onions until the vegetables are tender. Spread the tomato sauce over each pita and top with the sautéed vegetables. Bake in the oven for 8-10 minutes. Remove and add sun-dried tomatoes and olives. Sprinkle the nutritional yeast on top of each pizza. Enjoy!

Chickpea Salad Chard Wraps

Ingredients for 2 servings

½ cucumber, seeded and diced   ¼ cup diced kalamata olives
2 scallions, diced   1 cup canned chickpeas
½ cup cherry tomatoes, halved   ¼ cup sesame dressing
¼ red bell pepper, cut into strips 4 rainbow Swiss chard leaves

Directions and Total Time: 20 minutes

Place chickpeas in a medium bowl and roughly mash with a fork until desired consistency. Add the cucumber, scallions, cherry tomatoes, bell pepper, olives, and sesame dressing and mix well. Pour the dressing into the bowl and stir toss to combine. Divide the salad between the rainbow chard leaves. Roll them tightly, folding them in the ends to secure. Serve and enjoy!

Vegetarian Paella

Ingredients for 3 servings

½ cup chopped artichoke hearts
½ cup sliced red bell peppers   3 tbsp hot sauce
4 mushrooms, thinly sliced   2 tbsp lemon juice
½ cup canned diced tomatoes   1 tbsp allspice
½ cup canned chickpeas   1 cup rice

Directions and Total Time: 50 minutes

Preheat air fryer to 400°F. Combine the artichokes, peppers, mushrooms, tomatoes and their juices, chickpeas, hot sauce, lemon juice, and allspice in a baking pan. Roast for 10 minutes. Pour in rice and 2 cups of boiling water, cover with aluminum foil, and Roast for 22 minutes. Discard the foil and Roast for 3 more minutes until the top is crisp. Let cool slightly before stirring.

Avocado-Cucumber Sandwiches

Ingredients for 2 servings

1 avocado, mashed	1 cup alfalfa sprouts
4 toasted bread slices	1 cup arugula
½ cucumber, thinly sliced	1 tsp lemon juice
1 scallion, diced	Salt and black pepper to taste

Directions and Total Time: 20 minutes

Spread the mashed avocado over two toasted bread slices. Top with cucumber slices. Add the sprouts and arugula on top of the cucumber slices. Season with lemon juice, salt, and pepper to taste. Scatter with scallion. Top with the other two slices of toast. Serve and enjoy!

Mouth-Watering Vegetable Casserole

Ingredients for 3 servings

1 red bell pepper, chopped	2 tbsp balsamic vinegar
½ lb okra, trimmed	1 tbsp allspice
1 red onion, chopped	1 tsp ground cumin
1 (28-oz) can diced tomatoes	1 cup baby spinach

Directions and Total Time: 45 minutes

Preheat your air fryer to 400°F. Combine the bell pepper, red onion, okra, tomatoes and juices, balsamic vinegar, allspice, and cumin in a baking pan and Roast for 25 minutes, stirring every 10 minutes. Stir in spinach and Roast for another 5 minutes. Serve warm and enjoy!

Buddha Bowl with Couscous

Ingredients for 2 servings

3 cups mixed greens	½ cucumber, seeded and diced
½ cup couscous	1 cup cherry tomatoes, halved
1 cup cooked chickpeas	½ cup Kalamata olives, halved
2/3 cup hummus	½ diced orange bell pepper

Directions and Total Time: 20 minutes

Place the couscous into a mixing bowl, pour 1 ½ cups of boiling water over, and set aside for 10 mins to absorb. Divide the greens evenly between 2 bowls and top with couscous, chickpeas, hummus, cucumber, cherry tomatoes, olives, and bell pepper. Toss to combine. Serve.

Lentil Balls with Tagliatelle

Ingredients for 2 servings

1 tbsp flaxseed	¼ cup quick oats
2 garlic cloves	6 oz whole-grain tagliatelle
1 tsp Italian seasoning	1 tbsp tomato paste
1 cup cooked red lentils	1 ¼ cups tomato sauce
1 cup steamed beets, drained	2 tbsp vegan Parmesan cheese

Directions and Total Time: 45 minutes

Preheat the oven to 370°F. In a blender, pulse the flaxseed, 3 tbsp of water, garlic, and Italian seasoning. Let sit for 3 minutes. Add the lentils and beets to the blender and blend until combined, but not pureed. Scoop out 1 tbsp of the mixture and roll it into a ball. Repeat for all the balls. Roast the balls on a baking sheet for 20 minutes.

Cook the tagliatelle according to the package directions while the lentil-beet balls are baking. In a saucepan, warm and stir the tomato paste and sauce over medium heat to avoid burning for a few minutes.

Meanwhile, remove the balls from the oven and let cool for 5 minutes. Divide the pasta between 2 plates. Add half of the balls to each plate, top with the tomato sauce, and sprinkle the vegan Parmesan over each dish to serve.

Original Stuffed Peppers

Ingredients for 6 servings

6 red bell peppers, halved lengthwise	
1 cup farro, rinsed	1 tsp chili powder
2 tbsp extra-virgin olive oil	1 tsp dried oregano
4 garlic cloves, minced	2 tbsp lemon juice
2 tbsp tomato sauce	¼ cup chopped fresh parsley
1 shallot, diced	

Directions and Total Time: 45 minutes

Preheat the oven to 420°F. Bring the farro and 2 cups of water to a boil over high heat in a saucepan. Lower the heat and cover the saucepan. Simmer for 15 minutes.

Place the bell peppers, cut-side down, in a baking tray, and roast them for 15 minutes. Meanwhile, heat the olive oil in a skillet over medium heat. Stir-fry the garlic, shallot, and chili powder for 3-4 minutes until the garlic is fragrant.

Pour the oregano, lemon juice, and parsley and stir-fry for 1 more minute. Transfer the cooked farro to the skillet and mix to combine. Remove the peppers from the oven. Spoon the farro mixture into the open peppers and return them to the oven to roast for another 5 minutes. Let cool slightly before serving.

Mediterranean Eggplant & Rice

Ingredients for 4 servings

2 cups mixed cherry tomatoes, chopped	
1 ½ cups basmati rice	Salt and black pepper to taste
1 cup chopped basil leaves	4 grilled eggplant slices
½ cup kalamata olives	2 cups baby spinach leaves

Directions and Total Time: 20 minutes

Place the rice and 2 ¼ cups of water in a large pot over medium heat, cover, and bring to a boil. Then lower the heat and simmer for 6-8 minutes.

In a bowl, mix the tomatoes, half of the basil, olives, salt, and pepper. Arrange the eggplant slices over the rice. Pour the tomato mixture over and cover. Let simmer for 5 minutes. Add the spinach leaves in an even layer to the pot over the eggplant slices and simmer for another 5 minutes. Garnish with the remaining basil and serve.

Roasted Root Vegetables

Ingredients for 4 servings

1 large sweet potato, cubed	2 tbsp balsamic vinegar
2 medium beets, cubed	4 garlic cloves, minced
1 medium turnips, cubed	2 tsp dried basil
2 medium carrots, cubed	2 tsp dried oregano
1 zucchini, cubed	2 cups cremini mushrooms
1 medium parsnip, cubed	1 red onion, chopped
2 tbsp olive oil	Salt and black pepper to taste

Directions and Total Time: 45 minutes

Preheat the oven to 420°F. Whisk the olive oil, balsamic vinegar, garlic, basil, salt, pepper, and oregano in a small bowl. Spread the vegetables, mushrooms, and onion in a single layer on a rimmed baking sheet and pour the oil mixture over the vegetables. Toss to coat. Roast in the oven for 25-30 minutes, stirring once, until the vegetables are tender. Serve and enjoy!

Harissa Cauliflower Purée

Ingredients for 4 servings

4 cups cauliflower florets	1 tsp dried thyme
4 garlic cloves, peeled	Sea salt to taste
2 tbsp olive oil	¼ cup almond milk
½ tsp Harissa seasoning	

Directions and Total Time: 30 minutes

Preheat oven to 370°F. Toss the florets and garlic olive oil, thyme, Harissa seasoning, and salt in a large bowl. Transfer to a rimmed baking sheet. Roast in the oven for 20 minutes, stirring after 10 minutes. Remove the roasted vegetables from the oven and place them into your food processor with almond milk and blend until smooth.

Spinach & Olive Linguini

Ingredients for 2 servings

4 oz linguini	2 tbsp olive oil
2 cups chopped spinach	1 tbsp nutritional yeast
¼ cup Kalamata olives	Salt to taste
1 tbsp lemon juice	

Directions and Total Time: 25 minutes

Bring a saucepan of salted water to a boil and add the linguini. Cook according to the package directions. Drain the pasta and rinse under cold water. Set aside.

Steam the spinach in the same saucepan over medium heat for 3-4 minutes until the spinach is soft and bright green. Put the linguini back into the pot. Add the lemon juice, olive oil, nutritional yeast, olives, and salt. Toss to combine. Serve warm and enjoy!

Bean & Broccoli Couscous

Ingredients for 2 servings

3 garlic cloves, minced	1 (16-oz) can white beans
4 ½ tbsp olive oil	3 tbsp lemon juice
1 ½ cups vegetable broth	4 tbsp fresh parsley
1 cup whole-grain couscous	Salt and black pepper to taste
3 cups broccoli, cut into florets	

Directions and Total Time: 20 minutes

Stir-fry the garlic in ½ tbsp of olive oil over low heat in a saucepan, until fragrant, 3-4 minutes. Pour the broth and couscous into the saucepan and cook for 4 minutes or until the broth is absorbed, and the couscous is soft and fluffy. Meanwhile, in a skillet, heat 1 tbsp of olive oil over high heat and sauté the broccoli for 5 minutes. Stir in the beans and cook for another 5 minutes, until warmed through. Mix the cooked couscous with the broccoli mixture. Pour the remaining olive oil, lemon juice, and parsley, and stir. Season to taste and serve.

Lentil & Bean Chili

Ingredients for 4 servings

2 tbsp olive oil	1 tsp cumin
1 yellow onion, diced	1 tsp paprika
1 red bell pepper, cut into strips	1 cup vegetable broth
4 garlic cloves, minced	1 (16-oz) can diced tomatoes
¼ cup tomato paste	1 (16-oz) can white beans
2 tsp chili powder	1 (16-oz) can lentils, drained

Directions and Total Time: 40 minutes

Warm the olive oil in a saucepan over medium heat. Add the onion, bell pepper, and garlic and sauté for about 4 minutes until tender. Stir in the tomato paste, chili powder, cumin, and paprika for 1 minute. Pour in the broth and deglaze by scraping the bottom of the saucepan. Add the diced tomatoes, mixed beans, and lentils and stir well. Simmer on medium-low heat for 25 minutes, stirring occasionally to keep the bottom from burning. Serve warm and enjoy!

Tofu & Eggplant with Vegan Béchamel

Ingredients for 4 servings

1 eggplant, cubed	⅛ tsp sea salt
¼ cup sesame oil	1 (16-oz) can diced tomatoes
1 cup extra-firm tofu, crumbled	1 tbsp tomato paste
2/3 yellow onion, diced	1 tsp paprika
3 garlic cloves, minced	¾ cup water, as needed

Béchamel Sauce

1/3 cup olive oil	2 cups soy milk
1/3 cup flour	Salt and black pepper to taste

Directions and Total Time: 45 minutes

Preheat the oven to 400°F. Toss the eggplant with 2 tbsp of sesame oil in a baking tray. Bake in the oven for 20 minutes or until tender.

Heat the remaining sesame oil in a saucepan over high heat. Cook the tofu for 2-3 minutes; set aside. In the same pan, stir-fry the onion and garlic for 5 minutes until translucent and soft. Add the tofu mixture, salt, tomatoes, tomato paste, paprika, and roasted eggplant and stir. Cook for 15 minutes, adding water as needed until you reach your desired consistency.

Warm the olive oil in a small saucepan over medium heat for the sauce. Add the flour and milk and whisk the mixture well; be sure no clumps are formed. Season to taste. Top with the béchamel sauce and serve.

Berlin-Inspired Sauerkraut

Ingredients for 2 servings

¼ cup sauerkraut	1 cup white beans
2 tbsp Dijon mustard	1 onion, chopped
2 tsp olive oil	Salt and pepper to taste

Directions and Total Time: 25 minutes

Preheat the oven to 370°F. In a bowl, mix the sauerkraut and mustard. In a skillet, heat half of the olive oil and sauté the onion for 3 minutes until soft. Add the sauerkraut mixture cook for 8 minutes. Transfer to a baking dish and mix with the white beans. Season with salt and pepper. Bake in for an additional 8 minutes. Remove and let cool for 5 minutes before serving.

Broccoli & Caper Linguine

Ingredients for 4 servings

2 tbsp olive oil	8 oz whole-grain linguine
2 garlic cloves, minced	½ cup pitted green olives
1 head broccoli, cut into florets	Salt and black pepper to taste
¼ cup red onion, diced	2 tbsp lemon juice
½ tsp chili flakes	¼ cup parsley, chopped
1 tbsp capers	

Directions and Total Time: 20 minutes

In a saucepan over medium heat, warm the olive oil. Stir-fry the garlic and red onion for 3 minutes, until fragrant. Add the broccoli and chili flakes and stir until warmed through. Pour the pasta and 3 cups of water into the saucepan, cover, and bring to a boil. Cook the pasta for 8 minutes, until al dente. Mix in the olives and capers and season with salt and pepper. Sprinkle with lemon juice and garnish with parsley. Serve and enjoy!

Basil Artichoke-Potato Casserole

Ingredients for 4 servings

2 cups canned artichoke hearts, chopped

2 cups basil leaves	¼ cup extra-virgin olive oil
2 garlic cloves	2 lb potatoes, sliced
¼ cup hemp hearts	½ cup assorted olives
¼ tsp red chili flakes	4 tomatoes, chopped
¼ tsp sea salt	

Directions and Total Time: 15 minutes

Preheat the oven to 450°F. Place the basil, garlic, hemp hearts, red chili flakes, salt, and olive oil in a food processor and pulse until smooth. Place the potatoes slices on a parchment-lined baking sheet and roast for 15 minutes. Then, cover the potatoes with artichoke hearts, olives, and tomatoes. Spread the basil mixture on top and bake for another 15-17 minutes. Serve and enjoy!

Oriental Vegetable Stir-Fry

Ingredients for 4 servings

¼ cup olive oil	8 cups broccoli florets
¼ cup white wine vinegar	4 orange bell peppers, sliced
2 tsp Dijon mustard	16 mixed cherry tomatoes, diced
Salt to taste	2 carrots, chopped

Directions and Total Time: 30 minutes

Preheat the oven to 370°F. In a bowl, whisk half of the olive oil, vinegar, mustard, and salt. Add the broccoli and bell pepper slices and gently toss until well coated. Spread the vegetables on a baking sheet.

Cover with the cherry tomatoes and drizzle with the remaining olive oil. Season with salt. Roast in the oven for 20 minutes, or until the vegetables are tender and slightly charred. Serve.

Mushroom Fettucine al Pesto

Ingredients for 4 servings

8 oz whole-grain fettuccine	1/3 cup Perfect Pesto
2 tbsp olive oil	Juice of 1 lemon
2 garlic cloves, minced	¼ tsp red chili flakes
1 lb mushrooms, sliced	2 tbsp chopped fresh parsley
¼ tsp sea salt	

Directions and Total Time: 20 minutes

Add the pasta to a large saucepan, and cook according to the package directions until al dente. Drain, saving ½ cup of the pasta water, and set aside.

Warm the olive oil in a skillet over medium heat and sauté the mushrooms and garlic for 5-7 minutes until soft. Season with salt. Stir in the pasta, reserved water, lemon juice, chili flakes, and parsley for 2 minutes until well combined. Serve and enjoy!

Chickpea Spaghetti

Ingredients for 4 servings

1 ½ cups chickpeas, cooked	1 white onion, diced
Salt and black pepper to taste	3 garlic cloves, minced
4 cups cauliflower florets	Juice of 1 lemon
8 oz cooked spaghetti	¾ cup unsweetened oat milk
2 tsp olive oil	1/3 cup vegan Parmesan

Directions and Total Time: 30 minutes

In a large pot filled with boiling water, add the cauliflower and cook it until fork-tender, 5-7 minutes. Remove and drain, then transfer the drained cauliflower to a blender.

In a skillet, heat the olive oil and stir-fry the onion and garlic for 5 minutes or until translucent and fragrant.

Transfer to the blender with the cauliflower. Pour in the lemon juice, ¼ cup of milk, salt, pepper and pulse until the sauce is creamy. Place the cooked spaghetti in serving bowl and pour in the cauliflower sauce and mix well. Top with chickpea and vegan Parmesan cheese and serve.

Pesto Bean Zoodles

Ingredients for 2 servings

2 zucchini, spiralized	1 cup cooked white beans
16 cherry tomatoes, halved	1 tbsp vegan pesto

Directions and Total Time: 15 minutes

Combine the zucchini noodles, tomatoes, white beans and pesto in a salad bowl and toss to coat. Enjoy!

Simple Spinach Lasagna

Ingredients for 4 servings

2 oz grated plant-based Parmesan cheese
5 oz grated vegan mozzarella   ½ tbsp dried oregano
½ cup parsley, chopped   Salt and black pepper to taste
2 tbsp plant butter   1 cup baby spinach
1 white onion, chopped   8 tbsp flax seed powder
1 garlic clove, minced   1 ½ cup vegan cream cheese
2 ½ cups crumbled tofu   5 tbsp psyllium husk powder
3 tbsp tomato paste   2 cups coconut cream

Directions and Total Time: 65 minutes

Melt plant butter in a pot and sauté onion and garlic until fragrant and soft, 3 minutes. Stir in tofu and cook until brown. Mix in tomato paste, oregano, salt, and pepper. Pour ½ cup of water into the pot, stir, and simmer the ingredients until most of the liquid has evaporated.

Preheat oven to 300°F. Mix flax seed powder with 1 ½ cups water in a bowl to make vegan "flax egg." Allow sitting to thicken for 5 minutes. Combine vegan "flax egg" with vegan cream cheese and salt. Add psyllium husk powder a bit at a time while whisking and allow the mixture to sit for a few minutes. Line a baking sheet with parchment paper and spread the mixture in. Cover with another parchment paper and flatten the dough into the sheet. Bake for 10-12 minutes. Slice the pasta into sheets.

In a bowl, combine coconut cream and two-thirds of the plant-based mozzarella cheese. Fetch out 2 tablespoons of the mixture and reserve. Mix in plant-based Parmesan cheese, salt, pepper, and parsley. Set aside. Grease a baking dish with cooking spray, layer a single line of pasta, spread with some tomato sauce, 1/3 of the spinach, and ¼ of the coconut cream mixture. Repeat layering the ingredients twice in the same manner, making sure to top the final layer with the coconut cream mixture and the reserved vegan cream cheese. Bake for 30 minutes at 400°F. Slice and serve with salad.

Kale Stuffed Zucchini Boats

Ingredients for 2 servings

1 cup grated plant-based mozzarella
2 tbsp tomato sauce   1 zucchini
1 tsp olive oi   1 ½ oz baby kale
4 tbsp plant butter   Salt and black pepper to taste
2 garlic cloves, minced

Directions and Total Time: 40 minutes

Preheat oven to 375°F. Use a knife to slice the zucchini in halves and scoop out the pulp with a spoon into a plate. Keep the flesh. Grease a baking sheet with olive oil and place the zucchini boats on top.

Put the plant butter in a skillet and melt over medium heat. Sauté the garlic for 1 minute. Add in kale and zucchini pulp. Cook until the kale wilts; season with salt and black pepper. Spoon tomato sauce into the boats and spread to coat the bottom evenly. Then, spoon the kale mixture into the zucchinis and sprinkle with the plant-based mozzarella cheese. Bake for 20-25 minutes. Serve.

Mushroom & Kale Pierogis

Ingredients for 4 servings

Stuffing:

3 oz baby Bella mushrooms, sliced
2 oz plant-based Parmesan cheese, grated
1 red onion, finely chopped   2 oz fresh kale
2 tbsp plant butter   Salt and black pepper to taste
2 garlic cloves, finely chopped ½ cup dairy-free cream cheese

Pierogi:

1 ½ cups grated plant-based Parmesan cheese
5 tbsp plant butter   4 tbsp coconut flour
Olive oil for brushing   ½ tsp salt
1 tbsp flax seed powder   1 tsp baking powder
½ cup almond flour

Directions and Total Time: 45 minutes

Put the plant butter in a skillet, melt over medium heat, and then add and sauté the garlic, red onion, mushrooms, and kale until the mushrooms brown. Season the mixture with salt and black pepper and reduce the heat to low. Stir in the cream cheese and plant-based Parmesan cheese and simmer for 1 minute. Turn the heat off and set the filling aside to cool. Make the pierogis: In a small bowl, mix the flax seed powder with 3 tbsp water and allow sitting for 5 minutes. In a bowl, combine almond flour, coconut flour, salt, and baking powder. Put a small pan over low heat, add, and melt the plant-based Parmesan cheese and plant butter while stirring continuously until smooth batter forms. Turn the heat off.

Pour the vegan "flax egg" into the cream mixture, continue stirring while adding the flour mixture until a firm dough forms. Mold the dough into four balls, place on a chopping board, and use a rolling pin to flatten each into ½ inch thin round pieces. Spread a generous amount of stuffing on one-half of each dough, fold over the filling, and seal the dough with your fingers. Brush with olive oil, place on a baking sheet, and bake for 20 minutes at 380°F. Serve with salad.

Tempeh & Brussel Sprout Gratin

Ingredients for 4 servings

10 oz grated plant-based mozzarella cheese
¼ cup grated plant-based Parmesan cheese
1 cup tempeh, cubed   1 ¼ cups coconut cream
1 ½ lb halved Brussels sprouts 3 tbsp plant butter
5 garlic cloves, minced   Salt and black pepper to taste

Directions and Total Time: 30 minutes

Preheat oven to 400°F. Melt the plant butter in a large skillet over medium heat and fry the tempeh cubes until browned on both sides, about 6 minutes. Remove onto a plate and set aside. Pour the Brussels sprouts, salt, pepper, and garlic into the skillet and sauté until fragrant. Mix in coconut cream and simmer for 4 minutes. Add tempeh cubes and combine well. Pour the sauté into a baking dish, sprinkle with plant-based mozzarella cheese, and plant-based Parmesan cheese. Bake for 10 minutes or until golden brown on top. Serve with tomato salad.

Tasty Zucchini "Pasta" a la Bolognese

Ingredients for 4 servings

1 tbsp Worcestershire sauce	3 cups crumbled tofu
2 tbsp olive oil	2 tbsp tomato paste
2 tbsp plant butter	1 ½ cups crushed tomatoes
1 white onion, chopped	Salt and black pepper to taste
1 garlic clove, minced	1 tbsp dried basil
3 oz carrots, chopped	2 lb zucchini, spiralized

Directions and Total Time: 45 minutes

Pour olive oil into a saucepan and heat over medium heat. Add onion, garlic, and carrots and sauté for 3 minutes or until the onions are soft and the carrots caramelized. Pour in tofu, tomato paste, tomatoes, salt, pepper, basil, and Worcestershire sauce. Stir and cook for 15 minutes. Mix in some water if the mixture is too thick and simmer further for 20 minutes. Melt plant butter in a skillet and toss in the zoodles quickly, about 1 minute. Season with salt and black pepper. Divide into serving plates and spoon the Bolognese on top. Serve immediately.

Tofu Cordon Bleu

Ingredients for 4 servings

1 ¼ cup grated plant-based cheddar cheese	
4 tbsp olive oil	1 tbsp mustard powder
2 cups grilled tofu	1 tbsp plain vinegar
1 cup smoked seitan	Salt and black pepper to taste
1 cup vegan cream cheese	½ cup baby spinach

Directions and Total Time: 30 minutes

Preheat oven to 400°F. Place the tofu and seitan on a chopping board and chop both into small cubes. Mix the vegan cream cheese, mustard powder, plain vinegar, and plant-based cheddar cheese in a baking dish.

After, top with the tofu, seitan, and season with salt and black pepper. Bake in the oven until the casserole is golden brown on top, about 15 to 20 minutes. Serve with some baby spinach and a generous drizzle of olive oil.

Curried Cauliflower & Tempeh Casserole

Ingredients for 4 servings

15 oz cauliflower florets	Salt and black pepper to taste
4 tbsp plant butter	2 tbsp red curry paste
1 oz plant butter for greasing	1 ½ cups coconut cream
2 ½ cups chopped tempeh	½ cup fresh parsley, chopped

Directions and Total Time: 30 minutes

Preheat oven to 400°F and grease a baking dish with 1 ounce of plant butter. Arrange the tempeh in the baking dish, sprinkle with salt and black pepper, and top each tempeh with a slice of the remaining plant butter. In a bowl, mix the red curry paste with coconut cream and parsley. Pour the mixture over the tempeh. Bake in the oven for 20 minutes or until the tempeh is cooked.

Season the cauliflower with salt, place in a microwave-safe bowl, and sprinkle with some water. Steam in the microwave for 3 minutes or until the cauliflower is soft and tender within. Remove and serve with tempeh.

Mixed Mushroom Pizza with Pesto

Ingredients for 4 servings

¾ cup grated plant-based Parmesan cheese	
2 tbsp olive oil	1 tsp baking powder
2 tbsp flax seed powder	1 cup sliced mixed mushrooms
½ cup vegan mayonnaise	1 tbsp vegan basil pesto
¾ cup whole-wheat flour	½ cup red pizza sauce

Directions and Total Time: 40 minutes

Preheat the oven to 350°F. In a bowl, mix the flax seed powder with 6 tbsp water and allow thickening for 5 minutes to make the vegan "flax egg." Mix in vegan mayonnaise, whole-wheat flour, baking powder, and salt until dough forms. Spread the dough on a pizza pan and bake in the oven for 10 minutes or until the dough sets.

In a medium bowl, mix the mushrooms, olive oil, basil pesto, salt, and black pepper. Remove the pizza crust spread the pizza sauce on top. Scatter mushroom mixture on the crust and top with plant-based Parmesan cheese. Bake further until the cheese melts and the mushrooms soften, 10-15 minutes. Remove the pizza, slice, and serve.

Fettuccine Alfredo with Cherry Tomatoes

Ingredients for 4 servings

¾ cup grated plant-based Parmesan cheese	
3 tbsp plant butter	16 oz whole-wheat fettuccine
2 cups almond milk	½ cup coconut cream
1 ½ cups vegetable broth	¼ cup halved cherry tomatoes
1 large garlic clove, minced	2 tbsp chopped parsley

Directions and Total Time: 20 minutes

Bring almond milk, vegetable broth, butter, and garlic to a boil in a large pot, 5 minutes. Mix in the fettuccine and cook until tender while frequently tossing for about 10 minutes. Mix in coconut cream, tomatoes, plant Parmesan cheese, salt, and pepper. Cook for 3 minutes or until the cheese melts. Garnish with parsley and serve.

Creamy Broccoli Gratin

Ingredients for 4 servings

1 (10 oz) can cream mushroom soup	
2 cups grated plant-based cheddar cheese	
1 cup vegan mayonnaise	3 tbsp coconut cream
1 tbsp olive oil	1 medium red onion, chopped
3 tbsp plant butter, melted	¾ cup bread crumbs
2 cups broccoli florets	

Directions and Total Time: 50 minutes

Preheat the oven to 350°F. Heat the olive oil in a medium skillet and sauté the broccoli florets until softened, 8 minutes. Turn the heat off and mix in the mushroom soup, mayonnaise, salt, black pepper, coconut cream, and onion. Spread the mixture into the baking sheet. In a small bowl, mix the breadcrumbs with the plant butter and distribute the mixture on top. Add the cheddar cheese. Place the casserole in the oven and bake until golden on top and the cheese melts. Remove the casserole from the oven, allow cooling for 5 minutes, dish, and serve warm.

Broccoli & Tempeh Fritters

Ingredients for 4 servings

3 tbsp olive oil	1 head broccoli, grated
4 ¼ oz plant butter	8 oz tofu, grated
4 tbsp flax seed powder	3 tbsp almond flour
1 tbsp soy sauce	½ tsp onion powder
1 tbsp grated ginger	½ cup mixed salad greens
3 tbsp fresh lime juice	1 cup vegan mayonnaise
½ tsp cayenne pepper	Juice of ½ a lemon
10 oz tempeh slices	

Directions and Total Time: 40 minutes

In a bowl, mix the flax seed powder with 12 tbsp water and set aside to soak for 5 minutes. In another bowl, combine soy sauce, olive oil, grated ginger, lime juice, salt, and cayenne pepper. Brush the tempeh slices with the mixture. Heat a grill pan over medium and grill the tempeh on both sides until golden brown and nicely smoked. Remove the slices to a plate.

In another bowl, mix the tofu with broccoli. Add in vegan "flax egg," almond flour, onion powder, salt, and black pepper. Mix and form 12 patties out of the mixture. Melt the plant butter in a skillet and fry the patties on both sides until golden brown. Remove to a plate. Add the grilled tempeh with the broccoli fritters and salad greens. Mix the vegan mayonnaise with lemon juice and drizzle over the salad. Serve and enjoy!

Vegetable Biryani

Ingredients for 4 servings

1 cup chopped cremini mushrooms

3 white onions, chopped	½ tsp cayenne powder
1 tbsp turmeric powder	½ tsp cumin powder
6 garlic cloves, minced	1 tsp smoked paprika
1 tsp ginger puree	3 large tomatoes, diced
3 tbsp plant butter	2 green chilies, minced
1 cup brown rice	1 tbsp tomato puree
¼ tsp cinnamon powder	1 cup chopped mustard greens
2 tsp garam masala	1 cup plant-based yogurt
½ tsp cardamom powder	2 tbsp parsley, chopped

Directions and Total Time: 50 minutes

Melt the butter in a large pot and sauté the onions until softened, 3 minutes. Mix in the garlic, ginger, turmeric, cinnamon powder, garam masala, cardamom powder, cayenne pepper, cumin powder, paprika, and salt. Stir-fry for 1-2 minutes. Stir in the tomatoes, green chili, tomato puree, and mushrooms. Once boiling, mix in the rice and cover it with water. Cover the pot and cook over medium heat until the liquid absorbs and the rice is tender, 15-20 minutes. Open the lid and fluff in the mustard greens. Top with plant-based yogurt and parsley.

Spicy Spaghetti Squash Bake

Ingredients for 4 servings

2 oz grated plant-based Parmesan cheese

1 tbsp coconut oil	Olive oil for drizzling
2 tbsp melted plant butter	2 lb spaghetti squash

Salt and black pepper to taste	2 oz vegan cream cheese
½ tbsp garlic powder	1 cup plant-based mozzarella
1/5 tsp chili powder	2 tbsp fresh cilantro, chopped
1 cup coconut cream	

Directions and Total Time: 40 minutes

Preheat oven to 350°F. Cut the squash in halves lengthwise and spoon out the seeds and fiber. Place on a baking dish, brush with coconut oil, and season with salt and pepper. Bake for 30 minutes. Remove and use two forks to shred the flesh into strands.

Empty the spaghetti strands into a bowl and mix with plant butter, garlic and chili powders, coconut cream, cream cheese, half of the plant-based mozzarella and plant-based Parmesan cheeses. Spoon the mixture into the squash cups and sprinkle with the remaining mozzarella cheese. Bake further for 5 minutes. Sprinkle with cilantro and drizzle with some oil. Serve and enjoy!

Pepper & Tofu Bake

Ingredients for 4 servings

1 tbsp melted plant butter	2 tsp dried parsley
3 oz vegan cream cheese	4 orange bell peppers
¾ cup vegan mayonnaise	2 ½ cups cubed tofu
2 oz cucumber, diced	1 tsp dried basil
1 large tomato, chopped	

Directions and Total Time: 20 minutes

Preheat the oven's broiler to 450°F and line a baking sheet with parchment paper. In a salad bowl, combine vegan cream cheese, vegan mayonnaise, cucumber, tomato, salt, pepper, and parsley. Refrigerate.

Arrange the bell peppers and tofu on the baking sheet, drizzle with melted plant butter, and season with basil, salt, and pepper. Bake for 10-15 minutes or until the peppers have charred lightly and the tofu browned. Remove from the oven and serve with the salad.

Spicy Tofu with Sautéed Cabbage

Ingredients for 4 servings

1 tbsp + 3 ½ tbsp coconut oil	½ tsp onion powder
4 oz plant butter	2 cups Napa cabbage, grated
½ cup grated coconut	Salt and black pepper to taste
2 cups tofu, cubed	Lemon wedges for serving
1 tsp yellow curry powder	

Directions and Total Time: 55 minutes

Drizzle 1 tablespoon of coconut oil on the tofu. In a bowl, mix the shredded coconut, yellow curry powder, salt, and onion powder. Toss the tofu cubes in the spice mixture. Heat the remaining coconut oil in a non-stick skillet and fry the coated tofu until golden brown on all sides. Transfer to a plate. In another skillet, melt half of the plant butter, add, and sauté the cabbage until slightly caramelized. Then, season with salt and black pepper. Dish the cabbage into serving plates with tofu and lemon wedges. Melt the remaining plant butter in the skillet and drizzle over the cabbage and tofu. Serve.

Baked Squash with Spicy Chimichurri

Ingredients for 4 servings

½ red bell pepper, chopped
1 cup olive oil
1 tbsp plant butter, melted
Zest and juice of 1 lemon
1 jalapeno pepper, chopped
½ cup chopped fresh parsley
2 garlic cloves, minced
1 lb butternut squash
3 tbsp toasted pine nuts

Directions and Total Time: 15 minutes

In a bowl, add the lemon zest and juice, red bell pepper, jalapeno, olive oil, parsley, garlic, salt, and black pepper. Use an immersion blender to grind the ingredients until your desired consistency is achieved; set aside the chimichurri.

Slice the butternut squash into rounds and remove the seeds. Drizzle with the plant butter and season with salt and black pepper. Preheat a grill pan over medium heat and cook the squash for 2 minutes on each side or until browned. Remove the squash to serving plates, scatter the pine nuts on top, and serve with chimichurri.

Grilled Vegetable Steaks with Greek Salad

Ingredients for 2 servings

5 oz plant-based cheddar, cubed
¼ cup coconut oil
1 eggplant, sliced
1 zucchini, sliced
Juice of ½ a lemon
10 Kalamata olives
2 tbsp pecans
1 oz mixed salad greens
½ cup vegan mayonnaise
Salt to taste
½ tsp cayenne pepper

Directions and Total Time: 35 minutes

Set oven to broil. Arrange eggplant and zucchini on a parchment-lined baking sheet. Brush with coconut oil and sprinkle with cayenne pepper and salt. Broil for 15-20 minutes. Remove to a serving platter and drizzle with the lemon juice. Arrange the plant-based cheddar cheese, Kalamata olives, pecans, and mixed greens with the grilled veggies. Top with vegan mayonnaise and serve.

Avocado Pasta a la Carbonara

Ingredients for 4 servings

½ cup grated plant-based Parmesan cheese
5 tbsp psyllium husk powder
¼ cup olive oil
8 tbsp flax seed powder
1 ½ cups vegan cream cheese
1 avocado, chopped
1 ¾ cups coconut cream
Juice of ½ lemon
1 tsp onion powder
½ tsp garlic powder
Salt and black pepper to taste
4 tbsp toasted pecans

Directions and Total Time: 30 minutes

Preheat oven to 300°F. In a bowl, mix the flax seed powder with 1 ½ cups water. Allow sitting to thicken for 5 minutes. Add the vegan cream cheese, salt, and psyllium husk. Whisk until smooth batter forms. Line a baking sheet with parchment paper, pour in the batter, and cover with another parchment paper. Use a rolling pin to flatten the dough into the sheet. Bake for 10-12 minutes. Remove, take off the parchment papers and use a sharp knife to slice the pasta into thin strips lengthwise.

Cut each piece into halves, pour into a bowl, and set aside. In a blender, combine avocado, coconut cream, lemon juice, onion powder, and garlic powder; puree until smooth. Pour the olive oil over the pasta and stir to coat properly. Pour the avocado sauce on top and mix. Season with salt and black pepper. Divide the pasta into serving plates and garnish with Parmesan cheese and pecans.

Bell Pepper & Cauliflower Gratin

Ingredients for 4 servings

4 oz grated plant-based Parmesan cheese
½ cup celery stalks, chopped
1 head cauliflower, chopped
1 green bell pepper, chopped
Salt and black pepper to taste
2 oz plant butter
1 white onion, finely chopped
1 cup vegan mayonnaise
1 tsp red chili flakes

Directions and Total Time: 35 minutes

Preheat oven to 400°F. Season onion, celery, and bell pepper with salt and black pepper. In a bowl, mix cauliflower, vegan mayonnaise, Parmesan cheese, and red chili flakes. Pour the mixture into a greased baking dish and add the vegetables; mix to distribute. Bake for 20 minutes. Remove and serve warm.

Home-Style Tofu Tzatziki

Ingredients for 4 servings

½ cucumber, shredded
2 garlic cloves, minced
14 oz medium-firm tofu, drained
2 tbsp extra-virgin olive oil
Juice of ½ lemon
1 tsp apple cider vinegar
¼ tsp dried thyme
1 tsp fresh dill
Salt and black pepper to taste

Directions and Total Time: 25 minutes

Place the tofu, garlic, olive oil, lemon juice, vinegar, thyme, dill, and salt and pepper into your food processor and blend until smooth. Transfer to a serving bowl. Add the shredded cucumber and stir to incorporate. Serve chilled.

Tempeh & Grilled Zucchini with Spinach Pesto

Ingredients for 4 servings

¾ cup olive oil
2 tbsp melted plant butter
3 oz spinach, chopped
1 ripe avocado, chopped
Juice of 1 lemon
1 garlic clove, minced
2 oz pecans
Salt and black pepper to taste
2 zucchini, sliced
1 tbsp fresh lemon juice
1 ½ lb tempeh slices

Directions and Total Time: 20 minutes

Place the spinach in a food processor along with the avocado, lemon juice, garlic, and pecans. Blend until smooth and then season with salt and black pepper. Add the olive oil and process a little more. Pour the pesto into a bowl and set aside. Place zucchini in a bowl. Season with 1 tbsp of lemon juice, salt, black pepper, and plant butter. Also, season the tempeh with salt and black pepper, and brush with olive oil. Preheat a grill pan and cook both the tempeh and zucchini slices until browned on both sides. Plate the tempeh and zucchini, spoon some pesto to the side, and serve immediately.

Artichoke-Broccoli Pizza

Ingredients for 4 servings

6 ¼ oz grated plant-based Parmesan cheese
2 tbsp flax seed powder
4 ¼ oz grated broccoli
2 tbsp tomato sauce
2 oz plant-based mozzarella

2 oz canned artichoke wedges
1 garlic clove, thinly sliced
1 tbsp dried oregano
Green olives for garnish

Directions and Total Time: 40 minutes

Preheat oven to 350°F and line a baking sheet with parchment paper. In a bowl, mix flax seed powder and 6 tbsp water and allow thickening for 5 minutes. When the vegan "flax egg" is ready, add broccoli, 4 ½ oz of plant-based Parmesan cheese, salt, and stir to combine. Pour the mixture into the baking sheet and spread out with a spatula. Bake until the crust is lightly browned, about 20 minutes. Remove from the oven and spread the tomato sauce on top, sprinkle with the remaining plant-based Parmesan cheese and plant-based mozzarella cheese. Add the artichokes and garlic. Sprinkle with oregano. Bake the pizza further for 5-10 minutes at 420°F. When ready, slice the pizza, garnish with olives, and serve.

Indian-Style Tempeh Bake

Ingredients for 4 servings

1 green bell pepper, diced
3 tbsp plant butter
3 cups tempeh slices

2 tbsp garam masala
1 ¼ cups coconut cream
1 tbsp cilantro, finely chopped

Directions and Total Time: 30 minutes

Preheat oven to 400°F. Place a skillet over medium heat, add, and melt the plant butter. Meanwhile, season the tempeh with some salt. Fry the tempeh in the plant butter until browned on both sides, about 4 minutes. Stir half of the garam masala into the tempeh until evenly mixed. Transfer the tempeh and spice to a baking dish.

Then, mix green bell pepper, coconut cream, cilantro, and remaining garam masala in a small bowl. Pour the mixture over the tempeh and bake in the oven for 20 minutes until golden brown on top. Garnish with cilantro.

Baked Tempeh with Garden Peas

Ingredients for 4 servings

½ cup grated plant-based Parmesan cheese
16 oz bow-tie pasta
2/3 lb tempeh, cubed
Salt and black pepper to taste
1 yellow onion, chopped
2 tbsp olive oil, divided
½ cup sliced white mushrooms
2 tbsp whole-wheat flour

¼ cup white wine
¾ cup vegetable stock
¼ cup oat milk
2 tsp chopped fresh thyme
¼ cup chopped cauliflower
3 tbsp breadcrumbs

Directions and Total Time: 50 minutes

Cook the pasta in 8 cups of slightly salted water for 10 minutes or until al dente. Drain and set aside. Preheat the oven to 375°F. Heat the 1 tbsp of olive oil in a skillet, season the tempeh with salt and pepper, and cook until golden brown all around. Mix in onion, mushrooms.

Cook for 5 minutes. Stir in flour and cook for 1 more minute. Mix in wine and add two-thirds of the vegetable stock. Cook for 2 minutes while occasionally stirring and then add milk; continue cooking until the sauce thickens, 4 minutes. Season with thyme, salt, black pepper, and half of the Parmesan cheese. Once the cheese melts, turn the heat off and allow cooling.

Add the rest of the vegetable stock and cauliflower to a food processor and blend until smooth. Pour the mixture into a bowl, add in the sauce, and mix in pasta until combined. Grease a baking dish with cooking spray and spread in the mixture. Drizzle the remaining olive oil on top, breadcrumbs, some more thyme, and remaining cheese. Bake until the cheese melts and is golden brown on top, 30 minutes. Allow cooling for 3 minutes. Enjoy!

Grilled Tempeh with Green Beans

Ingredients for 4 servings

1 lb tempeh, sliced into 4 pieces
1 lb green beans, trimmed
1 tbsp plant butter, melted
2 tbsp olive oil

Salt and black pepper to taste
2 sprigs thyme
1 tbsp pure corn syrup
1 lemon, juiced

Directions and Total Time: 15 minutes

Preheat a grill pan over medium heat and brush with the plant butter. Season the tempeh and green beans with salt, black pepper, and place the thyme in the pan. Grill the tempeh and green beans on both sides until golden brown and tender, 10 minutes. Transfer to serving plates. In a small bowl, whisk the olive oil, corn syrup, lemon juice, and drizzle all over the food. Serve warm.

Tomato & Mushroom Lettuce Wraps

Ingredients for 4 servings

4 oz baby Bella mushrooms, sliced
1 iceberg lettuce, leaves extracted
1 cup grated plant-based cheddar
1 ½ lb tofu, crumbled

2 tbsp plant butter
1 large tomato, sliced

Directions and Total Time: 25 minutes

Melt the plant butter in a skillet, add mushrooms, and sauté until browned and tender, about 6 minutes. Transfer to a plate. Add the tofu to the skillet and cook until brown, about 10 minutes. Spoon the tofu and mushrooms into the lettuce leaves, sprinkle with the plant-based cheddar cheese, and share the tomato slices on top. Serve the burger immediately.

Arugula & White Bean Pitas

Ingredients for 6 servings

4 tsp olive oil
1 (14-oz) can white beans
2 scallions, minced
¼ cup fresh parsley, chopped
2 Kalamata olives, chopped
1 tbsp tahini
1 tbsp lemon juice
½ tsp ground cumin

¼ tsp paprika
6 whole-grain wraps, warm
1 cup hummus
1 cup arugula, chopped
2 tomatoes, chopped
1 cucumber, chopped
¼ cup chopped avocado

Directions and Total Time: 60 minutes

In a blender, place the white beans, scallions, parsley, and olives. Pulse until finely chopped. In a bowl, beat the tahini with lemon juice. Add in cumin, paprika, and salt. Transfer into beans mixture and mix well to combine. Shape the mixture into balls; flatten to make 6 patties.

In a skillet over medium heat, warm the oil and cook the patties for 8-10 minutes on both sides. Spread each wrap with hummus and top with patties, tomatoes, cucumber, arugula, and avocado. Roll the wraps up. Serve.

Picante Tomato Seitan with Brown Rice

Ingredients for 4 servings

2 tbsp olive oil	2 carrots diced
1 lb seitan, cut into cubes	4-5 cloves garlic
Salt and black pepper to taste	1 cup vegetable broth
1 tsp chili powder	1 tsp oregano
1 tsp onion powder	1 cup chopped tomatoes
1 tsp cumin powder	3 green chilies, chopped
1 tsp garlic powder	1 lime, juiced
1 yellow onion, chopped	1 cup brown rice
2 celery stalks, chopped	

Directions and Total Time: 50 minutes

Add brown rice, 2 cups of water, and salt to a pot. Cook for 15-20 minutes. Heat the olive oil in a large pot, season the seitan with salt, pepper, and cook in the oil until brown, 10 minutes. Stir in the chili powder, onion powder, cumin powder, garlic powder, and cook until fragrant, 1 minute. Mix in the onion, celery, carrots, garlic, and cook until softened. Pour in the vegetable broth, 1 cup of water, oregano, tomatoes, and green chilies.

Cover the pot and cook until the tomatoes soften and the liquid reduces by half, 10 to 15 minutes. Open the lid, adjust the taste with salt, black pepper, and mix in the lime juice. Dish and serve warm with brown rice.

Cauliflower Seitan Gratin

Ingredients for 4 servings

5 oz grated plant-based Parmesan cheese	
2 oz plant butter	2 cups crumbled seitan
1 leek, coarsely chopped	1 cup coconut cream
1 white onion, chopped	2 tbsp mustard powder
2 cups broccoli florets	4 tbsp fresh rosemary
1 cup cauliflower florets	Salt and black pepper to taste

Directions and Total Time: 40 minutes

Preheat oven to 450°F. Melt half of the plant butter in a pot over medium heat. Add in leek, white onion, broccoli, and cauliflower and cook for about 6 minutes. Transfer the vegetables to a baking dish.

Melt the remaining butter in a skillet over medium heat and cook the seitan until browned, 5-7 minutes. Mix the coconut cream and mustard powder in a bowl. Pour the mixture over the vegetables. Scatter the seitan and plant-based Parmesan cheese on top and sprinkle with rosemary, salt, and pepper. Bake in the oven for 15 minutes. Remove to cool for a few minutes and serve.

Mushroom Pizza Bianca

Ingredients for 4 servings

¾ cup grated plant-based Parmesan cheese

2 tbsp olive oil	1 tsp baking powder
2 tbsp flax seed powder	2 oz mixed mushrooms, sliced
½ cup vegan mayonnaise	1 tbsp plant-based basil pesto
¾ cup almond flour	Salt and black pepper to taste
1 tbsp psyllium husk powder	½ cup coconut cream

Directions and Total Time: 35 minutes

Preheat the oven to 350°F. Combine flax seed powder with 6 tbsp water and allow sitting to thicken for 5 minutes. Whisk in vegan mayonnaise, almond flour, psyllium husk powder, baking powder, and salt. Allow sitting for 5 minutes. Pour the batter into a baking sheet and spread out with a spatula. Bake for 10 minutes.

In a bowl, mix the mushrooms with pesto, olive oil, salt, and black pepper. Remove the crust from the oven and spread the coconut cream on top. Add the mushroom mixture and plant-based Parmesan cheese. Bake the pizza further 5-10 minutes until the cheese has melted.

Basil-Cashew Fettucine with Peas

Ingredients for 4 servings

½ cup cashew butter, softened	¾ cup flax milk
1 tbsp olive oil	2 garlic cloves, minced
16 oz whole-wheat fettuccine	1 ½ cups frozen peas
Salt and black pepper to taste	½ cup chopped fresh basil

Directions and Total Time: 25 minutes

Cook the fettuccine in a large pot over medium heat until al dente, 8-10 minutes. Drain the pasta through a colander and set aside. In a bowl, whisk the flax milk, cashew butter, and salt until smooth. Set aside.

Heat the olive oil in a large skillet and sauté the garlic until fragrant, 30 seconds. Mix in peas, fettuccine, and basil. Toss well until the pasta is well-coated in the sauce and season with black pepper. Dish the food and serve.

Hot Chickpea Burgers with Avocado Spread

Ingredients for 4 servings

1 avocado, pitted and peeled	2 tbsp quick-cooking oats
4 hamburger buns, split	¼ cup chopped fresh parsley
3 (15 oz) cans chickpeas	1 tbsp hot sauce
2 tbsp almond flour	1 garlic clove, minced
1 tomato, chopped	¼ tsp garlic salt
1 small red onion, chopped	1/8 tsp black pepper

Directions and Total Time: 20 minutes

In a medium bowl, mash avocados and mix in the tomato and onion. Set aside the dip. In another bowl, mash the chickpeas and mix in the almond flour, oats, parsley, hot sauce, garlic, garlic salt, and black pepper. Mold 4 patties out of the mixture and set aside.

Heat a grill pan over medium heat and lightly grease with cooking spray. Cook the patties on both sides until light brown and cooked through, 10 minutes. Place each patty between each burger bun and top with avocado dip.

Nutty Tofu Loaf

Ingredients for 4 servings

1 lb firm tofu, crumbled
2 tbsp olive oil
1 cup diced mixed bell peppers
2 white onions, finely chopped
4 garlic cloves, minced
2 tbsp soy sauce
¾ cup chopped mixed nuts
¼ cup flaxseed meal
1 tbsp sesame seeds
Salt and black pepper to taste
1 tbsp Italian seasoning
½ tsp pure date syrup
½ cup tomato sauce

Directions and Total Time: 65 minutes

Preheat the oven to 350°F and grease a loaf pan with olive oil. Heat 1 tbsp of olive oil in a small skillet and sauté the onion and garlic until softened and fragrant, 2 minutes. Pour the onion mixture into a large bowl and mix with the tofu, soy sauce, nuts, flaxseed meal, sesame seeds, bell peppers, salt, black pepper, Italian seasoning, and date syrup until well combined. Spoon the mixture into the loaf pan, press to fit, and spread the tomato sauce on top. Bake the tofu loaf in the oven for 45 minutes to 1 hour or until well compacted. Remove the loaf pan from the oven, invert the tofu loaf onto a chopping board, and cool for 5 minutes. Slice and serve.

Roasted Asparagus with Cashew Mash

Ingredients for 4 servings

½ lb asparagus, hard stalks removed
1 tbsp olive oil
2 oz plant butter, melted
3 oz plant butter
3 oz vegan cream cheese
4 tbsp flax seed powder
½ cup coconut cream
Powdered chili pepper to taste
Juice of ½ a lemon

Directions and Total Time: 15 minutes

In a microwave bowl, mix the flax seed powder with ½ cup water. Let sit to thicken for 5 minutes. Warm the vegan "flax egg" in the microwave for 1-2 minutes, then pour it into a blender. Add in plant butter, vegan cream cheese, coconut cream, salt, and chili pepper. Puree until smooth.

Heat olive oil in a saucepan and roast the asparagus until lightly charred. Season with salt and black pepper and set aside. Melt plant butter in a frying pan until nutty and golden brown. Stir in lemon juice and pour the mixture into a sauce cup. Spoon the creamy blend into the center of four serving plates and use the back of the spoon to spread out lightly. Top with the asparagus and drizzle the lemon butter on top. Serve immediately.

California-Style Veggie Bowls

Ingredients for 4 servings

1 yellow onion, finely diced
1 avocado, sliced
1 cup grated plant-based cheddar
1 tbsp olive oil
1 lb extra firm tofu, cubed
Salt and black pepper to taste
½ cup cauliflower florets
1 jalapeño pepper, minced
2 garlic cloves, minced
1 tbsp red chili powder
1 tsp cumin powder
1 (8 oz) can sweet corn kernels
1 (8 oz) can lima beans, rinsed
1 cup quick-cooking quinoa
1 (14 oz) can diced tomatoes
2 ½ cups vegetable broth
2 tbsp chopped fresh cilantro
2 limes, cut into wedges

Directions and Total Time: 30 minutes

Heat olive oil in a pot and cook the tofu until golden brown, 5 minutes. Season with salt, pepper, and mix in onion, cauliflower, and jalapeño pepper. Cook until the vegetables soften, 3 minutes. Stir in garlic, chili powder, and cumin powder; cook for 1 minute. Mix in sweet corn kernels, lima beans, quinoa, tomatoes, and vegetable broth. Simmer until the quinoa absorbs all the liquid, 10 minutes. Fluff quinoa. Top with the plant-based cheddar cheese, cilantro, lime wedges, and avocado. Serve.

BBQ Bean-Oat Burgers

Ingredients for 4 servings

3 (15 oz) cans black beans
4 hamburger buns, split
2 tbsp whole-wheat flour
2 tbsp quick-cooking oats
¼ cup chopped fresh basil
2 tbsp pure barbecue sauce
1 garlic clove, minced
Salt and black pepper to taste

For topping:

Red onion slices
Tomato slices
Fresh basil leaves
Additional barbecue sauce

Directions and Total Time: 20 minutes

In a medium bowl, mash the black beans and mix in the flour, oats, basil, barbecue sauce, garlic salt, and black pepper until well combined. Mold 4 patties out of the mixture and set aside.

Heat a grill pan to medium heat and lightly grease with cooking spray. Cook the bean patties on both sides until light brown and cooked through, 10 minutes. Place the patties between the burger buns and top with the onions, tomatoes, basil, and barbecue sauce. Serve warm.

Tofu Balls with Jalapeño Mayo

Ingredients for 4 servings

4 oz grated plant-based cheddar cheese
2 tbsp plant butter
1/3 cup vegan mayonnaise
¼ cup pickled jalapenos
1 tsp paprika powder
1 tbsp mustard powder
1 pinch cayenne pepper
1 tbsp flax seed powder
2 ½ cup crumbled tofu

Directions and Total Time: 40 minutes

In a bowl, mix vegan mayonnaise, jalapeños, paprika, mustard powder, cayenne powder, and plant-based cheddar cheese; set aside. In another bowl, combine flax seed powder with 3 tbsp water and allow absorbing for 5 minutes. Add the vegan "flax egg" to the cheese mixture, crumbled tofu, salt, and pepper and combine well. Form meatballs out of the mix. Melt plant butter in a skillet and fry the tofu balls until browned. Serve and enjoy!

Tempeh & Bean Brown Rice

Ingredients for 4 servings

1 (8 oz) can black beans, drained
2 tbsp olive oil
1 ½ cups crumbled tempeh
1 tsp Creole seasoning
2 red bell peppers, sliced
1 cup brown rice
2 cups vegetable broth
Salt to taste
1 lemon, zested and juiced
2 chives, chopped
2 tbsp freshly chopped parsley

Directions and Total Time: 50 minutes

Heat the olive oil in a medium pot and cook in the tempeh until golden brown, 5 minutes. Season with the Creole seasoning and stir in the bell peppers. Cook until the peppers slightly soften, 3 minutes. Stir in the brown rice, vegetable broth, salt, and lemon zest. Cover and cook until the rice is tender and all the liquid is absorbed, 15 to 25 minutes. Mix in the lemon juice, beans, and chives. Allow warming for 3 to 5 minutes and dish the food. Garnish with the parsley and serve warm.

Chili Quinoa a la Puttanesca

Ingredients for 4 servings

4 pitted Kalamata olives, sliced	1/8 tsp salt
1 ½ tbsp capers	4 pitted green olives, sliced
4 cups plum tomatoes, diced	2 garlic cloves, minced
1 tbsp olive oil	1 tbsp chopped fresh parsley
1 cup brown quinoa	¼ cup chopped fresh basil
2 cups water	1/8 tsp red chili flakes

Directions and Total Time: 30 minutes

Add the quinoa, water, and salt to a medium pot over medium heat. Cook for 15 minutes. In a bowl, mix tomatoes, green olives, Kalamata olives, capers, garlic, olive oil, parsley, basil, and red chili flakes. Allow sitting for 5 minutes. Serve the puttanesca with the quinoa.

Green Pea & Potato Stir-Fry

Ingredients for 4 servings

2 tbsp olive oil	1 tsp cumin powder
4 medium potatoes, diced	¼ tsp turmeric powder
1 medium onion, chopped	Salt and black pepper to taste
1 tsp red chili powder	1 cup fresh green peas
1 tsp fresh ginger-garlic paste	

Directions and Total Time: 21 minutes

Steam potatoes in a safe microwave bowl in the microwave for 8-10 minutes or until softened. Heat the olive oil in a wok and sauté the onion until softened, 3 minutes. Mix in the chili powder, ginger-garlic paste, cumin powder, turmeric powder, salt, and black pepper and cook until fragrant, about 1 minute. Stir in the green peas, potatoes, and cook until softened, 2-3 minutes. Serve.

Basil Bean & Quinoa Burgers

Ingredients for 4 servings

4 hamburger buns, split	1 shallot, chopped
4 small lettuce leaves	2 tbsp chopped fresh celery
½ cup vegan mayonnaise	1 garlic clove, minced
1 (15-oz) can pinto beans	2 tbsp whole-wheat flour
1 tbsp olive oil	¼ cup chopped fresh basil
1 cup quick-cooking quinoa	2 tbsp pure maple syrup

Directions and Total Time: 35 minutes

Cook the quinoa with 2 cups of water in a pot until the liquid absorbs, 10 to 15 minutes. Heat the olive oil in a medium skillet over medium heat and sauté the shallot, celery, and garlic until softened and fragrant, 3 minutes.

Transfer the quinoa and shallot mixture to a medium bowl and add the pinto beans, flour, basil, maple syrup, salt, and black pepper. Mash and mold 4 patties out of the mixture and set aside.

Heat a grill pan to medium heat and lightly grease with cooking spray. Cook the patties on both sides until light brown, compacted, and cooked through, 10 minutes. Place the patties between the burger buns and top with the lettuce and vegan mayonnaise. Serve and enjoy!

Tempeh Filled Zucchini Rolls

Ingredients for 4 servings

1/3 cup grated plant-based Parmesan	
2 cups grated plant-based mozzarella cheese	
¼ cup chopped basil leaves	3 zucchinis, sliced lengthwise
1 ½ cups marinara sauce	¾ lb crumbled tempeh
1 tbsp olive oil	1 cup crumbled tofu cheese
2 garlic cloves, minced	

Directions and Total Time: 60 minutes

Line a baking sheet with paper towels and lay the zucchini slices in a single layer. Sprinkle each side with some salt and allow releasing of liquid for 15 minutes. Heat the olive oil in a skillet and cook tempeh for 10 minutes; set aside. In a bowl, mix tempeh, tofu cheese, plant-based Parmesan cheese, basil, and garlic.

Preheat the oven to 400°F. Spread 1 cup of marinara sauce onto the bottom of a baking pan and set aside. Spread 1 tbsp of the cheese mixture evenly along with each zucchini slice; sprinkle with 1 tbsp of plant mozzarella cheese. Roll up the zucchini slices over the filling and arrange in the baking pan. Top with the remaining marinara sauce and sprinkle with the remaining plant-based mozzarella cheese. Bake for 25-30 minutes or until the cheese begins to brown. Serve immediately.

Tempeh Bites with Crunchy Asparagus

Ingredients for 4 servings

¼ cup diced red bell pepper	1 lb tempeh, crumbled
1 lb asparagus, trimmed	1 tsp garlic powder
1 tbsp lemon juice	1 tsp onion powder
1 tbsp almond flour	1 tbsp vegan mayonnaise
2 tbsp plant butter	Salt and black pepper to taste
1 tbsp flax seed powder	2 tbsp pure maple syrup

Directions and Total Time: 40 minutes

Preheat the oven to 400°F and line a baking sheet with parchment paper. In a bowl, mix flax seed powder with 3 tbsp water and allow thickening for 5 minutes. Add in tempeh, bell pepper, salt, pepper, almond flour, garlic powder, onion powder, and vegan mayonnaise.

Mix and form 1-inch balls from the mixture. Arrange on the baking sheet, brush with cooking spray, and bake for 15-20 minutes; set aside. Melt butter in a skillet and sauté asparagus until softened with some crunch, 7 minutes. Mix in maple syrup and lemon juice. Cook for 2 minutes and plate the asparagus. Serve warm with tempeh balls.

Seitan Patties with Mashed Broccoli

Ingredients for 4 servings

2 oz grated plant-based Parmesan cheese
4 oz plant-based butter   ½ white onion
5 oz cold plant butter   1 lb broccoli
1 tbsp flax seed powder   2 tbsp lemon juice
1 ½ lb crumbled seitan

Directions and Total Time: 30 minutes

Preheat oven to 220°F. In a bowl, mix the flax seed powder with 3 tbsp water and allow sitting to thicken for 5 minutes. When the vegan "flax egg" is ready, add in crumbled seitan, white onion, salt, and pepper. Mix and mold out 6-8 cakes out of the mixture. Melt plant butter in a skillet and fry the patties on both sides until golden brown. Remove onto a wire rack to cool slightly.

Pour salted water into a pot, bring to a boil, and add in broccoli. Cook until the broccoli is tender but not too soft. Drain and transfer to a bowl. Add in cold plant butter, Parmesan, salt, and pepper. Puree the ingredients until smooth and creamy. Set aside. Mix the soft plant butter with lemon juice, salt, and pepper in a bowl. Serve the seitan cakes with broccoli mash and lemon butter.

Rice Bowls with Soy Chorizo

Ingredients for 4 servings

1 (8 oz) can pinto beans   2 cups vegetable broth
2 tbsp olive oil   ¼ cup salsa
2 cups chopped soy chorizo   1 lemon, zested and juiced
1 tsp taco seasoning   1 (7 oz) can sweet corn kernels
2 green bell peppers, sliced   2 green onions, chopped
1 cup brown rice   2 tbsp freshly chopped parsley

Directions and Total Time: 50 minutes

Heat the olive oil in a medium pot and cook the soy chorizo until golden brown, 5 minutes. Season with the taco seasoning and stir in bell peppers; cook until the peppers slightly soften, 3 minutes. Stir in the brown rice, vegetable broth, salt, salsa, and lemon zest. Cook the food until the rice is tender and all the liquid is absorbed, 15 to 25 minutes. Mix in the lemon juice, pinto beans, corn kernels, and green onions. Allow warming for 3-5 minutes. Garnish with parsley and serve.

Hot Chili Brussel Sprout Sauté

Ingredients for 4 servings

4 oz plant butter   Salt and black pepper to taste
4 shallots, chopped   1 lb Brussels sprouts, halved
1 tbsp apple cider vinegar   ½ cup hot chili sauce

Directions and Total Time: 15 minutes

Put the plant butter in a saucepan and melt over medium heat. Pour in the shallots and sauté for 2 minutes, to caramelize and slightly soften. Add the apple cider vinegar, salt, and black pepper. Stir and reduce the heat to cook the shallots further with continuous stirring, about 5 minutes. Transfer to a plate after.

Pour the Brussel sprouts into the saucepan and stir-fry with more plant butter until softened but al dente. Season with salt and black pepper, stir in the onions and hot chili sauce, and heat for a few seconds. Serve immediately.

Asian Chickpea Wraps with Peaches

Ingredients for 4 servings

2 cups torn Iceberg lettuce   Sea salt to taste
1 (14-oz) can chickpeas   1 cup diced peaches
3 tbsp tahini   1 red bell pepper, diced small
Zest and juice of 1 lime   ½ cup fresh cilantro, chopped
1 tbsp curry powder   4 large whole-grain wraps

Directions and Total Time: 15 minutes

In a bowl, beat tahini, lime zest, lime juice, curry powder, 3-4 tbsp of water, and salt until creamy. In another bowl, combine the chickpeas, peaches, bell pepper, cilantro, and tahini dressing. Divide the mixture between the wraps and top with lettuce. Roll up and serve. Enjoy!

Grilled Zucchini & Kale Pizza

Ingredients for 4 servings

½ cup grated plant Parmesan cheese
3 ½ cups whole-wheat flour   1 pinch sugar
1 tsp yeast   1 cup marinara sauce
3 tbsp olive oil   2 large zucchinis, sliced
¼ cup capers   ½ cup chopped kale
1 tsp salt   1 tsp oregano

Directions and Total Time: 30 minutes

Preheat the oven the 350°F and lightly grease a pizza pan with cooking spray. In a bowl, mix flour, nutritional yeast, salt, sugar, olive oil, and 1 cup of warm water until smooth dough forms. Allow rising for an hour or until the dough doubles in size. Spread the dough on the pizza pan and apply marinara sauce and oregano on top.

Heat a grill pan, season the zucchinis with salt, black pepper, and cook in the pan until slightly charred on both sides. Sit the zucchini on the pizza crust and top with kale, capers, and plant-based Parmesan cheese. Bake for 20 minutes. Cool for 5 minutes, slice, and serve.

Basil Fidelini Primavera

Ingredients for 4 servings

8 oz fidelini pasta   2 garlic cloves, minced
12 cherry tomatoes, halved   1 cup dry white wine
½ tsp paprika   Salt and black pepper to taste
1 small red onion, sliced   1 lemon, zested and juiced
2 tbsp olive oil   1 cup packed fresh basil leaves
3 tbsp plant butter, cubed

Directions and Total Time: 25 minutes

Heat the olive oil in a pot over medium heat. Mix in fidelini, paprika, onion, garlic, and stir-fry for 2-3 minutes. Pour white wine and season with salt and pepper. Cover with water. Cook until the water absorbs and the fidelini is al dente, 5 minutes. Mix in the cherry tomatoes, butter, lemon zest, lemon juice, and basil. Serve warm.

Sticky Northern Bean Bake

Ingredients for 4 servings

2 (155-oz) cans Great Northern beans
1 (14.5-oz) can diced tomatoes 2 garlic cloves, minced
2 tbsp olive oil 1 ½ tsp dry mustard
½ cup pure date syrup ¼ tsp ground cayenne pepper
1 onion, minced Salt and black pepper to taste

Directions and Total Time: 25 minutes

Preheat the oven to 350°F. Heat the olive oil in a pot over medium heat. Place in onion and garlic and sauté for 3 minutes. Add in tomatoes, date syrup, mustard, cayenne pepper, salt, and pepper. Cook for 5 minutes. Pour the beans into a baking dish and stir in the sauce to coat. Bake for 10 minutes. Serve warm and enjoy!

Cabbage & Tempeh Stir-Fry

Ingredients for 4 servings

1 green bell pepper, cut into strips
1 (28-oz) can whole tomatoes 1 can (8 oz) tomato sauce
1 small head cabbage, sliced 2 tbsp plain vinegar
1 lb crumbled tempeh 1 tbsp pure date sugar
1 large yellow onion, chopped 1 tsp dried mixed herbs

Directions and Total Time: 30 minutes

Drain the tomatoes and reserve their liquid. Chop the tomatoes and set aside. Add the tempeh to a large skillet and cook until brown, 10 minutes. Mix in the onion, tomato sauce, vinegar, date sugar, mixed herbs, and chopped tomatoes. Close the lid and cook until the liquid reduces, 10 minutes. Stir in the cabbage and bell pepper; cook until softened, 5 minutes. Serve and enjoy!

Kale & Tofu Filled Mushrooms

Ingredients for 4 servings

4 large portobello mushrooms, stems removed
Garlic salt and pepper to taste ½ tsp olive oil
1 small onion, chopped ¼ cup crumbled tofu cheese
1 cup chopped fresh kale 1 tbsp chopped fresh basil

Directions and Total Time: 25 minutes

Preheat the oven to 350°F and grease a baking sheet with cooking spray. Lightly oil the mushrooms with some cooking spray and season with black pepper and garlic salt. Arrange the mushrooms on the baking sheet and bake in the oven until tender, 10 to 15 minutes.

Heat the olive oil in a skillet over medium heat and sauté the onion until tender, 3 minutes. Stir in kale until wilted, 3 minutes. Spoon the mixture into the mushrooms and top with tofu cheese and basil. Serve and enjoy!

Cajun-Style Stuffed Mushrooms

Ingredients for 4 servings

½ head broccoli, cut into florets
1 lb cremini mushroom caps 1 bell pepper, chopped
1 onion, finely chopped 1 tsp Cajun seasoning mix
1 tsp garlic, minced Salt and black pepper, to taste
2 tbsp olive oil ¼ cup plant-based mozzarella

Directions and Total Time: 35 minutes

Preheat oven to 360°F. Bake mushroom caps in a greased baking dish for 10-12 minutes. In a food processor, place broccoli and pulse until it becomes like small rice-like granules. In a heavy-bottomed skillet, warm olive oil; stir in bell pepper, garlic, and onion and sauté until fragrant. Place in pepper, salt, and Cajun seasoning mix. Fold in broccoli rice. Divide the filling mixture among mushroom caps. Top with cheese and bake for 17 minutes. Serve.

Baked Sweet Potatoes with Hot Corn Salad

Ingredients for 4 servings

1 (15-oz) can corn kernels ¼ tsp cayenne pepper
½ tbsp plant butter, melted 2 scallions, thinly sliced
4 sweet potatoes, cubed 1 large green chili, minced
2 limes, juiced 1 tsp cumin powder

Directions and Total Time: 35 minutes

Preheat the oven to 400°F and lightly grease a baking sheet with cooking spray. In a medium bowl, add the sweet potatoes, lime juice, salt, black pepper, and cayenne pepper. Toss well and spread the mixture on the baking sheet. Bake until the potatoes soften, 20-25 minutes. Transfer to a serving plate and garnish with scallions. In a bowl, mix corn kernels, butter, green chili, and cumin powder. Serve the sweet potatoes with the corn salad.

Avocado & Spinach Pizza with Chickpeas

Ingredients for 4 servings

¼ cup grated plant-based Parmesan cheese
1 (15 oz) can chickpeas 1 tsp salt
3 tbsp olive oil 1 pinch sugar
1 tsp oregano 1 cup red pizza sauce
3 ½ cups whole-wheat flour 1 cup baby spinach
1 tsp yeast 1 avocado, chopped

Directions and Total Time: 40 minutes

Preheat the oven the 350°F. In a bowl, mix flour, nutritional yeast, salt, sugar, olive oil, and 1 cup of warm water until smooth dough forms. Allow rising for an hour or until the dough doubles in size. Spread the dough on a greased pizza pan and apply the pizza sauce on top. Top with oregano, baby spinach, chickpeas, avocado, and plant-based Parmesan cheese. Bake in the oven for 20 minutes or until the cheese melts. Remove from the oven, cool for 5 minutes, slice, and serve. Enjoy!

Faux Parmesan Cheese

Ingredients for 3 servings

¼ cup hemp hearts ¼ cup nutritional yeast
¼ cup raw cashews 1 tsp garlic powder
1 tbsp raw sunflower seeds

Directions and Total Time: 10 minutes

Place hemp hearts, cashews, sunflower seeds, nutritional yeast, and garlic powder in a blender and blitz quickly until the mixture resembles grated Parmesan. Store in an airtight container in the fridge for up to 14 days.

DINNER

Hot Mushroom Fried Cauli Rice

Ingredients for 4 servings

1 cup white button mushrooms, sliced
1 cup grated purple cabbage   1 onion, chopped
1 large head cauliflower   3 tbsp tamari
3 garlic cloves, minced   Salt and black pepper to taste
1 cup frozen peas   2 tbsp chives, sliced
1 cup sliced carrots   2 tbsp hot sauce
2 tbsp olive oil

Directions and Total Time: 30 minutes

Grate the cauliflower in either a food processor or box grater to make about 4 cups of cauliflower rice. In a large skillet, heat 1 tablespoon oil over medium heat. Sauté onion and mushrooms for 5 minutes until softened. Sauté garlic for 1 minute until aromatic. Next, add another tablespoon of oil along with the cauliflower rice. Cook for 2 minutes stirring often. Then stir in peas, carrot, cabbage, and tamari sauce. Cook for another 4 minutes, stirring occasionally. When the rice starts to get tender, season with salt and pepper and stir. Transfer to a serving dish and top with chives and hot sauce. Serve.

Andalusian Spinach & Chickpeas

Ingredients for 4 servings

1 tbsp olive oil   1 (15-oz) can chickpeas
1 onion, chopped   1 (14-oz) can diced tomatoes
2 garlic cloves, minced   1/3 cup raisins
2 tsp ground cumin   Salt and black pepper to taste
½ tsp sherry vinegar   5 oz baby spinach
2 tsp Spanish paprika

Directions and Total Time: 15 minutes

In a large skillet, heat oil over medium heat. Sauté onion for 3 minutes until soft, then stir in garlic, cumin, vinegar, and paprika. Sauté for another minute until aromatic. Stir in chickpeas, tomatoes and the juice, raisins, salt, and pepper. Combine to coat and stir occasionally for 3 minutes. Stir in spinach and cook for another 3 minutes until it is wilted. Serve warm and enjoy.

Potato Wedges with Mushroom Gravy

Ingredients for 2 servings

2 large russet potatoes, cut into wedges
Salt and black pepper to taste   ½ tsp chili powder
½ tsp Italian seasoning   ½ cup mushroom gravy
½ tsp garlic powder

Directions and Total Time: 30 minutes

Preheat the oven to 475°F. Line a baking sheet with parchment paper. In a large bowl, toss potatoes, Italian seasoning, garlic powder, and chili powder. Arrange the potatoes on the baking sheet and lightly spray them with cooking oil. Bake for 10 minutes, then flip the wedges. Bake for another 5 to 10 minutes until fork-tender. Serve warm with mushroom gravy. Enjoy!

Hush Puppies with Sriracha Mayo

Ingredients for 6 servings

1 (15-oz) can chickpeas   ½ cup all-purpose flour
2 chopped spring onions   2 tsp baking powder
2 garlic cloves, minced   Salt to taste
6 tbsp almond milk   4 tbsp canola oil
¾ cup yellow cornmeal   1 cup sriracha mayo

Directions and Total Time: 20 minutes

Mash chickpeas in a large bowl along with spring onions, garlic, almond milk, cornmeal, flour, baking powder, and salt. In a heavy, deep skillet or saucepan, add 2 inches of oil. Heat to 350°F. Test with a drop of batter. If the batter sizzles when it hits the oil, it is ready. Roll out a heaping teaspoon of batter to make a hush puppy. Set aside until the oil is hot enough. Use a slotted spoon to carefully add hush puppies to the oil. Do not overfill the pot. Fry for 1 to 2 minutes or until golden. Transfer to a plate lined with paper towel. Continue frying the rest of the hush puppies. Serve warm with sriracha mayo.

Caribbean Roasted Kabocha Squash

Ingredients for 4 servings

2 lb kabocha squash, sliced   ¼ cup vegan butter
½ cup dark rum   ¼ tsp ground cinnamon
1/3 cup maple syrup   Salt to taste

Directions and Total Time: 40 minutes

Preheat the oven to 425°F. Line a baking sheet with parchment paper. Arrange the squash in a single layer on the baking sheet. Roast for 20 minutes. While the squash is roasting, heat rum, maple syrup, and butter in a small saucepan over low heat. Stir until combined. Flip the squash and spoon over rum sauce. Season with cinnamon and salt. Bake for 8 to 10 minutes until the squash is fork-tender and caramelized. Serve warm.

Cauliflower Governator

Ingredients for 4 servings

1 head cauliflower, cut into florets
1 cup almond milk   1 tsp dried oregano
1 tbsp apple cider vinegar   1 tsp dried coriander
1 cup all-purpose flour   ½ tsp dried thyme
1 tbsp chili powder   ½ tsp shallot powder
Salt and black pepper to taste ½ tsp garlic powder

Directions and Total Time: 40 minutes

Preheat oven to 450°F. Whisk milk and vinegar in a small bowl. Whisk flour, chili powder, salt, pepper, oregano, coriander, thyme, shallot powder, and garlic powder in a medium bowl. Dip cauliflower first in the milk mixture, then dredge it in the flour mixture. Arrange on a parchment-lined baking sheet. Repeat the process for the rest of the cauliflower. Lightly spray the cauliflower with nonstick cooking spray. Bake the cauliflower for 15 minutes, then flip the cauliflower. Spray again with nonstick cooking spray and bake for another 15 minutes until golden and crunchy. Serve warm and enjoy.

Sherry Tofu with Mushrooms

Ingredients for 4 servings

2 cups baby Bella mushrooms, sliced
1 (14-oz) block tofu, drained
1 tbsp sesame oil
1 onion, chopped
3 garlic cloves, minced
½ cup dry sherry
1 tsp soy sauce
1 cup vegetable broth
1 tbsp tomato paste
1 tbsp corn starch
Salt and black pepper to taste
2 tbsp chopped parsley

Directions and Total Time: 30 minutes

Preheat oven to 425°F. Cut tofu horizontally into 3 thin strips, then cut each strip in half crosswise. Take each piece and cut on the diagonal to make 12 triangles. Arrange the tofu in a single layer on a parchment-lined baking sheet and bake for 10 minutes. Flip the triangles and bake for another 10 minutes until golden. Heat oil over medium heat in a skillet. Sauté onion for 3 minutes. Sauté garlic for 1 minute until aromatic. Stir in sherry and mushrooms and cook for 5-7 minutes to reduce the wine. Make a slurry by whisking soy sauce, broth, tomato paste, and corn starch in a small bowl. Add the slurry to the skillet and continue stirring for 3 minutes until the sauce has thickened. Add salt and pepper. Dip the tofu in the sauce until coated. Remove to a serving platter. Drizzle with the remaining mushroom sauce. Top with parsley.

Barbecued Mushroom Sandwiches

Ingredients for 4 servings

1 cup white button mushrooms, stemmed and sliced
2 garlic cloves, minced
1 tbsp avocado oil
1 onion, chopped
½ cup barbecue sauce
1 tsp smoked paprika
½ tsp ground cinnamon
4 vegan hamburger buns
¼ red onion, thinly sliced

Directions and Total Time: 30 minutes

Heat oil in a large skillet over medium heat. Sauté onion for 3 minutes until softened. Sauté mushrooms for 5 minutes. When reduced in size, sauté garlic for 1 minute until aromatic.Stir in barbecue sauce, paprika, and cinnamon. Reduce heat and simmer for 10 minutes for the sauce to reduce. Scoop ¼ of the mixture onto a bun and top with red onion. Repeat for the rest of the buns and mixture. Serve warm and enjoy.

Beet Tartare with Homemade Vegan Ricotta

Ingredients for 4 servings

1 lb beets, peeled and cubed
1 tsp olive oil
½ tsp lemon juice
Salt and black pepper to taste
1 scallion, minced
¾ cup cashew
½ tsp garlic powder

Directions and Total Time: 25 minutes

Combine beets, oil, lemon juice, salt, pepper, and scallion in a large bowl. Set to the side. Add cashews, ½ cup water, garlic powder, and salt to a blender jar. Blend until it comes together like ricotta cheese. Portion the cashew sauce among 4 plates, then top with the beets. Serve.

Balsamic Quinoa & Couscous Burgers

Ingredients for 4 servings

2 tbsp olive oil
¼ cup couscous
¼ cup boiling water
2 cups cooked quinoa
2 tbsp balsamic vinegar
3 tbsp chopped olives
½ tsp garlic powder
Salt to taste
4 burger buns
Lettuce leaves, for serving
Tomato slices, for serving

Directions and Total Time: 20 minutes

Preheat oven to 350°F. In a bowl, place the couscous with boiling water. Let sit covered for 5 minutes. Once the liquid is absorbed, fluff with a fork. Add in quinoa and mash them to form a chunky texture. Stir in vinegar, olive oil, olives, garlic powder, and salt. Shape the mixture into 4 patties. Arrange them on a greased tray and bake for 25-30 minutes. To assemble, place the patties on the buns and top with lettuce and tomato slices. Serve.

Dijon Black Bean Sandwiches with Pecans

Ingredients for 4 servings

2 tbsp olive oil
1 onion, chopped
1 garlic clove, crushed
¾ cup pecans, chopped
¾ cup canned black beans
¾ cup almond flour
2 tbsp minced fresh parsley
1 tbsp soy sauce
Salt and black pepper to taste
½ tsp ground sage
½ tsp sweet paprika
Bread slices
1 tsp Dijon mustard
4 lettuce leaves
4 tomato slices

Directions and Total Time: 20 minutes

Put the onion, garlic, and pecans in a blender. Pulse until roughly ground. Add in the beans and pulse until everything is well combined. Transfer to a large bowl and stir in the flour, parsley, soy sauce, mustard, salt, sage, paprika, and pepper. Mold patties out of the mixture. Heat the oil in a skillet over medium heat. Brown the patties for 10 minutes on both sides. To assemble, lay patties on the bread slices. Top with mustard, lettuce, and tomato.

Thyme Mushroom Stroganoff

Ingredients for 6 servings

1 onion, sliced into half-moons
1 cup baby Bella mushrooms, sliced
1 cup shiitake mushrooms, sliced
4 garlic cloves, minced
¼ cup vegetable broth
1 tsp paprika
1 tbsp olive oil
Salt and black pepper to taste
¼ cup vegan sour cream
½ tsp Dijon mustard
4 tbsp chopped thyme
1 lb tagliatelle, cooked

Directions and Total Time: 25 minutes

In a large skillet, heat oil over medium heat. Sauté onion and mushrooms for 5 to 8 minutes until softened. Sauté garlic for 1 minute until aromatic. Next, add broth, paprika, salt, and pepper. Cook for 5 minutes, stirring occasionally. Remove from heat, then stir in sour cream, mustard, and 2 tablespoons of thyme. Combine with pasta and garnish with the rest of the thyme. Serve warm.

Italian Seasoned Summer Squash Skillet

Ingredients for 4 servings

2 zucchinis, sliced into half-moons
1 yellow summer squashes, sliced into half-moons
2 tbsp olive oil   1 tsp Italian seasoning
1 red onion, sliced   ¼ tsp ground nutmeg
3 garlic cloves, sliced   Salt and black pepper to taste
10 cherry tomatoes, halved

Directions and Total Time: 20 minutes

In a large skillet over medium heat, heat the olive oil. Sauté red onion for 5 minutes until softened. Sauté garlic for another minute until aromatic. Stir in zucchini, squash, tomato, Italian seasoning, nutmeg, salt, and pepper until combined. Cook for 4 to 6 minutes stirring occasionally. Adjust the seasoning with salt and pepper if needed. Cook until the zucchini and squash become golden and fork-tender. Serve warm and enjoy.

Rich Kitchari

Ingredients for 5 servings

4 cups chopped cauliflower and broccoli florets
½ cup split peas   ½ tsp ground ginger
½ cup brown rice   1 tsp ground turmeric
1 red onion, chopped   1 tsp fennel seeds
1 (14.5-oz) can diced tomatoes Juice of 1 large lemon
3 garlic cloves, minced   1 tsp olive oil
1 jalapeño pepper, seeded   Salt and black pepper to taste

Directions and Total Time: 40 minutes

In a food processor, place onion, tomatoes with juices, garlic, jalapeño pepper, ginger, turmeric, and 2 tbsp of water. Pulse until ingredients are evenly mixed. Heat the oil in a pot over medium heat. Cook the fennel seeds for 2-3 minutes, stirring often. Pour in the puréed mixture, split peas, rice, and 3 cups of water. Bring to a boil, then lower the heat and simmer for 10 minutes. Stir in cauliflower, broccoli, and cook for another 10 minutes. Mix in lemon juice and adjust seasoning. Serve.

Curried Lentil Burgers with Walnuts

Ingredients for 4 servings

2 tbsp olive oil   1 tbsp tomato puree
1 cup dry lentils, rinsed   ¾ cup almond flour
2 carrots, grated   2 tsp curry powder
1 onion, diced   4 whole-grain buns
½ cup walnuts

Directions and Total Time: 70 minutes

Place lentils in a pot and cover with water. Bring to a boil and simmer for 15-20 minutes. Meanwhile, combine the carrots, walnuts, onion, tomato puree, flour, curry powder, salt, and pepper in a bowl. Toss to coat. Once the lentils are ready, drain and transfer into the veggie bowl. Mash the mixture until sticky. Shape the mixture into balls; flatten to make patties. Heat the oil in a skillet over medium heat. Brown the patties for 8 minutes on both sides. To assemble, put the cakes on the buns and top with your desired toppings.

Piri Piri Mushroom Burgers

Ingredients for 4 servings

4 large portobello mushroom caps, stemmed
Salt and black pepper to taste   4 vegan hamburger buns
1 cup Piri Piri spicy sauce   4 tomato slices
¼ cup vegan butter, melted   ¼ red onion, thinly sliced
4 Boston lettuce leaves   2 tbsp vegan ranch dressing

Directions and Total Time: 25 minutes

Preheat the oven to 425°F. Line a baking sheet with parchment paper. Whisk piri piri sauce and butter in a small bowl. Set to the side. Season mushroom caps with salt and pepper and place on the baking sheet. Drizzle with 2 tablespoons of the piri piri mixture. Bake for 10 minutes, flip the mushroom caps and drizzle another tablespoon of piri piri sauce. Bake for another 10 minutes until the mushrooms have reduced in size. Serve in buns garnished with lettuce, tomatoes, onion, and dressing.

Oat & Black-Eyed Pea Casserole

Ingredients for 4 servings

1 (15-oz) can black-eyed peas   ¾ cup quick-cooking oats
1 carrot, shredded   ½ cup breadcrumbs
1 onion, chopped   ¼ cup minced fresh parsley
2 garlic cloves, minced   1 tbsp soy sauce
¾ cup whole-wheat flour   ½ tsp dried sage

Directions and Total Time: 25 minutes

Preheat oven to 360°F. Combine the carrot, onion, garlic, and peas and pulse until creamy and smooth in a blender. Add in flour, oats, breadcrumbs, parsley, soy sauce, and sage. Blend until ingredients are evenly mixed. Spoon the mixture into a greased loaf pan. Bake for 40 minutes until golden. Allow it to cool down for a few minutes before slicing. Serve immediately. Enjoy!

Smoked Bean Burgers

Ingredients for 4 servings

4 tbsp olive oil   ¼ cup almond flour
1 minced onion   1 tsp smoked paprika
1 garlic clove, minced   ½ tsp dried thyme
1 (15.5-oz) can fava beans 4 burger buns, toasted
1 tbsp minced fresh parsley 4 lettuce leaves
½ cup breadcrumbs   1 ripe tomato, sliced

Directions and Total Time: 15 minutes

In a blender, add onion, garlic, beans, parsley, breadcrumbs, flour, paprika, thyme, salt, and pepper. Pulse until uniform but not smooth. Shape 4 patties out of the mixture. Refrigerate for 15 minutes. Heat olive oil in a skillet over medium heat. Fry the patties for 10 minutes on both sides until golden brown. Serve in toasted buns with lettuce and tomato slices.

Green Bean & Rice

Ingredients for 4 servings

3 hot green chilies, chopped   1 roasted bell pepper, chopped
3 tbsp canola oil   2 ½ cups vegetable broth

½ cup chopped fresh parsley
1 onion, chopped
2 garlic cloves, chopped
Salt and black pepper to taste

½ tsp dried oregano
1 cup long-grain brown rice
1 ½ cups cooked black beans
2 tbsp minced fresh cilantro

Directions and Total Time: 35 minutes

In a food processor, place bell pepper, chilies, 1 cup of broth, parsley, onion, garlic, pepper, oregano, salt, and pepper and blend until smooth. Heat oil in a skillet over medium heat. Add in rice and veggie mixture. Cook for 5 minutes, stirring often. Add in the remaining broth and and simmer for 15 minutes. Mix in beans and cook for another 5 minutes. Serve topped with cilantro.

Cauliflower & Quinoa Sauté with Swiss Chard

Ingredients for 4 servings

1 head cauliflower, break into florets
2 tsp untoasted sesame oil
1 tsp toasted sesame oil
1 cup quinoa
Salt to taste
1 cup snow peas, cut in half

2 cups chopped Swiss chard
2 scallions, chopped
2 tbsp water
1 tbsp soy sauce
2 tbsp sesame seeds

Directions and Total Time: 30 minutes

Place quinoa with 2 cups of salted water in a pot over medium heat. Bring to a boil, lower the heat and simmer for 15 minutes. Do not stir. Heat the oil in a skillet over medium heat and sauté the cauliflower for 4-5 minutes. Add in snow peas and salt and stir well. Mix in Swiss chard, scallions, and 2 tbsp of water; cook until wilted. Drizzle with sesame oil and soy sauce and cook for 1 minute. Divide the quinoa between bowls and top with the cauliflower mixture. Garnish with sesame seeds.

Black Bean & Faro Loaf

Ingredients for 6 servings

2 (15.5-oz) cans black beans, mashed
3 tbsp olive oil
1 onion, minced
1 cup faro
½ cup quick-cooking oats

1/3 cup whole-wheat flour
2 tbsp nutritional yeast
1 ½ tsp dried thyme
½ tsp dried oregano

Directions and Total Time: 50 minutes

Heat the oil in a pot over medium heat. Place in onion and sauté for 3 minutes. Add in faro, 2 cups of water, salt, and pepper. Bring to a boil, lower the heat and simmer for 20 minutes. Remove to a bowl.

Preheat oven to 350°F. Add the mashed beans, oats, flour, yeast, thyme, and oregano to the faro bowl. Toss to combine. Adjust the seasoning. Shape the mixture into a greased loaf. Bake for 20 minutes. Slice and serve.

Cilantro Bean & Millet Pot

Ingredients for 4 servings

1 (15.5-oz) can black-eyed peas
2 tbsp olive oil
1 onion, chopped
2 zucchinis, chopped
2 garlic cloves, minced

1 tsp dried thyme
½ tsp ground cumin
1 cup millet
2 tbsp chopped fresh cilantro

Directions and Total Time: 40 minutes

Heat the oil in a pot over medium heat. Place in onion and sauté for 3 minutes until translucent. Add in zucchinis, garlic, thyme, and cumin and cook for 10 minutes. Put in peas, millet, and 2 ½ cups of hot water. Bring to a boil, then lower the heat and simmer for 20 minutes. Fluff the millet using a fork. Serve garnished with cilantro.

Vegetable Fried Rice

Ingredients for 4 servings

1 head broccoli, cut into florets
2 tbsp canola oil
1 tbsp toasted sesame oil
1 onion, chopped
1 large carrot, chopped
2 garlic cloves, minced
2 tsp grated fresh ginger

3 green onions, minced
3 ½ cups cooked brown rice
1 cup frozen peas, thawed
3 tbsp soy sauce
2 tsp dry white wine

Directions and Total Time: 20 minutes

Heat the canola oil in a skillet over medium heat. Place in onion, carrot, and broccoli, sauté for 5 minutes until tender. Add in garlic, ginger, and green onions and sauté for another 3 minutes. Stir in rice, peas, soy sauce, and white wine and cook for 5 minutes. Add in sesame oil, toss to combine. Serve right away and enjoy!

Cilantro Wild Rice Pilaf

Ingredients for 6 servings

3 tbsp olive oil
1 onion, minced
1 carrot, chopped
2 garlic cloves, minced
1 cup wild rice

1 ½ tsp ground fennel seeds
½ tsp ground cumin
Salt and black pepper to taste
3 tbsp minced fresh cilantro

Directions and Total Time: 30 minutes

Heat the olive oil in a pot over medium heat. Place in onion, carrot, and garlic and sauté for 5 minutes. Stir in rice, fennel seeds, cumin, and 2 cups water. Bring to a boil, then lower the heat and simmer for 20 minutes. Remove to a bowl and fluff using a fork. Serve topped with cilantro and black pepper. Enjoy!

Gingery Mushroom Red Lentils

Ingredients for 4 servings

2 tsp olive oil
2 cloves garlic, minced
2 tsp grated fresh ginger
½ tsp ground cumin
½ tsp fennel seeds

1 cup mushrooms, chopped
1 large tomato, chopped
1 cup dried red lentils
2 tbsp lemon juice

Directions and Total Time: 25 minutes

Heat the oil in a pot over medium heat. Place in the garlic and ginger and cook for 3 minutes. Stir in cumin, fennel, mushrooms, tomato, lentils, and 2 ¼ cups of water. Bring to a boil, then lower the heat and simmer for 15 minutes. Mix in lemon juice. Serve and enjoy!

White Bean & Bulgur with Green Onions

Ingredients for 4 servings

2 tbsp olive oil	Salt to taste
3 green onions, chopped	1 ½ cups cooked white beans
1 cup bulgur	1 tbsp nutritional yeast
1 tbsp soy sauce	1 tbsp dried parsley

Directions and Total Time: 55 minutes

Heat the oil in a pot over medium heat. Place in green onions and sauté for 3 minutes. Stir in bulgur, 1 cup of water, soy sauce, and salt. Bring to a boil, then lower the heat and simmer for 20-22 minutes. Mix in beans and yeast. Cook for 5 minutes. Serve topped with parsley.

Cumin Black Beans

Ingredients for 4 servings

2 tsp olive oil	1 (14.5-oz) cans black beans
4 shallots, chopped	1 cup vegetable broth
1 tsp ground cumin	2 tbsp sherry vinegar

Directions and Total Time: 25 minutes

Heat the oil in a pot over medium heat. Place in shallots and cumin and cook for 3 minutes until soft. Stir in beans and broth. Bring to a boil, then lower the heat and simmer for 10 minutes. Add in sherry vinegar, increase the heat and cook for an additional 3 minutes. Serve.

Buckwheat & Rice Croquettes

Ingredients for 6 servings

¾ cup cooked buckwheat groats	
½ cup cooked brown rice	1/3 cup whole-wheat flour
¼ cup minced onion	¼ cup chopped fresh parsley
1 celery stalk, chopped	3 tbsp olive oil
¼ cup shredded carrots	Salt and black pepper to taste

Directions and Total Time: 25 minutes

Combine the groats and rice in a bowl. Set aside. Heat 1 tbsp of oil in a skillet over medium heat. Place in onion, celery, and carrot and cook for 5 minutes. Transfer to the rice bowl. Mix in flour, parsley, salt, and pepper. Place in the fridge for 20 minutes. Mold the mixture into cylinder-shaped balls. Heat the remaining oil in a skillet over medium heat. Fry the croquettes for 8 minutes, turning occasionally until golden. Serve and enjoy!

Navy Bean Fussili with Chimichurri Salsa

Ingredients for 4 servings

½ cup chopped pitted black olives	
8 oz whole-wheat fusilli	1 cup chopped tomatoes
1 ½ cups canned navy beans	1 red onion, chopped
½ cup chimichurri salsa	

Directions and Total Time: 25 minutes

In a large pot over medium heat, pour 8 cups of salted water. Bring to a boil and add in the pasta. Cook for 8-10 minutes, drain and let cool. Combine the pasta, beans, and chimichurri in a bowl. Toss to coat. Stir in tomato, red onion, and olives. Serve right away and enjoy!

Tangy Chickpeas

Ingredients for 6 servings

1 onion, cut into half-moon slices	
2 (14.5-oz) cans chickpeas	2 tsp dried oregano
3 tbsp olive oil	Salt and black pepper to taste
½ cup vegetable broth	

Directions and Total Time: 5 minutes

Heat the olive oil in a skillet over medium heat. Cook the onion for 3 minutes. Stir in chickpeas, broth, oregano, salt, and pepper. Bring to a boil, then lower the heat and simmer for 10 minutes. Serve and enjoy!

Trick-or-Treat Mac & Cheese

Ingredients for 4 servings

2 cups elbow macaroni	1 cup canned pumpkin puree
1 ½ cups almond milk	1 (16-oz) can navy beans
2 tsp garlic powder	Salt and black pepper to taste
½ cup nutritional yeast	¼ tsp red pepper flakes
2 tsp Dijon mustard	

Directions and Total Time: 20 minutes

Bring a large pot of salted water to a boil. Add and cook the macaroni according to the package directions until al dente. Warm the almond milk in a saucepan over medium heat. Add the garlic powder, yeast, mustard, and pumpkin puree and whisk until well combined. Reduce the heat to low and cook for 5 minutes.

Combine 1 cup of the pumpkin mixture with navy beans in a food processor and blend until smooth. Pour the mixture back into the saucepan and mix well. Pour the sauce over the cooked, drained macaroni noodles, stir, and season with salt and pepper. Top with red pepper flakes.

Bell Pepper & Seitan Rice

Ingredients for 4 servings

2 tbsp olive oil	1 green bell pepper, chopped
2 cups water	1 tsp dried basil
1 cup long-grain brown rice	½ tsp ground fennel seeds
1 onion, chopped	¼ tsp crushed red pepper
8 oz seitan, chopped	Salt and black pepper to taste

Directions and Total Time: 35 minutes

Bring water to a boil in a pot. Place in rice and lower the heat. Simmer for 20 minutes. Heat the oil in a skillet over medium heat. Sauté the onion for 3 minutes until translucent. Add in the seitan and bell pepper and cook for another 5 minutes. Stir in basil, fennel, red pepper, salt, and black pepper. Once the rice is ready, remove it to a bowl. Add in seitan mixture and toss to combine.

Pistachio-Mushroom Bulgur with Dried Cherries

Ingredients for 4 servings

1 cup chopped dried cherries, soaked	
1 tbsp plant butter	1 cup chopped mushrooms
1 white onion, chopped	1 ½ cups bulgur
1 carrot, chopped	4 cups vegetable broth
1 celery stalk, chopped	½ cup chopped pistachios

Directions and Total Time: 45 minutes

Preheat oven to 375°F. Melt butter in a skillet over medium heat. Sauté the onion, carrot, and celery for 5 minutes until tender. Add in mushrooms and cook for 3 more minutes. Pour in bulgur and broth. Transfer to a casserole and bake covered for 30 minutes. Once ready, uncover and stir in cherries. Top with pistachios to serve.

Meatless Paella

Ingredients for 4 servings

2 tbsp olive oil	3 cups Spanish rice
4 cups vegetable broth	1 tsp turmeric
1 tsp paprika	1 lemon, cut into wedges
2/3 cup diced white onion	1 cup peas
4 garlic cloves, minced	1 (16-oz) can cannellini beans
1 cup diced red bell pepper	1 tbsp parsley, chopped

Directions and Total Time: 40 minutes

Warm the olive oil in a large skillet over medium heat. Stir-fry the onion, garlic, and bell pepper for 2-3 minutes until the onion is translucent. Season with paprika, salt, and pepper. Stir in the rice for 2 minutes. Add the warm vegetable broth and turmeric and stir. Bring to a boil and reduce the heat. Simmer for 10 minutes or until the broth is absorbed by the rice and it is slightly tender.

Add the frozen peas and cannellini beans and mix well to combine. Continue cooking for an additional 5-10 minutes or until the rice is tender. Top with parsley. Serve with lemon wedges and enjoy!

Lemon Couscous with Green Peas

Ingredients for 6 servings

1 cup green peas	2 tbsp chopped fresh thyme
2 ¾ cups vegetable stock	1 ½ cups couscous
Juice and zest of 1 lemon	¼ cup chopped fresh parsley

Directions and Total Time: 15 minutes

Pour the vegetable stock, lemon juice, thyme, salt, and pepper into a pot. Bring to a boil, then add in green peas and couscous. Turn the heat off and let sit covered for 5 minutes until the liquid has absorbed. Fluff the couscous using a fork and mix in the lemon zest and parsley. Serve.

Instant Pot Green Lentil Stew

Ingredients for 6 servings

3 tbsp coconut oil	2 garlic cloves, sliced
2 tbsp curry powder	1 cup green lentils
1 tsp ground ginger	Salt and black pepper to taste
1 onion, chopped	

Directions and Total Time: 30 minutes

Set your IP to Sauté. Add coconut oil, curry powder, ginger, onion, and garlic. Cook for 3 minutes. Stir in green lentils. Pour in 3 cups of water. Lock the lid and set the time to 10 minutes on High. Once ready, perform a natural pressure release for 10 minutes. Unlock the lid and season with salt and pepper. Serve and enjoy!

Chickpea & Quinoa Pot

Ingredients for 2 servings

2 tsp olive oil	1 bunch arugula chopped
1 cup cooked quinoa	1 tbsp soy sauce
1 (15-oz) can chickpeas	Salt and black pepper to taste

Directions and Total Time: 15 minutes

Heat the olive oil in a skillet over medium heat. Stir in quinoa, chickpeas, and arugula and cook for 3-5 minutes until the arugula wilts. Pour in soy sauce, salt, and black pepper. Toss to coat. Serve immediately and enjoy!

Parsley Buckwheat with Pine Nuts

Ingredients for 4 servings

2 tbsp olive oil	¼ cup pine nuts
1 cup buckwheat groats	½ onion, chopped
2 cups vegetable stock	1/3 cup chopped fresh parsley

Directions and Total Time: 25 minutes

Put the groats and vegetable stock in a pot over medium heat. Bring to a boil, then lower the heat and simmer for 15 minutes. Heat a skillet over medium heat. Place in the pine nuts and toast for 2-3 minutes, shaking often. Heat the oil in the same skillet and sauté the onion for 3 minutes until translucent. Once the groats are ready, fluff them using a fork. Mix in pine nuts, onion, and parsley. Sprinkle with salt and pepper. Serve and enjoy!

Festive Mushroom & Quinoa Stuffing

Ingredients for 4 servings

1 cup button mushrooms, sliced	½ cup raisins
3 garlic cloves, minced	½ cup chopped walnuts
¼ cup plant butter	2 cups cooked quinoa
1 onion, chopped	1 tsp Italian seasoning
2 celery stalks, sliced	Sea salt to taste
½ cup vegetable broth	2 tbsp chopped fresh parsley

Directions and Total Time: 25 minutes

In a skillet over medium heat, melt the butter. Sauté the onion, garlic, celery, and mushrooms for 5 minutes until tender, stirring occasionally. Pour in broth, raisins, and walnuts. Bring to a boil, then lower the heat and simmer for 5 minutes. Stir in quinoa, Italian seasoning, and salt. Cook for another 4 minutes. Serve topped with parsley.

Olive & Endive Salad

Ingredients for 6 servings

1 lb curly endive, chopped	10 black olives for garnish
1/3 cup vegan mayonnaise	¼ tsp ground black pepper
¼ cup rice vinegar	¼ tsp smoked paprika
2 tbsp vegan yogurt	¼ tsp chipotle powder
1 tbsp pure date sugar	Salt to taste

Directions and Total Time: 10 minutes

In a bowl, mix the vegan mayonnaise, vinegar, vegan yogurt, sugar, salt, pepper, paprika, and chipotle powder. Gently add the curly endive and mix with a wooden spatula to coat. Top with black olives. Serve and enjoy!

Okra & Mushroom Fried Rice

Ingredients for 6 servings

1 cup sliced shiitake mushrooms
2 tbsp sesame oil   2 garlic cloves, minced
1 onion, chopped   ¼ cup soy sauce
1 carrot, chopped   1 cups cooked brown rice
1 cup okra, chopped   2 green onions, chopped

Directions and Total Time: 25 minutes

Heat the oil in a skillet over medium heat. Place in onion and carrot and cook for 3 minutes. Add in okra and mushrooms, cook for 5-7 minutes. Stir in garlic and cook for 30 seconds. Put in soy sauce and rice. Cook until hot. Add in green onions and stir. Serve warm and enjoy!

Artichoke Rice & Beans

Ingredients for 4 servings

1 cup artichoke hearts, diced   2 tbsp olive oil
2 grape tomatoes, quartered   3 garlic cloves, minced
1 ½ cups brown rice   3 cups vegetable broth
1 tsp dried basil   Salt and black pepper to taste
1 ½ cups cooked navy beans   2 tbsp minced fresh parsley

Directions and Total Time: 35 minutes

Heat the olive oil in a pot over medium heat. Sauté the garlic for 1 minute. Stir in artichokes, basil, navy beans, rice, and vegetable broth. Sprinkle with salt and black pepper. Lower the heat and simmer for 20-25 minutes. Remove to a bowl and mix in tomatoes and parsley. Using a fork, fluff the rice. Serve right away and enjoy!

Instant Pot Green Chickpeas

Ingredients for 5 servings

1 cup chickpeas, soaked   1 celery stalk, chopped
1 onion, chopped   3 tsp ground cinnamon
2 garlic cloves, minced   ½ tsp ground nutmeg
2 tbsp olive oil   1 cup spinach, chopped
1 tbsp coconut oil

Directions and Total Time: 50 minutes

Place chickpeas in your IP with the onion, garlic, celery, olive oil, 2 cups of water, cinnamon, and nutmeg.

Lock the lid in place; set the time to 30 minutes on High. Once ready, perform a natural pressure release for 10 minutes. Unlock the lid and drain the excess water. Put back the chickpeas and stir in coconut oil and spinach. Set the pot to Sauté and cook for another 5 minutes.

Green Bean & Rice Alfredo

Ingredients for 3 servings

1 cup Alfredo arugula vegan pesto
1 cup green beans   2 cups brown rice

Directions and Total Time: 25 minutes

Cook the rice in salted water in a pot over medium heat for 20 minutes. Drain and let it cool completely. Place the Alfredo sauce and beans in a skillet. Cook over low heat for 3-5 minutes. Stir in the rice to coat. Serve warm.

Lentil Paella

Ingredients for 4 servings

1 ½ cups cooked lentils   1 tbsp capers
¼ cup sliced black olives   ¼ tsp crushed red pepper
1 ½ cups brown rice   1 green bell pepper, chopped
2 tbsp olive oil   2 garlic cloves, minced
1 onion, chopped   2 tbsp minced fresh parsley
1 (14.5-oz) can diced tomatoes   3 cups vegetable broth

Directions and Total Time: 50 minutes

Heat oil in a pot over medium heat and sauté onion, bell pepper, and garlic for 5 minutes. Stir in tomatoes, capers, red pepper, and salt. Cook for 5 minutes. Pour in the rice and broth. Bring to a boil, then lower the heat. Simmer for 20 minutes. Turn the heat off and mix in lentils. Serve garnished with olives and parsley. Enjoy!

Cannellini Beans with Curry & Artichokes

Ingredients for 4 servings

1 (14.5-oz) can artichoke hearts, quartered
1 (14-oz) can cannellini beans   2 tsp curry powder
1 small onion, diced   ½ tsp ground coriander
2 garlic cloves, minced   1 (5.4-oz) can coconut milk
1 tsp olive oil   Salt and black pepper to taste

Directions and Total Time: 25 minutes

Heat the olive oil in a skillet over medium heat. Sauté the onion and garlic for 3 minutes until translucent. Stir in beans, artichoke hearts, curry powder, salt, pepper, and coriander. Add in coconut milk. Bring to a boil, then lower the heat and simmer for 10 minutes. Serve.

Mango & Cauliflower Tacos

Ingredients for 6 servings

1 head cauliflower, cut into pieces
16 cherry tomatoes, halved   1 cups shredded watercress
2 tbsp whole-wheat flour   2 carrots, grated
2 tbsp nutritional yeast   ½ cup mango salsa
2 tsp paprika   ½ cup guacamole
1 tsp cayenne pepper   8 small corn tortillas, warm
2 tbsp olive oil   1 lime, cut into wedges
Salt to taste

Directions and Total Time: 40 minutes

Preheat oven to 350°F. Brush the cauliflower with oil in a bowl. Mix the flour, yeast, paprika, cayenne pepper, and salt in another bowl. Pour into the cauliflower bowl and toss to coat. Spread the cauliflower on a greased baking sheet. Bake for 20-30 minutes. Combine the watercress, cherry tomatoes, carrots, mango salsa, and guacamole in a bowl. Once the cauliflower is ready, divide it between the tortillas, add the mango mixture, roll up and serve with lime wedges on the side. Enjoy!

Gochugaru Millet

Ingredients for 4 servings

1 cup dried millet, drained   Salt and black pepper to taste
1 tsp gochugaru flakes

Directions and Total Time: 30 minutes

Place the millet and gochugaru flakes in a pot. Cover with enough water and bring to a boil. Lower the heat and simmer for 20 minutes. Drain and let cool. Transfer to a serving bowl and season with salt and pepper. Serve.

Barbecued Pinto Beans

Ingredients for 6 servings

1 green bell pepper, cut into strips
1 serrano pepper, cut into strips   2 carrots, chopped
1 red bell pepper, cut into strips   2 garlic cloves, minced
1 (18-oz) bottle barbecue sauce   3 (15-oz) cans pinto beans
1 onion, chopped   ½ tsp chipotle powder

Directions and Total Time: 30 minutes

In a blender, place the serrano and bell peppers, onion, carrot, and garlic. Pulse until well mixed. Place the mixture in a pot over medium heat. Add the pinto beans, BBQ sauce, and chipotle powder. Cook for 15 minutes. Season with salt and pepper. Serve warm and enjoy!

Smoked Chipotle Black-Eyed Peas

Ingredients for 4 servings

1 cup black-eyed peas, soaked   1 ½ tsp onion powder
8 sun-dried tomatoes, diced   1 tsp dried oregano
2 tsp ground chipotle pepper   ¾ tsp garlic powder
1 ½ tsp ground cumin   ½ tsp smoked paprika
2 tbsp olive oil   Salt to taste

Directions and Total Time: 35 minutes

Place the black-eyed peas, 2 cups of water, olive oil, chipotle pepper, cumin, onion powder, oregano, garlic powder, salt, and paprika in a pot over medium heat. Cook for 20 minutes. Mix in sun-dried tomatoes. Let sit for a few minutes. Serve and enjoy!

Spinach Quinoa Curry

Ingredients for 4 servings

4 tsp olive oil   1 cup canned diced tomatoes
1 onion, chopped   4 cups chopped spinach
2 tbsp curry powder   ½ cup non-dairy milk
1 tsp ginger powder   2 tbsp soy sauce
1 ½ cups quinoa   Salt to taste

Directions and Total Time: 35 minutes

Heat the oil in a pot over medium heat. Sauté the onion, curry powder, and ginger powder for 3 minutes until tender. Pour in quinoa, and 3 cups of water. Bring to a boil, then lower the heat and simmer for 15-20 minutes. Mix in tomatoes, spinach, milk, soy sauce, and salt. Simmer for an additional 3 minutes. Serve and enjoy!

One-Skillet Chickpeas with Kale

Ingredients for 4 servings

4 tbsp olive oil   2 garlic cloves, minced
1 (15-oz) can chickpeas   1 tbsp Italian seasoning
Juice and zest of 1 lemon   2 cups kale, chopped
1 onion, chopped   Salt and black pepper to taste

Directions and Total Time: 20 minutes

Heat the olive oil in a skillet over medium heat. Place in the chickpeas and cook for 5 minutes. Add in onion, garlic, Italian seasoning, and kale and cook for 5 minutes until the kale wilts. Stir in salt, lemon juice, lemon zest, and pepper. Serve warm and enjoy!

Turkish-Style Pizza

Ingredients for 2 servings

1 tbsp olive oil   Salt to taste
½ eggplant, sliced   2 prebaked pizza crusts
½ red onion, sliced   ½ cup hummus
1 cup cherry tomatoes, halved   2 tbsp oregano
3 tbsp chopped black olives

Directions and Total Time: 25 minutes

Preheat oven to 390°F. Combine the eggplant, onion, tomatoes, olives, and salt in a bowl. Toss to coat. Sprinkle with olive oil. Arrange the crusts on a baking sheet and spread the hummus on each pizza. Top with the eggplant mixture. Bake for 20-30 minutes. Top with oregano.

Basil Pesto Millet

Ingredients for 4 servings

1 cup millet   ½ cup vegan basil pesto
2 ½ cups vegetable broth

Directions and Total Time: 50 minutes

Place the millet and broth in a pot. Bring to a boil, then lower the heat and simmer for 25 minutes. Let cool for 5 minutes and fluff the millet. Mix in the pesto and serve.

Tomato Lentils with Brown Rice

Ingredients for 4 servings

2 tbsp olive oil   1 tbsp dried rosemary
4 scallions, chopped   1 tsp ground coriander
1 carrot, diced   1 tbsp garlic powder
1 celery stalk, chopped   2 cups cooked brown rice
2 (15-oz) cans lentils, drained Salt and black pepper to taste
1 (15-oz) can diced tomatoes

Directions and Total Time: 25 minutes

Heat the oil in a pot over medium heat. Place in scallions, carrot, and celery and cook for 5 minutes until tender. Stir in lentils, tomatoes, rosemary, coriander, and garlic powder. Lower the heat and simmer for 5-7 minutes. Mix in rice, salt, and pepper. Cook for another 2-3 minutes.

Red Pepper Steamed Broccoli

Ingredients for 6 servings

1 head broccoli, cut into florets
Salt to taste   1 tsp red pepper flakes

Directions and Total Time: 15 minutes

Boil 1 cup water in a pot over medium heat. Place in a steamer basket and put in the broccoli florets. Steam covered for 5-7 minutes. In a bowl, toss the broccoli with red pepper flakes and salt. Serve and enjoy!

Asian Kale Slaw

Ingredients for 4 servings

1 tbsp toasted sesame oil	2 tsp soy sauce
¼ cup tahini	1 (12-oz) bag kale slaw
2 tbsp white miso paste	2 scallions, minced
1 tbsp rice vinegar	¼ cup toasted sesame seeds

Directions and Total Time: 15 minutes

Combine the tahini, miso, vinegar, oil, and soy sauce in a bowl. Stir in kale slaw, scallions, and sesame seeds. Let sit for 20 minutes. Serve immediately and enjoy!

Baked Chili Carrots

Ingredients for 4 servings

2 lb carrots, chopped into ¾ inch cubes	
½ tsp chili powder	2 tsp olive oil
½ tsp smoked paprika	½ tsp garlic powder
½ tsp dried oregano	Salt to taste
½ tsp dried thyme	

Directions and Total Time: 35 minutes

Preheat oven to 400°F. Line with parchment paper a baking sheet. Rinse the carrots and pat dry. Chop into ¾ inch cubes. Place in a bowl and toss with olive oil. Mix the chili powder, paprika, oregano, thyme, salt, and garlic powder in a bowl. Pour over the carrots and toss to coat. Transfer to a greased baking sheet and bake for 30 minutes, turn once by half. Serve and enjoy!

Herby Green Cabbage

Ingredients for 4 servings

1 lb green cabbage, halved	1 tsp dried oregano
2 tsp olive	½ tsp dried rosemary
3 tsp miso paste	1 tbsp balsamic vinegar

Directions and Total Time: 50 minutes

Preheat oven to 390°F. Line with parchment paper a baking sheet. Put the green cabbage in a bowl. Coat with olive oil, miso, oregano, rosemary, salt, and pepper. Remove to the baking sheet and bake for 35-40 minutes, shaking every 5 minutes until tender. Remove from the oven to a plate. Drizzle with balsamic vinegar and serve.

Tamari Eggplants

Ingredients for 4 servings

2 unpeeled eggplants, sliced	1 tbsp dry sherry
1 tbsp canola oil	½ tsp pure date sugar
1 tsp toasted sesame oil	2 green onions, minced
1 garlic cloves, minced	10 pitted black olives, chopped
2 tbsp tamari sauce	

Directions and Total Time: 20 minutes

Combine the garlic, tamari, sherry, sesame oil, and sugar in a bowl. Set aside. Heat the oil in a skillet over medium heat. Place in the eggplant slices, fry for 4 minutes per side. Spread the tamari sauce on the eggplants. Pour in ¼ cup water and cook for 15 minutes. Remove to a plate and sprinkle with green onions and black olives. Serve.

Mushroom & Broccoli Skillet with Hazelnuts

Ingredients for 4 servings

½ cup slivered toasted hazelnuts	1 cup sliced white mushrooms
2 tbsp olive oil	¼ cup dry white wine
1 lb broccoli, cut into florets	2 tbsp minced fresh parsley
3 garlic cloves, minced	Salt and black pepper to taste

Directions and Total Time: 20 minutes

Steam the broccoli for 8 minutes or until tender. Remove and set aside. Heat 1 tbsp of olive oil in a skillet over medium heat. Add in garlic and mushrooms and sauté for 5 minutes until tender. Pour in the white wine and cook for 1 minute. Stir in broccoli florets, parsley, salt, and pepper. Cook for 3 minutes until the liquid has reduced. Remove to a bowl and add in the remaining oil and hazelnuts and toss to coat. Serve warm and enjoy!

Sautéd Okra

Ingredients for 4 servings

Salt and black pepper to taste	4 cups okra, halved
2 tbsp olive oil	3 tbsp chopped fresh cilantro

Directions and Total Time: 10 minutes

Heat the oil in a skillet over medium heat. Place in the okra, cook for 5 minutes. Turn the heat off and mix in salt, pepper, and cilantro. Serve immediately and enjoy!

Lemony Asparagus

Ingredients for 4 servings

1 tbsp olive oil	1/3 cup fresh lemon juice
1 onion, minced	Salt and black pepper to taste
2 tsp lemon zest	1 lb asparagus, trimmed

Directions and Total Time: 15 minutes

Combine the onion, lemon zest, lemon juice, and oil in a bowl. Sprinkle with salt and black pepper. Let sit for 5-10 minutes. Insert a steamer basket and 1 cup of water in a pot over medium heat. Place the asparagus on the basket and steam for 4-5 minutes until tender but crispy. Leave to cool for 10 minutes, then arrange on a plate. Serve drizzled with the dressing. Enjoy!

Edamame, Zucchini & Rice Sauté

Ingredients for 4 servings

1 red bell pepper, chopped	1 ½ cups brown rice, rinsed
2 cups cooked shelled edamame	4 shallots, chopped
1 medium zucchini, chopped	2 tomatoes, chopped
2 cups corn kernels	3 tbsp chopped parsley
2 tbsp olive oil	

Directions and Total Time: 40 minutes

Boil 3 cups of salted water in a pot over high heat. Place in rice, lower the heat, and cook for 20 minutes. Set aside. Heat the oil in a skillet over medium heat. Add in shallots, zucchini, and bell pepper and sauté for 5 minutes until tender. Mix in edamame, corn, tomatoes, salt, and pepper. Cook for 5 minutes, stirring often. Put in cooked rice and parsley, toss to combine. Serve warm and enjoy!

Tofu & Haricot Vert Pilaf with Mushrooms

Ingredients for 4 servings

5 shiitake mushroom caps, sliced

1 tbsp grapeseed oil	3 green onions, minced
1 tbsp toasted sesame oil	8 oz firm tofu, crumbled
1 cup haricots vert	2 tbsp soy sauce
1 onion, minced	3 cups hot cooked rice
1 tsp grated fresh ginger	1 tbsp toasted sesame seeds

Directions and Total Time: 25 minutes

Place the haricots in boiled salted water and cook for 10 minutes until tender. Drain and set aside. Heat the grapeseed oil in a skillet over medium heat. Place in the onion and cook for 3 minutes until translucent. Add in mushrooms, ginger, green onions, tofu, and soy sauce. Cook for 10 minutes. Share cooked rice into 4 bowls and top with haricot and tofu mixture. Sprinkle with sesame oil. Garnish with sesame seeds. Serve warm and enjoy!

Orzo Stuffed Tomatoes

Ingredients for 4 servings

2 tsp olive oil	1 tsp orange zest
2 cups cooked orzo	4 large ripe tomatoes
Salt and black pepper to taste	1/3 cup toasted pine nuts
3 green onions, minced	¼ cup minced fresh parsley
1/3 cup golden raisins	

Directions and Total Time: 40 minutes

Preheat oven to 380°F. Mix orzo, green onions, raisins, and orange zest in a bowl. Set aside. Slice the top of the tomato by ½-inch and take out the pulp. Cut the pulp and place it in a bowl. Stir in orzo mixture, pine nuts, parsley, salt, and pepper. Spoon the mixture into the tomatoes and arrange on a greased baking tray. Sprinkle with oil and cover with foil. Bake for 15 minutes. Uncover and bake for another 5 minutes until golden. Serve and enjoy!

Cherry Tomato & Potato Bake

Ingredients for 5 servings

10 cherry tomatoes, halved	2 tbsp rosemary
2 tbsp olive oil	Salt and black pepper to taste
5 russet potatoes, sliced	

Directions and Total Time: 55 minutes

Preheat oven to 390°F. Make several incisions with a fork in each potato. Rub each potato and cherry tomato with olive oil and sprinkle with salt, rosemary, and pepper. Arrange on a baking dish and bake for 40-45 minutes. Once ready, transfer to a rack and allow cooling. Serve.

Caramelized Root Veggies

Ingredients for 4 servings

3 sweet potatoes, cut into chunks

2 parsnips, cut into chunks	4 medium shallots, halved
2 turnips, cut into chunks	¼ cup water
½ cup pure date sugar	¼ cup sherry vinegar
1 tbsp olive oil	2 large carrots, cut into chunks
2 garlic cloves, minced	Salt and black pepper to taste

Directions and Total Time: 30 minutes

Heat oil in a skillet over medium heat. Place in garlic and shallots and sauté for 3 minutes. Stir in sweet potatoes, carrots, parsnips, and turnips; cook for 5 minutes until tender. Pour in the sugar and 2 tbsp of water, cook for 5 minutes until the sugar dissolves. Stir in the remaining water and vinegar, simmer for 2-3 minutes. Season with salt and pepper. Lower the heat and cook for 25 minutes.

Port Wine Parsnips & Carrots

Ingredients for 4 servings

½ lb parsnips, sliced lengthways

2 tbsp plant butter	½ cup Port wine
½ lb carrots, sliced lengthways	¼ cup chopped fresh parsley
Salt and black pepper to taste	

Directions and Total Time: 25 minutes

Melt the butter in a skillet over medium heat. Place in carrots and parsnips and cook for 5 minutes, stirring occasionally. Sprinkle with salt and pepper. Pour in Port wine and ¼ cup water. Lower the heat and simmer for 15 minutes. Uncover and increase the heat. Cook until a syrupy sauce forms. Serve garnished with parsley.

Roasted Broccoli Brown Rice

Ingredients for 4 servings

1 head broccoli, cut into florets

¾ cup pure date sugar	2 tbsp cornstarch
2/3 cup water	4 cups cooked brown rice
1/3 cup apple cider vinegar	2 tbsp olive oil
1 tbsp ketchup	2 scallions, chopped
¼ cup soy sauce	Sesame seeds

Directions and Total Time: 30 minutes

Preheat oven to 420°F. Line with parchment paper a baking sheet. Coat the broccoli with oil in a bowl. Spread on the baking sheet and roast for 20 minutes, turning once. Add the sugar, water, vinegar, and ketchup to a skillet and bring to a boil. Lower the heat and simmer for 5 minutes. Whisk the soy sauce with cornstarch in a bowl and pour it into the skillet. Stir for 2-4 minutes. Once the broccoli is ready, transfer into the skillet and toss to combine. Share the rice into 4 bowls and top with the broccoli. Garnish with scallions and sesame seeds.

Spaghetti Squash with Tahini Sauce

Ingredients for 4 servings

1 (3-lb) spaghetti squash	1 tbsp tahini
1 tbsp rice vinegar	Salt and black pepper to taste

Directions and Total Time: 50 minutes

Preheat oven to 390°F. Line with wax paper a baking sheet. Slice the squash half lengthwise and arrange on the baking sheet skin-side up. Bake for 35-40 minutes. Let cool before scraping the flesh to make "noodles." Place the spaghetti in a bowl. Whisk 1 tbsp hot water, vinegar, tahini, salt, and pepper in another bowl. Add into the spaghetti bowl and toss to coat. Serve.

Provençal Zucchini & Squash Stir-Fry

Ingredients for 4 servings

2 yellow squashes, sliced half-moons
2 zucchinis, sliced half-moons   3 garlic cloves, sliced
2 tbsp olive oil   1 tsp herbs de Provence
1 red onion, sliced   Salt and black pepper to taste

Directions and Total Time: 20 minutes

Heat the olive oil in a skillet over medium heat. Sauté the onion and garlic for 3 minutes until tender. Mix in zucchini, squashes, herbs de Provence, salt, and pepper. Cook for 4-6 minutes, stirring often. Serve and enjoy!

Curry-Glazed Sweet Potatoes

Ingredients for 6 servings

2 tbsp olive oil   2 tbsp pure date syrup
1 lb sweet potatoes, sliced   Juice of ½ lemon
2 tbsp curry powder   Salt and black pepper to taste

Directions and Total Time: 20 minutes

Cook the sweet potatoes covered with salted water for 10 minutes. Drain and return the potatoes to the pot. Lower the heat. Add in oil, curry powder, date syrup, and lemon juice. Cook for 5 minutes. Season with salt and pepper. Serve warm and enjoy!

Mixed Cole Slaw with Apples

Ingredients for 6 servings

1 head white cabbage, grated   2 tbsp pure date sugar
2 tbsp olive oil   ¼ cup cider vinegar
1 onion, sliced   1 tsp cumin seeds, crushed
1 head red cabbage, shredded   Salt and black pepper to taste
2 apples, sliced

Directions and Total Time: 30 minutes

Heat the olive oil in a pot over medium heat. Place in onion, shredded cabbages, and apples and sauté for 5 minutes until tender. Stir in date sugar, 1 cup water, vinegar, cumin seeds, salt, and pepper. Lower the heat and simmer for 20 minutes. Serve right away and enjoy!

Spicy Beet Pasta

Ingredients for 4 servings

1 tsp olive oil   ½ tsp dried basil
1 garlic clove, minced   ½ tsp dried oregano
4 medium beets, spiralized ½ tsp red pepper flakes

Directions and Total Time: 20 minutes

Heat the olive oil in a skillet over medium heat. Place in garlic, beets, basil, oregano, pepper flakes, salt, and pepper. Cook for 15 minutes. Serve and enjoy!

Eggplant Fritters with Tofu & Tomatoes

Ingredients for 2 servings

2 tbsp olive oil   Salt to taste
½ cup non-dairy milk   2 eggplants, sliced
½ cup breadcrumbs   4 tbsp tomato sauce
2 tbsp nutritional yeast ½ cup tofu, crumbled

Directions and Total Time: 25 minutes

Pour the milk into a bowl. In another bowl, mix the breadcrumbs, nutritional yeast, and salt. Dip the eggplant slices in the milk, then coat in the breadcrumbs. Remove to a plate. In a skillet over medium heat, warm the oil. Fry the eggplant slices for 10 minutes on both sides. Remove to a baking sheet. Top with tomato sauce and tofu. Place the sheet under the broiler for 6 minutes until the tofu begins to brown. Serve and enjoy!

Eggplant Pizza with Tofu

Ingredients for 4 servings

1 cup grated plant-based Parmesan cheese
⅓ cup melted plant butter   12 oz crumbled tofu
2 eggplants, sliced lengthwise 7 oz tomato sauce
2 garlic cloves, minced   ½ tsp cinnamon powder
1 red onion   ¼ cup chopped fresh oregano

Directions and Total Time: 45 minutes

Preheat oven to 400°F. . Brush the eggplants with some plant butter. Transfer them to a parchment-lined baking sheet. Bake until lightly browned, about 20 minutes. Heat the remaining butter in a skillet and sauté the garlic and onion until fragrant and soft, about 3 minutes. Stir in the tofu and cook for 3 minutes. Add the tomato sauce and season with salt and black pepper. Simmer for 10 minutes. Remove the eggplants from the oven and spread the tofu sauce on top. Sprinkle with plant-based Parmesan cheese and oregano. Bake further for 10 minutes or until the cheese has melted. Serve and enjoy!

Sriracha Cole Slaw

Ingredients for 4 servings

1 ½ lb green cabbage, grated   2 shallots, thinly sliced
3 tbsp apple cider vinegar   Salt and black pepper to taste
3 tbsp olive oil   ½ tsp sriracha sauce

Directions and Total Time: 25 minutes

Heat the oil in a skillet over medium heat. Place in shallots and cabbage and cook for 10 minutes until tender. Pour in vinegar and scrape any bits from the bottom. Mix in sriracha sauce. Cook for 3-5 minutes, until the liquid absorbs. Sprinkle with salt and pepper. Serve and enjoy!

Mushroom & Bel Pepper Medley

Ingredients for 4 servings

3 tbsp olive oil   1 green bell pepper, sliced
1 cup mushrooms, sliced   2 garlic cloves, minced
1 red bell pepper, sliced 3 tbsp red wine vinegar
1 orange bell pepper, sliced 2 tbsp chopped fresh basil
1 yellow bell pepper, sliced

Directions and Total Time: 25 minutes

Heat the oil in a skillet over medium heat. Place in mushrooms, garlic, and bell peppers and sauté for 7-10 minutes. Pour in vinegar and scrape any bit from the bottom. Cook for 2-3 minutes until the vinegar is reduced. Top with basil. Serve and enjoy!

Pine Nut & Raisin Zucchini Rolls

Ingredients for 4 servings

8 diced sun-dried tomatoes
2 tbsp olive oil
4 zucchinis, sliced lengthwise
Salt and black pepper to taste
1 garlic cloves, minced
4 green onions, chopped

¼ cup ground pine nuts
3 tbsp golden raisins
3 tbsp grated vegan Parmesan
1 tbsp minced fresh parsley
2 cups marinara sauce

Directions and Total Time: 50 minutes

Preheat oven to 360°F. Arrange the zucchini slices on a greased baking sheet. Season with salt and pepper and bake for 15 minutes. Set aside. Heat the oil in a skillet over medium heat. Place in garlic, green onions, and pine nuts and cook for 1 minute. Stir in tomatoes, raisins, Parmesan cheese, parsley, salt, and pepper. Spread the mixture onto the zucchini slices. Roll up and transfer to the baking dish. Top with marinara sauce. Cover with foil and bake for 30 minutes. Serve hot and enjoy!

Kale & Chickpea Patties

Ingredients for 6 servings

1 roasted red bell pepper, chopped
1 (19-oz) can chickpeas
1 cup ground almonds
2 tsp Dijon mustard
2 tsp date syrup

1 garlic clove, pressed
Juice of ½ lemon
1 cup kale, chopped
1 ½ cups rolled oats

Directions and Total Time: 50 minutes

Preheat oven to 360°F. In a blender, place the chickpeas, almonds, bell pepper, mustard, date syrup, garlic, lemon juice, and kale. Pulse until ingredients are finely chopped but not over blended. Add in the oats. Pulse until everything is well combined. Shape the mixture into 12 patties and arrange on a parchment-lined baking sheet. Bake for 30 minutes until light brown. Serve and enjoy!

Mirin Wine Buckwheat

Ingredients for 4 servings

1 cup buckwheat groats
¼ cup unseasoned rice vinegar

¼ cup Mirin wine

Directions and Total Time: 25 minutes

Boil 2 cups of water in a pot. Put in the buckwheat groats, lower the heat, and simmer covered for 15-20 minutes until the liquid absorbs. Let cool for a few minutes. Using a fork, fluff the groats and stir in vinegar and Mirin wine. Serve.

Mediterranean Spaghetti Squash

Ingredients for 4 servings

1 (4-lb) spaghetti squash, halved and seeded
2 cups chopped artichoke hearts
½ cup sliced green olives
1 cup halved cherry tomatoes
3 garlic cloves, minced
1 ½ tsp Italian seasoning
2 tbsp pine nuts

2 tbsp grated vegan Parmesan
1 onion, chopped
3 tbsp olive oil
Red pepper flakes
Salt and black pepper to taste

Directions and Total Time: 50 minutes

Preheat oven to 390°F. Line with parchment paper a baking sheet. Rub each squash half with some oil on all sides. Arrange on the sheet cut-sides down and bake for 40-45 minutes until tender. Let cool. Meanwhile, heat the olive oil in a skillet over medium heat. Place in onion, garlic, and artichoke and cook for 5 minutes. Add in olives and tomatoes and cook for another 3-5 minutes.

Take out the squash flesh, using a fork, and separate into strands. Transfer to the veggie skillet. Season with Italian seasoning, salt, and pepper; toss to combine. Share into bowls and garnish with pine nuts, Parmesan cheese, and pepper flakes. Serve and enjoy!

Vegetable Paella

Ingredients for 4 servings

1 yellow onion, chopped
1 red bell pepper, diced
3 garlic cloves, chopped
2 tbsp olive oil
2 medium carrots, sliced
1 celery stalk, sliced
8 oz green peas
1 cup Spanish brown rice

1 (14.5-oz) can diced tomatoes
2 ½ cups vegetable broth
½ tsp crushed red pepper
½ tsp ground fennel seed
¼ tsp saffron
2 cups oyster mushrooms
1 cup asparagus, chopped

Directions and Total Time: 35 minutes

Heat the oil in a pot over medium heat. Place in carrots, celery, onion, bell pepper, and garlic. Cook for 5 minutes until tender. Stir in green peas, rice, tomatoes, broth, salt, red pepper, fennel seeds, and saffron. Cook for 20 minutes. Mix in mushrooms and asparagus. Cook covered another 10 minutes. Serve warm and enjoy!

Tangerine Quinoa Pilaf with Peanuts

Ingredients for 4 servings

1 tbsp olive oil
1 medium red onion, minced
1 ½ cups quinoa, rinsed
3 cups vegetable broth
2 (15.5-oz) cans chickpeas

¼ tsp ground cayenne
1 tbsp minced fresh chives
1 tangerine, chopped
½ cup peanuts

Directions and Total Time: 30 minutes

Heat the oil in a pot over medium heat. Place the onion and cook for 3 minutes until softened. Add in quinoa and broth. Bring to a boil, then lower the heat and sprinkle with salt. Simmer for 20 minutes. Stir in chickpeas, cayenne pepper, chives, tangerine, and peanuts. Serve.

Garlicky Red Potatoes

Ingredients for 4 servings

1 ½ lb baby red potatoes, halved
3 garlic cloves, minced
2 tbsp plant butter

1 tbsp minced fresh dill
Sea salt to taste

Directions and Total Time: 35 minutes

Preheat oven to 430°F. Mix in the potatoes, butter, garlic, dill, and salt and spread evenly on a parchment-lined baking sheet. Bake for 30 minutes until golden brown.

DESSERTS

Smoothie Popsicles

Ingredients for 6 servings

2 cups chopped fresh raspberries
1 cup chopped mango   ½ cup shredded coconut
¾ cup canned coconut milk   ½ tsp maple syrup

Directions and Total Time: 5 minutes + freezing time

In a food processor, blend everything until almost smooth. Transfer to ice pop molds, leaving a bit of space at the top. Freeze up until solid.

Seedy Choco-Banana Muffins

Ingredients for 6 servings

3 bananas   ¼ cup muscovado sugar
1 cup almond milk   1 tsp baking powder
2 tbsp almond butter   ½ cup cocoa powder
1 tsp apple cider vinegar   ¼ cup sesame seeds
1 tsp pure vanilla extract   A pinch of salt
1 ¼ cups whole-grain flour   ¼ cup dark chocolate chips
½ cup rolled oats

Directions and Total Time: 45 minutes

Preheat the oven to 350°F. Lightly spray 12-cup muffin tin with cooking oil. Puree bananas, almond milk, almond butter, vinegar, and vanilla in a blender. In a large bowl, add the rest of the ingredients. Pour the wet ingredients with the dry ingredients and stir until combined. Scoop batter into the prepared muffin cups. Bake for 20-25 minutes. Let the muffins cool completely in the muffin tins. Serve and enjoy.

Matcha Pudding

Ingredients for 4 servings

1 lime, zested and juiced   ½ tsp vanilla extract
1 (14-oz) can coconut milk   2 tbsp chia seeds
1 tbsp coconut sugar   2 tsp matcha powder

Directions and Total Time: 5 minutes + chilling time

In a food processor, blend all the ingredients until smooth. Transfer to the fridge for 20 minutes to chill before serving. Enjoy!

Peach-Coconut Tart

Ingredients for 6 servings

½ cup rolled oats   1 cup almond milk
1 cup Brazil nuts   2 peeled peaches, chopped
1 cup soft pitted dates   ½ cup shredded coconut

Directions and Total Time: 10 minutes + freezing time

Put oats, nuts, and dates in a food processor. Blend until it holds together. Transfer the mixture into a pie pan. Press firmly. In a blender, add the almond milk, ½ cup of water, peaches, and shredded coconut. Purée until smooth, 1 minute. Pour the filling into the crust, and level with a spatula. Freeze the pie for 30 minutes. Once frozen, remove from the freezer for 15 minutes to soften.

Almond Cookies with Chocolate Chips

Ingredients for 6 servings

¼ cup non-dairy chocolate chips
2 tbsp ground flaxseed   1 tsp lemon zest
1 banana, mashed   1 tsp pure vanilla extract
½ cup demerara sugar   1 tsp baking powder
½ cup almond butter   1 ¼ cups ground almonds
2 cups cooked quinoa   ½ cup chopped pistachios
3 tbsp lemon juice

Directions and Total Time: 45 minutes

Preheat the oven to 360°F. Prep a baking sheet by lining it with parchment paper. Combine flaxseed and 3 tablespoons of water in a small bowl. Let sit for 5 minutes until it comes together in a jelly-like texture. In a large bowl, combine banana, sugar, and almond butter until smooth. Stir in quinoa, flax jelly, lemon juice, lemon zest, and vanilla until well mixed. Carefully stir in baking powder and almonds until just mixed. Fold in pistachios and chocolate chips. Scoop and shape into 12-16 balls. Arrange the balls on the baking sheet and flatten them with your hand. Bake for 20 minutes. Cool for a few minutes on the baking sheet before cooling them completely on the cooling rack. Serve and enjoy.

Avocado-Berry Cake

Ingredients for 6 servings

1 cup rolled oats   1 cup raspberries
1 cup walnuts   2 tbsp rice syrup
1 cup soft pitted dates   4 tbsp lemon juice
1 tsp lemon zest   2 tbsp mint, minced
2 avocados, peeled and pitted

Directions and Total Time: 10 minutes + freezing time

Add oats, walnuts, dates, and lemon zest in a food processor. Blend until the mixture holds together. Transfer the mixture into a pie pan. Press firmly. Pour avocados, raspberries, rice syrup, lemon juice, and mint in a blender and blend until smooth. Pour the filling into the crust, and level with a spatula. Freeze for 2 hours.

Festive Apple & Pear Crumble

Ingredients for 6 servings

3 peeled apples, chopped   2 tbsp almond butter
2 peeled pears, chopped   2 tbsp rice syrup
½ cup applesauce   1 ½ cups rolled oats
3 tbsp maple syrup   ½ cup walnuts, chopped
1 tsp ground cinnamon   ½ tsp ground cinnamon
A pinch of salt   3 tbsp date sugar

Directions and Total Time: 40 minutes

Preheat the oven to 350°F. Combine apples, pears, applesauce, maple syrup, cinnamon and salt in a baking dish. Blend the almond butter and rice syrup in a medium bowl. When it is smooth, stir in oats, walnuts, cinnamon, and date sugar. Top the apples with the oat mixture and bake for 20-25 minutes. The fruit will be soft and the topping will be golden. Serve warm and enjoy.

Sweet Quinoa Balls

Ingredients for 6 servings

2 tbsp cashew butter
2 tbsp rice syrup
¾ cup cooked quinoa
¼ cup sesame seeds, toasted
1 tbsp chia seeds
½ tsp vanilla extract
1 orange, zested
1 tbsp raisins
¼ cup ground almonds

Directions and Total Time: 25 minutes

Mix cashew butter and syrup in a medium bowl until smooth. Mix well with the remaining ingredients until they can hold their shape together. Shape into 12 balls and arrange on a parchment-lined baking sheet. Refrigerate for at least 15 minutes. Serve and enjoy.

No-Bake Energy Bites

Ingredients for 6 servings

¾ cup ground macadamia nuts
1 cup dates, pitted
1 cup shredded coconut
¼ cup chia seeds
¼ tsp protein powder
¼ cup cocoa nibs

Directions and Total Time: 25 minutes

Add all the ingredients to a food processor and puree until crumbly and just coming together. Scoop out 24 portions and shape into balls. Arrange on a parchment-lined baking sheet. Refrigerate for at least 15 minutes to set. Serve.

Vanilla-Lemon No-Bake Cookies

Ingredients for 6 servings

3 tbsp plant-based butter
1 ¼ cups almond flour
2 tbsp date sugar
1 tsp lemon zest
1 tsp vanilla extract
A pinch of salt

Directions and Total Time: 15 minutes + chilling time

Put the plant-based butter in a pan and melt it on low. Mix the plant-based butter, almond flour, date sugar, lemon zest, vanilla, and salt in a bowl and stir well. This mix will have the consistency of cookie dough. Make 1-2 inch balls out of the mix and put them on a plate. Put in the refrigerator for an hour, then serve.

Mexican Hot Chocolate Fat Bomb

Ingredients for 5 servings

¼ cup coconut butter
¼ cup coconut oil
¼ cup plant-based butter
2 tbsp cacao powder
½ tsp vanilla extract
¼ tsp cayenne pepper
½ tsp ground cinnamon
2 tbsp pure date sugar
A pinch of salt

Directions and Total Time: 10 minutes + freezing time

Put the coconut butter, coconut oil, and plant-based butter in a skillet and melt on low. After the mix is completely melted, toss in the cacao powder, vanilla, cayenne, cinnamon, date sugar, and salt. Put the mix in ice cube trays and put in the freezer for 30 minutes. Set them on the counter for a few minutes, then crack them gently out of the ice cube tray. Store in the fridge.

Pistachio Clusters

Ingredients for 6 servings

3 tbsp plant-based butter
¼ cup coconut cream
1 tsp vanilla extract
1 tbsp maple sugar
1 cup chopped pistachios
¼ cup dark chocolate chips

Directions and Total Time: 15 minutes + chilling time

Put plant-based butter in a pan and melt it on medium. Stir throughout to make sure it doesn't burn. When gold, take off the heat. Lower the heat to low, return the pan to the burner, and add the coconut cream, vanilla, and maple sugar. Cook for 5 minutes on low, stirring throughout. The mix should be thick and dark; take off the burner and add the pistachios. Lay parchment paper or a silicone mat on a cookie sheet, then place 2 or 3-inch piles of the mix on it. Place the cookie sheet in the fridge for 10 minutes. Put the chocolate in a bowl that can go in the microwave and melt it, which takes about 30 seconds. Drizzle the chocolate on top of the pistachio clusters.

Coconut Fat Bomb

Ingredients for 6 servings

½ cup pecans
¼ cup pecan butter
¼ cup coconut oil
¼ cup plant-based butter
½ tsp vanilla extract
1 tsp pumpkin pie spice
½ tbsp shredded coconut
1/3 cup date sugar
A pinch of salt

Directions and Total Time: 15 minutes + freezing time

Place a skillet on the stove and turn the burner on medium. Toss the pecans in and roast them. Stir often to keep them from burning. Put the pecans on a cutting board and chop them up. Lower the heat to low and put the skillet on the burner. Toss in the pecan butter, coconut oil, and plant-based butter. Allow this mix to melt, then pour in the vanilla, pumpkin pie spice, date sugar, shredded coconut, and salt. Put the pecans in equal amounts in ice cube trays. Ladle the coconut mix into the ice cube holes over the pecans. Put in the freezer for 30 minutes. Once frozen, put on the counter for a few minutes, then crack them out of the ice cube tray gently. Store in the fridge or freezer.

Caramel Popcorn

Ingredients for 6 servings

½ cup popcorn kernels
¼ cup vegetable oil
1/3 cup muscovado sugar
1 tsp sea salt

Directions and Total Time: 10 minutes

In a medium saucepan, stir in all of the ingredients to coat the kernels. Cover and cook over medium heat. When you hear popping, shake the pot back and forth over the heat until the kernels pop more frequently. Remove the pot from the heat after 30 seconds on rapid popping. Continue shaking until the popping happens about every 1 to 3 seconds. Pour the popcorn into a large bowl and let cool for 10 minutes. Gently break apart the popcorn with a spatula. Serve and enjoy.

Overnight Strawberry-Chia Pudding

Ingredients for 4 servings

2 tbsp chopped macadamia nuts
1 (15-oz) can coconut milk
1 tbsp pure date sugar
1 tsp vanilla extract
¼ cup chia seeds
1 tbsp blueberries
1 tbsp raspberries
1 tbsp diced strawberries
2 tbsp shredded coconut

Directions and Total Time: 25 minutes + chilling time

Open the can of coconut milk without shaking it. Dip out the solid cream and put it in a food processor or blender. Add the date sugar and vanilla, then blend until the mix gets thick. Toss in the chia seeds and fold them into the mix. Put the blueberries, raspberries, and strawberries in a pan and simmer on low heat for 15 minutes. Smash them with a fork. In 4 glasses or bowls, add ½ the coconut/chia seed mix, then pour in the berry mix, then the other ½ of the coconut/chia seed mix. Put lids on the glasses or bowls and put them in the fridge overnight or for up to 3 days. Add some macadamia nuts and shredded coconut when you're ready to serve.

Agave-Peanut Butter Chia Pudding

Ingredients for 4 servings

1 (15-oz) can coconut milk
2 tbsp peanut butter
1 tbsp agave syrup
1 cup mixed berries
1 tsp vanilla extract
¼ cup chia seeds
1 tbsp cacao nibs
1 mango, sliced for topping

Directions and Total Time: 10 minutes + chilling time

Open the can of coconut milk without shaking it. Dip out the solid cream and put it in a food processor or blender. Add the peanut butter, agave syrup, and vanilla. Blend until the mix gets thick, then add the chia seeds and fold them in. In 4 glasses, add ½ the coconut/chia seed mix, then pour in the mixed berries, then the other ½ of the coconut/chia seed mix. Put lids on the glasses or bowls and put them in the fridge overnight or for up to 3 days. Add some cacao nibs and mango slices when ready to serve. Enjoy!

Easy Rum Brownies

Ingredients for 6 servings

½ cup cocoa powder
¾ cup all-purpose flour
¾ cup organic cane sugar
½ cup olive oil
1 tsp vanilla extract
1 tbsp corn starch
1 tsp baking powder
½ tsp sea salt
½ cup almond milk
1 tsp dark rum

Directions and Total Time: 35 minutes

Preheat oven to 360°F. Whisk flour, sugar, cocoa powder, corn starch, baking powder, and salt in a large bowl. Stir almond milk, oil, rum, and vanilla in a medium bowl. Pour the wet ingredients into the large bowl with the dry ingredients. Stir until well combined without overmixing. Pour the batter into a greased baking pan and bake for 30 minutes. A toothpick in the middle with come out clean. Cool completely. Serve and enjoy!

Salted Chocolate Chip Cookies

Ingredients for 6 servings

1 ½ cups vegan chocolate chips
2 ½ cups all-purpose flour
1 cup dark-brown sugar
½ cup organic cane sugar
2 tbsp corn starch
1 tsp baking soda
1 tsp sea salt flakes
1 cup sunflower oil
½ cup pumpkin puree
2 tsp vanilla extract

Directions and Total Time: 30 minutes

Preheat the oven to 360°F. Line 2 baking sheets with parchment paper. Whisk flour, brown sugar, cane sugar, corn starch, and baking soda in a large bowl. Stir in sunflower oil, pumpkin puree, and vanilla until it comes together in a thick dough. Fold in chocolate chips. Scoop 1 heaping tablespoon of the cookie dough and roll into a ball. Place the cookie dough balls on the baking sheet with at least 2 inches of space in between. Bake for 10 to 12 minutes until the edges start to brown and the center is set. You may have to bake in batches. Top with salt and cool on a rack for at least 10 minutes. Serve and enjoy.

Fresh Banana Pudding

Ingredients for 4 servings

3 bananas
1 (15-oz) can coconut milk
¼ cup maple syrup
1 tbsp corn starch
1 tsp vanilla extract
1 tsp lemon zest
1 tsp ground cinnamon

Directions and Total Time: 10 minutes + freezing time

Add 1 banana, coconut milk, maple syrup, corn starch, and vanilla to a blender jar. Blend until the mixture is smooth. Pour the banana mixture into a saucepan and let it come to a boil over medium heat. When it starts to boil, reduce the heat and whisk for 3 minutes while it simmers. When the mixture has thickened and sticks to the spoon, remove it from the pan and let it sit in a container to cool for an hour. Cover and refrigerate for at least 4 hours. To serve, slice the rest of the bananas. Layer each dessert dish with a layer of pudding and a layer of bananas. Repeat the layers until all of the ingredients are used. Top with lemon zest and cinnamon. Serve.

Homemade Chips Ahoy

Ingredients for 4 servings

1 tbsp coconut oil, melted
1 tbsp maple syrup
1 tbsp almond milk
½ tsp vanilla extract
¼ cup oat flour
2 tbsp coconut sugar
¼ tsp salt
¼ tsp baking powder
2 tbsp chocolate chips

Directions and Total Time: 20 minutes

Combine the coconut oil, maple syrup, almond milk, and vanilla in a bowl. Add the oat flour, coconut sugar, salt, and baking powder. Stir until combined. Add the chocolate chips and stir. Preheat oven to 350°F. Pour the batter into a greased baking pan, leaving a little room in between. Bake for 7 minutes or until golden. Do not overcook. Move to a cooling rack and serve chilled.

Lemon Pie Bars

Ingredients for 6 servings

½ cup confectioners' sugar
1 cup all-purpose flour
1/3 cup coconut oil
½ cup lemon juice

½ cup almond milk
1 cup organic cane sugar
1 tsp peppermint extract
3 tbsp corn starch

Directions and Total Time: 20 minutes +chilling time

Preheat the oven to 350°F. Lightly spray a baking pan with cooking oil. Mix flour, oil, and confectioners' sugar in a medium bowl until it comes together in a dough. Press the dough into the baking pan with about ¼-inch thickness. Bake for 8 minutes. The crust will still be white and soft. While the crust is in the oven, add lemon juice, almond milk, cane sugar, and peppermint in a small saucepan. Stir over medium heat. In a small bowl, whisk corn starch and ½ cup of water. When the lemon juice starts to boil, reduce to slow and stir in the slurry slowly. Simmer for 3 to 5 minutes, stirring occasionally. The lemon mixture will thicken and stick to the spoon. Pour the lemon mixture evenly over the crust. Cover and refrigerator overnight. Before serving, take the lemon bars out of the refrigerator, cut, and dust with confectioners' sugar. Served chilled and enjoy.

Chocolate-Almond Fudge Loaf

Ingredients for 6 servings

¾ cup creamy almond butter
½ cup corn syrup
1/3 cup coconut oil, melted

6 tbsp cocoa powder
1 tbsp chopped almonds
1 tsp flaked sea salt

Directions and Total Time: 15 minutes + cooling time

Line the bottom and sides of a loaf pan with two layers of plastic wrap. One layer goes in horizontally with many overhangs, and one layer goes in vertically, also with a lot of overhangs. Gently combine almond butter, corn syrup, and coconut oil in a medium bowl until smooth. Stir in cocoa powder and almonds until creamy.

Transfer the mixture to the loaf pan. Top with sea salt. Wrap the fudge mixture with the excess plastic wrap. Freeze for at least 1 hour. When the fudge is firm, lift the fudge from the loaf pan and unwrap. Cut into 1-inch pieces. Serve and enjoy.

Avocado Chocolate Mousse

Ingredients for 2 servings

1 (15-oz) can coconut milk
1 avocado, pitted and peeled
3 tbsp cacao powder
2 tsp vanilla extract
½ tsp lemon zest

1 tsp ground cinnamon
2 tbsp pure date sugar
1 cup fresh spinach
A pinch of salt

Directions and Total Time: 10 minutes

Open the can of coconut milk without shaking it. Dip out the solid cream and put it in a food processor or blender. Add the avocado, cacao powder, vanilla, lemon zest, cinnamon, date sugar, spinach, and salt. Blend until creamy. Serve and enjoy!

Birthday Vanilla Cupcakes

Ingredients for 8 servings

½ cup vegetable shortening, softened
3 ½ cups organic confectioners' sugar
1¾ cups all-purpose flour
1 cup organic cane sugar
1 tsp baking powder
1 tsp baking soda
½ tsp sea salt
1 cup cashew milk

½ cup canola oil
1 tbsp lemon juice
2 tsp vanilla extract
½ cup vegan butter, softened
½ tsp orange extract
1 tbsp edible glitter flakes

Directions and Total Time: 25 minutes

Preheat the oven to 350°F. Place cupcake liners in 16 muffin cups. Whisk flour, cane sugar, baking powder, baking soda, and salt in a large bowl. Combine cashew milk, oil, lemon juice, and vanilla in a medium bowl. Pour the wet ingredients into the bowl with the dry ingredients and stir until just combined. Scoop the batter into each cupcake liner to about 2/3 full. Bake for 16 to 18 minutes. A toothpick in the middle of the cupcake comes out clean. Cool. While the cupcakes cool, cream the vegan butter, shortening, and orange extract in a mixing bowl. Add confectioners' sugar one cup at a time. Beat until the frosting is fluffy. Frost the cooled cupcakes with a butter knife and top with edible glitter flakes.

Cinnamon Tortilla Crisps

Ingredients for 4 servings

1 (8-inch) tortilla
Cooking oil

2 tsp muscovado sugar
½ tsp cinnamon

Directions and Total Time: 10 minutes

Preheat oven to 350°F. Slice the tortilla into 8 triangles like a pizza. Put the slices on a plate and spray both sides with oil. Sprinkle muscovado sugar and cinnamon on top, then lightly spray the tops with oil. Place in a baking sheet in a single layer. Bake for 5-6 minutes or until they are light brown. Serve warm and enjoy.

Mango Cobbler with Raspberries

Ingredients for 4 servings

1 ½ cups chopped mango
1 cup raspberries
1 tbsp brown sugar
2 tsp cornstarch
1 tsp lemon juice
2 tbsp sunflower oil
1 tbsp maple syrup

1 tsp vanilla
½ cup rolled oats
1/3 cup flour
3 tbsp coconut sugar
1 tsp cinnamon
¼ tsp nutmeg
⅛ tsp salt

Directions and Total Time: 30 minutes

Preheat the oven to 320°F. Place the mango, raspberries, brown sugar, cornstarch, and lemon juice in a baking pan. Stir with a rubber spatula until combined.

In a separate bowl, add the oil, maple syrup, and vanilla and stir well. Toss in the oats, flour, coconut sugar, cinnamon, nutmeg, and salt. Stir until combined. Sprinkle evenly over the mango-raspberry filling. Bake for 20 minutes or until the topping is crispy and golden.

Orange-Chocolate Cake

Ingredients for 6 servings

¾ cup flour	½ tbsp orange juice
½ cup sugar	2 tsp vanilla
7 tbsp cocoa powder	2 tsp orange zest
½ tsp baking soda	3 tbsp peanut butter, softened
½ cup almond milk	1 ¼ cups powdered sugar
2 ½ tbsp sunflower oil	A pinch of salt

Directions and Total Time: 35 minutes

Use a whisk to combine the flour, sugar, 2 tbsp cocoa powder, baking soda, and a pinch of salt in a bowl. Once combined, add almond milk, sunflower oil, orange juice, and orange zest. Stir until combined. Preheat oven to 350°F. Pour the batter into a greased cake pan and bake for 25 minutes or until a knife inserted in the center comes out clean. Use an electric beater to beat the peanut butter and powdered sugar together in a bowl.

Add the remaining cocoa powder and vanilla and whip until fluffy. Scrape the sides occasionally. Refrigerate until ready to use. Allow the cake to cool completely, then run a knife around the edges of the baking pan. Turn it upside-down on a plate so it can be frosted on the sides and top. When the frosting is no longer cold, use a butter knife or small spatula to frost the sides and top. Cut into slices. Serve and enjoy!

Exotic Mango Granita

Ingredients for 6 servings

2 peeled mangoes, chopped	2 limes, juiced and zested
3 cups cubed watermelon	2 cups apple juice

Directions and Total Time: 10 minutes + freezing time

Combine all of the ingredients in a food processor and blend until smooth. Pour into a 1-quart freezer-proof container with a cover. Freeze for 4 to 5 hours. Before serving, let the granita thaw for 10 minutes. Use a strong spoon to scrape the amount of granita desired. It will resemble shaved ice. Transfer to a dish. Serve cold.

Apple-Carrot Cupcakes

Ingredients for 6 servings

1 cup grated carrot	1 tsp ground cinnamon
1/3 cup chopped apple	½ tsp ground ginger
¼ cup raisins	1 tsp baking powder
2 tbsp maple syrup	½ tsp baking soda
1/3 cup almond milk	1/3 cup chopped walnuts
1 cup oat flour	

Directions and Total Time: 25 minutes

Preheat the oven to 350°F. Combine carrot, apple, raisins, maple syrup, and almond milk in a bowl. Stir in oat flour, cinnamon, ginger, baking powder, and baking soda until combined. Divide the batter between 6 cupcake molds. Top with chopped walnuts each and press down a little. Bake for 15 minutes until golden brown and a toothpick comes out clean. Let cool completely before serving.

Date Oat Cookies

Ingredients for 6 servings

¼ cup vegan butter, softened	3/4 cup flour
2 ½ tbsp almond milk	¼ tsp salt
½ cup sugar	¾ cup rolled oats
½ tsp vanilla extract	¼ tsp baking soda
½ tsp lemon zest	¼ tsp baking powder
½ tsp ground cinnamon	2 tbsp dates, chopped

Directions and Total Time: 20 minutes

Use an electric beater to whip the vegan butter until fluffy. Add the almond milk, sugar, lemon zest, and vanilla. Stir until well combined. Add the cinnamon, flour, salt, oats, baking soda, and baking powder in a separate bowl and stir. Add the dry mix to the wet mix and stir with a wooden spoon. Pour in the dates. Preheat oven to 350°F. Drop tablespoonfuls of the batter onto a greased baking pan, leaving room in between each. Bake for 6 minutes or until light brown. Make all the cookies at once, or save the batter in the fridge for later. Let them cool and enjoy!

Banana-Lemon Bars

Ingredients for 6 servings

¾ cup flour	¼ cup lemon juice
2 tbsp powdered sugar	⅛ tsp salt
¼ cup coconut oil, melted	¼ cup mashed bananas
½ cup brown sugar	1¾ tsp cornstarch
1 tbsp lemon zest	¾ tsp baking powder

Directions and Total Time: 40 minutes

Combine the flour, powdered sugar, and coconut oil in a mixing bowl. Place in the refrigerator. Mix the brown sugar, lemon zest and juice, salt, bananas, cornstarch, and baking powder in another mixing bowl. Stir well.

Preheat the oven to 350°F. Spray a baking pan with oil. Remove the crust from the fridge and press it into the bottom of the pan to form a crust. Place in the oven and bake for 5 minutes or until firm. Remove and spread the lemon filling over the crust. Bake for 18-20 minutes or until the top is golden. Cool for an hour in the fridge. Once firm and cooled, cut into pieces and serve.

Healthy Chickpea Cookies

Ingredients for 6 servings

1 cup canned chickpeas	2 tbsp almond butter, melted
2 tsp vanilla extract	1/3 cup flour
1 tsp lemon juice	½ tsp baking powder
1/3 cup date paste	¼ cup dark chocolate chips

Directions and Total Time: 25 minutes

Preheat oven to 320°F. In a blender, blitz chickpeas, vanilla extract, and lemon juice until smooth. Remove it to a bowl. Stir in date paste and almond butter until well combined. Then mix in flour, baking powder, chocolate chips. Make 2-tablespoon balls out of the mixture. Place the balls onto a parchment-lined cake pan, flatten them into a cookie shape, and bake for 13 minutes until golden brown. Let cool slightly before serving.

Berry Streusel Cake

Ingredients for 6 servings

2 tbsp demerara sugar	¾ cup oat milk
2 tbsp sunflower oil	2 tbsp olive oil
¼ cup almond flour	1 tsp vanilla
1 cup pastry flour	1 cup blueberries
½ cup brown sugar	½ cup powdered sugar
1 tsp baking powder	1 tbsp lemon juice
1 tbsp lemon zest	⅛ tsp salt

Directions and Total Time: 60 minutes

Mix the demerara sugar, sunflower oil, and almond flour in a bowl and put it in the refrigerator. Whisk the pastry flour, brown sugar, baking powder, lemon zest, and salt in another bowl. Add the oat milk, olive oil, and vanilla and stir with a rubber spatula until combined. Add the blueberries and stir slowly. Coat the inside of a baking pan with oil and pour the batter into the pan.

Preheat the oven to 310°F. Remove the almond mix from the fridge and spread it over the cake batter. Put the cake in the oven and bake for 45 minutes or until a knife inserted in the center comes out clean and the top is golden. Combine the powdered sugar and lemon juice in a bowl. Once the cake has cooled, slice it into 4 pieces and drizzle each with icing. Serve and enjoy.

Banana-Almond Delights

Ingredients for 4 servings

1 ripe banana, mashed	1 cup almond flour
1 tbsp almond liqueur	¼ tsp baking soda
½ tsp ground cinnamon	8 raw almonds
2 tbsp coconut sugar	

Directions and Total Time: 30 minutes

Preheat oven to 300°F. Add the banana to a bowl and stir in almond liqueur, cinnamon, and coconut sugar until well combined. Toss in almond flour and baking soda until smooth. Make 8 balls out of the mixture.

Place the balls onto the parchment-lined baking pan, flatten each into ½-inch thick, and press 1 almond into the center. Bake for 12 minutes, turn and bake for 6 more minutes. Let cool slightly before serving.

Holiday Pear Crumble

Ingredients for 4 servings

2 tbsp coconut oil	2 cups finely chopped pears
¼ cup flour	½ tbsp lemon juice
¼ cup demerara sugar	¾ tsp cinnamon
⅛ tsp salt	

Directions and Total Time: 40 minutes

Preheat oven to 320°F. Combine the coconut oil, flour, sugar, and salt in a bowl and mix well. Stir the pears with 3 tbsp of water, lemon juice, and cinnamon into a baking pan until combined. Sprinkle the chilled topping over the pears. Bake for 30 minutes or until they are softened and the topping is crispy and golden. Serve.

Raisin & Apple Puffs

Ingredients for 6 servings

1 tsp raisins	6 phyllo dough sheets
2 apples, finely diced	½ tsp vanilla
2 tsp cinnamon	½ cup maple syrup
½ cup sugar	¼ cup coconut oil
⅛ tsp salt	½ tsp salt

Directions and Total Time: 30 minutes

In a bowl, combine raisins, apples, cinnamon, 2 tbsp sugar, and salt; set aside. Unwrap the phyllo dough carefully. Put a large piece of phyllo on a clean, dry surface. Fold it into thirds and spray each portion with oil.

Preheat oven to 320°F. Spoon 1/3 cup of the apple mix at the base of the rectangle. Fold the bottom of the phyllo over the mix. Continue to fold up, forming a triangle. Put the apple-filled triangle in a greased baking dish. Repeat for all the remaining phyllo and apple mix.

Bake the triangles for 10 minutes or until browned. Add the vanilla, maple syrup, coconut oil, remaining sugar, and salt to a small pot. Boil over medium heat, stirring constantly, until it simmers and eventually thickens. Plate the apple puffs and add the caramel sauce. Serve warm.

MEASUREMENTS & CONVERSIONS

	US STANDARD	US STANDARD (OUNCES)	METRIC (APPROXIMATE)
VOLUME EQUIVALENTS (LIQUID)	2 tablespoons	1 fl. oz.	30 mL
	¼ cup	2 fl. oz.	60 mL
	½ cup	4 fl. oz.	120 mL
	1 cup	8 fl. oz.	240 mL
	1 ½ cups	12 fl. oz.	355 mL
	2 cups or 1 pint	16 fl. oz.	475 mL
VOLUME EQUIVALENTS (DRY)	¼ teaspoon		1 mL
	½ teaspoon		2 mL
	1 teaspoon		5 mL
	1 tablespoon		15 mL
	¼ cup		59 mL
	⅓ cup		79 mL
	½ cup		118 mL
	⅔ cup		156 mL
	¾ cup		177 mL
	1 cup		235 mL
	2 cups or 1 pint		475 mL
	3 cups		700 mL
	4 cups or 1 quart		1 L
WEIGHT EQUIVALENTS	½ ounce		15 g
	1 ounce		30 g
	2 ounces		60 g
	4 ounces-		115 g
	8 ounces		225 g
	12 ounces		340 g
	16 ounces or 1 pound		455 g

	FAHRENHEIT (F)	CELSIUS (C) (APPROXIMATE)
OVEN TEMPERATURES	250°F	120°F
	300°F	150°F
	325°F	180°F
	375°F	190°F
	400°F	200°F
	425°F	220°F
	450°F	230°F

Made in United States
North Haven, CT
12 April 2022

18177058R00076